DAGHESTAN
TRADITION & SURVIVAL

CAUCASUS WORLD
SERIES EDITOR NICHOLAS AWDE

Other books in the series include:

Georgia: Mountains and Honour *Peter Nasmyth*
The Russian Conquest of the Caucasus *J.F. Baddeley, with a new Preface by Moshe Gammer*
A Bibliography of Articles on Armenian Studies in Western Journals, 1869-1995 *N.V. Nersessian*
Ancient Christianity in the Caucasus (Iberica Caucasica vol. 1) *edited by Tamila Mgaloblishvili*
Armenian Sacred and Folk Music *Komitas (Soghomo Soghomonian)*
The Armenian Neume System of Notation *R.A. At'ayan*
Armenian Monodic Music *Kh.S. Khushnaryan*
Armenian Perspectives *edited by Nicholas Awde*
Madder Red *Robert Chenciner (forthcoming)*

PEOPLES OF THE CAUCASUS HANDBOOKS
1. The Armenians *edited by Edmund Herzig*
2. The Georgians *edited by Nicholas Awde*
3. The Azerbaijanis *edited by Laura LeCornu*
4. The Chechens *Anna Zelkina*
5. The Abkhazians *edited by George Hewitt*

Forthcoming volumes include: 6. The Circassians   7. The Peoples of Daghestan   8. The Ossetes
9. The Ingush   10. The Turkic Peoples of the Caucasus   11. The Iranian Peoples of the Caucasus
12. The Mountain Jews   13. The Georgian Jews   14. The Laz, Mingrelians and Svans
15. The Ubykh   16. The Displaced Peoples of the Caucasus in Soviet Times
17. The Caucasus in Diaspora   18. The Hemshin   19. The Kalmyks
20. The Cossacks   21. The Ancient Peoples of the Caucasus

CAUCASUS LANGUAGES
1. Chechen Dictionary and Phrasebook
2. Georgian Dictionary and Phrasebook
3. Armenian Dictionary and Phrasebook *(forthcoming)*
4. Azerbaijani Dictionary and Phrasebook *(forthcoming)*

Previous page:
'Djigits' decorate a Daghestani carved wooden spoon box next to the hearth (Quyada village).

DAGHESTAN
TRADITION & SURVIVAL

Robert Chenciner

CURZON
CAUCASUS WORLD

CAUCASUS WORLD

First published in 1997
by CURZON PRESS
15 The Quadrant, Richmond
Surrey TW9 1BP
U.K.

Typeset and designed by Nicholas Awde/Desert♥Hearts
Scans by Emanuela Losi
Maps by Kieran Meeke & Nick Awde
Photos by Robert Chenciner unless otherwise credited

Printed and bound in Great Britain by
Biddles Ltd, Guildford and King's Lynn

British Library Cataloguing in Publication Data
A catalogue record for this book is available from the British Library

ISBN 0 7007 0632 1

Contents

Acknowledgements

This book has been more than ten years in the making. This was in part because of the complexity of arrangements needed to carry out the research in mountain villages. In addition, the development of scanning technology has only now permitted the inclusion of so many illustrations which are used as the equivalent of textual reference from an oral society. Lastly, the tragic violence in the Caucasus has given rise to broader interest in the region. Who had heard the names *Daghestan* or *Chechenia* five years ago?

This was no simple book to produce; as well as essential local help on expedition and at the Academy of Sciences in Daghestan, I needed what became an international network of facilitators, permission granters, protectors. Next, a variety of technical expertise was called on including Russian, photography and cartography; philology, history, agriculture and library technology; and an additional huge pool of energy from people helping to support my idea over a long period. My wife Marian has had to share my attentions with Daghestan – at our wedding I gave my occupation to a bemused clerk as "Eastern Caucasologist" – and the next generation in the form of my daughter Louisa appeared more quickly than the book. May I thank those who helped without regard to rank or position; with this kind of work, it was a humanitarian act on their part.

First thanks go to my chief collaborator Dr Magomedkhan Magomedkhanov, and my mentor Dr Ramazan Khappoulaev – both in Daghestan.

In Daghestan, as in the rest of the Caucasus, when you have a friend you are also a friend of their family and their clan, so it is impossible to record all the names. Among them: From the Scientific Centre of the Daghestan Filial of the Academy of Sciences of Russia: Ac. Hadji Gamzatov, Dr Abdurakhman Abdurakhmanov, Prof. Enver Kisriev, Dr Paruk Debirov and Prof. Sasha Koudriavsev. From the government, H.E. Dr Bagauddin Akhmedov (Vice-President) and Naida Abdulgamidova (Minister of Culture), the late Gamid Gamidov (Finance Minister), and Daghestan's cultural icons Rasul Gamzatov and

Facing page (right to left from top): Diana of the Ephesians-like painted egg displays on giant bread loaves known as 'kulucha' prizes at the Kaitag-Dargin 'Vruchat Veterani' festival (photo: G. Bartikhanov); Zoroastrian fire jumping reconstruction by academics at the First Furrow Festival in Korkmaskala; Marx's bust crowns the roll of honoured workers at the entrance to Party HQ in Batlaich, pop. 1200; brass stamp of Hand of Fatima, a talisman against the evil eye to mark the plaster outside front doors (coll. Daghestan Kraevecheskii Museum, Makhachkala; photo: Justin Thomas); barbed Scythian bronze arrow heads excavated near Derbent by Prof. A Koudriavsev; tug-of-war at the Lezgin Spring fire festival, Chiryurt; Khilikh' shepherd family grandmother who specialised in making appliqué swaddling bands for her many children; double-storey columns in Mishlesh mosque; wooden spoon for stirring wedding soup (Lezgin), Akhti Museum; Lezgin Rain Festival in Akhti – pagan-Islamic spring fertility parades continued under Socialism (photo: G. Bartikhanov, c. 1970).

Patimat Gamzatova. The grist of this book was provided by my *konaks* who give me their hearths in more than a hundred villages in the mountains and the plains.

I am especially grateful to Niamh O'Mahony, who travelled with me and contributed to the research about women.

I would like to thank the others who helped me, in elliptical geographical order which somehow reflects the contents of this book.

In Soviet Moscow: H.E. Michael Stepanovich Kapitsa, formerly Deputy Foreign Minister of USSR, Mikhail Borrisov and Sergei Klokov, sometime of the USSR Foreign Ministry, who together gained the first invitation for me to visit Daghestan; Terry Sandell, formerly Cultural Attache at the British embassy; Dr Dmitri Chirkov, formerly Curator at the Moscow Eastern Museum, and Dr Anatoly Ivanov of the State Hermitage, Leningrad.

In Britain – at St Antony's Oxford: Dr Theodore Zeldin and Lord Ralph Dahrendorf, my sponsors, Dr Harry Shukman, in connection with our Shamil Symposium and Alan Davidson and Harlan Walker of the Oxford Food Symposium(a), both of which took place there. Peter Brown and Jane Lyddon of the British Academy, Dr Francis Herbert of the Royal Geographic Society, John Roberts, former director of GB-USSR Association, Godfrey Goodwin former director of the Royal Asiatic Society. Distinguished philologists generously helped me: The late Prof. Sir Harold Bailey, Dr Ilya Gershevitch and Anna Chaudhri, Prof. Edmund Bosworth, Prof. Donald Rayfield, Dr George Hewitt, Dr Simon Crisp, Prof. Ricks Smeets, Dr Helma van den Berg, and Prof. Michael Zand. Valuable anthropological thoughts emanated from Prof. Malcolm McLeod, Iris Barry, Dr Jeremy MacClancy, Minou Williams and Dr John Campbell. Cary Wolinsky, Josephine Powell, Frederique Brenner and Michael Anikst gave me authoritative advice on how to photograph and Emanuela Losi selflessly scanned the results into the Apple Mac, while Kieran Meeke oversaw preparation of the maps. Tatiana Dunbar helped with massive translation, Dr Stephen Carter acted as my cheery Russian tutor, and Anthony North of the Victoria & Albert Museum first introduced me to Daghestan through metalwork.

In various more mysterious ways, I was sustained by advice and encouragement from Marcus Grant, Gillian Goodwin, Andrew Harman, Rupert Knowles, Zinovy Zinik, Prof. Claudio Scazzocchio, Prof. Sasha Kennaway, John Wright and John Parker.

In addition to several of those mentioned above, revision of my writing beyond the call of duty was given by Robert Irwin, Helen Irwin, Dr Mary Abbott and Prof. Andrew Crowcroft; and in the final production, my editor Nicholas Awde and publisher Malcolm Campbell.

A surprisingly large proportion of those mentioned above were and are firstly friends as well as advisers. I have been told that I am changed by this book, so thank you all for your interest and professional help in making it possible and may it go some way towards meeting your standards.

Foreword

There seems to be a time for things in history. The unique changes in the Caucasus during that recent special period between totalitarian Soviet socialism and early capitalism beset by interethnic conflicts and, especially, the Russian-Chechen war in the mid 1990s, provided a chance to explore wider problems appearing through the prism of Daghestan.

Events combined with my personal life, or rather the lack of it, to take advantage of this opportunity. Subsequent timing finds me in London, an old father, with my loving wife Marian, doting on our mercurial three-year-old daughter Louisa.

In contrast, history leaves my younger friend Gamid Gamidov, sometime champion wrestler, finance minister and a brilliant future president of Daghestan, dead, assassinated by a remote-control car bomb in October 1996. Grozny is destroyed, and the future for neighbouring Daghestan – at the whim of a hostile, lurching Russia — is bleak and uncertain.

The only response is to build a monument to a rich and varied culture in celebration of the perseverance and diversity of the Daghestanis. Please join them in a wry laugh and forget nothing . . .

LONDON 1997

The Great Caucasian Mountains

VILLAGES, TOWNS & CITIES

Map of villages

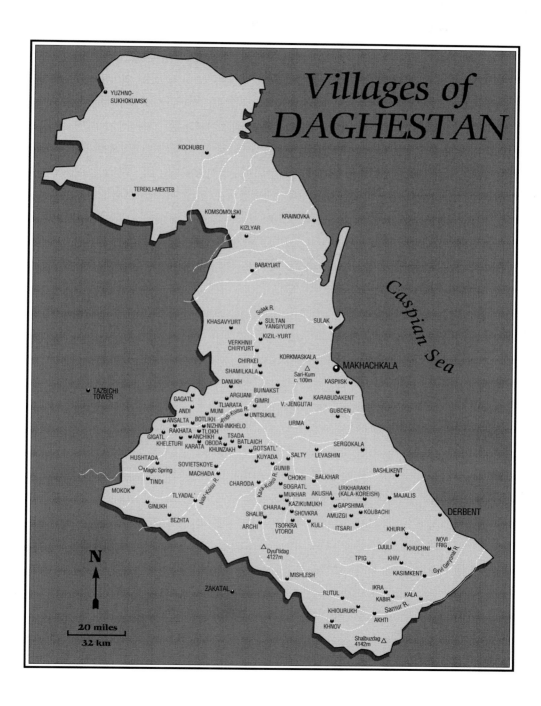

The pass between Tliarata and Arguani villages.

·1·

Introduction: survival & tradition

"When a raven is in charge, he will lead you to the rubbish dump."
People's Front of Daghestan, samizdat No. 1, April 1990.

As our Red Army jeep drove into the next mountain village, my non-Daghestani Soviet ex-collaborator started our usual argument. "There is no ethnography in this village. This village is like all the others. Why don't you believe me?" he droned. I felt desperate, how could this Iron Curtain part for me? "I am going to find ethnography here. This village is different. Why should I believe anyone? If only there was more time." "Then ask them for more time," he taunted. "Of course of course," the Daghestan authorities replied, "we would like you to have more time, but you see, the *komandirovka* permit and the *programma* have been fixed . . ."

ૐ

Daghestan is the size of Scotland, where the claws of the Great Caucasian Mountains grab south-eastwards at the Caspian Sea. The two million inhabitants, two thirds of whom live in 700 villages, still speak thirty-two languages, even after over a century of Tsarist control followed by seventy years of repressive Soviet rule. I was looking for non-Soviet life in a non-Soviet way. I tried to record only what was happening, leaving my opinions on the survival of their culture till later. To some extent that culture was already defined by what the Soviets had tried to suppress. Definition of traditional or present culture is not only a problem in Daghestan.

The effects of this century are universal, as can be seen from the embalming of our own European lowland villages, as they become weekend holiday homes for city-dwellers, while mountain villages in Switzerland, Turkey, France or Spain have suffered depopulation due to lack of work. Daghestan, with its tapestry of national groups, is a microcosm of the ethnic problems of the Soviet Union. Yet, the great liberating changes still sweeping the ex-USSR have hardly reached here, where only ten per cent of the new deputies are non-Communist, representing ninety per cent of the electorate.

❧

The words 'a closed USSR republic' meant that Daghestan was not open to non-Soviet-bloc tourism, which, in any case, was confined to tourist camps or hotels. It also meant that the local people were unaccustomed to foreigners and, because of the totalitarian regime, they were frightened of them, unless someone they knew explained why the stranger was there. For my first three trips, I was accompanied by Russians or their friend, an Azeri, so the Daghestan people were suspicious.

I was frustrated. My first problem was gaining access to ordinary life, not officials or their Soviet idea of what a visitor should see. Ethnography is finding out what makes people different at some identifiable level of their humanity. "What exactly do you want to see?" they asked. "It is hard to say until I have seen it," I replied (meaning: "I want to see what you might not want to show me"). There are few parts in the world where so many indigenous nationalities are crammed into such a small area. How would it be possible to assimilate such a polyglot mixture of past and present cultures? Only with the help of the Daghestan villagers. After eight visits during the first four years, I had gained many *konaks*, or kinsmen, effectively providing family bonds in many villages. My only barriers then were those of propriety, albeit in a different social framework to the one that I am used to, rather than suspicion.

Daghestan societies are diverse, yet akin, from village to village, mountains to plains, the North Eastern Caucasus to the whole Caucasus. Time has also caused changes, just as English villages have changed their nature since the War. This made the many close comparisons of life today with before the Revolution all the more remarkable. Because of Daghestan's bloody resistance to the Revolution, it has always been under extra close control from Moscow. Even so, there ought to be changes emerging after glasnost, based on what has happened elsewhere. How much has this wild land been sovietised by the abrasive onslaughts of Moscow Socialism? Villages were destroyed during the war in the 1920s, the mosques in the 1930s, the people transported in the 1940s and 1950s and the villagers pushed to move down-country to the towns during the 1960s and 1970s, following the unreported earthquakes. Had Moscow attacked the wrong weak points, while trying to suppress their traditions, and so, by mistake, preserved a complex culture which glasnost, Pepsi-Cola and pop culture may finish off, arriving as by-products from an unknown world?

❧

At the beginning I felt like a spaceman. They thought so too. Four years later my Irish friend was walking alone around the town of Akhti. At the town centre, in front of the Party headquarters, a temporary stage had been erected for a festival. Her guide pointed to it. "That is where the Great Pink One danced," he announced, as she winced. Was I turning into a modern Gulliver in Lilliput? I had unwittingly lived outside in freedom. But in this land, a knowing native said, in shame, about his own countrymen who had joined the Party, "What sort of people would ever denigrate and despoil their own homeland?" Journeying into the dark side of a Thomas More's Utopia, there were no Virgils to be my guides, they had all been brain-killed by the system. But maybe there was a little Virgil in everybody. That was my hope.

❧

The only way to go on my own – or, by that time, just to go, as I had nothing more to offer my previous Soviet sponsors, was through the Daghestan Filial of the USSR Academy of Sciences, for which I needed a recommending letter from the British Academy. But I had no official British academic affiliation. I heard about the Oxford Food Symposium at St Antony's College. The theme that June was Staple Foods, so I offered a talk on little known aspects of North-East Caucasian mountain ram and other dishes. This was my first venture into *bas-cuisine*, where the symbolic meaning of food was more important than its taste. This came over vividly from the photographs I took while eating, and drinking. By November, the letters were sent, outlining my proposed itinerary to forty villages.

The buildings of the USSR Academy of Sciences in Moscow stretched along two kilometres. At House Number 7, the Foreign Relations Department, they smiled and said that I was the first person who had ever asked to go to Daghestan. They had sent telegrams. When I arrived, the local director, in view of his assessment of the importance of my work, which had never exactly been described to him, had allocated me two distinguished senior scholars as guides. One, Paruk Debirov, now a good friend, was a massive man, over seventy. After we met, he tactfully made it clear that he was too old for this sort of thing. We laughed. The other, a historian, had disappeared ill and I did not come across him until some years after.

Consequently, a special meeting of the Academy had to be called to decide who on earth should look after me. Magomedkhan Magomedkhanov, an ethnographer, volunteered. I had been waiting in a little office to which I had been given a key, wondering how I could escape to the mountains, as I knew how hopeless it was when plans were changed. A shiny-faced stocky man of about thirty-five entered, beaming. He ambled forward, looked straight ahead at my chest and simply said, "I like your face." The face was not so wonderful, he meant the me-behind-the-face, he explained. Was it some sixth sense? "If I did not approve of you, I would not work with you," he added. "Thank you," I replied.

I meant it. It was impossible to overestimate the worth of friendship in

3

Daghestan. That day marked the start of serious work. Following his example, others helped. We have since even begun to study how emigrants from Daghestan to Turkey have kept their traditional life, attempting to find a better answer to the question: was capitalism or Communism the more destructive force?

ᴥ

The variety of both warriors and settlers who journeyed down the road between the Great Caucasian mountains and the Caspian sea, has engaged the curiosity of historians since Herodotus. The walls of Derbent, built by the Sassanian Persians during the sixth century, shut off the southward migration route. Successive waves of nomads forced previous settlers to found villages in invincible mountain refuges. But others already lived there. I asked a man from the remote alpine village of Archi, where his people originally came from. "Other people come from us," he stated.

Although mountaineers married within their communities, they were not entirely isolated. Some villages had adjacent quarters inhabited by different nationalities, and the difficult tracks between them were passable on horseback. There was always the *konak* surrogate family village-to-village hospitality system. So, many customs are common over the whole mountain region.

A custom is a way of combining rituals to reconcile both everyday and special occasions with metaphysical contradictions and so make life bearable. Perhaps any mountain peoples who share such a difficult life would have evolved similar customs on their own, whether Scots, Basques, Swiss or Andeans. Traditional society is fragmentary, ironically similar to the opposed "progressive" society, which is still portrayed in many Soviet publications. Much material has been published by Soviet ethnographers. The weight of the books gives them a reassuring feeling of completeness and accuracy which, when studied closely, proves insufficient for outsiders. In the corset of Marxist structuralism, every function of society was fitted into a straining diagram. The word 'scientific' was made to stand for only parts of the true research process – postulating the same Party slogans, backed up by supportive research, leading to information without new theories. I wanted to break out of their Disneyland.

ᴥ

The usual visitor's story during the Soviet period, was that the rare traveller was accompanied by a Party Official, as local guide. My Soviet 'collaborators' used to answer the questions that I asked the locals. The visitor was only allowed to meet National Cultural Heroes and Party officials and visit places where everyone had been forewarned. Extended feasting made sure that the so-called explorer was never free to wander about, especially as he risked offending the rules of hospitality. On my first visit in Untsukul, I arrived after dark, was

Chokh village. The road zigzags down past the local khan's palace in the heart of Imam Shamil Avar country.

feasted and had a shotgun fired in my honour, but was not even allowed to walk around the village next morning.

The brief restricted visits by a small number of Europeans this century meant that they wrote the small sections of their travellers tales from library armchairs, if at all, judging from the recent comments of Susan Richards, the author of *Epics of Everyday Life*. In Tsarist times too, in spite of customary hospitality, foreign civilians never stayed long in Daghestan. John Baddeley, who rode through in ten days in 1901, wrote the best work, *The Rugged Flanks of the Caucasus*, published posthumously in 1940.

My heart rose when, range by range, the great mountains appeared as we left the road along the plain. It was selfish of me to sit in the front seat. "But you are only looking out for exceptional things, you must admit that most life here is just Soviet," arguing again. "But it is only the unusual which makes them different." That was partly right. Was there enough to be significant? Was there anything left to be found? They had so much time on their annual expeditions while I had so little. I became a cultural commando, making raids on unknown targets, which unexpectedly appeared and were gone. My findings must be an incomplete sample, added to local unpublished research work, generously given to me in writing or recordings, and compared with published, but largely unobtainable, recent books and earlier sources in Russian. The result differs from what outsider Soviets have seen and local specialists have written.

Almost all publishing is still state controlled from Moscow, excepting two brief political samizdats, *Impuls* and *NFD*, which appeared after February 1990. For example, the richest treasure of Daghestan – a thousand folktales, gathered over twenty-five years – remained largely unpublished in Russian or English, unlike Russian stories, although a proportion has been published in the main local languages. Was this a form of subtle censorship, dampening the existence of a culture different from Moscow?

The mountain villages of Daghestan have survived as a separate culture because the people share an observable, if partly conscious, vocabulary of real and abstract symbols. This is the link which connects their everyday lives to traditions more ancient than their current rulers, making them perpetual anarchists and so targets for sociological culling. I tore apart and resurrected this idea by recording what was different – both in their physical surroundings and how they behaved. Only then could I try to assess the value of what remains – a substitute custom (like our Christmas), a child's game, or a folk tale. At the end, we were still arguing, where was the ethnography, and which system won? I gradually realised that the answer to this question was also the reason for my selections – to discover the equation of the 'loyalty structures' of the mountain peoples of Daghestan and the rate at which these are changing. My collaborators in Daghestan were unaware of what I was seeking – just like me – so they were unable to conceal anything.

ঝ

Stalin understood how to use loyalty structures. In 1913 he defined the 'nation' as a stable community of human beings, which has accrued historically and was founded on an identity of language, territory and economy, and shared the same spiritual values. By early 1921, Stalin was warning the Conference of Communists of the Turkic Peoples of the Russian Federation, RFSFR, of the dangers of nationalism. In 1923, Sultan Galiyev, the most important Muslim in the Party, was named an enemy of the proletariat and a pan-Turk nationalist, expelled from the Party and imprisoned. It marked the start of the persecutions.

Stalin's method of terror was based on manipulating the loyalty structure. In earlier years both Muslim and Russian Communists argued with varying conviction that individual, family, clan, national and Communist Party bonds were linked. Later when these fidelities diverged, initially at Party and then at local level, Party members found themselves in a position of conflicting allegiance with their colleagues. Willing or unwilling betrayal occurred. By tradition, suspected or actual denunciation would have been treated equally in Daghestan by their adat or customary law, where serious offences of honour were resolved by the inter-family blood feud. The break-up of their loyalty structure must have been fast and nasty. The recovery period, towards a decent trust between individuals, is still incomplete.

The author visiting shepherds on the alpine plain above Archi, atop a mountain pony, saddled with a large metal towing ring on the front which was too large on too small a saddle.

The form of my own investigation emerged after reading about whether, on the eve of the Revolution, the Muslims of Russia were conscious of belonging to a single community, in *Islam in the Soviet Union*. Written in the 1960s, reflecting a depressing period of repressions, there was great similarity between the authors' necessarily brief discussion – they were not allowed into Daghestan – of the extended family, clan, endogamy, village commune and language problems and what I saw a quarter of a century later. The threads of interwoven topics were falling into an order. Imagine a magic tree where the branches represent the many allegiances of an individual. At the crown there are the

A typical old mountain village, Amuzgi, with flat rolled earth roofs – and not the current gable tin/asbestos. (Photo: Dmitri Chirkov)

personal loyalties to family – down to the broad lower boughs of national fealty.

The family is so central and pervasive to the Daghestan and mountain Caucasian accountability that it permeated their whole lives. By their nature, every theme involves an array of obligations, almost changing the magic tree into a hedge.

҂

I started puzzling about loyalty in the 1970s, while I taught management to postgraduates in London. During case studies, which were designed to illustrate new ideas, it was startling that within minutes, the students reacted emotionally to numbers, which I called out. They clearly held different values to me, in their aims, the way they lived and their responses. Also, they worked for large corporations, unlike me. Every individual is bound by obligations of differing strength or of perceived, rather than real, importance to a variety of organisms. In order of increasing size these are: the family, from spouse and children to parents and relatives, sib (an individual-centred family to sixth cousins) and clan; the work circle of job, colleagues, employer; both the inherited culture of language, tradition, religion, and the acquired environment of school and university, passions of sport or pastimes, clubs and political creed; the surroundings of village community, region, nationality by race or political boundary; and lastly – all humanity. The way these loyalties are counted defines cultural identity, which explains why I first looked for customs, which did *not* involve loyalty to the Communist Party or USSR in Daghestan. This was only half possible as, in reality, the local clans, or *tukhums*, had often subverted the Party power system.

꙳

I reached Daghestan at walking pace. It took three years to travel the four hour drive, north from Baku to Derbent. I first became curious about Daghestan 16 years ago, when I bought what appeared to be a rare 15th-century Persian bronze inlaid-silver napkin-ring – it turned out to have been made in Koubachi village in Daghestan in the late nineteenth century. Further tantalising riddles began to accumulate, which intrigued me more about Daghestan. Hundreds of *kinjal* daggers began to appear in London salesrooms. Then in 1984, a Moscow friend gave me Russian book on Koubachi, which illustrated not only *kinjals*, but extraordinary felt masks. Near the British Museum, I found an ancient grammar of Avar, a main language of Daghestan. Even the regular verbs looked impossible, with 24 gerunds. I borrowed books on carved stone and wood, filled with what looked like Celtic motifs, which confirmed that Daghestan had design in the blood. I found two books in English about the curious family customs, such as the blood-feud.

My first chance occurred in 1983, when I was invited to a conference in Baku to talk about rugs. There was scant first-hand knowledge of Caucasian rugs, felts and embroideries then, so I arrived five days early and reached Kuba village, just south of Daghestan, which I felt must be full of textiles. Three years later, after several visits to Azerbaijan, I had discovered that a group of virtually unknown woollen tapestry rugs, called *dumi* and *davaghin*, came from Daghestan. I wanted to give a talk about the rugs at the International Carpet Conference in Vienna and Budapest in 1987, which meant that I had a reason to go to Daghestan.

I had to obtain a visa, which was only possible with an invitation, because Daghestan was closed to Westerners. But nobody knew me in Daghestan, so I first needed a telegram asking them to invite me from a Soviet ministry. I had worked in Azerbaijan with the USSR National Commission for UNESCO, who said they could only help if the Carpet Conference were sponsored by UNESCO. But Britain had just withdrawn from that organisation, so I had to obtain support of the National Commissions of seven other countries as well as the USSR.

It was a surprise that Oriental rugs were, deservedly, considered to be important. At last, a means of getting a visa appeared. Deputy Foreign Minister, Mikael Stepanovich Kapitsa, Chairman of the USSR National Commission for UNESCO, was prepared to be taken to lunch by the *National Geographic Magazine*, whom I had indirectly introduced and so I was allowed to come along, armed with a letter from the ill-starred Secretary General of

UNESCO – His Excellency Amaktar M'Bow had once given me a bear hug, when I was hitching a ride on his jet aeroplane from Baku to Moscow, and was standing in the gangway, accidentally blocking his path to the toilet. (M'Bow, a former Minister of Health of Senegal, resigned in 1986 after various scandals, including his £1 million luxury flat in Paris, massively inefficient authoritarian spending of UNESCO funds and finally, proposing a Third World press corps to exclude the Western press).

We met in the authentic Japanese restaurant in Armand Hammer's Hotel Mejdunarodny in Moscow. Professor Kapitsa was a big man, and I am not small, and we made elaborate jokes, as we nodded glistening pates and squeezed our legs under the low table and ate in exquisite discomfort, served by Russian geisha girls, who would not let me take their picture. The bill came to a hundred pounds each. Kapitsa had been Stalin's Chinese interpreter, as a young man, and was, unusually for a Soviet politician, both educated and an orientalist. He had recently returned from undermining President Reagan's South East Asian policy, before the American's visit. Gorbachev surely threw away one of his best diplomats, when he was rumoured to have dismissed Kapitsa for his extravagant lifestyle. He became director of the Oriental Institute at the Academy of Sciences. I was amazed that Kapitsa had the time to send a telegram, requesting the First Secretary of Daghestan to invite me. And so I finally got my visa. During a week of receptions, I was invited to his Caspian seaside residence and after a swim and a talk, I presented him with my first Koubachi bronze – poetic justice for the object. Later that year, at the conference, I gave the talk about the rugs and a second on Daghestan felts. We had invited three Daghestanis and I remember their look of wonder as they saw six hundred people, obviously captivated by the textiles of their country.

That was the starting point for more journeys I realised were needed there. There is no substitute for field-work on your own, outside a Soviet mission-style group. The results of my visits over the past ten years have often led me to change my first impressions. Some ideas have grown stronger, but others more self-contradictory. What I first saw as the intrusion of politics over the first four years, has now taken on a relevance, if not always a meaning. To develop my thoughts, Daghestan became a subject for me to talk about in Britain.

Two years after my talk about rams, Dr Magomedkhanov, my collaborator, arrived in Oxford with the now celebrated ram gut sausages and gave a talk, Traditional Table Manners in Daghestan, where he was attacked for the way women were treated there. A full house at the Royal Geographical Society seemed to indicate that there was further interest in Daghestan in London, which encouraged the Zamana Gallery in London to sponsor the exhibition Daghestan Today. But in Glasgow at the Scottish Royal Geographical Society, an old lady whispered loudly to her husband "but it's nee as beautiful as Scotland!"

At St Antony's, I was ordered to learn Russian to make my work easier, which proved true during four one-man British Academy–Academy of Sciences expeditions from 1988 to 1990. Events moved fast. I had arranged a 1990

Mist fingers along the Great Caucasian Chain above the Samur River. The frontier with Azerbaijan here artificially divides the historic homeland of the Lezgi people.

seminar entitled 'Why there does not appear to be a Popular Front in Daghestan', but by the time I spoke, there was, and I handed round the first Popular Front samizdat.

ð.

Firstly, however, I had to discover how to obtain information in Daghestan. Through the hangovers, the feasts, the gifts (which were not bribes) and my doing everything everyone wanted, I had come to realise that if I stopped worrying, I would be relaxed enough to notice a little of the knowledge which passed my way.

It did not come easily. On an early trip, I took a professional tape-recorder and managed to interrupt every interview, exactly at the moment before something important would have been said. Even after I learnt to pause, more patience was needed to wait for imaginary jeeps to get out of Makhachkala, the capital, and into the mountain villages. After about a week, jeeps, drivers and fuel would appear and we would depart. The rewards included over two thousand slides of people, villages, homes and objects, and many sound recordings – simple samples of twenty of the thirty-two languages, and songs, including a lullaby, felt-rolling chants, a bride's ululation on her car ride to her wedding night, and a 93 year old, singing his people's epic poem.

My friends in Daghestan, both within and outside the Institute of History, Language and Literature at the Daghestan Filial of the Academy of Sciences, enthusiastically answered my thousand questions and shared their books, photographs, time, drink and wry humour. I often got it wrong, for instance wearing what I thought were smart white slacks, which to Daghestanis look like Red Army winter underwear, but at least I was not from Moscow, like the man in the next story . . .

Not so long ago, a Russian lecturer was explaining to a group of Daghestan mountain villagers all about the Soviet conquest of space. He warmed to his subject as his audience politely listened, gazing at the stars in the mild summer night. After three hours, the address had finished, everyone clapped, and the lecturer asked if there were any questions.

The respectful silence was eventually broken by a village elder. He thanked the speaker and confirmed that indeed they now knew everything thing about the cosmos, but as they were in the presence of a scientist, perhaps he could ask him about a problem which had for long puzzled him. "How did they get the soft jam into the centre of the hard sugar sweets?"

The story points to a dogged fight against the constant Russian denigration of Daghestan. A Russian member of the London embassy once came up to me after a talk I gave, which, according to other people who heard it, had put forward their different cultures honourably, The official said with an embarrassed smile, "I enjoyed your talk, but I did not realise how primitive it was."

This symbolises Russian racial prejudice towards North East Caucasians, born of colonial disdain and a fear of their legendary courage, immortalised by Russian Romantic literature. Something is surviving, but what is it? In the long term, the first enemy may be the Russians, but the real battle, a kind of faith-war, is taking place between three religious powers in Daghestan. The legacy of the Leader, or *vozhd*, as Stalin was known by all Soviet peoples, underpinned the Communist Party faith. The hand of the 19th-century rebel Imam Shamil is present behind the spiritual resurgence in the new Islamic movement. The pagan Ram is the symbol of the old pagan traditions and customary laws, which survive in the villages, inspiring both the opposition and Green movements. Like their tapestry woollen rugs, the warps and wefts of their interwoven loyalties picked out all three forces, and nothing was black and white. This conflict was even reflected in the unusual names of the people of Daghestan.

Until after the Revolution, the Old Testament practice was followed of using a first name plus the father's name, e.g. 'Gamid the son of Magomed'. As the years passed and it became safer to become more 'Soviet,' so the second name was Russianised with the addition of an *-ov* or *-ova*. Then, an invented patronymic was introduced to achieve the usual three Russian names. Soviet names were introduced, like Mischa or Vladimir, Traktor or even Mels (standing for Marx-Engels-Lenin-Stalin). But today their names still remain of Muslim or Daghestan origin – like so many other Soviet designs, it never worked.

·2·

Kung-fu in the evenings: the strongman cult

*I*n the quiet before dusk, high on a deserted valley between two mountain ridges, where the greens and sepias were turning into blues and violets to the sound of a burbling stream, there was a distant movement. I peered closer and made out three young men, who were silently practising the karate reverse foot drop-kick. Was this the significance of the modern Olympic Latin motto, *citius, altius, fortius*, meaning 'faster, higher, stronger,' painted on the Spartak gym wall in Makhachkala?

Down the road, in Market No. 2, there was a crowded stall next to the main entrance, where they sold images of heroes. The current hagiography encompassed Imam Shamil, with his haunting stare, framed by his dark beard (which should have been red), Bruce Lee attacking, in full kung-fu flight and the Austro-American film-star Arnold Schwartzenegger, bunching his pectorals and rippling his deltoids. These pictures, together with modest pin-ups of sari-clad Indian dancing-girls, were taken home and carefully displayed, pinned on to modern rugs adorning bed-room walls, next to family photographs. The mutual admiration of Daghestan (and other Caucasian) men for their machismo, however displaced it may be from its historical context, was a lone attempt to avoid the steamrollering conventionality of *homo sovieticus*.

At the Last Judgement, the Daghestan mountain man knows that he will be recognised as a fighter, who only submitted to God, Shamil and Stalin. On a bus, Niamh my Irish, Russian-speaking friend, sat next to a 50-year-old man, who rapidly fell to arguing with her. "How many statues of Stalin are there in Britain?" When she replied "None," he complained: "Why not, if you have statues of Roosevelt and Churchill?"

When Niamh volunteered that there were hardly any Churchills either, he persevered: "But why are there no statues of Stalin in Britain?" Niamh said it was because we did not respect him. "Why not?" "Because he was a cruel dictator who killed his own people." He looked at Niamh in disgust and said that Stalin was *muzhestvenni*, a real man. Thinking he would put down Britain, he asked if there were a lot of "black people" in London.

When Niamh answered yes – *and* yellow *and* pink *and* brown – he said smugly that there were no black people in Daghestan and promptly stopped talking to her as a sign of his contempt.

Above the side of the driver's windscreen, there was a photo triptych of Stalin, the Virgin Mary and a female body-builder in a cut-away leotard. My gifts of coloured postcards of Madonna, the popular singer, whose torso was being held by hands of all nations, were eagerly snatched away. Over the middle of the front windscreen was another picture of Stalin upon a bunch of plastic red roses. There is always a place for a small portrait in the home, either in the form of a postcard-sized photograph or a wall-mounted chromed plaque. A truck in Gunib even had Stalin's portrait painted on the door. Although he transported and murdered large numbers of the peoples of Daghestan, he is still revered as the archetypal strongman.

Truck with portrait of Stalin on the door on the road from Gunib, Shamil's fortress.

This masochistic worship has something akin to the fascination exerted by serving in the Red Army. In villages locally painted recruiting posters with handsome Slav faces asserted "glory to the armed forces of the USSR." When call-up day came, the Red Army conscript was probably leaving his Daghestan for the first time, so the army gave him a chance to see the world – or rather, the Eastern Bloc, Afghanistan and the USSR. Daghestan conscripts formed close-knit groups to resist intense racial prejudice, starting officially with their being obliged to eat pork, or nothing.

Their experience was commemorated in a professionally prepared *Pamiat v Sluzhbe* – a 'Memorial of Service'. One such treasured album was covered in Red Army greatcoat felt, with bullets as terminals on the binding, and red and green painted moulded tin tanks and lettering. Inside I saw a curious pre-call-up party picture, where the boys were wearing girl's headscarves and dresses. On every page, there were paintings of Red Army symbols and photographs of the recruit and his army friends. The last page had a tin moulded fist, punching through a wall shaped into the number 730 – the number of days of service (see pages 165 & 220). Recruits liked their new-found "liberty," which gave rise to the popular song of the plaintive but frisky Kumyk maiden from Daghestan, hoping that her betrothed who had left for his military service, would not fall for a Russian blonde.

Many didn't return from the Great Patriotic War, as the Soviets called the Second World War. Some villages lost half their men. Almost fifty years later they were building a new monument to the war dead in the centre of Bezhta

A post-perestroika stall in Market No. 2, Makhachkala, showing popular icons Shamil, Arnold Schwartzenegger, Indian girl film idols and Italian pin-up Sabrina. The stall has since vanished.

village. Their enthusiasm contrasted with the confused embarrassment of the curator of the Akhti museum, when I asked if I could photograph the four freshly painted names on the memorial roll of the dead, the results of the Afghan war. He was happier about the large oil painting of 'The capture of 22 Germans' by Ibraghim.

As well as the war sections in local museums, which were common throughout the USSR, there were naive-style portraits of war heroes on the walls of municipal village gardens, and on some houses square cameos of swarthy Daghestanis, and not the expected Slavic war heroes. In the village of the tightrope-walkers, mentioned below, there were several one-legged war veterans, wearing their medals, standing in front of the painting of their air-ace, who shot down two hundred enemy planes. In a different mountain town there was a portrait of the local sailor hero, while on another village school wall, a battered poster proudly announced: "In our school from 1927-34 studied a hero of the Soviet Union Zsed Babastanovich Salnikov." A simpler memorial was a bent and twisted four-inch T-section rolled steel joist embedded in a great rock in Buglen village, the handiwork of the Kumyk strongman, Ali Kilich, who died fighting in the Civil War (1920). Like a self-appointed guardian of this shrine, an eagle swooped in the background.

It reminded me of the Moscow victory parade, where the bands were led by remarkable standard-bearers, holding high their micro-cosmic symbols, direct

Painting by Franz Rubo, court painter to the Tsar, of the storming of Salti (September 21st 1847) after a six week siege.

descendants of those carried by the conquering Central Asian hordes. The delightfully pagan standards were made of pairs of hanging horse tails, flanking brass ram or bulls horns, surmounted by a spherical finial. The Red flags had tear-drop shaped flat finials in old Persian-style, though here they were simply filled with a cut-out brass Red star.

After the breach of the Great Caucasian mountain chain by the construction of the Georgian military highway during the 1780s, until Imam Shamil finally surrendered Daghestan with honour in 1859, a significant part of the Tsars' army was tied up in the Caucasian wars. This distracted the Russians from their wars with Turkey, and removed pressure from Persia and the British trade routes to India. The Daghestanis (and their neighbours, the Chechens) who resisted Russian rule from 1800 were called *murids*.

They were followers of the Naqshabandi Sufi order, and their aspirations can be read from the Arabic inscriptions on the green banner of the Murid leader Imam Gamzatbek, taken by the Russians at the storming of Chekmeshkent village on December 1, 1831: "Once you have gone to war, be cautious and patient during the horror of conflict; you must survive until the end. Victory to he who upholds the faith, defeat to the unbelievers! May God forgive your past and future sins. May his love carry you on the straight path, and may God help you. Allah, Allah, Allah!"

While Imam Shamil took an active part in the resistance from 1830, he was only chosen as leader after Gamzatbek's murder in 1834. But from the Tsar downwards, the Russians admired and had suffered at the hands of Shamil and his men. The Russian court painter Nikolai Svetchkov portrayed the Imam on horseback in 1859 and thirty years later the Tsar's historical painter Franz Rubo filled huge canvases with scenes of battles and Shamil's surrender. The reputation of Shamil was denied by the Communist Party until recently, when there was an academic conference in Daghestan, which turned into a celebration of Shamil's spiritual homecoming.

It seemed to snowball from there. In 1990 two calendars with Shamil's portrait were printed, one with his name in Arabic (albeit wrongly spelt). In the Kraevedcheskii Museum in Makhachkala there is a display case for his holsters of leather with mounted velvet panels, decorated with couched and laid silver threads, his saddle, covered in red silk velvet, embellished with silver stars and discs of Crimean Tatar or Turkish work, his *shashka* Caucasian sabre and some of the medals, which he presented to his *naibs* or commanders. The silver gilt and niello discs are the size of the palm of a hand. Recalling Shamil's magnificent fight against the Russians, where it was said that one of his Daghestani mounted warriors, locally known as a *djigit*, could match a hundred of the Tsar's troops. The medals boast traditional Arabic inscriptions such as "He who thinks what will happen after the battle, is not brave," and "That is our son, he is very brave and in battle he was a lion." Shamil stylishly never wore medals, but gave them to his *naibs* to indicate their rank.

1870s photograph of Gurusi village. Moshe Gammer in his book 'Muslim Resistance to the Tsar' noted that during the 19th-century Caucasian War, the Russians had to destroy villages like this every three years in rotation – apart from burning the roofs there was nowhere to throw the stones.

'Haji-Murat' and his djigits on parade at the First Avar Festival (Khunazkh). The historical pageant excluded re-enactment of Russian defeats.

Only seventeen out of two thousand mosques had been permitted to function in Daghestan since the severe repressions from 1928 to 1938. During 1991, mainly in northern Daghestan, over two hundred mosques were re-opened, caught up in the new dawning of Shamil. Reinforcing this revival, in 1990, the Fond Shamilia, an academic centre for studies of the previously banned

A local acting Shamil with a microphone, at the festival of the renaming of the village of Shamilkala ('Fortress of Shamil'), previously known as Svetagorsk ('Light of the Mountains'), in 1990.

nationalist and anti-Russian hero, was started at the Daghestan branch of the (then) USSR Academy of Sciences. Even in Bezhta, a remote alpine village, the first question we were asked at an official village meeting in 1989 was: "Did Shamil visit our village?"

The reinstatement complete, modern portraits of Shamil are now seen everywhere. My first sighting of one was at the Writers' Union Festival in Makhachkala in 1988, where a painting was stood significantly beside the door of the war museum. At the 2,500th Anniversary Festival in Khunzakh in July 1989, no Russian was spoken by any official there, only Avar – Shamil's language. The main posters were portraits or sayings of Shamil. While the mounted historical pageant featured Haji-Murat, the fearsome rebel commander who broke with the Imam only to be betrayed and decapitated by the Russians, there was tactfully no re-enactment of fighting against the Tsarist Russians, against a massive background sheet painted with Shamil and the Tsar having a sword-fight on horseback. The old Obkom council building had been given new stone walls and was transformed into a fortress, which various generations of Daghestanis attacked, wearing appropriate costumes. Over the main gate, the white cement bust of Lenin had to be boxed in for protection against the blank charges fired from the cannon. There was the rare sight of horsemen swathed in *bourkas* galloping past.

The first Shamil demonstration led by religious elders in 'papaka' hats at the renaming of the village of Shamilkala.

At all festivals men and boys performed traditional dances dressed in the *cherkess* – the traditional black flared coat with a bandirole for charges sewn across the chest – while old men singers comfortably wore the *cherkess* decked with Soviet war medals. Shamil's final official recognition came in August 1990 at the renaming of a recently-built village, previously called Svetagorsk, a Stalinist-style name, meaning in Russian 'Light of the Mountains'. The village was rechristened Shamilkala, meaning 'Fortress of Shamil' – *kala* is a local word borrowed from Turkish. The parade with banners and slogans of the Imam continued with an energetic ride-past in old costume accompanied by gunshots and cannon firing blanks. The speech from the local First Secretary was read in Russian, while the local imam spoke without notes in Avar. There was a disappointing actor playing Shamil on horseback. He needed notes for his incongruous speech in Russian which he muttered into an out-of-place microphone. The men were followed by three important women, a poet, a singer and a scholar who spoke of the role of women in Shamil's struggle. Then rows of men in front of rows of women prayed on the football pitch.

By 1993 the pictures were no longer sold in the market in Makhachkala when either the mafia required too much protection money from the tin-pot stall or the bearded religious men disapproved of the company Shamil was keeping. The most fantastical image has to be in a smart new private restaurant on a remote road, crammed with specially commissioned oil paintings and exotic beaten metal screens. On one huge canvas covering an entire wall, Shamil is depicted flourishing his sabre at the gallop, racing alongside an unusually lean Rasul Gamzatov, national poet and member of the supreme soviet of the USSR, who was clutching his book *My Daghestan*. The image of

Gamzatov seemed to reflect his political future. It was not clear if he was waving or falling off.

Shamil exhibits had been discreetly on display alongside diagrams of a faked class structure in the Kraevedcheskii museum in Makhachkala for many years, but by 1993 an enlarged objective display had been opened. There is still, however, no statue of Shamil in Daghestan. The question remains whether the inspirational memory of Shamil, such as my colleague Magomedkhan felt, standing before the portraits of his forebears who fought with Shamil, will not be trivialised into a mindless Stalin-style personality cult.

ം

Every man and boy in Daghestan carefully keeps and venerates the uniform and arms of his grandfather and great-grandfather, the original *djigits*. The *djigit* was a dare-devil mounted warrior, whose sure-footed horse could float over the terrain, scattered with loose and protruding rocks, punctuated with fast deep rivulets and sudden ravines. I experienced this scary thrill in the summer of 1993. After staying with some alpine shepherds I was gently walking back on horseback over an uneven grass and rock murrain between two mountain ranges towards the village of Archi. I was thinking of a hot bath, being sore and raw and increasingly too large for my saddle, when up rode a young man, who greeted me. We smiled and he unexpectedly gave my horse a whack which sent us off at the gallop. I chose life and cameras akimbo about my neck I pulled back the horse's mane. He stopped with several jolts. It hurt. The young man laughed. I swore.

Horses hold an important place for Daghestanis. Horses which won special funeral races symbolically took their dead masters to the next world, even in this century in the North Caucasus. It is not unexpected to find that horse-racing was and is an all-male affair. After much preparation, the meet was held in late spring, when planting was completed. Among the Tsakhurs, for instance, the elders selected the *bek* or organiser, who had to be middle-aged and respected in the village. He chose the date for the races, which was announced at the village meeting place, called *godekan* in Avar and other local languages. The event was held in a field five kilometres from the village. The *bek* had to order supplies and nominate reliable men to transport them up to the mountains on the day. He had to check all the horses and harnesses of the competitors and allocate entrants to races.

On the great day, all gathered on the outskirts of the village and, led by the elders, the procession of horses, carrying men and food, samovars and wood, set off to the accompaniment of music. The women were left behind with the musicians and had their own feast. Races were run in series of heats of four and went on till there was an overall winner, who received a prize of a length of cloth or a shawl. As a parallel competition, everyone was given painted eggs, which were used in a game of striking egg against egg to find the strongest, like

Two portraits of Imam Shamil –
above: pastel, artist unknown; right:
oil painting by Nikolai Svetchkov,
1859 (photo: Justin Thomas)

a bizarre game of conkers. The lavish festive meal with roasted meat was followed by music, singing, dancing and games. The return procession had a strict order: first the *bek*, then the winning horse, with both his owner and jockey on his back, next the second horse, and so on, to the last. All the others followed, with boys running at the back. At the edge of the village they were met by all those left behind and women draped brocade over the winning horse and tied ribbons on his mane. In the evening the owner entertained his close friends and the whole village continued celebrating.

Every son, in his proud father's eyes, was a future *djigit* warrior. When boys did something wrong, they were not hit, but told a story. Tales of the Nart giants provided both a fascinating lesson and a good yarn, which was why they survived. The Narts were the central characters of ancient Iranian myths. During the rule of the Iranian Sassanians, before the seventh-century Arab conquest of Daghestan, their culture became mixed with the Avars and much later, after the Mongol invasions, with that of the Turkic Kumyks. The first record of a mounted warrior from Daghestan appears in Movses of Chorene's seventh-century AD account of a cavalry attack on the Armenians from the north-east, led by an invincible Nart-like giant covered in felt armour.

The first generations of Nart giants were strong but stupid. Legends attributed natural phenomena to the work of Narts, as assistants to the creator of the world. Mountains, rivers and pastures were all products of their colossal strength. The two-metre volcanic stone balls, scattered in the fields around Tlokh and Kharakh certainly look like marbles that once belonged to a boy colossus. According to one legend, a Nart divided the turbulent waters of the river Sulak into the Avar-Koisu and Andi-Koisu rivers. The latter, it was also said, came from seven streams, each guarded by a Nart. Two of them had a quarrel and fought, so God became angry and made an earthquake and an enormous gorge appeared, which filled with water to become the river.

By the road to Khasavyurt stands a freak sand-dune five kilometres long which moves randomly half a kilometre every year. Stranger still, the yellow sand is only found in Turkmenistan on the far side of the Caspian Sea. Scientists are baffled by this. A fantastic explanation according to a Lak legend, is that the dune, called Sari-Kum, the nearby mountain of Vatzilu and the Kazi-Kumukh-Koisu river were formed as a result of the love of two Narts, Barkhu and Arin, for a beautiful Pari, an angelic mythical fairy, who lived on a snowy mountain. When the Pari saw how the sun rose out of the sea, she wanted the sea at the foot of her mountain and so she offered herself to whoever could bring it to her. Barkhu, with his huge hands, dug an enormous space for the sea, throwing all the earth in one place to form Mount Vatzilu. But the Nart, on his way to the sea to fetch water for the pit, noticed Arin filling his helmet with sand and pouring it in one place, which created Sari-Kum. Arin saw that Barkhu had already created a sea, so he shot an arrow into Barkhu's back and he fell dead into the water. The news reached Pari, the snow-beauty, and she wept bitterly, for she loved Barkhu and her hot tears formed the Kazi-Kumukh-

Koisu, which poured into the village of Tzudakar. The river continued to the sea, in symbolic union between Pari and Barkhu, while Arin was cursed by the snow-beauty to roam the steppes for ever. Vatzilu was considered a holy mountain and people often climbed to the top to pray for a good harvest.

Another cosmic manifestation was the advent of the one-eyed Nart, recalling Homer's Odessy, where the cyclops are called "circular-eyed" – this could indicate why the story cycles are believed to date from the seventh-century BC. The Avars called this giant "plate-eyed," and to the Laks, he was "bread-eyed" and "cup-eyed." His cyclopean eye, big, round and brilliant, stood for the sun. Narts bowed in the direction of the setting sun and the sun answered to their bidding by pausing to allow them to complete their day's work.

A second breed of Nart was also strong, but wiser and kinder. This Nart slept for weeks to gather his Herculean strength, then roamed through the woods, leaving enormous footprints. He loved to hunt and then hang the game he had killed, from the uprooted plane tree, which he carried on his shoulders, like the north European Wild-Man, an often green, always hairy figure who lived in the primal forests and who symbolised the uncontrolled passions of men (and women), most notably illustrated in 15th-century South German tapestries.

In one tale a villager fell asleep after ploughing, and when he awoke, he saw a great Nart beside him, who was examining what he thought was a wooden stick. The Nart asked him what it was, and the man told him that it was a weapon, which could shoot a great distance. The Nart was amazed that a thing like that could exist in his lifetime. He pondered for a while and then asked if the gun could kill a bull he could see some way in the distance. Without moving from where he was, the man shot it. The Nart thought that if people had become clever enough to invent a stick like that, it would be difficult to beat them. But when the Nart said that he would go to a nearby mountain, the man became suspicious. So, after the Nart left, the villager stood his *bourka* felt cape up in his place, while he moved out of the way to safety. From the top of the mountain, the Nart plucked a great tree from the ground and hurled it at what he thought was the villager. But on his return, the Nart saw that the man was alive, and he admitted: "Now that man has become wiser and more cunning and invented such a weapon, there is no place for us." And that is how Narts disappeared from the face of the earth.

Yet a third spawning of Narts proved to be less strong, but wiser and technically more advanced. Legends of the Kumyks, Laks and Avars even attribute the construction of the 130-odd kilometres of the walls of Derbent to Narts. In folklore, the Nart symbolised the best human virtues. There was no higher compliment than to say that someone was as manly as a Nart.

One Nart had two wives. He asked his younger wife if there was anyone stronger than him or more beautiful than her. She answered, "Wherever could there be people like that?" He asked the same question to his older wife, who said, "The world is very large, so perhaps you could find them." The Nart was enraged and threw out his older wife. "Why should I keep a woman like that?" he muttered. But he decided to find out for himself. He searched far and wide and eventually lay down to rest beneath a tree. At that time, there were other Narts, stronger than him, living in these parts, whose son was grazing their horses. The son greeted him, saying "*Salaam aleikum!*" (as good Muslims do), he then captured him and took him home, where his brothers said that they were happy to have him look after the geese.

The smaller Nart ate and ate to get stronger so he could escape. One day he unexpectedly saw an even larger Nart, dragging nine carts loaded with salt in one hand, and great cured bull pelts in the other. He begged him to save him from the family of Narts and he readily agreed and hid him in his mouth. When his captors returned on horseback, they asked his rescuer where was the little Nart and he replied that he had not seen him. They asked him again, pointing out that he had only recently run past, and the great Nart shook his skins at them and chased them away. Later, when he returned home and sat down to eat, he thought that he had a loose tooth, until he remembered the little Nart and took him out of his mouth. He invited him to eat with him and asked him how he came to be there. The little Nart told his story and in return, the great Nart started: "We were forty brothers. One day we were out hunting and it became dark, so we decided to rest in a cave, out of the rain. When we woke up in the morning, we discovered that the chamber was actually the skull of a Nart. That moment an even bigger Nart rode by, and his dog picked up the skull and ran off. The Nart took his whip, and flicked away the skull, which rolled for forty days and nights. That's the way my thirty-nine brothers were killed, but I, by chance, was saved. So don't think you are the strongest or the most beautiful in the world, the world is large. Go home and get rid of your foolish younger wife and take back the older, who told you the truth."

❧

In other epic poems, Narts were renowned for dancing on point, as are young men in Daghestan and other parts of the Caucasus today. The steps were prodigiously difficult. A typical solo toe-dance sequence is made up of nine different parts, including straight and sideways runs and alternating gallops, pirouettes, leaps with an arched back, landing half-squatting and hopping while holding a leg. This Caucasian tradition set fire to the sensational ballet coming out of the Marinski Theatre and Diaghalev's Ballets Russes, who only half acknowledged their debt.

After the Revolution, only Caucasian dancers were allowed to wear daggers and swords, which were forbidden in the rest of the USSR. The highlander was never parted from his weapons, even when dancing, or his music, even when fighting. In the eighteenth century, a Russian Tsar wanted to invade Daghestan through the Kumyk plains beside the Caspian sea. His spy visited a few places, and returned to the Tsar with this curious report: "They are few, their army is small and lightly armed, yet these people are invincible unless you destroy one small three-stringed musical instrument, called the *achaka kupuz*. For, unless it is silent, their spirit will never be defeated."

Another form of dance is tightrope-walking. The ancient secrets of the wire are as well known in Daghestan as in distant Uzbekistan and China. The end of a day's celebrations was marked by the magic sight of a man on the rope at dusk, silhouetted against the lurid pink and violet sky. The Lak village Tsofkra-Pervoy, with a hundred houses, is known as the village of the tightrope-walkers. When I arrived, they were all away of course, working in circuses as far away as Moscow. Their skills seemed impossible. A master walker would jump up and

grab the wire or walk up the guy rope, but never use a ladder. At an Akhti festival, I watched one such walker called Khadirov balance two glasses on a wooden T-shaped platter held in his mouth, while standing inside a vertical bicycle wheel rim on the wire.

One Avar managed to upstage the entire Daghestan national dance troupe. First off, a glass filled with water balanced on his forehead, he walked up the guy-rope and lay down on the main rope. Next, without spilling a drop, he stood up and passed two bicycle wheel rims around his body, and then stood inside a rim and skidded along the wire. The 'official' state-sponsored artiste had walked blind inside a sack, whereas the local man hopped blindfold. Finally, he walked the wire, with two toddlers in rope cradles, suspended from each of his feet, after which he danced down the guy-rope. Others could stand on toe-point on the wire, and also on a tin tray, which they eased along the wire.

Khunzakh 2,500th Anniversary Festival. Ancient warriors are strong too. The young venerate and listen to the old in Daghestan.

They even made pyramids of three people on piggyback, like the man with his eight-daughter tightrope-walking troupe. The acts were always accompanied by the reedy wail of the broad mouthed *zurnah* horn and insistent drums, while money was collected by two masked clowns, one wearing a goat's head or skin, the other dressed as a devil or a bear. They would tease individuals in the audience, with shouts of "You look like a rich fellow, how about a generous donation?!" as they collected five to ten roubles a head.

Wrestling was even more popular than tightrope-walking. As in Ancient Greece, before the start of a wrestling match, a dance was performed, but this custom disappeared in the 1850s, dourly banned by Imam Shamil because it

There is no trick in sledgehammering this heavy stone placed on a carpet on the strongman's stomach at the Khunzakh Festival.

was "a time of danger for their land." Their technique was similar to Cumberland wrestling, the aim being to flip the opponent onto the ground, using only hands or knees, while remaining standing. The fights were umpired strictly by the elders, or *aksakali* – a tradition which reappeared in a different form last year when a potentially nasty inter-ethnic conflict between Lezgins and Avars was avoided when the elders suddenly appeared and ordered the young bloods to go home which they promptly did.

But forget those stories of the weak but cunning fighters beating their heavier opponents. It is the epic tales of the strong men of Daghestan forged in the wrestling or circus rings, which are the currency of the oral tradition today. Here, for example, is the tale of Kochap Mamma, a Kumyk-Avar, later known as Sali Suleiman of international fame. Incalculable physical strength and an iron will made him the invincible king of wrestling, having fought in Poland, Iran, India, Turkey, Denmark and Sweden. He was honoured as Champion of Champions in his native town, Buinakst, and lived until 1972 when he was over ninety.

Mama was born to a poor highland family, and worked from childhood. At sixteen, he went to work as a loader for a wine merchant. He could easily break a chain, make a knot in a steel rod, or bend a train rail over his shoulders. I once saw an ancient long-haired straggling-moustachioed strongman in Baku lift twenty men standing on both ends of a length of railway track and then bend the track with his neck, as if he was being crucified. He had turned grey as he staggered away exhausted, the fat flowing over his corset-truss.

But back to Mama's story. Once, on his way home, he came upon two men with daggers at each other's throats. Mama snatched the blades, broke them as if they were wood and held the two men apart. The wine merchant was impressed and began putting on demonstrations of Mama's strength. When a circus came to Buinakst, Mama went to see the wrestling. A Turk had defeated all comers, and the crowd demanded that Mama had a go. He lifted the Turk off the ground and threw him down. Out came a well-known 131kg wrestler to teach the boy a lesson, but Mama dropped him harder and broke his nose.

When he won the championship of Azerbaijan, Mama became known as the Lion of Daghestan. Next he beat the Persian champion and progressed to Turkey, to fight the Sultan's gladiator. The two men, smeared with oil (as is the custom in Turkey) had a hard match, but finally, Mama caught the Turk around the torso in a vice-grip, squeezing him into submission. The Sultan pronounced Mama champion and renamed him Sali-Suleiman after a historic hero. Sali-Suleiman toured with the famed circus 'Maksa'. Once, in Rostov, he saw and was fascinated by classical wrestling, but when he asked advice from Le Bushe, the French champion, he was invited to a teaching demonstration and derisively thrown, by surprise. In St Petersburg, Mama took the opportunity to train professionally. After a contest in the Zoological Gardens there, a defeated Spaniard, in revenge, opened the cage of a Bengal tiger which leaped on Mama, who grabbed it by the throat and killed it, despite his wounds.

At the regional mini-Olympic games in Odessa, the circus was packed to see the greatest wrestlers in the world. First in the ring was Mama – his opponent was the elegant Le Bushe, who was still smiling when Mama lunged forward and threw him with his own hold. Le Bushe had to be carried out. At the World Championships in Florence, Sali-Suleiman defeated his remaining rival, the world champion Dane, Pederson; and in Paris, the following year, he defended his title. Sali-Suleiman also won in Chicago, Washington and Rome, Madrid and Stockholm, Warsaw, and even London. Paruk Debirov, a huge laughing Avar, and one of my collaborators at the Academy of Sciences, once met him and said that he was a fine figure of a man, but utterly mad.

Other strongmen threw donkeys, held revving cars immobile or twisted rail track with their bare hands. The most bizarre act I saw was a Lezgin, who started off by lifting three 16kg iron balls, tied together with cloth, in his teeth. He then twisted four-inch nails with his hands. Next, he lifted another man sitting on a chair by taking the back of the seat in his teeth. Finally, he lay on his back and a worn rug was placed on his body. A large rock was manoeuvred across the platform by three assistants who lowered the rock onto his torso, with his head and feet protruding. An assistant then took a sledge-hammer and smashed the rock like an energetic convict. As it was going slowly, another helper got to work with a second sledge-hammer. I was barely able to lift some of the smaller bits of rock. There was no trick involved. The crowd loved it, particularly the boys.

Wrestling is taken seriously by the State too. The entrance to Makhachkala wrestling school, built in 1935, may be flanked by giant social-realist Soviet-style statues of revealingly-clad and well-endowed Russian youth and girl athletes, but inside the transformation of boys into men was in progress.

International coaches instructed 12- to 16-year-olds and their little brothers. Even the handicapped son of one of the coaches had been helped to walk through wrestling. The nine pairs of older and ten pairs of younger boys trained obsessively five times a week for one hour in the morning and from 3.30 till 5 in the afternoon. They all danced as well. Next, the senior class started with a line-up and the Muslim greeting *salaam aleikum* 'peace to you!', from the coach, followed by a roar of *aleikum salaam* 'and peace to you!' from the class. There were two small and wiry champions in the senior group. "Why are they so tough?" I questioned the coach. It was obvious. "Because, unlike the Russians, they don't eat pork."

The Russian wrestling team invited to Manchester for the 1994 British open championships, was entirely made up of nine Daghestani champions. Their Daghestani sponsor was Gamid Gamidov, a retired champion and also president of the national savings bank and a

Two wrestling champions (one of the three Gamidov champions is on the left), at the Makhachkala Wrestling Academy.

director of the Daghestan central bank. Many of his bank staff are ex-wrestlers – at least they are used to winning. But they never arrived – airfares had been hit by inflation and were unaffordable.

❧

Both in the USSR and Eastern Europe, when the Communist Party totalitarian system dissolved, there was little to take its place except nationalist fascism and simplified religion. In Daghestan, however, if the schools disappeared, the eight hundred *medreses*, or Islamic religious schools, could return – and are returning. Piles of Marxist books in sheds and corridors outside schools and libraries wait to be recycled and supposedly less dogmatic and history is being rewritten in multi-ethnic Daghestan by historians who were never allowed to think before. If the Soviet Pioneer camps, which were for indoctrinating the under-14s, and Komsomol, which took them up afterwards, have vanished, then a far older local education system, known as the pre-Islamic Men's Houses and Men's Unions, might well revive.

The Men's Union, first mentioned in 'On Scyths or Friendship' (the presence of Scyths in Daghestan is confirmed by the discovery of typical barbed Scythian arrowheads in several different places there) by the ancient Roman writer Lucian, is between a one term a year all-male violent English public-school and a German student co-operative of the early 1800s, with its obligatory sabre duels.* About that time, the Christian Cherkess princes in the North West Caucasus held similar six-week secret sessions in isolated huts, after the harvest. All participants had to wear masks, so that existing inter-family blood-feud vendettas would not interfere with their training. They went out on violent robbing expeditions and even spoke a secret language 'Cherkobza'. The Houses derive from a pre-Islamic tradition perhaps linked to Spartan training which would have been known in ancient Colchis which was located in present-day Georgia. Thus the Houses differ from the full-time Futuwwa or Akhi mystical Orders of Chivalry, which flourished in the Muslim world. The Men's Unions of Koubachi was called 'Chabkoun', and in Gidatl village and the Lak villages, they were called 'Chadkin', and those of the Bagulaal 'Igibi', the last two meaning 'devastation'.

As an example of life in the Men's Union in Daghestan, unmarried men and boys over fifteen in Koubachi entered their Union and left at twenty-five. Forty men, a fixed number, lived in each of the five towers spread around Koubachi; no one was allowed in to see them, not even a mother. A large part of the day was spent in competitive sports and games, the same method which is used today for military training. The Union performed exercises to the beat of a drum. They wrestled and raced in bare feet – hardened in cold water – and played games in snow and on ice. On the first day of spring, all Union members joined the villagers to take part in games, competitions and general merry-making, but, in order to avoid old blood-feud enemies, they had to remain unrecognised, so they wore masks.

Fifteenth-century stone carvings of the Union members in Koubachi depict wrestling, fisticuffs, horse-racing, polo and archery. In the Igibi (Bagulaal) and Chadkin (Laks from Gidatl) Unions the mastery of weapons and horse-riding was of prime importance. In Gidatl, they invented the Pamplonaesque Union horse-race. Unsaddled horses, without bridles, were gathered at the outskirts of the village and chased down a narrow street, where the Union members waited with bridles and whips in hand. Each man had to spot his own galloping horse, mount it at a run, put the bridle on and race along the route through narrow streets with low overhanging roofs, steep climbs and slopes, sharp turns and over fences.

---

* German students followed their professors from university to university and stayed at commercial lodgings with others who came from their local area. These semi-political organisations had the macho tradition of fighting other co-operatives in the three-stroke alternating sabre duel resulting in 'honourable' scars on the unprotected cheeks of the adversaries.

The Unions provided the core of defence in the community, protected the weak and old and acted as vigilantes. As training for security, the Chadkin invented a game, where three men were chosen to enter a house, late at night, and take something out unnoticed. If they succeeded, the house-owner was fined; but if they were spotted, the village crier would announce the householder's vigilance and he was rewarded with an exemption of one month's obligatory payment towards the maintenance cost of the Union.

The code of the Unions included self-sacrifice. In 1735, during the invasion of Daghestan by the Persian Nadir Shah, who had already conquered much of India, troops laid siege to Koubachi. The Union there fought valiantly but was so heavily outnumbered that the villagers begged them to surrender. Like the Spartans, they replied, "The Persians may enter our village over our dead bodies." The situation grew desperate, and further bloodshed seemed in vain, so a second group went to plead with the members. This time it was the fathers of those still left alive, thinking that they would be obeyed, but to no avail. Then, for the sake of the children and the old, and to save their village from complete destruction, the villagers themselves set fire to the towers of their protectors. The Chabkouni came out, but only to fling themselves at the enemy in a last stand. Every one of them was killed.

Education in the Unions was not only directed towards military prowess, but harshness toward enemies, devotion to community, dignity in victory or misfortune, and loyalty in friendship; all of which followed a strict social and moral code. Like a knight of the Round Table, the Chadkin member respected the elderly, behaved with courtesy to strangers, was amiable and convivial, but self-controlled, especially in eating or joking. In all, as Dr Sergei Luguev wrote in his thesis (1980-81) about the Lak Chadkin, there was a saying that "the heart of a Chadkin should be so big that you could ride a horse within it."

By the end of the 19th century, Men's Houses were widely spread over Daghestan. These were for boys of twelve to fifteen, and sometimes older, but always unmarried. In some cases, at the parents' request, even a child of seven or eight was admitted. In Koubachi these houses were called *gulala-aku-bukon*; the Gidatls, Akhwakhs, Balugaals, Chamadins, and others called them *hortlo ruk'*, meaning 'communal house'; the Khushtada, Tlondada and Tindi – *shchebili*; and in Lak *chartu batin*. As payment for their upkeep, the boys brought rations of meat, cheese, milk, flour or money.

The Men's Houses occupied large buildings, which were also used for meetings of clan-members, known locally as *tukhum*,* or for major feasts at births, weddings or funerals, with payment, again, in produce. Frequently such houses were taken over for the duration of the boys' assembly, lasting from one to three months each year. But the youngest boys – or sometimes all – spent nights at home. Unwritten regulations were strictly enforced by a *shah*, a sort of

---

* A *tukhum* is usually made up of blood kinsmen also joined by marriage, but can have honorary members from other villages or ethnic groups as well.

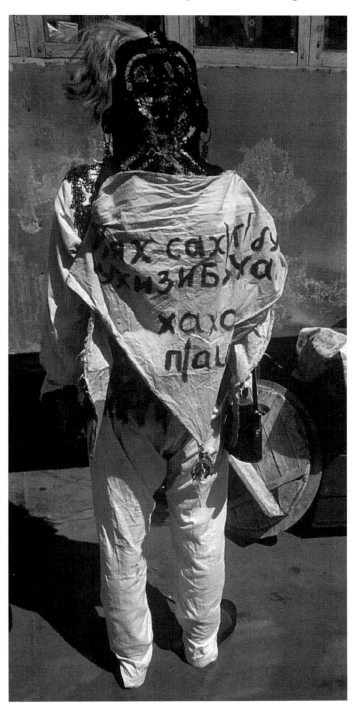

Koubachi boy on the roof of his house, dressed in painted plumed mask, tassled cape, with Koubachi slogans written in adapted Cyrillic, a whip, binocular case doubling as a 'kashkul' and Red Army issue long-johns. The costume is for Koubachi Union of Men rituals.

prefect, who usually had contributed generously to the rations, but also had authority and influence. He and his assistants had full power to see that all the rules were obeyed and duties were carried out: all procedures in the house had to be kept secret and no member was ever to appear in a drunken state. Any violation of rules was punished by a fine. The strict daily regime included competitive archery, duelling, horse racing, athletics and wrestling.

The Men's Houses and the Men's Unions existed side by side. Moreover in Koubachi, the administration of the Union organised the attendance of youths at the House, where members over fifteen automatically moved up to the Union, as did the Gidatls and Bagulaals. The Lak assembly for boys, called *chartu batin* 'stone-collecting', was not only connected with the useful community work of clearing stones from fields, but had a deeper association with the Lak Union of chivalry. In Daghestan, small round stones were slung or fired from bows in battle, and for that reason slings were used as children's toys. The Rugujda paid the villagers of Chokh for pasturage with three measures of small round stones which, in the past, they shot at enemies with a bow. It is written that such battles were mimicked in a favourite sport of Lak boys, during the festival of farewell to winter and welcome of spring. The Ingush and Chechens were still hunting birds early this century, using bows which fired stones, which were carried in a shoulder-bag.

In the Men's Unions, there were over eighty traditional games and contests, of which many were unique to the 'prep-school' Men's Houses. Most games were warlike, cruel or tormenting, reflecting their tough life. For example, a boy was sent out late at night to leave his cap somewhere in the cemetery and another, selected by lot, was sent to find it, not knowing that others were hidden there to frighten him. In the Rutul game of *daradugma*, a circle three metres across was drawn on the ground. The two teams of six drew lots, and the losers stood inside the circle. Each defender had a whip at his feet, with the end just over the perimeter; the attackers tried to snatch them from the circle and lash the shins or calves of those inside who, to protect their whips, kicked out and tried to pull their attackers into circle. When the circle was breached, the teams changed places. This game required – and taught – the ability to jump high. To develop a healthy mind there were a variety of board games, learning and reciting poetry and tongue twisters, guessing riddles, explaining proverbs, finishing a story started by another, and composing fables. Much time was also devoted to singing and dancing to music.

ૐ

Nowadays, in contrast, when the men of Daghestan met together, they usually acted like all Soviets from Moscow to Novosibirsk. They prepared their own food, sometimes with the help of male servants, such as their chauffeurs, and drank themselves stupid. *"Davai vypit' eshyo sto gramm!"* ("Come on let's drink another hundred grammes!") was intoned with a religious fervour. When I had drunk 31 – my other host was counting in wonder – toasts of vodka, with the present vice-president of Daghestan, who had once studied philosophy, he declared that I was a true *djigit*. The men made a fuss of toasting each other in their own languages. The purpose of these meetings seemed to be to reaffirm clan bonds, to introduce neophytes and transact business. It ended in hearty embraces and avowals of eternal friendship. I thought it was time to start frequenting the Rotary or Lions clubs back in Europe. I felt awkward, obliged to witness hours of ceremonial of which I was the unwilling focal point. There is even a ritual clinking of glasses where the toaster tries to touch the bottom of the toastee's glass with the top of his glass as a mark of respect. And vice versa.

One Saturday, Ramazan, then the director of Daghestan libraries who had kindly arranged the trip, took me to the town of Majalis in the Daghestan library minibus. I think it was the cold sheep's tail I ate there (allegedly to preserve me from the effects of the vodka) that did not mix with the acidic dry white wine and the thick sweet *kreplonnoye* doloroso madeira, which I had to drink by the glassful at every toast. Later that night, I opened the back window of the speeding white car of the First Secretary of Majalis, known as Number One, just in time to vomit the concoction as we hit another bump, narrowly missing him and his chauffeur at the front.

Majalis is near Derbent both geographically and in clan relations. The First Secretary of Majalis was entirely round and sly, in contrast to the tall and jolly 57th mayor of Derbent, whose city had aged 3,000 years during his short tenure. This was thanks to the archaeological discoveries of Sasha Koudriavsev, who had commanded us to drink with them at 6.00pm. Or was it the lunch I had already eaten at three? By eleven, the table was a battlefield of cold ram chunks, *khingali* dumplings congealed in white grease, pomegranates, red water melon and bread ends. But then, it could have been the whole clove of pickled garlic I chewed at lunch. When the car stopped outside the Number One's home, for him to pee in the road, I staggered out into a skewed wooden telegraph pole and retched four times, leaving nothing inside, except my bowels, which had turned to liquid. I rushed through the front door to the outside privy, where the cartouche-shaped hole was flanked by two plaster foot pads. Crouching, I tried to focus my lurching eyes two feet away, on a triangle of small holes, joined by shallow runnels – yes, it was the 'Chintamani' sign of Tamerlane the Conqueror, also known as three leopard spots over two tiger stripes! Only then did I notice that there was no water in the grey plastic ewer. How I wished I had not left behind my travelling bag with the carefully preserved paper roll. My once white trousers were already covered in vomit, thicker towards the feet, so I gave them a rinse too when I finally emerged. Then into Number One's house, where four of our party of nine remained. His wife had thoughtfully prepared another meal. Dargin dancing followed and I was obliged to take part. At last, the mayor of Derbent drove off in his black car at miraculous speed, and I was released down the road to sleep in a room, shared with a snoring archaeologist.

I awoke at eight with the phone ringing in my head, to find that in the outside world my toothbrush and clean clothes were miles away at the VIP's dacha in the Pioneers' camp. The white car arrived with surprisingly few traces of my nocturnal emissions, streaking away from the back window, like the crow's feet around my eyes. It was invigorating to race towards a road full of cattle with spiky horns next to a sign declaring in Russian "Peace on earth," first thing into a hangover. We reached the camp where I stripped and washed in the artesian fountain and then started leaking again, as the liquor had broken my digestion, so off to a twin-hole deluxe privy where the ammonia stung my eyes. In place of water or paper, it was furnished with leafy switches, which I could not work out how to use.

The others were still asleep, as I drove back ten kilometres to pick up my camera. I declined a large breakfast of cold mutton and dumplings in Number One's yard, in order to visit the Sunday market. Among the wares laid out on cloths on the ground, I bought what I took to be a large smoker's pipe carved from a single piece of wood, but which, appropriately, turned out to be an excreta tube for a girl baby's cradle. I blended in well, wearing my host's Soviet red track-suit bottoms, and was invited to watch a black and white kung-fu jumping combat film in the darkened village cinema, called the *video-zaal*, packed with boys and young men. I wandered back, as my washed white trousers should have been ready to iron now.

At the house, three people tried to hustle me away before my trousers had dried. My lone visit to the market had evidently broken some rule. I had been reported to Number One, who, grotesque in his sky-blue tracksuit, bloated and hungover, blocked his doorway and demanded our departure. My friends were embarrassed as we drove away and the chilled atmosphere was only broken when one of them asked me how old I had been before I was circumcised, having observed me as I washed earlier. He had thought that circumcision was only done in Asia. I was thankful when we got back to Makhachkala that evening, pursued by relentless vows of eternal friendship.

Such drunken fellowship was not confined to local high officials who had funds for entertainment. In Bezhta, I had been reluctantly adopted by Magomed, the German-speaking teacher, who looked like the young Jean-Paul Belmondo in the final reel of a crime film. We had visited some of his up-village friends in a three-storey house. Upstairs we had a bowl of soup and mutton, with three young men, playing cassettes of Avar songs. We discovered that Bezhta men have large feet, sized 41-42. Downstairs, all the women, girls and children sat eating in another room.

We left and while we were walking along an unpaved road in Bezhta, an old crone, carrying a great bundle of hay, walked up to Magomed. She asked him, in Bezhtin,* if it was true that she had heard that he was going back to his first

---

* The language common to 3,000 inhabitants in the village and different from the languages in the next village.

34

wife, who lived in another village. He replied that he was happy with his second wife and two children and hadn't heard anything about this, and where had she heard it from, as everyone talked to everyone in the street? We then went to his sister's house, drank tea and played with his little daughter. After lunch, I walked back with my staggering keeper. He couldn't find his key, so he smashed off the padlock on the door of his own house.

Inside, after a sharp rain storm, it suddenly became very hot and I fell asleep on the raised platform known as a *takhta*. My host had also passed out, to judge from the snoring drone when I awoke at two, drowning the noise of a helicopter landing. We were next to the landing field. The village was so often cut off by snow or landfalls that the helicopter was a vital link to the outside world. When I opened my eyes again, he had prepared more food. I howled the Spanish civil war cry *¡no pasarán!*, embraced my host, mockingly strangled him and left.

Daniel, the dog-fighting authority and historian was also there on a field trip. He had been visiting Bezhta every summer expedition time for 23 years to look into its history. He told Magomedkhan that it was fine to drink clean spirit in the mountains, and that it was impossible to get a hangover here. He believed it until he awoke late next day, with an internal balaclava and parts of his head missing, in reaction to the bootleg *chacha*, a spirit I think is quite poisonous. *Chacha* comes on horseback from Georgia in 70-litre oxygen cylinders. It sells for five roubles a litre, half the price of Daghestan state vodka, and the Georgians take back the local salty sheep cheese, paying eight roubles a kilogram. *Chacha* is 60-70 degrees proof – and allegedly better when clearer, not pale yellow – whereas vodka is 40 degrees.

I estimated that over half the adult males here in Bezhta are regularly drunk or suffering apocalyptic hangovers. This, together with Socialism, might account for why the town street is not paved, drained or filled and that there is no mains drainage, which could easily be dug. At a wedding, a young doctor told me, as we were gazed over Bezhta from a rooftop, that "there was no need for drainage, as we had the river." No one seemed to work there, except for the few who were rebuilding their houses, the school and the war memorial. Any work immediately stopped for a guest. Yesterday we bathed upstream, near two large drained rectangular ponds, which were built two years ago as a trout farm. But as an example of typical Soviet shortage, there was no food to feed the fish to be found, so the trout died. It seemed that the Russians used vodka to weaken the locals, as the British once used opium in China, and *chacha* finished the job. Fifteen years ago there was little drinking in Daghestan, however the Russians had used it before against the men of Daghestan in the 1830s as part of the attempt to crush the Islamic uprisings.

Magomed the German was shouting-drunk, reciting Teuton poems, until I silenced him with a souvenir £5 note and Michael Jackson photographs for his wife. On my other side was Jamal, sixtyish, our haggard host who used to be a village official, before his drink problem took control. I slept on the veranda to escape the drunken snoring. There were strange noises about. Next day I discovered the source: a donkey munching purposefully through the garden, followed by a three-legged cat.

Men could be sober too – but bellicose. Through the window of our Niva jeep in Bezhta, I spotted three men restraining a fourth, while another was smashing his fist into the man's body and face. I saw his eyes blazing through the blood. My suggestion to stop and take a picture was firmly declined and when I asked, "But wasn't it bad?", my friends replied, "No, he was standing, he was not killed." Whenever a Daghestan man made a sharp remark like that, he beamed, inclined his head, raised his eyebrows and in a slow, sweeping movement smacked the ends of the fingers of his right hand against mine.

By 1990 the blood-feud had reappeared in Grozny, the capital of Chechen-Ingushetia, where the current price was five hundred roubles per death. Subtler methods have been employed by Daghestan men to get out of difficult situations without losing face or resorting to violence. It helps to have languages like Avar with its tortuous verb forms and its twenty-odd participles, to avoid being directly offensive. One day we had commandeered an empty bus. When we stopped to pick up 20 passengers so our driver could pick up some extra money and we could ask them questions, six rowdy young men got on too. One of them had a screeching radio, which he would not turn off. So we stopped the bus and Magomedkhan asked them to get off, darting off archaic commands in Avar. Surprisingly, to me, they went quickly.

"What did you do?" I asked Magomedkhan.

"I changed the idea of leaving into a question of them keeping face," he patiently explained.

èa

It often puzzled me what was the right time to get an obstinate man to change his mind. One evening we arrived at Sergokala, renamed after the Communist butcher-general Sergo Orzhonokidze. Daniel, the dog-fighting historian, took me for a snack in the seedy beer hall. When we returned to our double hotel room, Daniel's three dried fish were beginning to stink, so I put them on the window sill. We also found a Dargin settled there, who introduced himself with the simple declaration, "My name is Elias."

It had been a long day. Dargins have a reputation for stubbornness and I remembered watching one making a reluctant sheep go forward by lifting its rear legs from behind and pushing it, as if he were steering a lawn-mower's handlebars. As I wrote, the dried Caspian fish, *leysh*, had just been moved in front of me, together with more 'Makhachkala Zhigolefskaya' beer, named after the Russian car. However, when the label was removed and neatly folded in a way that hid certain letters, those letters spelt out a Russian word for male member. This was repeatedly and painstakingly explained to me; it was such a laugh . . . "Do you understand? Let me explain again!"

Kung-fu in the evenings

An old Dargin woman, who helped run the boarding house, came to our room to talk to Elias, who did not want to move. I disappeared to wash my shirts downstairs, in re-used water from the tap, and then Daniel and I went back to the village beer house and shop. We bought more beer, vodka, tomatoes, hard-boiled eggs, bread and sausage. We watched gangs of Dargins drinking beer, sitting around tables littered with more dried fish ends. I could not stand that smell. Daniel smiled knowingly when we returned, and Elias had found another room.

Men normally only greet other men with a handshake or a kiss on the lips for a real or adopted kinsman; in contrast, it was not done for me or any other

My collaborator and friend Magomedkhan Mogomedkhanov, wearing a ceremonial 'bourka' before a picture of his ancestors. The old man in the centre of the portrait was an 'alim' of Shamil's.

Daghestani to kiss a friend's woman relative on the cheek). The correct form is very important. If a hand (or a drink for clinking glasses after a toast) is proffered and then ignored, there is cause for offence. One bright morning, by eight, after a mercifully light breakfast, we were at a gathering place for men who were going to work. The buzzing words *"inalshe, inalshe,"* Lezgin for "come over here," echoed against the sharp mountain light, as over a hundred men interminably shook hands with each other, and us. It happened twice every day.

Kung-fu in the evenings, strongman cults . . . even greetings can have their bizarre side, particularly to Daghestan visitors in English-speaking places. Rasul Gamzatov, the national poet, was introduced to a glamorous young lady in Britain as "Miss X." In Avar *miss* means 'vagina', so he immediately replied, "This is *mekhir* (meaning 'prick') Gamzatov!"

ᕫᕍ

Before Communism, the more sober Council of Elders, or *djamat* was of primary importance in each village, as it provided rules, organisation and justice for the community. Members had to be over forty. There are many legends and folk tales about how the Elders came to be revered. Three hundred years ago in the villages of Hushtada, Kvanada and Tlondada, there was a Bagulaal Avar tradition to kill off old men over sixty, because there was insufficient food. They put them in a basket and threw them off a special rock on the mountain.

Once an enemy besieged the village of Hushtada, where a young man had hidden his clever father, so he would not be killed. The father told his son how to beat the enemy. It was an old ruse or well-used tactic, or something . . . The trick worked and the villagers asked how he had thought of the idea. He told the villagers about his father and so they stopped killing their elders there. In another village, after a battle, the losers were to pay compensation in land or cattle. At a meeting they decided it had to be cattle, for they could not part with precious land. But one young man said that the cattle should be kept and the land given away. Everyone was surprised and asked him why. "Because we will soon be strong again and win back our land, but we will lose our cattle forever." All agreed and asked where he had learned such wisdom. The young man said it was from his old father, whom he had hidden. Another story tells of a young man, who was weaving a large basket, when his old father looked over and whispered, "Weave it strong, of good, thick reeds." The son asked, "Why?" and the old man replied, "So it does not break and can be used again for you." The son thought over his father's words and decided to let him go free.

Such stories mark the start of veneration of the Elders for their wisdom. Boys too are a part of the male hierarchy. Male ancestor worship has survived, with prominent framed hand-coloured photographs in most homes and the upkeep of cemeteries. The Khilikh' village schoolteacher had even drawn his family tree, five generations back. His grandfather was a revolutionary and he had kept his flag, a shiny cloth appliqué of a hammer and sickle emerging from burning young birch logs, with the slogan *Smena smene idyot*, 'Changes lead to changes'.

A few years earlier my academic colleague and friend Magomedkhan posed in front of his ancestor's portraits, wearing his ritual black *bourka* felt cape, golden fleece *papakha* hat and dagger. It may have been dignified but at the time the posing seemed slightly ridiculous to me. I was wrong.

In 1991 his father died of a heart attack in his village aged sixty. By chance I had helped save his life on an earlier occasion by delivering a large syringe from a British charity. It was the only such syringe in Daghestan and was used to draw off a litre of fluid from his lung which would have killed him. I learnt indirectly that he had been a famous underground Sufi leader. Hundreds of men came up the awful mountain road to Archi to mourn at his grave every day for the prescribed week. Magomedkhan is now the head of his *tukhum* or village clan of one hundred males. He is the final arbiter on any problems or disputes which any member of his clan brings to him. He has inherited his father's mantle.

I saw him during his own forty days of statutory mourning. He questioned how he could combine the old open-door traditions of his new archaic position with a modern working life. It is a problem for all the men of Daghestan. Is it a strength or their weakness?

·3·

Inventing the wheelbarrow: women & sex in the mountains

"Wagidat flicks the ball to Aminat, Aminat to Patimat, Patimat tackled by Aisha, Aisha to the other Patimat, the other Patimat passes back to Wagidat, Patimat again over to Aminat, beats Kalimat on the wrong foot . . ." The sunny Korkmaskala festival crowd of headscarfed women and girls, wearing long dresses over long trousers, screamed with laughter as the stand-up Kumyk comic did a spoof commentary on the Daghestan Olympic women's hockey match. It was impossible. It was so funny. Meanwhile, on the floor in a house in distant, mountainous Andi, barefoot women in white headscarves and red tartan shawls, sat and watched the television, where mini-skirted, deep-cleavaged singers jerked through their leggy dances at the Sopot International Song Contest. As they peered, they knitted, kneaded dough, embroidered or chopped food for dinner. Whatever were they thinking?

The women of Daghestan live in a state of self-contradiction: as guardians of tradition, work-horses and breeding machines. In Makhachkala, in 1989, I gave a 20-minute talk about women's liberation to a surprised 300 girls, studying English. Their reactions were giggles, but no questions, and after I was presented with Russian-type carnations, a miniature samovar and exquisitely bound English translations of Pushkin, the only comment was that they usually have much longer talks.

Women were guardians of tradition because they used to be isolated at home from harvest to spring, while the men went away to work in neighbouring Georgia or Azerbaijan. In the 1850s Laks worked as far away as Orenberg and Tabriz. It was reported that a young Kumyk bridegroom had just three days, before leaving his bride to be a 'widow' for eight months. When there was no work, mountaineers went to fight or pillage. Since the Revolution, the women's seclusion has been interrupted by sending them off to be educated, giving them jobs away from the village and by the creation of a transport service. The bus service to mountain villages is good (for example, six buses a day from Akhti to Rutul), but is often cancelled by bad weather or landslides.

The women of Daghestan have a well-defined role in traditional life, which may be one of its chief attractions, giving them what has been described in Europe as 'philosophical space', so they do not suffer from the same kind of depressions brought on by the modern woman's identity crisis. However their lives are subservient, hard and, depressingly (both to them and to us), circumscribed. They are kept so busy that they do not have the time, nor the energy, to ponder on a solution to their plight.

Men, by tradition and often nowadays, never addressed their wives by name, especially in front of strangers, saying *gei!* in Kumyk, *you!* in Avar or *gui!* in Dargin, all of which means "hey!" or "listen, you!" One reason given for this custom was that if a wife's name was mentioned, it would attract the attention of the evil eye and harm would befall her, similar to the effect of praising children. In Georgia too, wives may not address their husbands by name or pronounce words containing the syllables of his name to avoid the same result. In Daghestan a wife, in turn, addressed her husband as "he," and spoke to him only when it was convenient to him, in a soft calm voice.

The oldest representations of women in Daghestan are cast bronzes, which all show evidence of matriarchal (or at least equal) societies. The earliest, a seven-inch second millennium B.C. naked figure of a woman, proudly giving milk from her breast into a jar, was found in the village of Sogratl. Daghestan was a possible homeland for the legendary Amazons of classical antiquity, which could explain a seventh-century B.C. figure of a naked female charioteer, holding the reins, again from Sogratl and later naked figures of a woman with crown and pronounced vagina, sitting across a horse, and another with a crown and wearing neck, waist and arm rings, holding two drinking-horns, both found near the village of Gigatl, in the Tsumadinskii rayon.

Other archetypal figures are of a woman, with her hands touching her ears, re-enacting the moment of creation in Zoroastrian mythology, made about the third century B.C., found in Tsuntinskii rayon. Another representation is found in a cylindrical Daghestan bronze, with a male on one side and a female on the other, with broken common arms and a plant stem, growing from their head. Another pendant of a madonna and child, stated to be from the fifth to eighth century A.D. (but I think earlier), was puzzlingly made before any Christians arrived in Daghestan. It was excavated some distance from the border with Christian Georgia, in the village of Verkhnii Karanai, near Chiryurt, in the Leninskii rayon.

The Kumyks have the legend of an Amazon-like giant woman called Maksuman. Forty Narts, the Kart-Kojak, were her brothers, but Maksuman was both the strongest of them all and gave them strength. The Amazon was sleeping when the brothers called her, and beat her as she did not answer. She was revived by her small horses, who snuffled her awake and pushed the Kart-Kojak back. They then fired their bows, but the arrows missed Maksuman, who shot back, scattering them, as she scolded, "Shame on your old mother." The Kart-Kojak next went to Maksuman's father for special swords to subdue her. But when they knocked off her helmet, they were astonished to see her hair,

Shamkhal's wife in Andi head-dress at the Khunzakh festival – part of the Botlikh Family Ensemble.

because they had not known that she was a woman.

The tradition of strong women survives. Daghestan women fought the Russians, both under Shamil and during the Revolution, and today carry double their own weight of hay, on their backs, in the village of Archi and elsewhere, where the wheelbarrow does not seem to have been invented. Niamh O'Mahony, who is Irish and speaks Russian and Arabic and was living in London, accompanied me on her second visit to Daghestan. Unlike her first visit alone, to sign a contract for small tours, when she was an honorary man, this time she had the role of wife, and so was ignored by virtually all the men, who would not even shake her proffered hand, or greet her, out of respect for me. Although she naturally found this offensive, it freed her to talk with the women which was the aim of the trip.

Women greet each other and say goodbye by throwing a straight right arm stiffly around the neck, and then touch cheeks, but do not kiss, unless they are making a sign of kinship. In Gagatl, the daughters and daughters-in-law stood up from a squatting position, whenever the mother of the house approached. This formality reflects the ritual religious nature of women. Uraza Bayram is an Islamic festival, when families visit their ancestors' graves. It was permitted in Daghestan from 1988, for the first time under Soviet rule. Makhachkala cemetery was filled with the living, and there were groups of women, dressed in black, sitting around tombstones, gently chanting from the Koran. This emphasised the role played by women as guardians of the faith, throughout the recently-ended atheistic period. Religion demanded blind obedience from wives towards their husbands, and clergy blamed women's failure in their obligations as the cause for natural calamities, such as droughts or floods.

With the sound of old women counting their worry beads and praying at home, it seems odd that in the villages of Daghestan women do not go to the mosque, even though there are women's areas set aside there. But this is also the custom throughout the Muslim world. In contrast, it is chiefly women who

Three generations of women collecting water with ten litre copper ewers. The village fount is an important social centre. Daghestanis are proud of their strong, straight-backed women.

visit the holy shrines, which are found throughout Daghestan, and were so hated by the Soviet authorities. Today, every shrine is covered with hundreds of new ribbons, fluttering in the wind. This is magic folk-religion, with its vestigial paganism. Women practise dream divination by themselves in Daghestan, unlike Russia where there are mediums, said one Daghestani woman. When she dreamt, she interpreted blood as good luck, a dog means that a man is saying bad things about you, while a snake means that a woman is. Tea-leaf divination was not known, whereas palm-reading was practised by local specialists for free, but only if they wanted to; for instance, they would not when they were in mourning.

The old women have a mystical attachment to the soil. I stopped on the plain near Khunzakh, when I saw two old women in the distance. One of them suddenly collapsed in a field. A closer look revealed that, in fact, she was working, tearing hay not with a scythe but with her bare hands, tying bales with twisted hay. As her 70-year-old daughter explained, the almost blind and deaf 89-year-old mother insisted on coming out to work beside her, sitting in the field, as she was no longer strong enough to stand.

My first reactions of shock and outrage, leading to thoughts that she should be resting in an old peoples' home, gave way to an understanding of the way families look after their old in Daghestan and that she was there because she wanted to be with her daughter and because she had always been there. I remembered how Watt-the-Croft, my now-dead ancient wild neighbour in the Borders between England and Scotland, had been finally insulted when they dragged him away from his stinking sheepdogs and gave him a bath in the old folks' home in Brampton.

While I was taking a break between four weddings, I paused, leaning over the bridge in Bezhta. Looking into the sun, upstream, down the gorge, I noticed an old woman, jumping or treading, thigh-deep, with her long dress in the rushing muddy river, pounding wool in a loose-woven wicker basket, first with her feet and then, bent over, with her hands. She then carried the dripping load back up the incline. The wool was then dried on stones outside her house, before it was spun, ready for knitting. Another old Avar widow, with her lovely smile, who always cooked special treats for me, became unwell if she stayed indoors and did not work in her kinsman's garden in Makhachkala. "I have been given my life from the land," she explained slowly, "and I feel strong only when I am working on it."

ஃ

While walking along a track, up a valley, towards a village, I greeted rows of women bent double, hand-scything hay, while the male overseer was sitting on a large rock, shouting encouragement. He proudly posed to have his picture taken and the women rushed up, adjusting their silver-chain-fringed scarves and bright clothes, which they wear to do hard labour in the fields near Archi.

A. Omarov in 1870 gave an unchanging description of spring weeding: "If one looks down from a high place onto a green field below, one sees shapes moving slowly, exactly like a grazing herd; only when the figures stand up briefly to rest their tired limbs does one realise that they are women." And reaping, when "one can see a whole caravan of women, loaded with grain coming slowly from the field, bent double under the heavy loads, so that their heads are down near the knees."

Archi women work like slaves for the collective farm, earning 30 to 50 roubles a month, compared with the Soviet average wage of 160 to 200. During harvest, they are paid by the load of hay they carry, as weighed, and the record is six and a half *poods* or 104kg. We saw many women, who weigh about 45kg, including a 60-year-old, carrying 50 to 60kg. There was a 90-year-old there, they bragged, who still cuts the hay and carries loads.

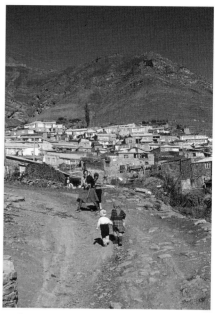

Women are blackmailed into this kind of work. As the *kolkhoz*, or collective farm, owns all the cultivated land,* hay could only be obtained from the collective farm, hay necessary to feed each family's two or three cows and forty-odd sheep. They allow women to take home one load in eight.

I was shocked by seeing women engaged in heavy work and challenged the *kolkhoz* chief: "Why don't you use wheels or a hand-pulled cart, or a hand-pushed cart, or a wheelbarrow?" "There's no point in having a wheelbarrow, the women would have nothing to do," he smiled at me, as though I had missed the most obvious point. Even in Lakhla, in the

Daghestani girls walking towards Kuli village – the largest mountain village in Daghestan, with 10,000 inhabitants. I was greeted by a teenager there in perfect English.

Tabassaranskii rayon, the pre-wheel transport method, where pairs of oxen pull wooden sleds, is a better option for women.

On the road near Lower Inkhelo village, I stopped the jeep to take pictures of three young women carrying large wooden beehives on their backs, supervised by a man. This is a method unchanged from last century, when a woman fetched stones for building jobs and fetched wood which she cut and brought back with a donkey in two loads – the heavier of which she carried

---

* Property changes since 1992 are described later in the chapter 'Daghestan avoids violence'.

herself. Men replied "That is our custom" when asked why women did all the heavy work. Anything to do with the home is women's work. A man's job is to provide security and travel. "Our women are very strong, they can carry all these weights," grinned the son of the house where we stayed in Gagatl.

Possible shame is ever-present in Daghestan, taking the place of sin in the Roman Catholic church. The Avar and Daghestan national poet Gamzat Tsadasa (Rasul Gamzatov's father – he is also national poet) declared that to do woman's work was considered disgraceful. A man played the leading role in the family, and his prayer was: "Save me, God, from the cold mountains and from a disobedient wife!" Dubrovin in the last century commented that "helping a wife in her work is considered shameful, and even when she is ill, a Daghestan mountaineer would not dream of doing her work, and asking a neighbour for such a favour would be a sign that he could not manage his household." Our passenger from Tsurib, a 45-year-old hunter, was amazed when he heard that I cooked in London. He admitted that in Archi women did all the work and men did nothing: "It's our way." However, there is an unexplained photograph of Shchinas men milking sheep, wearing traditional moccasins, taken in 1968.

There was a correct way, too, to do male work. For example, a man from Kharakh was skinning a sheep with a wooden wedge – but it should be done with the hand if he was a "real" man. By tradition, the man took upon himself only ploughing, sowing and hay-making, but gathering it and taking it away was woman's work.

The division covered games too. One evening, my absent host, Abdurakhman-the-Storyteller's lovely 17-year-old lodger student Zulfiya, and her two girlfriends, who all spoke Kumyk, taught me a three-handed card game called *durak*, or 'fool' in Russian, played with a six-to-ace pack and a trump suit. Trumps were wild. The loser was left with cards in his or her hand. Two played against each other, leading low for tricks. When one could not continue, he had to pick up from the discard pile and the third started to play against the other. Usually you took enough from the stack to make up your hand to six cards, but sometimes I was landed with the whole stack. I was mystified by the rules but it did not matter. Zulfiya whispered to her friend, who giggled, that they were playing cards with a man!

Women's work begins as girl's work. Archi girls carry twenty litres of water home from the communal fount twelve times a day, when washing clothes. They always wash at home, not at the fount. Dirty water is thrown out of the gate or door into the street, as there is no drainage. "Why don't you take the washing to the water?" suggested Niamh, dangling the principle of the laundrette. "We don't do things like that here," they shrugged.

Girls start serious cooking, like *khinkal* dumplings or *chudu* pancakes, from the age of nine, so by marriage at eighteen they are expert. They are expected to go to the fount several times a day, depending on the numbers of working women in the house. The Gagatl women were all up at six to milk the cows. After breakfast they went to move hay 500 metres from the truck to a store (where it could have been driven), for the *kolkhoz*. Each carried two 40-kilo bales at a time. Even a six-year-old girl carried a reduced load. Another girl complained about all the work women had to do all day long. When it was suggested that she refused, she muttered, "That's the way it is here, it's impossible to change."

In Khunzakh, teenage daughters are captive home labour. They can never go out even with girlfriends. Kalimat was a 15-year-old daughter, working in a field in Gagatl. It was a religious house were the men did not smoke or drink – the father was teaching himself to read the Koran in Arabic and was a stern man. Kalimat never stopped working, in silence, with her head always bowed. She was quick and lightfooted, and the only person who could get the picture right on the television.

Kalimat carried a couple of 20-litre aluminium canisters, slung over her shoulder with canvas webbing, from the fount half a kilometre away, up a steep path, slippery with cow-dung, five or six times a day. At the fount, when two other women were asked if they liked this work because they could meet other women and gossip, they scoffed at this purely male opinion. They agreed, laughing, that in Daghestan the women do all the work and the men do nothing, adding that they had no time to dawdle and left. When we asked why they let it go on, they chuckled and said that this was always the way here, explaining that if they waited for the men to do the work, then nothing would get done. It was the same story in Andi, where a woman was building a stone wall in an unconventional way. They always seemed to be doing things the hard way.

It is not only carrying heavy weights, but also the long hours of awkward work, which eventually breaks these women's backs, as Dubrovin also sadly noted in the 1860s. "The burden of work, required from early years, stunts their development and they age quickly, preserving for a long time only their beautiful eyes full of pain and indomitable spirit." Kalimat milked the family's four cows with her new 19-year-old sister-in-law, the two of them squatting on their heels in the field. Back at home, she had to make *chudu* pancakes, crouched on the floor.

Kalimat said that she would marry at seventeen to someone she did not want, and it had all been decided. The sister-in-law loathed the rewards of her marriage. She had come from a smaller family with less work. In poor Russian, they asked Niamh how many cows she had back in London. Milking cows is women's work. It would be shameful for a man to be connected with cow work. Men buy and sell and slaughter cattle. There was a village where a man once milked a cow, and it is now known as the Village Where a Man Milked a Cow.

The hand making of cow-dung patties for fuel, called *kizlyak*, is also girl's work. A young Archi girl, her mother and sisters, were all covered in cow dung, above the elbows and she splatted the round black slime against the wall, where it would dry and then be stacked like flat bricks. They laughed in embarrassment at being photographed. This was just progress from 1870, when a Mrs Omarov was reported to have remembered a little girl who could have been her great-grandmother. She came out early each morning to the place where in summer cattle were gathered to be taken to pasture, she stood in the middle of the herd and as soon as she noticed an animal lift its tail, she dashed to catch the dung in her bare hands – she soon had enough to make ten pieces.

People used to say "what a fine wife she'll make – lucky man who gets her!"

The wife of the mayor of Khunzakh was proud of her own traditional image, yet she admitted that 90 per cent of the women of Khunzakh go to work outside the home at the *kombinat*, or factory. She said that the women in Gagatl are free, as they only have to do housework. In addition to housework, women sew, knit and embroider, and some weave rugs and make felts, and felt shoes and resole shoes. In spite of their unending commitment, women had no rights in the social organisation or to attend public meetings and no voice in established social order, one thing the Party attempted to change, with limited success.

Taking snuff in Khunzakh. Snuff, or 'ts'unt' ', is especially popular with old women.

There is little work done purely for pleasure, excepting the manufacture of snuff, which is mainly taken by the old women. Surprisingly, women do not smoke cigarettes, not even home-produce with tobacco-stem woodshavings for a softer smoke. Daniel the dog-fighter's mother from Karata took snuff to cure her runny eyes – then his father started. But we also saw men taking it in Bezhta, Khunzakh and Kheleturi villages. At Botlikh market, women sold snuff for one rouble for a two-inch-long paper cone. Snuff, *ts'unt'* in Avar, is made from especially strong tobacco. Dried tobacco leaves are ground between a hand-sized and a round loaf-sized stone. The powder is mixed four to one, with perfumed ash from a local prickly bush, called *ts'ere* in Avar.

Snuff is kept in a used shotgun cartridge case, closed by a crumpled cloth plug, or ideally a wooden stopper. The plug is removed with the right hand and placed in between the thumb and index finger of the left, and a little snuff is tipped into the left palm. The cartridge is placed upright between the fourth and little fingers of the left hand, freeing the right hand to take a pinch between the right thumb and index finger, which is then snorted into each nostril – and elegantly done too.

The hard work of women is only part of their load. They also bear many children, and, as their husbands confirmed, preferably boys. Details of sexual practice were always kept secret in Daghestan, though the rituals, which enshrined the act, such as marriage, were frequently described, both late last century and more recently, as propaganda for Sovietisation. The customs which surround the salient points of the journey through a regular life, namely, birth, engagement and marriage, and death, are described in elsewhere in this book. However, attitudes towards sexual taboos, which are erected to protect the normality of life from largely inarticulated threats, are where the battle between Soviet, Muslim and pagan traditions has been waged, as was trumpeted in the 1940s anti-traditional Soviet poster of a veiled woman, with the slogan "Under the power of *adat* traditional law . . ."

Both a male and female informants have confirmed that up to the 1970s, female circumcision was widespread in Daghestan. It is not clear why it decreased or stopped, but it must have been partly due to the influence of regional hospitals and better education for girls. When a girl of ten to twelve seemed oversexed, her female relatives took her to a woman who cut the end off the girl's clitoris. The circumcision did not affect her marriage prospects, rather it was considered to ensure that she was not tempted to lose her virginity. There was also the background accepted attitude that women were not supposed to enjoy sex, which this 'operation' helped ensure.

Until they pass 60, the women of Daghestan are almost invisible due to their reserve, humility and modesty in public. They must never appear to be attractive to men. For example, in Khunzakh, where the people there are more traditional, if a woman tries to look modern, she is generally scorned. Such lack of social communication between members of the opposite sex, who are outside the family, even gave rise to secret languages for women in Koubachi village and others.

It follows that lively banter between adult male and females does not occur in public. Only old women cackle with men. Once on a bus, young Andi men from Gunkho, the village where everyone laughs, and an eighteen-year-old married woman were loudly, but innocently, giggling and teasing each other. They were sternly reprimanded by a 30-year-old woman and the bus driver, both from neighbouring Gagatl.

But the most bizarre instance of communal modesty happened in 1921, after

An old woman rolling the packed-earth flat roof of her terraced home in Koubachi. The roller is made out of an old stone column. (Photo: Dmitri Chirkov)

the Civil War, as related by *'Parteigenosse'* S. M. Kirov after an inspection visit: "Hunger and deprivation have reached the limit of human endurance," he reported, when the merciless destruction had left many villagers, not only starving, but in rags or without clothes. Every morning, in one village, the men stayed indoors, so as not to see the women go naked to the fount to fetch the water. It would have been dishonourable for the men to carry water.

The opposite happened to me in Bezhta, at three o'clock one afternoon, when two girls silently arrived, with their ten-litre tinned copper ewers filled with water, to do housework, while I was naked, washing, standing in a small bowl in the garden. One giggled when she saw me later, whereas the other averted her eyes. When we entered a house where a friend of ours was drinking, the girl standing at the gate turned her back to us. Another quickly peeked at us before getting a matronly smack from her mother for her immodesty. Near Bezhta, returning from a hot spring, in the middle of nowhere, we passed a girl carrying a load, who turned her face away from us, so we would not stop. Our local car-owning driver even knew her, she was a philology student at Makhachkala.

When Niamh and the girls were walking home in Gagatl, they met old men who were walking to the mosque, and they had to hide themselves if possible,

Winning the dancing at the Khunzakh festival.

or if not, stand with their faces to the wall. It seemed that in 1901, it was more liberal near Gimri, when pretty girls laughed at goat horns slung around a man's neck, but I think the observant traveller saw a small part of a more elaborate traditional joke, judging by what happened ninety years later. When Magomedkhan's 23-year-old unmarried sister, a biology teacher, wanted to come riding with us, the men and her relatives were against it. It was not suitable for a woman to ride or be with men. They even didn't want Niamh to come. But I asked as their guest, so they had to let her come. As Niamh and she crossed the river in town, both riding on one horse, she was teased by her girlfriends, who were washing clothes in the river: "You should be ashamed of yourself!" – both because she was riding and riding astride the horse. Girls do not ride bicycles either – only boys; the same problem as Niamh's mother had in Ireland in the 1940s.

There is, however, some contact between young members of both sexes at wedding dances and in games. One widespread agent of love is the Wedding Stick, which can look like a white or pink curly cloth leek, or a white flowery rod, or even a shish kebab. In the village of Shovkra the wedding-usher, with his red arm band and his whip, started the dancing by offering the Wedding Stick to his partner for the dance, inside a circle of villagers. They danced round three times, when he retired and she then chose her new partner, and so on, in a chain of single pair dances. It was a convenient way for girls to indicate to boys, and vice versa, that they are keen on one another. In south Daghestan, teenage boys and girls played hide-and-seek in springtime, and there were festivals, where they could spend the whole day together, but always in a group, such as the Flower Festival in Akhti.

Meetings were not always so formal. Near Tlokh, in 1901, the English traveller Baddeley, then a news-reporter, saw a handsome Dargin shepherd boy playing his pipes, with a pretty girl sitting beside him. According to the grandmother of Alla Umakharanova,* Kumyk young people were much freer in meeting each other than mountain boys and girls. The lowland Kumyks have a Stick of Love, *suidun taiak* in Kumyk and *palochka lyubvi* in Russian (really the same as the Wedding Stick), which is used by 20-year-olds, who still play the following game, which was popular in the 19th century. All the boys and girls in the village gather together and the leader orders a boy to sit on a stool, in the middle of the room or field. The leader then chooses a boy or girl to beat hard with the Stick on the shoulders of the seated victim, who is blindfolded and must guess who it was. The beater shouts "I am beating you black!" to help the victim guess who it is. If he is right, they change roles. But before that, he or she must tell a story, dance or sin. "If you can't beat the Stick of Love, you must burn it in the fire or break it." They even had magic for enticement: touch the girl you love anywhere with a rabbit tail, and she will fall in love with you.

---

* A former classical ballet dancer now working on traditional dances in the Art Department of the Daghestan Scientific Centre at the Academy of Sciences, Makhachkala.

Women pay attention to their appearance within complicated limits, which are now gradually changing. For example, hair is only shown in public by unmarried girls. An 18-year-old girl, studying trade economics, told us that women dye their hair red with a mixture of half henna and half basmata (?). A natural redhead, like Niamh, is considered to be hot tempered and difficult. It is most beautiful to have black hair and bright blue eyes. The beautiful dark hair of Raziyat, Magomedkhan's wife, reaches all the way down her back, but is always kept in a bun, according to custom. In Gagatl bazaar, in the upper, or woman's, part of the segregated market, Niamh was applauded by one woman for not wearing a scarf, adding that their men would never allow it there.

Women show their sexual status by their headscarf colours, such as in Archi, where young girls and women wear a green and red *kaz* headscarf, whereas old women wear black and brown. Another time, in the Kasimkent hotel, my Daghestan companion did not want me to share a room with nine people, including two sons and their mother, who were already asleep. Following mysterious lengthy arrangements, I was given a bed between mother and son. At seven, she got up first, having slumbered fully dressed with headscarf, and departed. Next, everyone else got up and left the room – I decided to remain asleep – and then she came back to comb her long oily hair, and replaced it in a bun under her snood, before going off to face the world.

Near Koubachi village there is a hut where the bus to Derbent stops so the women can change into, or out of, their traditional clothes or townwear. Botlikh village was known throughout Daghestan as the second Paris, because they are so *kul'turnye*, that is the women wear make-up and short sleeves. Botlikh girls wear gold earrings from the age of three, when their mothers pierce their ears. In Khunzakh, the mayor's wife had two dresses, for weddings only, bought five years before from *spekulianty* traders, labelled 'Made in England by Gee-Gee'. Made from synthetic material, they had cost her 250 and 300 roubles. In Khunzakh, like everywhere, no one wants to wear Soviet clothes. Festivals are a time for dressing up and exotica. At the Khunzakh festival, a woman singer wore 4-inch stiletto heels and had no trouble in dancing in them, while the state Lezginka dance troupe looked out of place, with the women wearing thick-painted foundation make-up, edged with scarlet lips and black-lined almond eyes, utterly unlike the Avar women watching them.

The male theory, in an unexpectedly candid admission, is that their women are so attractive that if they were not hidden away, they would be seduced and/or raped. In the alpine village Kurush, any man who seduced a girl was killed. In Tsunta-Akhwakh, the most traditional district in Daghestan, betrothed couples might sleep together, but the girl could only be touched above the waist, a custom called 'bundling' in England. In the mid-19th century a girl was applauded for stabbing her lover who had broken this rule. If a maiden or widow became pregnant, she could legitimately break into the home of her seducer and give birth to the child there. He would then have to marry her. When one Avar's grandfather, who naturally was living at home with his grandson, heard that he had slept with a girl, he was silent for a week. Then he broke his silence, saying that he was 70 and had only known his wife, and was entirely happy. Another time, the grandfather caught sight of the couple embracing and pronounced that "it is not our family tradition – this could be a serious matter."

The most serious sex offences were those of rape and incest. If an Ingush woman was raped, the attacker would be killed on the spot. If he escaped, a blood feud broke out between the sibs, or extended group of relatives, of the two parties. In *adat* law-courts, confession of the rapist or accusation of the victim were considered undeniable evidence. The accused could only prove himself innocent by swearing with five character-witnesses, two of whom must be relatives. The poisoned chalice of temptation was offered in the Tsunta-Akhwakh district, (but not elsewhere), in 1901, where it was the custom for the host to give his guest one of his daughters or another girl, to look after his horse, his baggage, his feeding and then sleep with him. Depending on the wishes of the girl, they might lie together naked, but the guest would be killed if he forced himself on her.

In the Dargin region, rape, attempted rape or a mere suspicious touch, were all equally punishable as rape. No inadvertent physical contact with a woman, or girl, was allowed while dancing. If her husband, brother or betrothed, saw it, he would take it as rape and stab the man on the spot. To prevent bloodshed at weddings (as is so graphically represented in a painting in the Akhti museum) and Bayram when tempers were frayed after fasting, the usher would order all men to leave their *kinjal* daggers at home. So, I danced with care at weddings at Kulag in Tabassaran, and Shokhra in Kumukh. Nowadays, men only shake hands with women who are over 65.

Men have a distressing view on the responsibility for rape, unless a victim has a husband or father, whose honour would be involved. Two stories show what men think of women's strength and physique. A woman from a mountain village cried one morning that she had been raped by a man from the next village. The man was summoned to the village council and denied it. The council deliberated and then gave them two sacks of flour each as compensation – to her, for being raped, to him, for mistaken identity which had marred his honour. The man took only one sack, explaining that he could not lift both, while the woman carried away her two sacks. Because of that, the council said she was stronger than the man and so, could not have been raped by him.

In another mountain village, men were discussing rape. One took out his *kinjal* dagger from its sheath and asked another to replace it while he twisted the sheath from side to side. Of course, it was not possible to replace it, just as, he said, it was impossible to rape a woman.

&

Despite the legendary faithfulness of Daghestan wives, who waited 20 years and more for their husband's return after the Stalinist expulsions and World War II, or the Great Patriotic War, there are severe customs to keep wives in their place after marriage. At home, the host's wife would never sit at the same table as guests, unless she was specially requested to do so. The host frequently scolds his wife in front of guests, displaying no affection, unless the guest is a close family friend. The same applies in public. Today, as in the last century, a Lezgin (or any other villager), would never put his arm around his wife while dancing at a wedding.

Back in Moscow, I was staying at Rasul Gamzatov's apartment where Aisha, an almond-eyed Kumyk beauty, had been asked to look after me, while she stayed in a nearby apartment. Aisha was 35 and married with two children, and worked in Makhachkala. She was in Moscow for treatment of her gall-stones which got bigger and smaller. I was a known guest and so outside any taboo. This was the same when some children in Archi took me around and we happened on a mother who continued suckling her baby in her yard, in front of all her family. Aisha said she would not sit alone in a room with me if I were not an honorary kinsman (i.e. if I were a Russian). We recorded her beautiful songs.

Next day, by mistake, we walked into the Soviet Victory Parade, which embarrassed her. I was feeling aggressive, so I asked sarcastically where were the banners for the victory in Afghanistan? In reply she silently nodded. In past years, girls from the various Soviet Republics had marched in the parade, dancing national dances in their brightly coloured national costumes. That day, for the first time, they did not want to and stayed at home, so they were replaced by fat Moscow girls, decked out as, for instance, Azeri dancing-girls. They were followed by drum majorettes and a wriggling bunch of go-go dancers. Bemused Russian matrons, medals on their heaving bosoms, who lined the boulevards, looked steadfast for the one solitary tank grumbling past. Moscow was changing faster than Daghestan.

Marriage in Daghestan is described elsewhere, but ideas of female humility are continued in marriage taboos, which concern monogamy, the bride's freedom to choose her partner, and her virginity. In spite of a man being permitted more than one wife by Islamic *shariat* law, and forbidden by Soviet law, monogamy has been usual for a long time, because the ratio of men to women only varies up to 100/105, providing too few local women.

Fifteen to twenty-five was the usual age for marriage (now after 18), and weddings and bride price were generally too expensive for repeats. However, two-wife marriages meant a second wife added to the work force – especially useful in the mountains; while in the lowlands, a dowry of additional land was the prize. "In 1929 there were 45 legal polygamous marriages, in 1930 – 34, and in 1931 – six," according to Professor B. K. Dalgat, writing in the 1930s. Another exception was an optional marriage of a widow to her brother-in-law or son-in-law. This prevented her marrying elsewhere, and so kept the widow working for the family, who would have had to return the bride price.

Marriage within the village sib, the extended family or *tukhum*, the larger clan, was strictly observed for the Lezgin, Kaitag, Tabassaran, Dargin and Rutul people. They could only marry out to prevent extinction. Lowie wrote that endogamy, or marrying-in is not primitive, but thrives where social rank is important and, in Daghestan, was probably of Mazdaic Iranian (that is pre-Islamic) origin, to preserve purity of blood. Lezgins are classless, so purity of the whole people was the aim. Islamic law forbids brother-sister, while allowing first-cousin-marriage.

One unmarried girl confided that there was still no choice in marriage in Gagatl village, where parents had total control and you married the man, whether you wanted to or not. A love match was considered bad by parents, and if they knew that the girl fancied the boy to whom they have arranged a match, they would find another. Young girls are frightened to protest because some years ago – in 1985 – an unmarried girl was strangled by her own father, because she was seeing – not even having an affair with – a local boy. He has now married another girl and the father was not even cautioned, let alone arrested – it did not count as murder. Most marriages are still arranged from the first introduction when love "happens."

Most village people will only marry within their nationality, even if some of them have settled far away in Central Asia. This was the case with Hadji Mohamet, our part-time driver, a 21-year-old jeweller from Koubachi, who married in 1986. His 18-year-old bride was born there, but years before, her family left for Ashkhabad, in Turkmenistan on the other side of the Caspian, and they came back for the first time, for a holiday, last year. Her sister got them together at the regular Thursday night village dance. Then their families discussed the marriage.

Mountain peoples also marry within their local group of villages, although locality can also be a reason for not marrying because of old inter-village enmity, such as Andi villagers never marrying Gagatl people, a mere three kilometres away – "We prefer our own," they explained. An educated city-dweller purred while telling how he had already been approached by two interested Lak fathers for his Lak daughters. But he had told them to come back later. In contrast, the women of the Kumyks, who live in the plains, were always freer to choose their husbands. Chechen and Ingush boys and girls had no choice in what was a family economic matter. Only girls had no choice among the Lezgins. However any Daghestan girl would be stabbed by her brother before her wedding night if she wanted to marry a Russian. One consolation for girls who had lost their virginity and so their value as a bride, was that they could choose who they wished to marry.

To generalise, Daghestanis like to think that last century's marriage customs largely survive and that there has been little increase in cross-nationality marriages today. Published statistics on inter-ethnic marriages are confusing, as they apply only to the capital Makhachkala and can be altered by changing definitions of ethnic groups. To promote international identity within the

USSR, it was part of Soviet policy to encourage such marriages or at least to report them. Cross-marriages, about one in ten to one in twenty, mainly occurred in the five large towns in Daghestan, and the numbers must have increased with urbanisation, as a third of the population now live there.

Today, as ever, a man does not sleep with his future bride before they are married. The bride should be a virgin, but if not, you tell a distant relative or good friend that you have already slept with her, but not her father or near relative. Historically, in the southern Samur region, on the morning after the wedding, the blood-stained sheet was given to the two relatives guarding the bridal suite, and the husband might have fired his gun, to confirm his bride had been a virgin. In contrast, the Dargin groom's gunshot signified that the bride's hymen was previously broken, and so she would be returned to her family with a financial penalty. A bride who was found to be unchaste, would, if she was denounced by her husband, have her lips and ears cut off and be driven out of the village. All Daghestan peoples, except perhaps the Chechen, had the virginity test as a condition of marriage. Honour was not always at stake, since accidental rupture of the hymen counted the same. Dubrovin wrote last century, that such incidents were frequent, both when young girls were carrying heavy loads on steep rocky slopes, covered with briers, and during regular ritual washing.

ॐ

Present sexual activity seems to be typical of a vigorous Muslim society. Transgressions are noted, but punishment seems less visibly violent than in the past. There is some sexual instruction. During the day of the marriage ceremony, before the bride and groom retire from the hundreds of guests, into a plushly decorated marriage bedroom, which contains his parent's normal bed, a distant male relative, who has children of his own, takes the groom for a stroll and explains to him what he can and what he cannot do. Perhaps the unnatural pressure upon the young couple on their wedding night gave rise to the Kumyk observation that if at a marriage party somebody shuts a flick-knife or sheathes a *kinjal* or closes scissors or makes knots, then the bride will be infertile.

Men talk about sex among themselves, but not in detail, and they think women do as well, but lovemaking must be private. In Gagatl, there was a new bride who was reluctant, or rather, afraid to discuss sex. Perhaps it was because she didn't like her new family, and found them dull, after only a week of marriage. In 1984, I visited a house in the village of Kuba, just south of present-day Daghestan. I was introduced to a family by the chief of the apple-growing *kolkhoz*, because he was proud that they had thirteen children, supporting the reputation of Lezgin fertility. In the 1989 census, the Lezgins had increased their numbers by 22 per cent over ten years, but this was still less than the fertile 25 per cent average for Daghestan.

How this achievement was possible became even more mysterious, when I

Koubachi woman carrying ten and five litre vessels, made of tin simulated to look like wood. Six trips a day to collect water from the village fount.

saw their traditional domestic architecture. There was a bedroom for the new bride in the groom's family house, where she would sleep alone for the first six months. She would then move into the main bedroom with the whole family. This was far more daunting than the old custom, where a Chechen or Ingush groom had to leave his new wife and live with neighbours for two or three weeks. When, eventually, a couple could get away by themselves, they cuddled for at least half an hour before love-making, or maybe all day (how they had time to do this, when the girls have to work all the time, is not clear either). They never see or look at each other's body or make love in the light. It is forbidden to touch each other's genitals when lying together, whereas hugging and kissing and fondling breasts is normal.

Men think that women masturbate. Men boasted that in one night they made love from two to twelve times. Until he is fifty, a man made love twice a night as a minimum, about four times a week. It was better to make love in the morning, before *namaz*, prayers. A man can be potent until his death.

In contrast to the claims of men about their sexual performance, we heard from women, that, just like anywhere else in the world, married men make love once, turn over and go to sleep. Perhaps this is the reason why, by the hearth of many houses, there is a bronze oil lamp, in the form of an erect phallus, whose testes are supported by a tripod. These were made in Koubachi since the 13th century and are similar to the earlier, slightly more explicit, bronze Roman winged lamps. The effectiveness of these talismans may be confirmed by the report that fathers and sons frequently have children at the same time. A 75-year-old and his 40-year-old wife had a son when his grandson was born, and the grandfather apologised. However, in the male cattle section at Gagatl market, Niamh was surrounded by young men, who took advantage of meeting a rare foreign woman to ask directly, "What is your relationship with that old man? Is it usual in Britain for young women to marry older men?" When she said no, they said for them, too, it was rare – five years was the maximum age gap. A drooling madman pinched her bottom, as she climbed up into the truck which was taking us away.

Marriage in Daghestan is for the purpose of having children. It is, however, merely considered bad luck, a chance of fate, for a woman to be barren, but it is considered, especially by men, a misfortune to have daughters. Niamh pretended to have been trying to have a child for three years, and asked for advice. An Avar village woman said that she didn't believe in herbal remedies, that Niamh was young and would soon have babies, many people waited for ten years and then had a lot of children. Her mother had no remedies either. However in Derbent there is a sacred place – a tenth-century walled shrine, with the Tombs of the Forty Arab Martyrs, killed fighting the Khazars, where people go to cure barrenness. Inside, a sacred tree is covered with tied-on cloth offerings belonging to the women, some in memorial of a ritual for barren or pregnant women, who come there, for picnics in the summer. There is one particular tomb, with an arched niche in the headstone, where the woman supplicant bends forward, to touch her forehead, in order to ensure children. Ethnic groups compare their relative fecundities with interest, when the results of the ten-yearly census are published, and the Lezgins are known for having more children than the other Daghestan nationalities – an exaggeration.

It is scarcely unexpected that barren women feel left out. At Tsada (meaning 'in the fire', because the mountains there look like orange flames at sunset), Niamh met the wife of an economist, who had returned to the village eight years ago, to run the *kolkhoz*. She had been married for ten years, and was barren. She was very depressed with nothing to do and wanted to return to Makhachkala, where she had trained as an art teacher. Sometimes she helped in the local museum, but she mostly stayed at home. So did the wife of the schoolteacher in Andi, Patimat, who asked endless questions, such as, "Do you have spoons, do you have sheep, do you have saucepans in England?" She married at 17, eight years ago, and still had no children – "It is in the hands of Allah."

Men want sons. A macho mountaineer Lak driver sneaked off to have his head and sternum anointed with oil by an old woman at the Tomb of the Forty Martyrs so that he would have a son, as he only had two daughters. A half-Rutul, half-Dargin urbane man living in Derbent even apologised for having no sons. At least he acted in a more restrained manner than the man in the next story. There was a Dargin mountain village woman, who had borne eight daughters. After the birth of the last daughter, the husband said he would leave her as she could not make him a son. Insulted, she immediately left him, the children and the new baby, and returned to her parents. His family begged her to come back to give milk to the baby, but she refused, saying that she would not stay with a man who could not make her a son. Eventually, she relented and next year had another baby – a daughter. Aisha with the almond eyes commented, "What a brave woman, to leave not only her husband and her children, but her baby, to make her point." Aisha had been very pleased when she had a second daughter, because it meant that her other daughter would have a friend to talk to and get over life's problems.

Women now at least have the possibility to deal with their personal birth rate. It is hardly surprising that economic deprivation stimulates birth control, but in Daghestan, this reason is deeply offensive to male pride. Three women's stories, told to Niamh in confidence, show the common physical and psychological problems of an urban mother, a pregnant villager and a villager who works in the town. At present, there are no satisfactory answers.

Patimat was thirty, pretty and educated, with a degree in sociology from Makhachkala. One of eight children – four boys and four girls, she married Kemal, a Dargin, who was one of seven children – three boys and five girls, ten years ago. Unlike him, she is an Avar from a mountain village. They have two daughters, aged nine and three. The girls speak only Russian, as do their parents, as it is their only common language. Patimat tried for a second child for six years, but she was not very well and tired all the time from working, looking after her child and supporting a student husband. At work, she earned 150 roubles a months. She received a small maternity allowance for one-and-a-half years, but after three she is still at home, by choice.

Kemal, an economist, was paid 200 roubles a month, plus extra work, advising in the village *kolkhozes* at 20 roubles a day, which he had to stop as he was appointed to a professional trade union post. He had a colleague, who was in charge of allocating some newly built flats, so he got a deservedly good one for his own family. After waiting ten years, they had got a new – though it didn't look it – three-room fourth-floor – the lift didn't work – flat in an seven-storey block with running water – still cold – and central heating. Before, they were living in overcrowded conditions, on one floor of part of one of a relative's shanty houses on the outskirts of Makhachkala, with a communal outdoor cold tap and shared lime-pit toilet, both in the yard.

Patimat wants to return to work, because she needed the money and was bored at home, as the younger child were now at kindergarten, three blocks away. Patimat loved children, but will have no more because she is too tired and it is too difficult to organise life. Kemal wants more children, especially sons, but Patimat does not want to lose her present children's material well-being after their long struggle, while there is a shortage of food. Having another child would force her to stay at home and lose her salary, so the coil stays in, and remains their major source of conflict.

Another Patimat, an eight-month-pregnant Botlikh woman, sat next to

Niamh on the bus to Gagatl. She was visiting relatives. She worked in a *kombinat* factory. Patimat married a year and a half ago, at 22, with a childhood sweetheart, her third cousin. But love marriages were unusual. She feistily said she wanted only three or four children and asked, why did one need more? This was the usual attitude in the larger villages, but in the mountains women have up to ten. They stopped having more by getting the coil, or *spiral*, fitted in the hospital. She did not think that the dangerously bumpy roads were bad for the baby – she was strong, they were mountain people. Patimat was honestly afraid of her first birth but that was life. She was happy with any baby as long as it is healthy, but husbands always wanted sons.

Wagidat, from a village near Khunzakh, is a 40-year-old who lives and works in a factory in Makhachkala and returns home for the holidays. She speaks Russian well, unlike the other village women. Wagidat has one son and one daughter and a *spiral* – "Two are enough. Life is too hard to have more. The situation in the country is bad and it will be worse in the future." Wagidat, like most people in Daghestan, is anti-Gorbachev and pro-Yeltsin (in 1990, but all changed since the Chechen War): "Gorbachev may be an educated man, but he is all talk and no action. Before him there was everything in the shops [selective memory, I think], now there is nothing because of the *spekulanty* who buy up everything. Life is very hard especially for women – in the country they do all the heavy agricultural work and in the towns they must go out to work."

Traditional methods of birth control include women jumping off three-metre-high rocks or walls, washing internally with soap and water, putting a propane cooking gas cylinder on your belly, sitting in scalding water to burn the baby out, or using poisonous herbs as an emetic to expel the foetus. Men say that these methods are not popular, as the women want large families. Women related that, in the country, women are still uncomfortable about contraception and they regard abortion as a sin.

The older generation of women are often more understanding. Patimat, the sociologist's mother had eight children and had difficult life. She would get up very early in winter to cut the grass under the snow, to feed the animals, before she went to work. She is the only one who supports Patimat's wish not to have many children – three is enough. Men also say that there are no abortions, but discreet abortion at the clinic in Makhachkala is common and takes a couple of hours in all. Village women take the bus up for the day on another pretext.

The main form of contraception in Daghestan is the copper wire *spiral*. This is unlike the non-Muslim USSR, where abortion is the widespread method of birth control. The coil is promoted in Daghestan and other Islamic parts of the USSR, while birth control devices are virtually unobtainable in Moscow. This is because of the high birth rates in the Muslim populations with more than three children, compared to the low Russian rate of half a child per couple. The army of babies is already starting to disturb the demographic balance, which kept the Muslim areas in a minority of 80 out of the 280 millions that made up the population of the USSR. It is therefore not surprising that the numbers of under-20-year-olds show a much higher proportion of Muslims, with the consequent implications for conscription, which became one of the reasons for Soviet withdrawal from Muslim Afghanistan.

The coil is now used even in the mountain villages, where families of over four children are no longer desirable. These are usually put in by a female *feldscher* (Russian for a medic trained to a standard between a nurse and a doctor) working in the larger villages. "It's not fair that women have all the pain, the responsibility, the unpleasant visits to the polyclinics, because of the rudeness of the staff and the queues, while the men get away with everything." The tragedy is that the coil, their only method of birth control, has, through bitter experience, become the least-favoured method of female contraception in the West, because it can get stuck high up the uterus and it is extremely painful and distressing to have removed. It can also cause infections with equally unpleasant consequences.

But in Daghestan, there are no alternatives. The Pill is known but not available and not trusted by women. Patimat did not understand how the Pill worked. She warned that it was necessary to wait three months between stopping the Pill and having a baby, as it is a poison and would poison the baby. Patimat wanted to use the calendar method of birth control, but for this to work she must be in excellent health, for the woman's cycle from day-nine to day-nineteen to be regular, and more difficult, her husband must be willing to comply. So she could not trust the method. There are no condoms either in the pharmacies – USSR 1987 production was estimated at about 250,000 per annum, or one for every 250 fertile women. They split or burst frequently, and were of such crude manufacture that they were known by women in Moscow scathingly, as the 'galosh'. I have noticed that brightly coloured condoms and other sexual aids are a popular purchase, as a joke, for Caucasian visitors to London.

There may be birth control, but menstruation has certainly been ignored by the Soviet system in 1990. I was waiting in the Soviet Embassy for my visa and I got talking to an elderly lady, who was picking up visas for the directors of her company. They had almost completed negotiations to build and commission the first four factories to manufacture tampons in the USSR. It was Women's Year – "All the other years had been Men's Years," a Daghestan woman wearily remarked. The elderly lady didn't get the visas.

In Daghestan, following tradition, no sex takes place during menstruation, which the woman keeps secret, and for which she uses cotton wool to soak up her blood. This, together with her cut hair, was burnt on the flat roof of a house or another ritually clean place. After birth, a woman was considered unclean for forty days and either stayed in a special house, which they had about forty years ago in Archi, for example, or with her mother, as they now do after spending a week in hospital.

In Makhachkala, when Patimat, the sociologist, was shown a tampon, she said that she had heard of them but never seen one. She read in *Zdorov'e*

*Wedding dowry –
brass and ceramic
plates on display in
Koubachi.*

*Prepared wedding-bed
in groom's parents'
bedroom – Magomed
Gapourovich Anjoyev
married Madimat
Abdukhaikovna
Kourbanova in
Bezhta.*

('Health') magazine that they are producing them in the USSR this year and thought they were a good idea, better than the cotton wool she uses at present. In the more isolated Archi village, a big 14-year-old girl was shown tampons, which she had never heard of and could not understand. A 19-year-old also could not comprehend and eventually thought that tampons were contraceptives. She found the idea repugnant, as she used cotton gauze.

As well as menses, there are other hygiene rules to be followed after sexual activity. After the wedding night the bridegroom went to the river and washed his naked body, secretly, to be clean. Both sexes should bathe before and after coitus. Water from the separate baths after coitus must be kept till morning and thrown out in a ritually clean place. If not, it would fall into the possession of bad spirits and one's health would be impaired. Early one morning, Magomed-khan and I saw one such filled bucket on the veranda of our host, the enthusiastic Communist mayor of Kriukh. As well as not having sex for forty days after giving birth, a man will not have sex with his pregnant wife after the fifth or sixth month. By Islamic law, a divorcee could not remarry before she has had three menses, to avoid doubt about paternity.

ða.

Last century the judgement taken of adultery (by women) was grim. Nika Bulat, a Lezgin, loved his mother. When he found out that she had an illicit lover he was enraged. He rushed to the adulterer's home, stabbed him with his *kinjal* and cut off his head and hands. He returned and dropped them at the feet of his mother, who burst into tears. This angered him further, and he stabbed his mother who fell on the head and hands she had loved. His two sisters were present and fell weeping on their mother's breast. Nika Bulat took this for approval of their mother's crime and killed them too.

But lovers' quarrels based on mere suspicion which ended in violence, were strongly condemned in the community. One ballad tells how Ali loved his wife Aishat. Ali was away in the mountains with his flocks and was told that his wife had given away the jewels that he gave her on their wedding day. On his return, he found that she was indeed not wearing them, so he stabbed her, only to learn from his dying wife that she had hidden the pearl and the ruby, so that they did not lose their lustre, and which she would not presume to wear when he was not there. The wretched husband pulled out his dagger and killed himself. Later, the *adat* laws for adultery became less severe. The offended husband formerly was entitled to clip off his wife's hair, then cut off her ear, arm or nose and finally kill her, so unfortunately becoming a blood enemy of her family. He usually preferred to divorce her instead and have his bride price returned.

At another village near Khunzakh, Aminat was an good-looking, yet unmarried, lady schoolteacher of about 35, who spoke English and had now, at last, met her first English-speaker. Aminat's parents from Tliarata, unusually, had allowed her to choose her own husband, but she was too fussy and found

63

no one. She says she has come to regret it, as she is now regarded as being very strange, yet at the same time very modern. She took off her headscarf inside the house of her friends to prove it. She lives on her own in the village, where she works, and returns to her family home during the holidays. But later, a friend told us that Aminat was married before, but was flighty, so her husband left her and she had to leave Tliarata because of her reputation. This version is more likely as hale and hearty spinsters are unknown. Moreover, Aminat didn't live alone, but with her brother, who is one of the three remaining full-time KGB staff in the Khunzakh region.

There are stirrings of a different attitude in the present generation. On the way back from Khunzakh to Botlikh, in the rattling old bus, a white-bearded *hadji** from Karakh, who was making sure that everyone realised he was a religious man, asked Magomedkhan if he knew why we had stopped by a shrine and he had led two minutes prayer, which everyone joined in, sitting in the bus. "No, please tell us," Magomedkhan replied.

The *hadji* explained: "A man and a woman were having an extra-marital and therefore illicit love affair. They drove together in his car, past the holy-man's shrine and then the car crashed, killing them both, because the spirit of the Sheik was displeased." Magomedkhan, who comes from an old Naqshbandi Sufi family and is older than he looks, immediately commented, "Maybe it was because she was unclean?" – after sex it is mandatory to wash according to religious and customary laws, so which transgression had offended the dead spirit? – the unexpected erudition silenced the old pedant.

Traditionally, whereas an offended husband could always take revenge, the break-up of a marriage caused pain without remedy for the wronged wife. Divorce was rare in Daghestan and always at the instigation of husband, but as the ethnographer Prof. B. Dalgat wrote in the 1930s, "a woman, without the agreement of her husband cannot divorce him, she can only complain about her situation and plead for his agreement to divorce. The husband always had custody of children when he divorced his wife. If she was pregnant during proceedings and gave birth in her father's home after the divorce, the child was taken away to her ex-husband." It happened in educated circles, too. A talented Kumyk woman, ex-wife of a Lak engineer, who went out with other women, recently died of a broken heart, six years after the divorce.

Among other versions of sex, buggery is unthinkable, as shown by this story – if a man buggers his wife, God will split the world to see it. Although I have seen men embracing each other and playing with each other's hair on an aeroplane, and there is much public contact between men, as in other Muslim countries, there is said to be no homosexuality in Daghestan (unlike Azerbaijan or Armenia, according to Daghestanis). Male homosexuality was punished as severely as illicit heterosexual relations, for example in the Dargin Hyuraki

* One of the few Daghestanis who had been given permission to make the hajj pilgrimage to Mecca.

area, two males caught in the act might have been killed on the spot by their relatives. If spared, they each had to pay a fine of three oxen to the community and they were both banished for a year. To get off a charge of homosexuality forty character witnesses were required (as for a murder charge) – like the Sligo Races alibi.

Among the Dargins, the penalty for homosexual rape was the same as for murder. The way I obtained much of the current information on male sexual habits was by a Mephistophelean exchange, where I gave a potted history of homosexuality in Britain – I forgot about the monasteries, but remembered the influence of pairs of soldiers in classical antiquity and how its ideals passed into English 18th-century culture and public schools. On reflection, there seem to be many parallel institutions in Daghestan, without an explicitly homosexual nature, which seems to explain their curiosity.

Daghestan town people talked about Aids like the Black Death, even though there are virtually no cases recorded there yet. On a local level there was at least concern about the possibility of infection through blood transfusions in the hospitals. But the authorities are certainly worried that any tourism will bring the virus. Precautions for the tourist complex under construction, south of Makhachkala, are planned. Tourists, of whom the much-travelled and 'virile' Poles are feared most, are permitted only single day expeditions to a few villages, such as Koubachi or Akhti, to stop them spreading Aids by nocturnal contact. They have a folk memory of such fears. Last century, syphilis was brought back to Daghestan by the migrant workers. But now the women say that Daghestan men will never wear sheath contraceptives – not that there are any – even to avoid Aids. Men are more likely to travel and sleep with women, say, in Moscow, so the risk is there.

It is difficult to imagine prostitution in villages because everybody knows what everybody else is up to. However, in the larger towns there are prostitutes. These might include the occasional 'fallen' Daghestani woman, but they are most likely to be Russian women. When Daghestani men travel alone to cities such as Moscow or St Petersburg, they often get drunk in the evenings and are vulnerable to approaches from Russian prostitutes. This frequently leads to altercations and trouble for the Daghestani men when they wake up in the morning, accused rightly or wrongly of some crime or misdemeanour in the unfriendly and effectively racist surroundings of Mother Russia.

· 4 ·
A way to be born . . .

I n Ginukh, like the whole world over, I saw little girls playing 'brides', dressed up in white gauze veils and plaited coloured girdles, jumping a few years, past puberty, to the time of betrothal. Meanwhile in Makhachkala, Patimat was chatting to Niamh, my Irish companion: "You must have a child soon, 31 is almost too late. Also Robert is old for children – he is nearly 50 [44 actually] and that's bad. Women are considered too old at 30 – because they are tired out by then. Why don't you marry Robert? The wedding is a woman's great day in Daghestan. I now have no more big days to look forward to. Getting a flat will be the last big day in my life . . ." From the age of 17 for a girl, and a little older for a boy, all their parents think about is betrothal. The oldest were in the village of Oboda, where brides were up to 25 and grooms five years older.

Even nowadays in a large town like Makhachkala, betrothals were orthodox. I was eating a breakfast of caviar and honeycomb prepared by Aminat, who taught English and was related to the Gamzatov clan, as she explained, where she had been the previous night, her round dark hair, eyes and gold-capped teeth gleaming with mischievous humour. Twenty years earlier she had been betrothed too. She always joked about her husband who was often away driving a truck.

"Last night," she began, "there was a party to introduce the families of the future groom and bride. Said Saidov, 22, was from Tsada village and Madina Abus, aged 19, was from Akhalchi village, both near Khunzakh. Said's mother's brother, Ali, was a neighbour of Mr Abus and told his sister about his daughter. She was clever, lovely, a good housewife and a good cook – unusually, there was nothing to do with money. The parents discussed the match – they knew the other family well. Late in May, after positive hints had been received, the boy's father came to the girl's home to ask permission for her hand. There were no drinks before her father consented. They talked for an hour about life, how many children they might have – it was always four. Said had finished car maintenance school and was in the army. He was not too academic, but much liked. The fathers agreed and the next day the boy's father returned with him,

One of five weddings on July 16th 1989 in Bezhta. Mothers and children sharing a wedding breakfast. In the countryside all the weddings happen when the harvest is in.

for them to meet for the first time. Madina was cooking and serving at table, helping her mother. Said was not enthusiastic and they did not talk privately. She did not sit at the table, but her mother did. During June, he visited her home every other day to get to know her better. If he didn't like her, he could tell his father who would apologise to her father: if she didn't like him she could tell her mother, who would tell her father, who would tell Ali. Both would give their reason – not beautiful enough, too tall, lame, blind, alcoholic, or dishonoured by a previous boyfriend (even only by repute). Also the betrothed couple could not have slept together before. There was no holding hands and no kissing, only eye contact was allowed, while they discussed common friends in the presence of her 18-year-old sister, mother or father. Mr Abus was good at repairing hi-fis and liked listening to tapes of Avar music, but the couple were very modern and liked pop music. There were 15 visits."

Aminat grinned and cut up some meat and onions for lunch before continuing. "By mid-June Said's parents sent an official delegation – his mother's brother and father's sister – with a gold engagement ring, set with a diamond worth a thousand roubles. The couple weren't present as they drank, talked, ate and danced to celebrate. A fortnight later, they went to the cinema with friends, as Madina was still too shy to go out alone with him. Every other day Said, with his parents, visited his bride-to-be's home, bringing presents of food, kerchiefs, cosmetics, clothes and shoes. Once, when his brother returned from the army, Madina's mother visited Said's family home, bringing gifts of sweets, cooked meats and other foods, such as buttered pancakes, halva with walnuts and – her speciality – cakes with cream and honey.

"Yesterday, Said's mother rang the couple's brothers and sisters and their children, to invite them to the betrothal feast. In all ten were able to come, out of 15 on the girl's side and ten on the boy's, because many were away on holiday. At six, the two boys, five girls, and four of the parents' generation arrived. In the main room, a line of five tables were laden with vodka, brandy, beer, mineral water, Pepsi, and champagne. They ate *stolichnaya* salad (a Moscow dish), cucumber and tomatoes, green peppers, onions, greens and herbs. Also vineleaves, tomatoes, cabbages and green peppers stuffed with meat and roasted spiral-cut potatoes." Aminat placed a pile of *chudu* cheese pancakes in front of me. They were covered in melted butter and *urbech* paste made from almond kernels.

"On one side, from the left, sat their cousins, with Said in

Wedding dance in Bezhta to the accompaniment of drum and horn music.

the middle and Madina's father, brother and mother's sister, facing the other relatives. She sat in a side room, with tables laid for her girl-friends. Said's mother made the introductions, then they sat down. Madina's girl friends invited Said to her room. He and his cousins went to her room to eat, joke and listen to music until midnight."

In villages, it was usual for proposals to be made similarly. At the first visit of the match-maker, if the host tasted the gifts, it was taken as a sign that he approved of the engagement – if not, he did not. His wife would have set a table for the guests and after some time the girl was invited to join them. If she would not sit with them, she tactfully turned down the match, while a spoken refusal would have been rude, with the possibility of offending the other family. Spurned suitors might take revenge, as was bloodily sketched in 'Murder at the Wedding' in the Akhti museum. Depicted so graphically in the painting was wedding party, on its feet, the feast untouched on the sagging tables. Slumped around the floor were male guests, stabbed, blood running down their white shirts. The groom was dying in the bride's arms. Young men with flashing eyes and daggers were making their getaways.

Betrothal was not so 'simple' for the disabled. In mountain villages, even today, parents tragically were unwilling to allow their disabled children to go to special schools, as it meant a public admission which they considered shameful. In turn, these children could not receive village schooling and so dropped further behind. I encountered a deaf and dumb girl, who had made the best of her isolation by constructing an exquisite dolls' house interior, laid out on the yard, sheltered from the rain under a balcony in Bezhta. If any child was "weak-brained," they were usually married to another with a similar defect, or, for example, a girl with a physical handicap might marry a man with a mental handicap. There was one beautiful eight-year-old Avar girl in Butsada, near Khunzakh, who had lost her leg below the knee in a combine harvester accident. She had been sent to Moscow for an operation three months earlier and now walked with a crutch. The mayor's wife commented, "It's a pity she was a girl, because now she will never marry as she cannot work hard enough."

If only they had listened to this Chechen story. A mouse decided to make a match for her daughter with the strongest creature in the world and asked the people who it was. The people sent her to the Shah, he to the fire, the fire to the water, the water to the sun, the sun to the clouds, the clouds to the wind, and the wind to a bush. She then asked the bush, "Is there anyone stronger than you?" "Yes," the bush admitted, "my roots are tougher than I am." "But we gnaw roots," the mouse swallowed, "so there's no one stronger than mice on earth."Aand she married her daughter off to the rodent in the next burrow. Since that time, Chechens have said, "Mouse came to mouse."

But problems surrounding engagements have always been the stuff of drama. Before the Revolution, the dowry or bride price could be extremely high – on the Kumyk plains, people there still pay a large bride price – anything up to 5000 roubles (then £5,000) – and this often proved too much for a youth, so he would kidnap his bride. To avoid being killed by her father or brothers, he would snatch her up as he galloped past on horseback. However, such a kidnapping would invariably by custom start an inter-family blood-feud. In Grozny, the capital of neighbouring Chechen-Ingushetia, bride-snatching has reappeared in the past few years. Today it is done by car, driving up to the girl and bundling her in. A 17-year-old Chechen girl's abduction was recently arranged by her sister and future sister-in-law, as her father was against the match. He only consented to meet the couple a year later. Up to half the weddings in Grozny are alleged to be the result of kidnaps, many of them with unwilling girls, so today girls are afraid to walk alone on the streets of Grozny.

A milder option was available earlier this century. If a Khvarshin couple wished to marry and the young man was unfairly refused by the girl's parents, all the respected people in the village would arrive together in his support, as the young man tied a saddled horse to the door of his fiancée, ready for a symbolic snatch. If he could not afford it, members of his clan and even the village council would help. This problem was cunningly solved in the following tale. Once there was a poor Khan's daughter of marriageable age, but nobody came from other villages to ask for her hand from one year to the next. One day the Khan of another village decided to go and discuss the marriage of his son with the first Khan. He arrived, greeted him, *salaam aleikum*, sat down, and said, "Our children have grown up. Your daughter and my son should get married. Life won't be bad for her with us. If they had 500 head of sheep, 50 cattle and 30 stallions, if they had a good strong house like a fortress, life won't be hard." The Khan was overjoyed and the girl left to be married. A month or two later, her father decided to visit her. He went to the village and found out where they lived and discovered a tumbled-down shack, without any livestock or any herds, only a couple of chickens, running around in the yard. He turned to the poor Khan in amazement and asked, "What have you done? Have you no shame?" The Khan replied, "What do you mean? I said nothing, I only said 'if'." In Avar, *bugoni* means 'if there is', but they always swallow the last syllable, saying *bugo*, meaning 'there is' – the same is true in Kumyk.

'The triumphant registration of marriage' is a clean-cut photo in the Akhti official photo album, which had been assembled over the past twenty years to record the town's traditions. Soviet-style marriage was thought to be a good way to subvert tradition, but it failed. Up the Andi-Koisu river, in Aguali village, boasting its modern town square and a restaurant, an obvious Party member, a 40-year-old woman, said that although she and her four brothers were of Muslim origin, they did not go to mosque, but they retained the complete white veil covering head and eyes for weddings. Staggering back to my room late one night, after about a litre of brandy at another wedding in a civic hall in Makhachkala, I was asked to be their photographer – it was "important." In between the vodka, brandy, champagne, sweet fizz and Soviet Pepsi, girls still sat at separate tables from everyone else. The bride wore white and the groom a dark suit and tie. They sat at the head table, in front of a machine-made carpet, tacked to the wall. The bride and groom, to wolf-whistles from his men friends, started the dancing, followed by single pairs, using a white flower as the Stick of Love to choose their next partner, while family and friends served in the kitchen and waited on the 500 guests.

Village weddings were different because of the music, dancing and customs. A professional four-man village band played outdoors. Two howling *zurnas*, or shawms, a double-reed instrument like an oboe, were accompanied by the rhythm of a *baraban* double-headed drum and the dirge-like groans of a local piano-accordian *garmon*, based on the mid-19th-century Russian model.

Stringed instruments usually accompanied singers. Most common was the strummed *pandur*, a two stringed fretted wooden lute, derived from the ancient three-stringed *achaka kupuz*, possibly meaning 'bard's lute', of the Turkic Kazakhs from the Steppes.

Among the myriad local dances, some were danced *en pointe*, reminiscent of the 'First Furrow' spring fertility dances. Lak, Dargin and Avar women danced the *kalmyayab*, meaning *en pointe*, while mixed Lak couples danced to a folk song with crossed steps, alternating with springs on to their toes. Women dancing together at weddings was unusual, unless they were relatives of the bride or groom. I have seen Daghestan men and women dance on their toes, wearing only soft leather boots or shoes with no blocks like Russian or Western women ballet dancers wear. They do not merely step up and do a few steps, but they leap in the air and down onto their points and hop on one toe. I met one boy who had danced *en pointe* in the Daghestan Children's Ensemble and he showed me his feet. They seemed absolutely normal with no sign of the damage *en pointe* dancers usually suffer. "No, it doesn't hurt," he explained patiently, "we've always danced like that."

Apart from music and dancing, wedding customs differed even from village to village, which confirmed that it was not the geographical barriers which isolated the villagers, rather the desire to retain individuality – a central thread in the survival of the old Daghestan. The four parts of different weddings, described below, show how rich the the variations were, even nowadays. I attended parts of three-day weddings in three different nationality-villages: Bezhta, Koubachi and the Lak Charah, as well as a stunning re-enactment of an Avar wedding in Khunzakh with hundreds of participants, in which they had collected every one of their customs.

The Khunzakh performance told the story from the betrothal up to the first day of the marriage, a few weeks later. It began with the mother and father, discussing their son's proposed match. The father said "yes," and the mother said "no," but the father was in charge, so at length she deferred. The family servant, wearing a pink shirt, served mutton and wine to celebrate, while their women relatives, in red, were discussing the news. After rearranging the house for the wedding, they were offered tea from a samovar and water from a ewer by the master of ceremonies, called variously *tamada*, *chauz*, *cardinal* or *eret kusgia*. The women then went to fetch the the bride. At the the bride's home, the women were gathering food and spoons as wedding gifts. The women's delegation from the groom's side sat down to eat the bride's food and drink a weak beer (brewed specially for women). Then back to the groom's house for the marriage party, where surrounded by their guests, with the women in white shawls, the groom's parents discussed how the party was going.

In typical married argument, he insisted "It's going to be this way!" and she retorted "It certainly won't!", covering her mouth with her hand as she looked away. The groom's grandmother held up a bent yellow fork, spearing the fat sheep's tail, saved for some special guest. The fork was bent to prevent meat

Day three of a Koubachi wedding. The richly ringed fingers of the bride hold a 'shashlik' Stick of Love used to pass from one of a pair of dancers at the wedding to the next. All who dance with the bride contribute to her wedding fund.

dropping off. The servant, who always had to have his hands filled, dished out mutton, pilaf, bread, cheese, *chudu* and beer. The six women accompanying the bride arrived with painted faces and hands and danced around the groom's father in his honour, while an old woman guest was singing and drumming on the back of a tin bath. (If she had been a professional, she would have been accompanied by a musician).

The bride's grandmother offered gifts to the men barring the groom's threshold with a rope, to be allowed in, while the mother danced with the servant, who was holding up a leg of mutton on a knife. All the bride's kinswomen brought sweets, such as dried apricot pilaf, raisins and halva, while the groom's mother stood by with a pot of honey to smear on the bride's lips to make the marriage happy. For a joke she also smeared it on the old woman's mouth. The groom's mother invited the groom's friends to sit, drink and sing, combining the symbols of home – the cooking pot, *pandur* guitar and triangular stool. The stool was left for the old woman, clowning that she was drunk. The servant offered beer to the young men, while the women danced separately in the bride's room.

For his wedding-night, the groom was given energy-food – apricot kernel *urbech* and a fried dumpling made from flour, liver, pepper, salt and vinegar. Everyone was also laughing at the bride's jester, dressed up as the bride. He was always making bizarre requests to the groom's people, such as "Oooo, I have a bad leg, roll me up and carry me off in a carpet." Then the bride's mother (or aunt) gave silk to perhaps 20 of the groom's relatives, to mark that they were now kinsmen. This time it was an embroidered bag, but scarves, handkerchiefs or hats were also given to keep as souvenirs.

At the climax, the veiled bride arrived at the groom's house, escorted by her young friends and her aunt, to be welcomed by the the groom's women relatives. Sometimes, if there was another youth who also liked the bride, he wrestled with the groom, who – if necessary – was given a chance to win and received a sheep as a prize (in the moutainous Charadinskii rayon) to mark an end to their rivalry. Children picked up money and sweets thrown in the air to mark the arrival of the bride. Before rice or paper confetti, walnuts were thrown to ensure at least four children. Recently, as an ironic comment on economic inflation, shredded rouble notes have been used as confetti. All the community joined in village weddings.

ða.

I moved between two of the four weddings in Bezhta village on a sunny July Sunday. There were about a hundred a year, mostly during the summer. The boys tended to be 22, the girls 18. At the first, Magomed Umar Rasoulov was marrying Mukhlizat Djemalova. At the groom's house, by 11am on the first day of the wedding, a feast was being consumed outside on a long table for a hundred women and children, while 50 young children upstairs squeezed along the balcony and another 50 of the groom's friends crammed into a separate room. We ate cabbage from Makhachkala and meat soup, cooked outdoors by men in a 1.5 metre cast-iron pot, standing on a trivet over the fire next to the house. The brown soup was ladled out with a great spoon into buckets. (The longest culinary spoon in the world may well be the 5' 5" one in Akhti museum, made in Kuyada, Gunibskii rayon.)

Much firewood was needed to cook a wedding feast, so several days before, all the young men in the village gathered to chop wood and afterwards held a party around the bonfire. We were sitting in the guests' room, where two Sticks of Love, decorated with curly white paper ribbons, were hung on the wall, ready for the dancing later. About 15 women entered and formed a circle to sing three old songs in Bezhtin, which was unusual, as Avar is the language of songs. The women cried when they sang how they lost their daughter to the groom.

At the second wedding in Bezhta, Anjoyev Magomed Gapourovich was the groom and Kourbanova Madinat Abdukhaikovna, his bride. I declined a heaped plate of the delicacy – stewed grey sheep guts – at midday. At about four in the afternoon, Said-the-Singer drove me in his Niva to pick up the bride, with her two closest girl friends. She had stayed with relatives in a nearby hamlet. According to custom, she put on her veil and left the house reluctantly, to encouraging shouts from young male relatives. She sat between her girl-friends in the back seat of our jeep, now festooned with balloons and ribbons. On the journey back we were escorted by four other motors. The girls ululated and sang to keep up her spirits, often reinforced by their radio cassette player. Twice the road was blocked by trucks, so the driver leading the procession, after much haggling, had to pay money and a bottle of vodka for them to let us pass.

When we arrived at the groom's family's three-storey house, the crowd was loudly dancing outside. The house had two storeys of balconies on two sides, full of guests in bright clothes. Children climbed onto the car as it and the bride were soaked by water, thrown by women from the balconies. The mother of the groom and her sister met the veiled bride and took her from the Niva.

Then it started. Three times the bride's way upstairs was blocked by dour young men. They were, I suspect, by tradition, making a last gesture that the bride was unworthy and trying to get a higher dowry. Everyone had been drinking and a scuffle broke out between the old man drummer and the young male 'resisters'. More water was poured onto the bride. She was dragged half-blinded from entrance to entrance by the women. It looked like a Spanish painting of Jesus going to Calvary, as the faceless bride stumbled and was borne up in the crush. They took her to a side entrance as a feint, but the men were not fooled, like in that medieval South German tapestry, where Wild Women stormed the Castle of Love.

At last they got in and I lost her, pressed in a crowd, surging up the stairs. When the groom was fetched back from his friends, he was given a symbolic *kalym*, bride price, of 50 roubles which he pretended to refuse. After the long and hectic day, the couple slept together in the groom's parents' bedroom, in their wedding bed, covered in dowry cushions and white gauze lace – their privilege for three nights. On the second afternoon, the bride and groom bathed separately with their respective friends. In the evening the bride's girl-friends organised a party for the girls, after which the bride and groom met and more friends came with more presents. On the third day, visits began after six, when the bride stayed at home to receive presents, like a scarf or a carpet, while the groom visited his friends. On the fourth day they were free.

In nearby Ginukh, weddings were similar, including the bride's soaking, but they did not keep her hidden away all day. They also danced more slowly with no jumping.

ò▪

The Koubachi August sky was overcast. The first day of the wedding had started with the slaughter of a cow, which reached the pot by midday. At four, the groom's young male friends came to his room with an accordion, to sing old songs about his imminent married life, while a hundred guests sat outside to listen. Then they all went to the bride's house. I missed the next day. To start the third day's wedding party on the hillside, three women, including the bride, in silk costumes and white head-scarves, carried symbolic ewers of water from the spring down under the arches. The large tinned copper 20-litre ewer was balanced in front by a smaller one, bound together with a canvas strap, slung over the shoulder. The women sat in a group, holding bunches of golden flowers, as a symbol of their wealth, like their gold embroidered head-scarves.

Fifty metres downhill, the men reclined on the steep grassy slope, feasting on stuffed cabbages and shashlik on wooden skewers and drinking champagne, vodka and brandy. They had their own *zurna* and drum players who wore sashes, like the ushers. One woman asked me if I was an ethnographer – she was one herself and worked at the Academy of Sciences in Makhachkala. The women wore dazzling thick gold brocaded silk dresses, some of which were heirlooms. The bride had large rings on every finger – every family in Koubachi is said to have a kilogram of gold hidden away, worth 75,000 roubles (which I have never seen). She and the other women danced slowly in two pairs with the men. They danced solemnly hunched over, holding their left hand hooked into their breast, with the right clenched behind the small of the back. Everyone who danced had to pay money – 25 or 50 roubles – to the bride, who passed the notes to a woman relative who gleefully counted it. The Society of Young Unmarried Men had not performed the day before, but they still did their wild masked dance at some weddings, depending on the family, though it was rarer nowadays.

I arrived late in the afternoon during a Lak mountain village wedding in Charah near Kumukh, just as the men's procession, from the groom's house to the boundary of village, emerged on the village green. There were hundreds of guests, with many from outside the village. I was immediately given a glass of vodka and a fatty knuckle of mutton. Next the women followed, singing to a tambourine accompaniment, surrounding the bride and carrying the white paper flower Wedding Stick to be offered and taken by each succeeding dancer. An old woman held a dish with the remains of caramel toffee wrapped in cloth. (Ingush brides also used to be presented with honey and butter by the groom's mother, on entering her house, so she would be "soft as butter and sweet as honey.") During the dancing, the second usher grasped his whip to keep order and a golden glazed ram's head, whose choicey knuckle I had been offered, symbolising strength and fertility.

Back at the groom's father's house, near the ten foot high stack of dowry cushions, the parents welcomed guests, pleased that eight of their ten sons were now married. In the yard, we passed the old male guests, still sitting quietly at their trestle table long after eating, while upstairs, filling the glazed verandah, the main table looked like a forest of bottles, abandoned after the feast. Off the verandah, next to the noisy old women and children's room, the girls were dancing in the bride's room, where the groom joined her. The groom's senior brother looked after me, as an honoured guest, at the men's table and we drank toasts and ate slices of creamy sponge wedding cake, surely of Russian influence, while downstairs even the old crones danced.

Daghestan people do not like being alone – they regard it as bad manners to leave a guest alone for even a moment. Even so, after the marriage, the claustrophobic pressure of living together in an extended family, combined with the duty of looking after older relatives with insufficient resources could

Proud Avar father: Magomed Pirbodagov, from Zaib village on the Avar-Koisu river, down the gorge from Khunzakh, with his swaddled newborn son Ali in a mosaic wicker basket. The last measured Avar birth rate increase from 1979-89 was 23 per cent.

become too much of a burden. However the newly-weds were often too poor to move out. After marriage in Britain, parents are left behind and inheritance happens on death, while in Daghestan inheritance theoretically happens on marriage and the parents remain. Before the Revolution – it is worse nowadays – the first son sometimes got his marriage 'portion' immediately to set up a separate household. There's an Avar saying that "the sooner you light your own hearth, the more salt you'll have," meaning that you'll live longer.

Following the marriage settlement agreed by the parents, the size of which reflected family honour, a highland bride would bring a considerable dowry in land or livestock, which made it possible to start a home. Sometimes a son had to wait just a few days for his share, maybe a couple of months and occasionally the not-so-newly weds had to live with his parents for two or three years. It all depended on the living space allotted to him and how quickly it could be enlarged or a new house built.

In the highlands, if the newly-weds moved quickly to their own home, a warm relationship was preserved, while in the plains, a swift departure was assumed to indicate difficulties within the family, described by the Kumyks and Nogai as "the cauldron is heavy, the cauldron can't be lifted" – there are too many people for the available resources. The eldest son was married first, and the father had to provide a house for him, or at least a space within the boundary of the village, as well as a share of his arable land, fields and herds. But a daughter merely received a third of the son's portion, excluding the dwelling or farm, so, "if a son is born, a house is built, but for a daughter, a house is demolished." If a father was poor, the principle was still "a share of everything, except the family home." The eldest son, having received his portion, had no further claim.

The rest of the inheritance was left to the youngest son(s) who continued to live in the family home. This arrangement often caused dissatisfaction amongst

District prosecutor Magomed and Khalimat Suleymanov's swaddled baby girl Patimat in Bezhta village.

brothers, and many popular ballads tell of their scheming. As one folktale goes, there were two brothers who enticed their younger brother to go out hunting for falcons. They led him to a nest in an inaccessible cave on a cliff and let him down on a rope, which they gently let drop. The young boy pleaded that he would give them a share of his inheritance, but his Cain-like brothers replied that if he died, especially not by their hand, they could take it all, so they left him in the cave.

Records have been kept of extended families since the 1880s. In 1886, Russian administrators surveyed 14,260 families from 340 villages, recording nationality, location in highland, foothills or plains, and occupation, but unfortunately omitting the position of individuals in the family or property owned. These early studies confirmed contemporary recollections of old men that younger brothers stayed on in the household, and ate from the same cauldron for ten years or more after they were married* and some even after their grandchildren had children.[†]

---

* Efendiev Gasan, born 1886 in Akhti; Alibek Gasanov born 1883 in Khurik; Efruz Pamaldanov born 1885 in Khuchni.
[†] Mamed-Dzhafar Makhmudov born 1894 in the village of Khnov.

The reason for leaving was often the death of the head of the family. The first picked out to leave was the son whose wife did not get on with the family, and was considered as a condemnation by the community. Wives, too, did not like leaving for they feared the despotism of their husbands, since all the bride's dowry of land or livestock was assimilated with her husband's and never referred to as belonging to her. As late as 1928 there were often "up to 40 people living under the same roof making up one household, for instance in Gidatl." The transportation into exile of these mistakenly called *'kulaks'* during the 1930s put an end to that.

The prime purpose of marriage was and is to have babies. It may be that "every time a Lak is born, it is a miracle," but it was less so for the mother. Babies and young children have always been loved and spoiled everywhere in Daghestan, but infant mortality – and death of the mothers – of these unusually tough people used to be high when the mothers gave birth in the villages. In Archi a woman used to have her first child at her parent's home and stay there for 40 days, while other villages had a special parturition hut, where the mother was exiled.

But today in Daghestan, women have their children in hospital and stay there for a week afterwards, much longer than in Britain. After leaving hospital, women and their babies still stay with their mothers for six weeks and then return to their husbands. Most women have children every year after marriage – on average five each – with the result that, for instance, the 35,000 children in the rayon of Botlikh have exceeded hospital and school capacity. The 25 per cent increase in the population of Daghestan from 1979 to 1989 shows the success of making mothers go to hospital. Today they also encourage them to name their babies then and there, which means more Mishas and less Magomeds – all part of Sovietisation policy to eradicate regional differences.

There are still problems. Dr Zulkip Magomedov, the 34-year-old Leningrad-trained chief doctor of the Bezhtinskii rayon, came early in the morning to see Magomedkhan, my collaborator. Old friends, they began wrestling together. Over breakfast Zulkip felt powerless as he explained that a recent Soviet report said that over 60 per cent of children in Daghestan were undernourished, confirmed by the shortage of vegetables and fruit – especially citrus fruit, which while available in season is expensive, i.e. £1 for a lemon as opposed to 20p in London. This is not the fault of the Daghestanis, but the government, who should start up a village nutrition education programme.

Residues off the baby were and are surrounded by superstition. Even recently, before cutting a baby's nails, its fingers were pressed on flour to stop it becoming a thief. When a baby's hair was cut, it had to be put in a hole in the wall of the house – what was locally described as a clean place, protected from malevolent beings or forces – as did the baby's nails. The baby's bath water had to be thrown out in the morning, so that no part of the infant fell into malevolent hands.

Male circumcision was widespread (even including Party officials), as was confirmed when they found out that I was circumcised. In the 1960s circumcision was one of the last external signs of belonging to the community of the faithful. The foreskin was also placed in a clean place in the eaves by the circumciser. It reminded me of the arguments surrounding the sanctity or profanity of similar relics of Christ, put forward by San Bernadino of Sienna in the 14th century.

In one village, when boys were over four, but before they had started school, they would play near the *godekan*. I was told the story of one such boy's circumcision, fixed for ever in the memory of the man, who chose to remain anonymous. His older friends teased him that he was not a true Muslim unless he had been circumcised, until, one day, he decided to have it done with a group of his friends. He was given a sort of kilt and set off, on his own, to the house of the village specialist. The operation was performed in the open air, on the verandah, so the boy would not be scared by being inside a room.

When he turned up to ask to be circumcised, there were four other boys already howling on the cots on the verandah. The specialist gave him a sugar-lump and made a few jokes, to put him at ease, and then pointed at something over his head, to make him look up at the vital moment. The boy had taken out his member and the specialist rapidly pulled the foreskin back to loosen it, revealing the head of the penis. He then pulled the foreskin as far forward as it would go and deftly clamped it between two finger-sized rectangular pieces of wood. He immediately cut off the foreskin in one stroke, along the straight edge of the wood.

The child screamed, but he was a tough little boy and he accepted another piece of sugar as his wound was disinfected with kerosene (sometimes herbs were used) and his hands were covered in talc, so he would not infect himself by touch. He did not lie down, but walked back home crying, which was thought of as brave behaviour, leaving his foreskin behind. The boys had a week off to heal, in their kilts, when they were allowed to do what they liked, which left a memory of fun. If they complained after then, their fathers ignored any residual pain and said it was nothing.

There were different lullabies for boys and girls. Most boys' lullabies of Daghestan and the North Caucasus were connected with the old forms of household economy: hunting and later, farming and shepherding. A few Avar, Dargin, Rutul and Lezgin lullabies survive about the wish for a son to be a hunter, summoning epic heroes, as these two examples in Avar:

> *May you kill a bear and a sharp-tusked boar.*
> *May you be able to light a bright fire on the blue sea.*
> *May your whip and horse, my darling, be all golden*
> *And your weapons steel, as those of 'Tzunta'.*

Old woman in the almost deserted hamlet of Khilikh' (near Archi) showing her talismanic swaddling bags (to ward off the evil eye) which she made for each of her ten grandchildren when babies. She is sitting with her husband on their rolled mud roof in the summer.

> *Yes, like 'Chilav' – you'll be a hunter.*
> *Valiant on your horse you'll sit*
> *With lightning speed you'll gallop.*
> *You'll be the most handsome in all the world.*
> *May a heavenly eagle sit on your shoulder,*
> *My beloved lion cub – and*
> *May 'Amast' help you in your hunting.*

The 'bright fire' may be a reference to the sun which was worshipped in the old Zoroastrian religion in Daghestan, as well as overcoming their ever-present fear of rivers and the sea. The work of a shepherd also called for courage and endurance, worthy of a mother's regard, as in this Avar lullaby:

> *You'll save a lamb from the hungry wolf,*
> *Obtain the tears from a tiger's eyes,*
> *Strike a way to the womb of a serpent,*
> *So your mother may see a man in you,*
> *And another, a son-in-law.*

A way to be born . . .

Yes, in your dark blue Andi coat of felt,
And your shining black boots,
You'll be a shepherd.

Similar lullabies were also found to the north-west, over the mountain range in Ossetia, Chechenia, Kabardia and Cherkessia. Shepherds required special training and festivals were held to test the lads. Reflecting his mother's worst fears, the future Lezgin shepherd babe was exorted to "kill a thousand wolves." Meanwhile, girls' lullabies ectolled the virtues of material well-being, daily life and practical accomplishments – all to prepare them for a life of toil. A girl was encouraged to be an industrious and talented worker: to weed, make hay, reap, care for herds, spin, weave and attend to all domestic duties.

ða

For the baby, lullabies may be the aural equivalent of breast suckling. But for the families involved, suckling from a woman of another family constituted kinship through adoption. In the last century, when a son was born to the ruler of the Karakaitags, he was sent from village to village to be suckled by all the women who could, in order to make him foster-brother of his entire generation. This was often a stronger tie than blood; Steder, a traveller-scholar of German origin, writing in 1797 noted that an Ingush murderer suckled his victim's mother at knifepoint, and so became part of her family, to avoid death by the blood-feud. Not long later, the Russian Karginov heard of an Ossete adulterer, who had been forced to kiss the breast of his beloved by her family, to terminate their relationship by making it incestuous. At the wedding at Khalag, I was careful while dancing, after I had jokingly been told that an inadvertent touch would be punished as attempted rape – with the same penalties as actual rape – the only escape being to find the girl's mother and suckle her breast at knifepoint.

As in Russia, swaddling is popular in Daghestan. It is thought to make the baby's legs grow straight, while in the West it is thought to restrict them. The baby, wearing a soft top and bottom garment, is covered in a sheet and blankets, slightly sticking out above the sides of the cot. The bundle is strapped in with a six-inch-wide cloth, wool or silk band. Strings attached to its pointed ends are tied together underneath the cot. I was given a photograph, taken in 1968, of Khutkhul mothers working in the fields, beside a line of swaddled babies in cots, shaded with linen covers. I passed a woman returning from a wedding in Bezhta, carrying on her back her swaddled baby in its cot, slung from her forehead with a strap. Nearby, the village prosecutor's swaddled baby seemed peaceful enough, watching us at lunch. Her parents said that she liked being swaddled. When she wanted a change, she cried out and they immediately undid her.

Cots are like those found in Corum in northern Turkey – a box with bent wooden semi-circular hooped ends with curved rockers. A proud Avar father had driven by car up the mountain track from his hamlet to Khunzakh, with his baby son swaddled in a wattle cot and in Kuli, a Lak woman walked by with her swaddled baby tied to her back with a shawl. Swaddling often seemed to act like a car's safety belt. In Ginichuk' village near Khunzakh, an Avar great-grandmother was singing a lullaby while vigorously rocking the baby, who was only held in by being swaddled into the cradle. I recognised the same melody I had recorded the previous year in our broken-down bus, when an Andi grandmother calmed down a strange baby which had driven its young mother to tears. She also made the same breathless growling sound to keep the baby quiet, in a rising and cut-off-at-the-end "wahahahahahahahah-khuh!" It even worked when I tried it out on London babies, but that could have been the effect of sheer astonishment.

Veiled bride and groom at their Andi wedding, July 1992. Good luck inscription in Andi in white foam on the carpet of honour. (Photo: M. Aglarov)

·5·

... and a way to die

Our jeep almost ploughed into the unexpected traffic jam. The road through Tashkapur was blocked by a large crowd, forming an amphitheatre around the bridge over the ravine, watching rescue operations to find the last two bodies from the car crash three days before. Daghestan people were both horrified and fascinated by accidents, like the Turks. This obsession was partly because of their fear of water, both in the dangerous rivers and the unpredictable Caspian, an ironic contrast to their dependence on water for agricultural survival. There was a hysterical dread of having your head forced under water, which caused another tragedy at Muni, where we had been invited to an Andi wedding.

There we met the bright young mayor who gave us portentiously bitter water to drink and continued on to the wedding house, where we ate soup. I then recorded some songs and was just tasting a home-made cherry wine when the party was interrupted by an intense quietly-spoken man. He explained that a 23-year-old man had been swept away while bathing nearby in the shallow, but fast-flowing Andi-Koisu river. We rushed to the jeep and everyone who could drove the five kilometres down the river, where it broadened into three main streams. Led by the mayor, the men undressed and fanned across the river, swimming an upright crawl to keep their heads above water, when it was too deep to walk. An old man in a golden *karakul* fleece hat came searching on foot with a group of women.

After thirty minutes they found him five kilometres downstream among the broken rocks, cold, eyes open, teeth broken, his skull fractured at the temple, still living. The villagers revived him so he was warm and we drove back feeling relieved. But back in the mayor's office, the man who had played the accordion came in to say that the man had died on the way home.

The deceased had been religious and had recently returned from serving in the Red Army where he prayed regularly and refused to eat pork (and so effectively starved). He was to have been married soon. He was bathing where the Muni tributary met the main river and was sucked under by a whirlpool. I asked Magomedkhan my collaborator how he could have drowned in such a

Gazi Magomedov Jakhfar travelled 200km to drink the healing waters at the spring at Inkhokvari to cure his stomach. He and his two sons also prayed on mats where the spring met the river. There is more gas in the magic spring water when the moon waxes and less when it wanes. This defies scientific explanation.

shallow river. He thought that the victim had panicked when his head went under and did not curl up in a ball, which could have saved his life. When he came up, he was immediately sucked down into a second vortex. But it was probably the bumps in the road that finished him off. His brother did not trust the hospital in Botlikh, an hour's drive away over rough roads, and instead had him brought back home, where they had herbal medicines. There he died.

Back at the wedding, the feast had been cleared away. Women were changing into black, the men were gathering at the *godekan*, all wearing hats. The closest male relatives were sitting on both sides of the mayor's porch. One held a shovel. The corpse would be buried in two hours. We were advised to leave and shook hands with all the men and then discovered that we had a puncture. While it was mended, we returned to sit outside the wedding house where the groom retold us the sad story. We drove back to Botlikh where a freak fierce gale started to blow. At the same time it was burning hot in the sun. A strange day.

꿈

Local services were also considered inadequate by members of the medical profession. Dr Zulkip Magomedov, chief doctor of the Bezhtinskii rayon, complained that there were only 150 hospital beds for 14,000 population, which is above average for Daghestan, compared to 150 beds for 25,000 in Britain in 1988-89! There are eight ambulances in the rayon, compared to an equivalent one in England. But in Daghestan, living conditions are poorer, so they get sicker. Also there are far fewer other vehicles to take people to hospital than in Britain, and the trips cover a longer distance and are slower because of the pot-holed dirt mountain roads. Programmed use of ambulances is non-existent, so efficiency must be lower, while maintenance takes longer, keeping the ambulances off the roads. By 1996, there were almost no medicines or medical disposables like syringes in Daghestan. The doctor expressed concern that the poor health service encouraged and maintained the widespread practice of folk medicine.

Spring waters, herbs and spells form an integral part of this medicine. Daghestan being a mountainous area, there is ample of each. The curing spring beside the waterfall at Inkhokvari, near Aguali village is one such mysterious example. When the moon waxes, there is more gas in the pungent waters, when moon wanes, less, and the flavour changes. Here I met the ailing Jakhfar Gazi Magomedov, whose sons had brought him 200 kilometres to cure his stomach by drinking the waters. They then prayed on mats by the river.

Earlier this century, on the night of the equinox, even ordinary spring water was considered to have medicinal properties by the Kumyks, who either bathed in the river or brought home ewers filled with its water to pour over themselves and their elderly relatives. They used special brass bowls, with central raised bosses and magical inscriptions, for drinking remedial waters. I too have simmered in the old Russian Officers' natural boiling-water baths near Akhti and soaked my feet in the gentler hot springs down-river from Bezhta, where strange children played in the sun with yellow flower petals stuck to their faces. Until early this century, there was a strong religious disbelief in man's ability to heal. Today in Makhachkala the bearded Khazar, El-Said, was renowned for his natural cures for asthma, rotting gums, rheumatism, arthritis and the common cold. He went so far as to claim five out of ten cures for cancer. There was a legacy of older lore as well, which only seemed to survive in folk-memory. An abundant range of preventative and treatment rites, as well as spells, were popular as in Tibet.

The evil eye was always held to be capable of bewitching and had to be avoided, as it could cause illness or even death. Even today, beads to keep the evil eye at bay are sewn on children's clothing from birth, or worn around their wrists or necks. Small glass beads, resembling eyes, were favoured by the Dargins, as were bones or teeth of boar, fox, wolf or goat, sea shells, bears' claws, and egg shells. The Lezgins protected themselves with amulets in red cloth bags or leather pouches, adapted in Muslim times to hold a few lines from the Koran, sewn into their clothing. Richer folk would keep an amulet box, containing barley, apricot kernels, quince or cornelian cherry, as fruit-bearing plants were thought to have healing properties.

These same powers were attributed to splinters from any tree struck by lightning, from the Zoroastrian belief, where fire from lightning was considered to be supernatural, and salt, alone or mixed with dog's excrement. Splinters of wood or grain also symbolised the imperishable or health. Snake-shaped bracelets were worn by sick or barren women and the reptile also decorated talismanic ceramic jugs and dishes. For additional protection, again as today, animal skulls were kept in the corner of a room or outdoors, and cattle horns were nailed to a fence or verandah. Metal charms included knives, sickles, scissors, pins, needles and horseshoes. A piece of metal was placed under the head of a new-born babe, and when a child started to walk, a small piece of metal was sewn to his clothing, to prevent a fall. Coal and soot were kept by Lezgins to ward off evil forces and youngsters were smeared with soot and dressed in torn clothes to make them unattractive to spirits.

Lezgins still use a profuse bean plant, locally called *uzelik* – or *paganum harmala* in Latin – thought to originate from Persia, which is dried in bunches and hung in houses, to keep away evil. The plant was also burnt to fumigate the sickroom, changing its role from a preventative to a curative agent. For instance, if the master of a household fell ill after giving dinner to a stranger, it was necessary to get a scrap of his clothing to burn with *uzelik*, to purify the house by cremating the miserable spirit which he had left behind. If this was impossible, a twig broom was used to sweep all the places where the guest's feet had trodden, and the dust collected, mixed with salt and incinerated with *uzelik*.

Both good and evil spirits were supposed to have interfered with the mentally ill, who were under the protection of Allah himself, and were called 'the poor of God', or 'the servants of God'. Pilgrims visited their sacred graves in times of illness, when their supernatural connections enabled them to chase away the spirits of sickness. For magical healing, the Lezgin resorted to a witch doctor, who performed various rites. He collected earth from holy places or shrines, such the Pyre of Suleiman on Mount Shalbuzdag, which was mixed with water and drunk as medicine. He also used the human-like Mary's hair, a fibrous plant which hangs from branches. If a prayer was said while a strand was tied around the wrist or ankle, magic powers of healing were activated. It is also used today in the manufacture of antiseptics. There were also many folk treatments for barren women, which are described elsewhere.

Three charms from the village of Archi were typical of sympathetic magic, connected with animals: if you kill a frog, your cow will die; if you eat cats, you get the 'trembling illness'; and if a child is agitated or afraid, feed it snake meat. A sick child's ear wax was dropped into a dish of cold water and the shape divined by the witch-doctor, usually as a snake or a frog, which was then caught and its skin rubbed over the child. Presumably, that was the more pleasant function of a bronze frog from Koubachi, now on show in a museum in Makhachkala.

If health and sickness can be thought of as opposites in a dualist magic system, then the negative side of curing was bewitching. Bewitching might occur if the evil eye was accidentally attracted by praising someone, celebrating recovery from illness, or even picking up a child in admiration. To harm a child on purpose, it was enough (and quite practical) to hold it close, after visiting a dying person and so pass on the illness. The Lezgins in particular had discovered a most effective way to kill: by burying some of the victim's hairs, knotted with a woollen string and a fatty sheep's tail in a sunny place. As the fat melted, so the victim would sicken and die in torment.

Within Daghestan murder was not common nowadays, however Daghestani workers in Central Asia faced greater risks. In 1989 air tickets to Makhachkala were hard to buy in Moscow because they were being bought up by Chechens fleeing racism in Kazakhstan.* Caucasians in general were skilled builders and became rich there, so the local jealousy grew into violence, particularly towards the Chechens. Magomedkhan's wife's 22-year-old cousin had just died in Kazakhstan. No one knew how. Magomedkhan put on his jacket and flat *aerodrom* peaked hat, a.k.a. the *furashka*, and immediately left for the man's village, six hours drive away, to break the news, as the senior member of his family. When his relatives saw him, they prayed and ate, but did not drink.

It later came out that in a dance hall in Kazakhstan, a Russian had insulted the young man's race and parentage, so he knocked him down and left. Later, while he was sitting outside his lodgings, telling what had happened to four friends, the Russian crept up behind and stabbed him in the back. The hospital was a hour away by car and he died from loss of blood. Next day the police arrested

---

* This was principally from Russians, and ignored by the Kazakh authorities, who later (post-Soviet) were to apologise for any such racism and invited the Chechens back.

the murderer who said he had been drunk and remembered nothing – though he must have remembered where his victim lived. No further action was taken.

&

Pre-Islamic burial customs have largely been replaced by Muslim traditions. In Avar legends, Nart giants lived on Mount Rechol, which rises over the village of Gagatl, peacefully farming and rearing pigs. Legends tell how they buried their dead in a knee-deep pit, surrounded and covered by slabs of stone, which was confirmed when a Late Bronze Age grave was excavated there. Horse death cults were first brought into the Caucasus by the Scyths, whose barbed arrowheads have been found widely in Daghestan, confirming Herodotus' history, written in the fifth century BC. In the first century AD, Strabo mentions that the west Caucasian Albani also had horse funeral cults. The last traces of this tribe were among the Uden in Georgia and in the villages of Nich and Vartashen in Azerbaijan, where there are several widely spread 17th to 19th-century horse tombstones, a partial survival.* Later Hun tribes settled in Ossetia, Circassia and Chechen-Ingushetia, and all these peoples were driven up the mountains by the Mongols, Tatars and Turks who also shared this practice.

Other archaeological finds, as well as later Turkic Kumyk epic songs, confirm that horses were buried with their owners. The southern Kumyks paraded horses in a circle around the corpse, like Atilla the Hun's horsemen. A carved stone relief from Koubachi, dating around the 13th century, shows a horse sacrifice. A man stands poised with a sword, with the horse in the background and a second man holds a beaker to pour a libation with the horse's blood, a religious offering taken from his ewer accompanied by a prayer. So, the following account of the cult among the Chechens was representative of northern Daghestan. However, the old heathen customs of the Ossetes and the Chechens, influenced by Zoroastrianism, the ancient Iranian religion, as well as medieval Christianity, were largely abandoned during the 19th-century Islamic struggle against the Russians, led by Imam Shamil.

"During a Chechen funeral, observed by Sjîgren in 1846, an animal was sacrificed and its right ear was cut off and thrown into the grave. He was told that 80 years earlier, the widow of the corpse also had her ear cut off and thrown into the grave. This was later replaced by the sacrifice of the top-knot of her hair."† This was the opposite of the Kumyk custom, noticed in Khasavyurt in 1963, where a small boy in mourning for a friend had all his hair shaved, except for a 'tail' of hair in the middle of his head. Many earlier travellers noted that Caucasian mountain families would bankrupt themselves on a funeral feast. "The

* Examples of unmounted horse tombstones are found in Kara Jemirli village (Shamkor rayon), Kirovaban village (Kelbajar rayon), Kazakh rayon, Gyanja, and Agdam village (Tauz rayon) – all in Azerbaijan.
† Quote taken from the extraordinary *Rossweihe und Pferderennen im Totenkult der Kaukasischen Volker* by R. Bleichsteiner.

Bezhta boys, who live 2,500 metres up near the Georgian border, love fighting with ancient Roman-style wooden swords.

corpse was dressed in new clothes and laid out for two to four days." (There is a photo of a Khevsur funeral, where the horse is being presented to the corpse, laid out on a rug, wearing a *karakul* hat, with his face covered by a cloth. Beer and bread were also provided for a comfortable passage to the next world.)

"On the day after the burial, the first memorial feast began and for three days, hundreds of guests were entertained. Everything they enjoyed benefited the soul of the dead and the belief therefore prevailed that those who partook of the feast could never be satisfied. This was rapidly followed by a second bed, or laying-out, feast to release the deceased into the after-life from the lying-down position. The main event of this feast was a horse race and the prize was the clothes of the deceased. The villagers picked the best available horses and sent them to a village several miles away." (This could be the origin of the 17 km horse-racing circuit in the mountains near Botlikh.)

"For the outward journey, the leader was given a small white flag as his badge and his companion riders held forked sticks with apples and nuts fastened on them to present to their host and the elders of the village. The following day (according to Shah Ahriev, quoted by Dubrovin), they would return, starting early. First the horses would walk, but nine miles from their village they would start to gallop. Meanwhile, the owners of the horses would each send out a few riders to meet the incoming horses and push them faster. Due to the whipping and the great distance of the race, the horses were so tired that even the winner only arrived at a slow trot. An elder who was an initiate of the cult would consecrate the winning horse to the dead man. The horse was given beer and the rider was given a piece of mutton and three

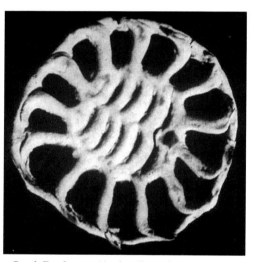

South Daghestan (Aguli village) funeral bread – sun sign-shaped. Traditional animist funerals dedicated a horse, beer, bread, a carpet and clothes to the deceased to speed their journey to the next world. Kaitag embroideries reflect this often with the representation of a microcosmic map and even horsemen and a sunbird in heaven. (Photo: 'Aguli', ed. A. Islammagomedov, Makhachkala, 1975)

loaves of bread. The elder asked the owner of the victorious horse if he would give it to the deceased to take it wherever he wished. The next three horses were pledged to the ancestors of the dead man."

A variant was the Kumyk custom, continued up to late last century, where they drove away the dead man's horse, after marking it by cutting off the tail or the mane, so that no one who had known the man would take it and so prevent him getting to the next world. "Then a shooting contest was held, with either bows or guns. Another Koubachi triptych frieze in Makhachkala Kraevedcheski museum may well depict funeral games." Bashkirov, 1928: "On the left, two riders charge each other, in the middle, two wrestlers are locked in combat and on the right, a mounted archer is shooting at a round target, beyond the lance with two flags, which – together with the embossed plate on the ground – were the prizes."

Kumyks also wrapped their corpses in felt, like the black undecorated felt found in the village of Durgeli when they dug the foundations for the House of Culture. There were strict rituals, varying from village to village, for mourning close relatives, governing who should do what, and the clothes and colours to be worn during their long walks around the yard of the dead person's home and barefoot visits to the grave – even in winter. Long ago, when a man and his wife were buried beside each other, there was a ritual burial dance, when they chanted a lament. Kumyk women cut their plaits, and the sister of a dead brother wore his clothes, flogged herself until she bled and even cruelly cut herself with glass.

Current funerals kept a few vestiges of the old customs. It was very difficult for me to attend funerals as it was considered wrong and bad luck for a stranger. No matter how important it was to record these customs, I also felt that to be too close would be an intrusion on their grief. It was too small a country, where everyone knew each other, and my own behaviour was also under observation. However, many people wanted to tell me about their funeral customs which allowed them to show me that they were following their traditions correctly and I could also look on from a distance. In Ginukh, we could not meet the imam there because a man had died and been buried yesterday and he was sitting with the family. Men had come from other villages for the funeral. A funeral lament was sung by the women in the Ginukh language – their only song which was not in Avar. Afterwards, most of the men stayed for *zikr*, the mystical chant where the men moved slowly in a circle, after which they drank a cup of milk and honey. Before they departed, the family of the dead man gave them bread and cooked meat. Although we were offered Havana pineapple rum in a china teapot, our hosts did not drink or make toasts, as it was during the first seven days of mourning.

In Botlikh nowadays, the corpse is wrapped in three layers of a 15-metre-long linen cloth, about one metre wide, which is tied, but never sewn. Male corpses have white shrouds and females green. The cloth is wrapped so that a man appears to wear trousers only, and a woman trousers, dress and head shawl. Propped up against the back wall of their mosque, you can see the body-sized tin washing tray and the stretcher to carry the corpse to its grave, with a cushion strapped to it under the *bourka* felt cape. The funeral takes place within a few hours of death, if it was nearby. Several men take turns to rapidly dig the rocky grave. After the shrouded corpse is gently lowered into the grave, the imam sprinkles water onto the eyes to simulate revival of the corpse for a last farewell. All the mourners, who must be male, throw earth on the grave which is then immediately filled in.

I did witness most of one funeral, simply because I happened to be staying on the route to the cemetery. Early one August morning, Mullasakinat (her name meant 'Mulla's daughter'), an old woman of 89, died peacefully in Alchuni, the next village upstream from Archi. The first person to enter her house, and discovered that she was dead, immediately closed her eyes. (If someone had died in agony, the *Sura Ya Sin* would be read from the Koran). One of the older religious women was next called to place cotton in the ears and nose and ritually wash the body on a wooden platter, like one I saw against the wall of the disused mosque in Djuli in Tabassaran. The body was dried and wrapped in a shroud. (In the case of a man, the imam or an elder who was a distant, but never a close relative, performed this task). One house only lit a smoky fire as a signal to the people of Archi, not to be confused with two for a wedding feast. All the men put on their hats and walked fast to the house. Only close family sat with the body or saw her face. She was wrapped in two layers of white linen shroud (more layers were used for younger corpses). At about nine in the morning, a dozen men in *aerodrom* peaked hats walked back briskly to dig her grave. More followed until about 30 in all were involved – even more are needed in winter when the ground is frozen and digging is harder.

Two hours later, a procession of 80 men – all the men in the village, with the elders wearing *papakha karakul*-fleece hats – escorted the body from the house as the women wailed. Following the old custom, no women attended any funerals. The shrouded body was covered entirely by a black *bourka* cape on a wooden stretcher, normally kept in the mosque, as in Botlikh. Men changed over for the honoured position of the four bearers during the five kilometre procession to the grave, along the old road which passed beneath the house where I was staying.

With only the *debir*, or imam – 78-year-old Ahmat Hadji – and the other men present, the shrouded corpse was gently lowered into the grave. After the funeral the men were given ritual sugar, boiled mutton and bread for refreshment, (while in Khunzakh they ate a special halva). Later, we met the four close male relatives in dark clothes, walking back home with a plastic packet of the remaining sugar lumps and another man wearing a black lace shirt, who had walked four kilometres from Khilikh' village. In the afternoon later that day, I went to the cemetery where the grave was wetted by the closest mourners inside a neat ring of egg-sized stones, to symbolise a continuation of life. A rock gravestone had already been erected and tied to it was a wooden pole with a white flag, in memory of the religious old lady. Next to it was a water pitcher outside a small tin house, inside which sat an old man (other times it was the imam), whose duty was to read the Koran for a week by her grave. The seven days of a week and 40 days after the death were significant dates, when the intensity of mourning decreased.

In Levashin we passed a *godekan* crowded with seated mourning men, wearing black, with silver *karakul*-fleece hats. In Khunzakh there were five town quarters, each with a mosque and a square, surrounded by the *godekans*,

Tombstone in Majalis cemetery with an Arabic inscription combined with the same microcosmic map in the niche under the roundel, as is found in the Kaitag embroidery on page 159. In Daghestan one finds animist and Islamic iconography side by side.

long simple benches where men would meet to mourn in their hats, dressed in the traditional *cherkess* jacket or *bourka* cloak, while the women mourned at home. In Kasimkent, women mourners were sitting in a home courtyard, on a bench covered with the brilliant coloured shaggy side of a *soumak* rug. The bereaved were being visited by well-wishers during the first week of the 40 days mourning and one year long period of remembrance.

Old women often spoke and wept about other people's misfortune, but never their own. In Batlaich, Shamil-the-School-Director said that after a funeral the bereaved relatives would sit outside their home for three days in sheepskin coats to keep warm, while they were consoled by visits of friends from other villages. Until the Kvarshins were deported in 1944 by Stalin, each of their households would leave logs on the doorstep of the bereaved, to be collected early in the morning for fuel to cook remembrance food. Old women also prepared for their own death. In Butsrah village, I met the ever courteous Aisanah Shaikhmagomedova, who was about 80. She proudly showed me a good number of small cushions which she had collected for the women mourners to be seated comfortably at her own wake.

Magomedkhan had been away from his village, Archi, for a year and so when he returned he was always visiting old people and bereaved families alone. We could not visit nearby hamlets where he knew a family which was in mourning. Neither could we get a lift, for any amount of money, from a village in mourning. At Tashkapur there was still a crowd around the curve of the bridge and far below in the ravine where three days before a new white Moskvitch car had leapt over to disappear into the fast current, said to be 50 metres deep. Two of the four bodies had not yet been found. They were all relatives of people we knew. I felt I was beginning to share the personal connection of a death, like anyone living in a small country. Back in Makhachkala, Magomedkhan's mother-in-law was upset because a young man who had been at school with her daughter was one of the dead. He was a bad driver and had evidently pressed the accelerator rather than the brake pedal. His male friend also drowned, but a child was saved.

In Daghestan widows are still visible. In Archi a widow had to wear a sheepskin coat in mourning for a year and thereafter the more typical black. The bereaved women speakers at one public ceremony wore black lace and satin. One had lost her son in the tragically usual car crash. Another dead young man had left his fiancée behind. "What would happen to her?" I wondered. Magomedkhan offered: "She might marry in one or two year's time if his parents give her parents their consent." Old Oboda village was reputed to be full of World War II widows. They were certainly very bent over. In one house an old woman jumped from room to room, through a two foot cube hole in the wall. In Khunzakh, Nurmagomed-the-Mayor's street was inhabited by 25 old women but no old men. My query about this state of affairs prompted the explanation: "Because men do less hard work, they die earlier!"

But perhaps there was a grimmer reality. It was mainly the men who were deported during the Stalin period and later. Many men too died in car crashes on the appalling roads, while women rarely drove or travelled. In Khunzakh there was only one woman – a schoolteacher – who drove a car. But her husband had died and she needed the money, and so sold the car when she got married again.

ra

Tombstone in Digbalik village with sun sign (see p160), next to another crowned with ram's horns.

94

As in other Muslim societies, there has been an Islamicisation of traditional ancestor-worship. On the day of the new moon before Uraza Bayram, the festival at the end of Ramadan, it was the custom to visit the graves of one's ancestors. Ramazan-the-Librarian took me to one of the Makhachkala cemeteries with many Lak and Azeri tombs. At the entrance there were some beggars and urchins collecting offerings of biscuits, wrapped sweets and rice, which the crowds were bringing to the graves of their dead relatives. The rice and biscuits were left on the graves for the birds to take to heaven, while the sweets were for the children. Half the town went, often during working hours.

Two years ago no one dared to go, but that day even the Minister of Culture told me that she would visit her graves in Buinakst. Whole families, including children came – I saw up to ten around a single grave, also a group of five women sitting around a grave, with one reading from the Koran. All the women wore black dresses and headscarves. On many tombstones, as well as the name of the deceased there was also written the name of their village. In Khunzakh, the Avar families also visited the graves of their ancestors and placed sweets and cakes on the graves for children, but not rice for the birds. They still made a thin round pancake-sized stodgy bread as *sadaka*, gifts for people they met. Children in the street got a quarter each, but house visitors were given a whole one.

With a few exceptions, tombstones have evolved from traditional forms. I was asked to take a picture of a neighbour of Magomedkhan's in Archi, because he was dying. He wanted the picture as a memory for his family wall. Happily, he had two large hunting hounds so I could make a genuine fuss about it. In town cemeteries, oval pictures of the dead were mounted on the headstones, but in the villages, older traditions were stronger, i.e. there no images of the deceased but floral motifs, motifs such as sheep shears describing occupations, cosmic symbols, arms, and so on. The eight-foot tall tombstones in Derbent from the tenth century and the decorated relief arabesques in Koubachi 400 years later came out of the Islamic tradition, unlike the huge number of anthropomorphic pagan stones standing throughout the mountain villages of Daghestan. For example, in the 19th-century cemetery at Yarakent (meaning 'Town of Arms'), a ruined village by the road from Akhti to Kasimkent, an eerie army of carved totemic tombstones stood in what appeared to be jaunty attitudes, pushed over by repeated earthquakes. On the front of each stone, a deep-cut small square with symmetrical diagonal lines on top of an upright rectangle, filled with archaic Kufic Arab script, represented a bearded head-and-shoulders figure, flanked by whirling sun signs.

Surrounding similar panels in Tabassaran, Celtic-style curved interlacing appeared, while diagonal rectalinear grids were more popular in the north, both like their wood carvings. On the other side of the stone, there were simple engravings of a star and crescent above what the dead man should take to the next world, occasionally on horseback, but always armed with his sword, dagger and gun, and with a water pitcher and a loaf for refreshment. Other tools of the dead man's trade appeared, such as the blacksmith's tombstone in Kandik, cockerels and even the 1980s truck driver's carved and painted vehicle on his headstone, beside a tall pole, with a cut-out tin finial of pre-Islamic facing sunbirds in Archi. In Karata, high in the mountains, beside each tombstone there was a memorial flag on a pole, up to five metres high, almost reaching to heaven, the tallest I have seen in Daghestan. There were also spherical volcanic (or meteorite) stones placed on top of stone slabs on some tombstones. In Koubachi, too, rectangular stone slabs rested on top of the headstones. I was

A cloth-covered animist-cum-Muslim shrine (5ft high) kept up throughout the Soviet period, when veneration of shrines was condemned in journals like the 'Atheist's Bulletin' (published until 1988).

told that it kept the rain off, but it seemed to me rather that they were for offerings, some survival of the following sky-burial rite.

"The 12th-century traveller Abu Hamed of Grenada wrote about the extraordinary burial rites of Sirihkeran, the village of the armourers, the Arab name for Koubachi. When a man died, his corpse was presented to some people who lived in wattle and earth huts – not the villagers in their fine stone houses – who chopped up the body, separating the bones from the flesh. The flesh was put out for the eagles, buzzards or other birds to eat (and take to heaven), as in Tibetan sky-burials while the cleaned bones were put in bags. Rich people had bags of gold embroidery, 'Greek' silk, or more simply bleached linen, which were then labelled and hung up in the houses" (R. Bleichsteiner – see Bibliography). In Koubachi, while I saw these unusual types of textiles, they were not made up as bags.

Hand-sized Old Georgian stone cross – a rare relic of Christianity in Daghestan under Queen Tamara of Georgia (13th century).

Beside the Andi-Koisu river, I passed a cluster of miniature one-metre-square, rectalinear stupa-shaped tombs for the fallen of the Second World War dead who did not return home. In the cemetery at Rakhata, puzzling white or green cloth bands were tied around the tombstones, one of which was dated 1950, where women came to pray outside the boundary fence. In Bezhta, shiny broken ceramics had been carefully placed all over the low mound of a child's grave by other children, supposedly to protect it from hail. In the North Caucasus, as presented in the St Petersburg Museum, rag-dolls were kept as symbolic playthings, burial offerings for a dead girl child, such as one I saw by a hearth in Kalajukh village. I was unusually, but politely, not allowed into Bezhta cemetery, but Daniel-the-Dogfighter-and-Historian reported three one-metre high tombstones engraved with simple crosses – Christian Georgia was just over the pass – and the indecipherable letters in the shape of 'N' and 'H'. It was often hard to see the tombstones as mountain land was valuable and hay was grown in cemeteries. But it was peaceful to see the shadows of rows of haystacks standing among the headstones in Kuli and the swish of the living reaper – a smiling woman – in Gagatl.

In Soviet times, the Communist atheist movement, the Society of Godless Zealots, had tried its utmost to eradicate the shrines of holy men, which acted as magnets for pilgrims. They failed, and today every village has one or two shrines and there are many more on the roadsides. They were usually simple stone huts, the older ones with domed roofs, but mainly noticeable by the innumerable white and coloured flags, dancing in the wind and lit up by the sun, set off against the deep-plunging mountains.

· 6 ·

King Khosrows' dumplings: food & feasts

First there is sex. But after that, of all human activities, food (especially stodge) seems to be the most resistant to cultural change. In Daghestan, culinary tradition stretches back to the sixth-century Sassanian Persians, through pagan and Islamic times, and there are even traces of Tsarist influence. The standard cooked dish in Daghestan is *khinkal*, oblong flour dumplings, which forms one of the oldest surviving recorded meals. In the tenth-century Arabic *Kitab at-Tabikh wa Islah al-Aghdhiya al-Ma'kulat* ('Book of Dishes'), there is a story about the Sassanian emperor Khosrows, who built his palace in Derbent during the middle of the sixth century. His favourite meal was virtually the same as today. Meat was boiled and flour pasta was added to the broth. The pasta was drained and garnished with the juice of crushed raw garlic and walnut. The broth and boiled meat were served separately.

The taste for *khinkal*, jokingly punned with *kinjal*, the Daghestan dagger, continued over the centuries. A story is told of the Daghestan man who went on a pilgrimage to Medina with his dried ram gut sausage and *khinkal*. The Arabs said that he would die from the heat, but changed their mind when they saw him eat his *khinkal* with broth. Kumyks make the smallest thimble-sized *khinkals*, while in Avar mountain villages like Botlikh, they make the largest, like handgrenades. If you start one, you must finish it. In Daghestan soup follows solids. The best broth I ever tasted was made by Kalimat in Bezhta, with chopped onions and stalks and herbs, fried in butter and tomato paste and sweet alpine potatoes. Ginukh *khinkals* were cooked with cumin and served in a tasty butter herb and tomato paste. In Khunzakh, I ate the filling 'super' *khinkal*, made for Uraza Bayram evenings, when, after the fast, many visits take place. Sweet corn and large black wild wheat grain (which is also tasty raw, when green) were heated on an iron dish over an oven until soft. They were mixed together and ground with a stone. The flour was compressed, lightly adding warm water and a little salt. A handful was then compressed gently (it could also be eaten then) and, for the last time, firmly, before being dropped into boiling water for 15 minutes. When ready, they were kept and fried in a little oil before eating. They are liked by older people, who say they clean out

Niamh (left) eating a boiled sheep with Archi shepherds. The sheep is cut into ten exactly equal portions – a custom of hungry shepherds who cannot usually afford to eat their flock. Lean and fat are not distinguished.

the digestive system. Daghestan foods can seem strange to western taste, but Daghestan people love their food for its symbolic and nutritional value. They have a self-sufficient agricultural system, which has not yet been divorced from nature, despite the mess created by the Soviet state farm system, which has reduced the area of land under the plough without any increasing yields. The oldest grains of rye and wheat in Daghestan – sixth millennium BC – were discovered near Chokh. Horse-towed sled-shaped threshing boards of wood, with hundreds of flints inserted underneath, have continued in use since the Neolithic period. The Iron Age began early here, during the eighth century BC, and since then the highlands were tilled by the spade.

I tasted some ancient foods, which had been specially reproduced for the Avar festival at Khunzakh. As well as boiled and baked mutton, there were cereal-based foods: a brown grain squeezed solid with butter sugar, honey, cheese and oil; baked grain, flat bread and a brown fermented grain paste and *buza* beer. Several of the modern cooked cereal foods also seemed like starchy white-beige baby mush. The most ancient way of eating meat which I saw, was in Gagatl, where a holy-idiot boy with mouth sores was chewing the marrow-filled end of a bloody sheep's horn.

In Daghestan, meat is meat. Lean meat was not separated from the fat, and there was no jointing of meat. At a picnic, near Archi, our hosts cut the throat, skinned and boiled a whole sheep, happily without the delicacy of the head. The carcass was then torn apart by hand and placed on the cloth to eat. Later when we had returned to Archi, a leg of calf appeared. I could not be restrained and showed a wondering circle of men, women and children how to cut the lean meat and make schnitzel, fried in egg and breadcrumbs. They liked it, so I

A 9-year-old Archi shepherd boy helping his father during the school holidays.

started thinking of what they could cook, but did not. Another time, while eating excellent boiled eggs, I noticed that this was the only way they were cooked in the area. Yet in another distant village, some of my host's relatives prepared me delicious scrambled eggs with herbs – but then the father had been transported from Archi village over 40 years before and had married a Lezgin. With the humility of an Escoffier, I 'invented' the omelette. Boiled eggs played a symbolic role in spring festivals, as described below.

❧

If there were no lemons in the mountain villages, unlike in Akhti or Makhachkala markets, there was always wine vinegar and oil, salt and pepper, though salad dressing was unknown. While the mountain woods were carpeted with mushrooms, the villagers did not pick them. A heterodox Koubachi woman intoned, "We Muslims do not eat mushrooms."

Daghestan was far richer in agricultural production before the Revolution. Although a resolution was passed by the Soviet congress in 1920 awarding up to five hectares of (their own) land to each family suffering from hardship, the soil was left barren both due to general devastation and the weakness of the men through famine. Cultivated land in Daghestan fell from 365,000 hectares in 1914 to 114,000 in 1923. Efforts to push the highlanders into the state collective farm system in 1930 were not successful because they were "not ready for it," so Party organisers reverted to the older and simpler form of co-operation, where groups of compatible friends shared pastures, and marketing. Even today, over two-thirds of the population live in villages, mostly in the mountains rather than the limited plains.

Mountain agriculture is obviously a tougher proposition. Terracing was historically used to maximum advantage in the struggle for space and sun, where each single fruit tree counted. Every inch of soil was important and arguments would frequently arise over ditches or stone-wall boundaries. Civil action were judged by two elders and if the plaintiff was considered to be in the right, the owner was ordered to take it down and "for each day's delay, he must pay a fine of one sheep."

Winter and summer pasturing for sheep and cattle was strictly controlled. Farms had enclosures for sheep and cattle, hay lofts, storage for farm products and living quarters for farm workers. Near Archi, a family recently resettled farm buildings which once supported 11 families. The sunny slopes, where grass grew quickly in the summer months, when each part reverted to its rightful owner for haymaking, were considered communal grazing ground in winter. To the chagrin of Communists, the more successful farmer with larger herds would take over his part of the slope as private property, and then bought a neighbouring field and so on. During a period of growth, not only meadows but pastureland far up the mountains fell into private hands, forcing less organised smallholders to travel far to find accessible grazing.

*Threshing the wheat by riding horses round in a circle in Mishlesh village.
The haystacks in the background are covered by woollen 'zilu' weave flat rugs normally only
found in 14th century Egypt.*

The owner of the new Red Bridge restaurant (see photo on page 146) on the banks of the turbulent Avar-Koisu river, used to have 800 sheep, until most of them were confiscated by a local Party boss for himself – under Communism, one man was only allowed 50 sheep. But before the Revolution there had existed sheep farms with up to 15,000 sheep. A hired shepherd on such farms received as payment food, clothing and one sheep per month of work. The domestic life of a shepherd was non-existent, as poignantly pointed out in the Avar joke: "Which is larger, the number of dead or the number of living?" – "The living – if you count shepherds as living." In spite of these hardships, the system worked for Daghestan. I met shepherds who drove flocks hundreds of kilometres up and down the valleys to market in Kizlyar in the northern plains. They were welcomed in the villages, especially by children and they passed news to the men, for "in one day, a rumour passes right through Daghestan."

Most villages profited from an ancient communal system. A complex property, called *miegh*, stretched around the village combining fields, pastures, cultivated land and the irrigation network. As the whole area is split by ravines, streams and tracks, it was divided into smaller sections. There were strict regulations for work on *miegh* for all the community. Every morning throughout the busy season, an elder would shout out the distribution of labour from the top of the minaret, from where he overlooked the holdings with a sharp eye.

King Khosrows' dumplings

One harvest date was set for the whole village to make sense of organising the shared work. With haymaking, anyone "who started early would be fined a measure of grain." Vineyard districts had special rules. By law and common conviction, it was forbidden to pick or even eat grapes till the 15th day of autumn. In some districts, if someone violated this rule he was driven through the village on a mule, his face smeared with soot. In ancient wine-making villages such as Mini and Ortokolo, if someone was caught "picking grapes, or if grape pips were found on somebody's doorstep, he would be fined one cow by the community." In spite of this, fines for eating one's own grapes were a matter of some sensitivity. A woman's position was worse than a man's, presumably because it was she who did the picking, and "if a pip was found on her or on her doorstep she was fined two bulls."

The day for harvesting grapes was selected by the community at a public festival. A crier announced the event throughout the village for five days in advance, so that no one left the village and there was time to clear away crops on the route to the vineyards. When the great day came, one woman from each household gathered at daybreak and set out to her vineyard, with her special basket, singing enthusiastically. They returned laden to a special feast and ate the first grapes of the year. Next day the whole community went to pick their grapes. In the lowlands, heavy soil, with a low organic content, required many hands to work the land – especially as fertiliser was seldom, if ever, used. This

Weighing the load of hay in Archi village.
Archi women carry one and a half times their body weight.

has now changed dangerously with the overuse of poisonous fertilisers. It was particularly difficult in summer to use the heavy wooden ploughs, drawn by four to ten oxen or buffaloes. Only a large family collective could own such a team, care for the cattle and work a typical farm of over six hectares, so it was not surprising that many smallholders got together to work each others' land.

In Daghestan survival depended on a sufficient harvest, which was at the mercy of rain and sun, which were thought to require placation through magic. All the peoples of Daghestan and the North Caucasus believed in the supernatural power of words, which was why the ceremonies were enshrined in poems, passed down through the generations. Symbolic offerings to invoke rain had evolved from human sacrifice to save crops in time of drought. This was confirmed by old men in Mezhgiul, who told that their ancestors stopped throwing humans into the river and started throwing stones instead. I saw a painting of a similar rite in Akhti.

In one village in the Agulskii rayon, the ceremony for rain took place near a river or a pond. People shouted

Hand scything in the fields near Arani by an 89-year-old mother unable to stand and her 70-year-old daughter. They are also tying bales with twisted hay. Old people like to feel the earth under their feet.

"O Allah, give us rain! Yes, there will be heavy rain. Yes, there will be rain!" as a shepherd – unnoticed – grabbed hold of a widow and jumped with her into the water. She tried to get away, screamed, and shouted for help, but all ignored her, re-enacting some archaic sacrifice to the water-god. Another variant was that of the Kumyks, who put a sack over a woman with a hole cut out for her head. She was led to the edge of the river by a rope, tied to her waist and water was poured over her. She was then thrown into the river and had to swim out of sight to escape.

Later rituals had three parts: the parading of a realistic votive object, the incantation, and the action itself. The votive object was usually a stuffed puppet animal or doll, made of grass or green branches. The incantation consisted of a repetition of words such as "May rain soak you!" and a song-prayer which the villagers repeated as they led a child dressed like a scarecrow around the village and then poured water over the stuffed puppet or the child – the action. Near Khoredzh, there was a large sacred stone resembling a man. In time of drought, people collected a spoonful of butter from each household. Six old men carried the butter up to the stone and smeared it on both the stone and themselves. In other villages they washed a sacred stone with water.

In Karabudakent, after a prolonged drought, a meeting was announced from the minaret. Those with milk herds were asked to bring milk, and the rest to bring produce for the sacrificial meal. In a separate ceremony the women went up to their sacred place, while the men sacrificed a horned animal at the sacred well, dressed in skin coats turned inside out. They chanted a special prayer, shouting "Yes, we will have rain!" and then poured the water from the well over each other. Young men were made to jump into the cold water, after which they all went to the mosque for the meal.

Until the 1900s, all over Daghestan, the mullah presented his village with a sheep's shoulder bone with Arabic inscriptions to encourage rain. In Khurik, the inhabitants gathered in their holy place, and after the sacrificial meal, they ran to river and poured water over each other. The Lak had a variety of scapegoat totems: straw-doll, straw-cat or straw-donkey. The Avar poet, Rasul Gamzatov wrote that when the earth cracked in the heat, trees drooped, and fields dried up and plants, birds, sheep and people longed together for heavenly water, (his Tsada) villagers picked a boy as a rain-donkey. Dressed up in coloured cloths, like grass faded by the sun, he was led on a rope through the village by children, chanting to Allah for rain. The women of the village ran out after the rain-donkey, with jugs or basins and poured water over him, while the children responded "Amen, amen!"

In the Kumyk coastal plains, the ancient Zemire* reappeared in the role of rain goddess, as reported about 1850 by a Russian writer, P. Prezhetslavskii. *Zemire* is a Balkar word for rain, related to widespread Turkic words *jamire* or *yamire*. Unlike in the mountains, only girls took part. In some villages, a totem of a wooden spade was decorated with a woman's face and, occasionally, snakes or frogs, in charcoal or red clay. In other places, they made a stuffed doll, dressed in old clothes, and attached it to a cross of sticks. The doll or the spade was carried from house to house in front of a procession of girls, chanting to

* Variants are: Zemire for the northern Kumyks; Zamure for the southern Kumyks; Murerek in the village of Majalis; Zamura in Geli; Zamnuge in Kakashura; Zemirkhan/Telekai in Alkhadzhakent.

Zemire for rain. Housewives poured water over both the totem and the girls, who were then rewarded with gifts of cake, meat, sugar, fruit or small pieces of silk. Odd fragments of these chants were written down, such as:

> *What is needed by Zemire? – Bread with milk.*
> *What is needed by the seedling? – Water from the stream.*
> *What is needed by the cattle? What is needed by the calves?*
> *   – Green grass up to the knee – Udders full of milk.*
> *What is needed by the miller? – A mill-race full of water.*
> *What is needed by the shepherd? – A girl with chestnut braids.*

Often in these Kumyk chants, the *Sut Katyn*, Kumyk for 'Milk-woman', appeared side by side with Zemire:

> *Oh Milk-woman – Milk-woman!*
> *A woman who has no breasts,*
> *Why is it she has no breasts?*
> *She soothes the weeping one,*
> *Oh Zemire, my joy!*

Popular mythic characters often undergo changes of identity or a switch from benevolent to evil. So perhaps Zemire and *Sut Katyn* were different names for the same goddess. Possibly "rain came to be identified with milk from a woman's breasts and cow's udders." To make quite sure of rain, the Kumyks had a third completely different deity, *Suv Anasy*, the sterile 'Mother of Water' who inhabited the earth. She was huge in size, like a Nart, with enormous strength and lived beside a river, guarding the water. She could deafen her victim with one blow, and even drown him, if he disrespectfully approached the river at night.

Invocations for the sun were similar. Girl mummers carried a doll-totem, made by dressing up a rake or fork as a woman, from house to house, singing songs of supplication to the sun, for which they received presents. In the painting of a 'Muslim ceremony' in the museum at Akhti, a mid-winter procession wound around the cemetery, following a raised totem of a white cloth torso on a pole. It is uncertain if the four horrid scarecrows raised above the fencing round a garden in Kamna village, near Chokh, were for rain or sun. The three Bosch-like torsos with cloth headcoverings, similar to 15th-century Teutonic tadpole-shaped helmets and a bull's skull were all impaled on steel tubes. I saw them twice, unchanged after three years (see page 186).

In Tabassaran, the villagers gathered beside springs, holy graves and on mountain peaks, to sacrifice a horned animal, which they had jointly acquired. In the village of Dubek, they gathered at their sacred tree to kill a sheep or ox. The gods were supposed to require the pure essence of the sacrifice, which was therefore boiled without herbs. After feasting on its meat, they broke a branch

Festival of the First Furrow in Akhti. The oldest (mobile) man in the village follows, planting the first seeds. Note the tractor in the background.

off the holy tree and with a stone tied to its crown, let it down into the spring, simulating the rain, which they believed would fall for as long as it remained under water. In Mezhgiul, they destroyed a raven's nest, so that the bird which was a scapegoat for the drought, would go away. In other villages, they opened up a saint's grave and put his remains in water for a few hours or moved the tombstone. Imitating rain, they would clean a sprig of silt or tie rags – usually red for riches – on the branches of a sacred tree or beat the water or ground with branches, chanting *"Ubg markh! Ubg markh!"* ("Pour, rain! Pour, rain!").

As a superstition, women kept a ewer of water, symbolising rain, near their gates, just in case a housewife passed in the street with an empty one and met someone carrying farm implements or seed to the fields, which was considered to be bad luck. Conversely, a full ewer meant good luck. To put a stop to hail, which damaged crops, metal implements such as axes, knives or daggers were thrown into the yard.

❧

The diversity of village population in Daghestan was and is so broad – 33 'nationalities' live in over 700 villages, sized from 300 to 10,000 – that there are too many variations in traditional local feasts to describe here. Simply, local feasts were linked with fertility. Firstly, family survival was celebrated at marriage, birth, male circumcision, first tooth (which looks like the festive corn-on-the-cob), and baby's first steps. Secondly, crop fertility was augured by feasts

Two angles of an unusual portrait of a bearded bronze fertility figurine (3rd–5th century BC) – a member of one of the 26 Albani tribes inhabiting the Caucasian mountains mentioned by several Classical authors.

Well endowed male bronze (Middle Iron Age, little-finger-sized) fertility figurines – with their hands forming antlers, following the legend of the formation of the founders of villages born of the union of a beast and a woman. More than 120 male, female and hermaphrodite figurines have been found at several mountain sites at different times since the 1870s.

for the First Furrow and separating the grain from the chaff. Thirdly, to ensure fecundity of livestock there were feasts on the spring day chosen for the ram to service his hundred sheep, on the autumn day when sheep (or a cow) were butchered for drying, and the winter day when a shepherd left with villagers' sheep for the higher south-facing slopes, with their untouched winter grass.

Muddy rivers meant the new year had come with spring. A professor at the Daghestan Filial was supposed to know when the First Furrow festivals began. In fact nobody knew. Even when we rang the village mayors, they said they did not know, maybe the farmers knew or perhaps they were waiting for the frost to go? The festival in Levashin had already taken place and we were too early for Khunzakh, where the snow was just melting.

But one crackling, sunny-windy March morning, we drove to a field, overlooked by a distant natural amphitheatre of bright snow-capped mountains outside Akhti, to join eight stocky men in the rite of the First Furrow. Two oxen were being yoked to an iron plough which had been unloaded from an open truck. With an air of purpose, the oldest man took the plough in his massive callused hands, while a younger man led the oxen, cutting the first groove a furlong across the plain and back. They were followed by a third man with a bag, brimming with seed which he was hand-casting over the exposed earth. But this was a contemporary procession, so they

Bronze figurine of a crowned mounted Amazonian woman from Gagatl village, in the Daghestan Krayechevski museum.

were closely followed by a tractor, cutting a second parallel furrow. They lifted the old plough back on the truck, while others opened a bottle of Daghestan cognac and we drank to a good crop and that was that.

As one of his labours, Hercules once ploughed a field, which sprouted spears of bristling warriors. This myth may share a common origin with the solemn dance for the First Furrow in Andi, recorded in 1876. Following the plough, dancing pairs circled slowly, with the man on point in the turned earth, alongside his woman. The Tabassarans practised more explicit fertility rites. In the village of Khoredzh, on the day before the First Furrow, all the men met at a holy grave and presented each other with *sadaka*, small gifts. In the evening, the ploughman performed a cleansing ritual, before making love with his wife. In the morning, he kept apart from his family and neighbours and, dressed in clean clothes, he went ploughing barefoot and for three days only he was entitled to sow seeds.

In north Tabassaran, men gathered to choose the first ploughman who was a real bull, usually an experienced farmer of about 45. On the morning he was obliged to shave his beard and head to go to the field entirely clean, so that his work should be impeccable. He ploughed for three days and no one was allowed to disturb him, ask him for implements or any other favour, while a fire was kept burning in his house. *Chudu* (stuffed pancakes), boiled eggs and bread were taken to the field with the seed-grain.

In the Akhti festival albums, there were mysterious photographs of other Lezgin customs. On the Day of the Gardener, the queen wore a gross Diana-of-the-Ephesians-style many-appled necklace, while another queen was presented with a round loaf upon a round stone. Khunzakh farmers decided on the date for the First Furrow ceremony, which they call *Otsbai*, from *ots* meaning ox, and *bai*, yoked. Children threw earth on the old man steering the plough, followed by another man sowing the seed. Women, who had given birth to sons during the past year, brought *urbech*, *chudu* and walnuts cooked with milk and honey, known as 'little birds'. Celebrations included running races, horse races, throwing the stone, cock fights, dog fights, bull fights, pre-rutting ram fights and tug-of war.

That dusk, I attended the New Year celebrations, called *Yaran Su'var* in Lezgin, in nearby Khriugh village. From the village square, lit by a bonfire of truck tyres, next to the Palace of Culture, I could see a dozen more fires on the surrounding mountains. Like yellow dotted lines, children wound up the mountain sides with flaming brands, towards the distant bonfires. When they arrived, streams of light appeared to shoot from some great fireworks, as they threw the torches down the mountain. The whole village was gathered now to hear the speeches. My speech was quick: "Ladies and gentlemen [not 'comrades'], boys and girls, the Fire Festival is as old as your people: may your fires burn!"

In front of the flaming tyres, two or three men in a ring danced fast, with small sharp steps, whooping to the repetitive frenetic call of the traditional three-piece of horn, flute and drums, which alternated with an amplified electric-guitar band. Next, one couple after another danced wildly, clutching their presentation certificates for labour, with pictures of Lenin, presented by the young mayor, in an ineffectual attempt to Sovietise the Zoroastrian festival. Boys first, then men pulled and fell in the tug-of-war, lit by the fire. They squabbled in excitement with the judge, who had folded the rope, to find the mid-point, so at least the start was fair. Strong villagers stepped forward to repeatedly lift and finally drop the 24kg iron ball. The winner was a 62-year-old man, who pressed the weight with one hand 31 times, but only after a younger man, with 39, had been disqualified for bending his legs to help.

That was nothing: a soldier from a nearby village had lifted it a record 124 times. There were fires everywhere, clear survivals of the Sassanian Zoroastrian New Year festival, which was further confirmed by excavations of several small bronze figures with their hands held by their ears, showing the Zoroastrian mythical moment of creation, in Tsundinskii rayon. At night by the road to Kasimkent, I passed men setting light to the boundaries of a field to ensure a good harvest, and was it entirely a joke when Abdurakhman, an Avar (like the Lezgins) led the leaping over the bonfire, followed by Ramazan, a Lak, and the Kumyk mayor of Korkmascala.

Near Makhachkala and near Buinakst, the mountains were still set alight at midnight on New Year, called *Novroz Bayran* in Kumyk and Azeri and on a smaller scale last century in Kazikumukh, Lak children threw fist-sized terra cotta balls with flaming twigs stuck into them.

My Lezgin New Year lunch was cooked by Velikhan, a rare male head cook, in the Akhti 'hotel restaurant'. The main dish was *git'*, a high calorie soup to feed up people for hard agricultural work in springtime. Dried feet and the jawbone of a one-year-old sheep, yellow corn, grain, and black beans were boiled in water until tender, when milk was added. The blotchy-coloured skin was a delicacy. There were two more dishes for ploughmen. A cold mixture of yogurt, mint, rice and tumin, was cooling in the heat and stopped any craving for water, while a warm thick soupy drink with a sweet-sour malty taste, made from barley, was a true tonic. The grain was soaked in water until it began to sprout. It was then dried and ground into a flour, which was added to a little water and left for a day to ferment. More water was then added and the mixture was boiled until thick. It was served in a bowl, sprinkled with beige flour, from baked grain.

The richness of Kumyk New Year dishes symbolised hope for a year of plenty. Thick pancakes in melted-butter, *chudu*, were filled with the finest greenery, bread was made with butter, and instead of boiled meat, there were plov and dolmas. In addition, large breads were baked in the shape of a ram, with horns twisted around his head, as the male symbol, and as the female, a partridge, sitting upon eggs. Large quantities of hard-boiled eggs, painted in bright colours, were gifts for the family and their many guests.

New Year heralded a string of other rituals throughout the year linking the land and the seasons. The three-day spring celebration over the March equinox – a spring festival – was called Bringing Out the Plough. Spring sowing for the Kumyks consisted of maize, spring barley or wheat and millet, as well as melon and watermelon, pumpkin, cucumber and onions. Preparations for the welcome of spring were lavish, yet done with the utmost care. Every house was whitewashed and cleaned, a great wash took place, special bathing was organised, women hennaed their hair and platted each other's and, as far as possible, everyone wore new clothes.

In summer the most popular celebration was Bringing Out the Sickle. Scythes, threshing boards and transport for grain were organised, a large circle of ground was cleared and levelled for threshing and a hut was built for breaks from the dusty work. The mutual aid system provided reapers, transport drivers, and threshers, for whom common food was prepared. The young – both boys and girls – worked side by side in the fields. For them, it was a time of enjoyment and always included singing, dancing and a valued chance to meet. When the grain had been sent to the granary, the owner celebrated the end of his threshing if there was surplus grain to pay for the feast. Families with neighbouring fields pooled together to provide roasted sheep, mountains of bread, fruit, and home-brew. As a rule, the guests were all men, who were supposed to behave with dignity, modesty and sobriety. Throughout a good harvest, this sort of party happened most evenings. In 1983, a sprightly 80-year-old woman in Karabudakent remembered that at the end of the summer, everyone used to go to the field and ceremonially re-light fires seven times.

For the plainsmen Kumyks, autumn sowing was more vital than the First Furrow, which was barely celebrated – unlike in the poorer highlands. The autumn climate changed fast and "good snow was a blanket, protecting the fields from frost." To magically simulate seedlings sprouting, women cooked wheat in water or milk, and offered it with mill-ground nuts to their neighbours, and gave children roasted wheat and maize. The Laks made "sacrificial offerings to the fields." An ox was bought by the *djamat*, or village council, and was paraded around the field, then had its throat cut and the meat was divided among the villagers. The Dargins from Itsari gathered together all the cows and bulls in a special large field for a ceremony called Uniting the Cow and the Bull. A woman officiated, walking among the cattle, scattering roasted barley, while intoning "In good time!" to promote a successful increase in healthy stock.

The farewell to winter, called the Burning of Winter, symbolised the end of the year. That day everyone brought out anything old from their homes and threw it into bonfires blazing in the yards, streets, or on the outskirts of the village, while inside every home a large fire filled the hearth, while halva and tasty little dumplings filled with a custard of eggs and milk were ready as gifts.

&.

Fasting, one of the Seven Pillars of Islam, brought its own variations. In Daghestan, fasting, in theory, occurs at the usual time in the Islamic calendar – during the festival of Ramadan. Nowadays, the fast tends to be observed by older people, while the feasts are celebrated by all. Traditionally there were also irregular instances of spontaneous fasting during mourning or when family honour was offended by the husband or wife, who then did not speak or eat with each other for one day. (Avars in Kuyada village were well known for this).

In Koubachi at midnight before the feast of Bayram, the family women were sitting on the floor, covered in newspapers, furiously preparing food. At six next morning, women began arriving in twos and threes to wish the house a happy

Novi Frig – making bread. A handful of goose quills are used to prick the dough before baking in the traditional oven which is so good it is rented by outsiders. A final flick of sour milk from the feather gives the bread its delicious crust. The scented fire is made of branches from pruned fruit trees.

Inside a water mill – a Bezhta village woman milling flour for customers who bring their own wheat. The mill was never owned by the Communist Party.

Bayram. The host greeted them at the door, but did not enter the women's room, which was in the charge of his mother. Soon a dozen women, wearing white headscarves, were sitting on the floor giggling and eating. They stayed for a while and moved on to other houses. In one, they crammed into a small blue back room with ten married women, who initially hid their faces when the son looked in. They were drinking tea and eating *khinkal* stuffed with nettles, to remind themselves of the hard years they had survived on the wild plant. Everyone was visiting everyone else, so either men or women occupied the feasting room, depending on who was in the majority.

The Archi people form a separate ethnic group, living in seven joined hamlets with a total population of 700. Every year they are snowed up for five months, over 2000 metres high in the Great Caucasian mountains on the ancient shepherds' trek south to Zakatal, now in Azerbaijan. After the fast of Ramadan, there was a feast with several special dishes, similar to the end of mourning for the dead. The imam (or, in Archi, *debir* – after the 12th-century saint who brought Sunni Islam there) announced the date two or three days in advance. A bereaved family was chosen and offered to prepare the ritual feast. As usual everyone was up and about by six. Later in the morning separate groups of the male elders who formed the village council, younger men, women, boys and girls went about the village. The elders first visited the *debir*, followed by the younger men, the women, the boys and lastly the girls.

Children took part as soon as they could walk. Next, the men visited the cemetery to venerate their ancestors, and went on to pray in the mosque.

They were then ready to visit the house of the bereaved (usually the most revered or the youngest person who had died during that, or the previous year, if there was none more recent). They entered the house, saying, "Let your fasting be noticed by God!", with the response "Yours too!" Then they ate the first feast in the house since the death, known as Putting Down the Planks (i.e. the table). They ate a breakfast of hot mutton, beef or veal, potatoes and herbs. The younger the deceased, the larger the feast, but there were no gifts of *sadaka* sweets, as was usual elsewhere. At the beginning and end of the meal, they prayed for the dead.

The groups then visited all the other houses in the village, staying about five minutes at each, only sampling what was on the table. Every household had prepared the dishes listed below, saving up the choicest ingredients throughout the year. It was a public day, with no private family meals, when no slaying of beasts or building was allowed. The feast ended with afternoon prayers.

Enforced fasting was caused by famine from war or a bad harvest. If a dairy cow died from starvation, the woman owner stayed at home and did not eat for a day. During the most recent famines from 1943-47 virtually all food was taken for the Front, including the final reserves of dried meat over one year old. Some villages, like Archi, had to beg for food from others in order to feed their pregnant women and children. It was reported that three women out of two hundred had died from eating earth. There were also no shoes (no leather)

A Tabassaran woman baking 'lavash' bread in a tandir oven near Khuchni village.
(Photo: Magomed Rasul Ibraghimov)

and everyone had lice. Young wild stinging nettles were gathered and the leaves were cut in shreds with scissors and dried for soup or stuffing *chudu* pancakes during the winter. People still eat them today, although they are embarrassed to offer nettles to a foreigner. Daghestan's aggressive enthusiasm for feasting is an understandable reaction to the tragic famines, caused by war and cruel nature.

ﻬ

Every event, every occasion – natural or man-made – seemed to be celebrated with a culinary accompaniment. Were these elaborate recipes part of some symbolic story, or did they merely reflect what was available? Was there some taboo to explain why had they never simply baked their cheese on *lavash*, their usual round leavened bread, like the pizza I cooked, which they greatly enjoyed? This would, of course, hardly apply to the main dishes of cold boiled meats, pilaf and raviolis with salads and normal bread, which appeared in everyday meals. The traditional funeral feasts were so popular that they continued to be celebrated throughout the Stalin period, when even Muslim funerals were forbidden. Everything was eaten at the same time, over several hours, i.e. there were no courses.

As well as *tandir* oven-baked bread without yeast, there was special bread. The beige malty-tasting flour was made from ground dried grain which had been soaked in the river for seven days till it sprouted. Two glasses of this flour were added to one of normal flour, and mixed with water, without salt, into a dough and squeezed into hand-sized balls. After baking, the crusty rolls had a sweet brown soft inside.

There were four types of pancake: 1. thin pancakes, locally described as 'tooth-thick'; 2. pancakes, described as 'finger-thick'; 3. thin pancakes, sandwiched between unleavened bread slabs, garnished with a melted piece of *kurduk*, fat-tailed sheep's tail, on the top and clarified butter on the bottom; and 4. cornflour pancakes boiled in milk into a porridge, to which was added boiled dried mutton intestine fat, diced onion, raisins, chabrets herb and caraway seeds – a centimetre of the mixture was sandwiched between sheets of rolled dough, which was then glazed with butter and baked.

There were six festive sweets. Eight-inch shortbread circles were made from eggs, clarified butter and sugar, baked the previous night and cut into rays, slices or squares next morning. Small sweet *khinkal* dumplings, made of flour and eggs, and eaten with honey. Halva, made by adding flour to clarified butter and mixing in granulated sugar. Sherbet, made by mixing two glasses of boiled milk with one of sugar and three tablespoons of flour; this was then boiled with one tablespoon of butter – the longer it was boiled, the harder the consistency of the white or beige toffee-like slabs. Then there was a beige rich sweet malty paste, made from half a litre of the malt flour, whipped up cold with half a litre of *buza* dregs and one tablespoon sugar. Lastly, rice was boiled in just enough milk to be swollen, put on a plate, leaving a space made in the middle for boiled

Dmitri Chirkov's photo of dried meat and gut sausages hanging out to dry on a round tower in Amuzgi village. Cows and sheep are killed in the autumn and preserved for winter food, which is relished by the carnivorous Daghestanis.

butter, alone or with malt flour, and *urbech* with honey.

In addition to home produce and barter in the village, there has always been a weekly market, where today trucks brought contact with the outside world. I went to all I could. They called one, 2000 metres up in Gagatl, an "international market." Men came from Vedeno in Chechenia, Khunzakh, Botlikh – everywhere. Three hundred people, trucks and animals were crowded onto a boot-shaped site, on two levels, spilling down a slope. The women occupied the top half of the market, overlooking a row of old men in *papakha* and *aerodrom* hats, sitting along the *godekan* log. Down below, the men dealt in horses, donkeys, cows, sheep and goats, while headscarved women's faces were shiny with unloading crates of plums and tomatoes from the backs of lorries. The boxes were too deep, so the tomatoes always got squashed, pounded by the jagged dirt roads.

Next to a starved foal in the lower men's market, dealers bought horses for 2000 roubles (£20 at the official or £80 at the then black market rate), as flocks of goats and sheep surged between the village terraces. Sheep cost 80-120 roubles each and a cow 6-700 roubles, after ten per cent bargaining. Lines of women vendors in violently coloured headscarves and long dresses, hands shading eyes, squatted next to their kerchiefs, on which they had displayed unripe green plums in tin buckets, red plums from wicker baskets padded with straw, garlic, tomatoes and apples, dried fruit, hazelnuts, walnuts and sunflower seeds. (Botlikh market also sold melons, red pepper, allspice, herbs, honeycomb, yogurt, cheese and butter). Between the rows of old or synthetic haberdashery, a girl carried a cage with silky white cocks and two boys brought on a hutch with smooth grey rabbits. I bought a nugget of black circular-chewing gum, which turned out to be pure rubber.

In subsistence village agriculture, there is never a great choice, even in the metropolis Makhachkala. Except for the private market No. 2, praised elsewhere, the food shops were bleak. In 1990 the usual staples, rice, flour and macaroni had disappeared from main-street shops. Everything was worse than before. There were only packets of salt, tasteless jars of conserved fruit and powdered baby food. Black pepper was sold under the counter to an old friend, with a warning that it was the last. Home produce had not, it was quite clear, been overtaken by the state distribution system. There are some home-processed food products which seem peculiar to Daghestan, but others are easily recognised as variants of Turkish, Georgian or Iranian recipes. In everyday meals, I ate bread, meat, tea, alcoholic drinks, cheese, ground seed paste, pickles and fish, which were all locally prepared. Soviet *ersatz* Nescafé, as at the feasts, was always on offer.

There was also plenty of bread, which had attracted its own traditions and rituals. In the older houses, the *takhta* was a knee-high seat and table platform in the living room. When Magomedkhan was small, he stepped over the bread placed on the *takhta* to get at some other food. His father made him kiss the bread as an apology, and promise never to do it again.

The first bread from new flour had always to be tasted by the head of house, and then by the youngest boy to ensure he grew up strong. Flat bread is never pierced with a knife, but only broken by hand. Also bread must always be placed right side up. There was an excellent *tandir* mud oven in Novi Frig for making the flat round bread *lavash*. Two women sisters and their children had come with their risen dough on a dish, under a cloth. They knelt to deftly roll out a melon-sized circle of dough with a thin stick rolling-pin. Then they stamped holes on the top with a bundle of goose quills. A final sprinkle of sour milk, flicked from a feather, gave the bread a crisp crust. While feeding the fire with branches from pruned fruit trees, one woman pulled out the bread on a wood slide to inspect it. When it was ready, golden-yellow with browned patches, she placed it on the other dozen, stacked on a low wooden table, covered with newspaper. The children kept eating the delicious bread. When their mothers had finished, another family arrived to bake their bread. In Aguli they baked special festival bread for the first day of spring, enriched with nuts and raisins. I was intrigued that loaves of bread were cut sideways, and then vertically down in half slices, and no one knew why – perhaps it was to keep it clean for guests.

૪

Mountain people professed not to like fish, which was confirmed by the dust gathered on the neat pyramids of tins of sild fish in tomato or shrimps from

Antartica in village shops. Fresh fish were harder to find. In some mountain torrents near Georgia, the small sweet Tsar's trout – Nicholas II liked to fish for them – were eaten raw. Kutum is an estuary fish, from where the Sulak river meets the Caspian. The deep burgundy-coloured fibrous meat of this large-scaled fish had been dried in the wind for four days, then salted once, dried for another week and salted again. The black-pudding-sized slices were sweet and tasty.

The pollution in the Caspian Sea, from Baku oil spillage and chemical effluent from there and the river Volga, almost killed off all the sturgeon, famous in England before Shakespeare, who praised it in Hamlet. A recent televised film about scientific breeding and conservation of sturgeon by the Daghestan Filial of the Academy of Sciences and the Moscow laboratories, apparently featured two four-foot-long young sturgeon. But was the interview with a plump white-fringed 65-year-old scientist simply old footage which had been inserted to give an optimistic message? I was often given addictive large grey pressed caviar in unmarked jars, except in March. It cost only forty roubles a kilo, but was unobtainable. Rich baked fresh sturgeon, delicious with thick pomegranate syrup, was also forbidden in order to conserve live fish.

At the village of Wachi I jumped out of the jeep, to witness a calf being slaughtered by the biblical or steppe-nomad method. The calf's hoofs were bound together and two men were sitting on top of it, while the local doctor was carefully cutting its throat with his sharp pocket-knife to bleed it, before chopping the head off. Cows or sheep were skilfully skinned, saving everything – there's a saying in alpine Archi, "Put the big spoon even on the sea shore," meaning don't waste a thing. Local pagan priests used to prophesy by examining the offal and other internal organs of the sacrifice, while the head was considered the most noble part of the animal, and was therefore reserved for the priest or the senior man. I may never have been offered any heads, though I saw them for sale in the markets, but the head was still considered as the meat, which turned a meal into a feast.

Another delicacy was *kurduq*, roasted fat tail of fat-tailed lamb – Shamil's favourite. It was better younger. In the words of Thomas Love Peacock, the Regency poet:

> *The mountain sheep are sweeter,*
> *But the valley sheep are fatter,*
> *We therefore deem it meeter,*
> *To carry off the latter.*

During autumn, in Archi (and everywhere else in the mountains), the whole cow and sheep, including heads broken at the jaw, hang in salted pieces, drying on the open verandas.

As well as the meat, there were baroque swags of cow-gut sausages, an inch across, the entire length of the gut casing, chunky herb-filled sheep's heart, a startling, small twisty sausage, a pair of stuffed testicles, and a pair of elongated stomachs. The mildly fermented sausages took half hour to boil. Khunzakh sausages were prepared at the end of October when the weather was fresh and the flies had gone – the higher the village, the earlier. One- to two-year-old cows or sheep were best for sausages. The meat was minced or cut up with onions, salt, berberis, cumin and thyme. The ram had only one short intestine, but the cow had a long gut and two stomachs, and so made more sausage. Cow tasted better than bull. Sausages were filled using a hand-mincer without the cutting front, with the intestine fitted over the end. There were both boiling and non-cooking sausages, which tasted like Italian *bresaola*.

In Untsukul, while dining on the balcony in the dark, I was served an unusual sausage of ram's intestine, surrounded by its orange bobbly gullet, bound together with string loops. It could not be cut or chewed, even when it reappeared at breakfast, next morning.

There are now four types of cattle in Khunzakh: Red Steppe, Caucasian Browns, Swiss and a small local breed, which gives an oily creamy milk. But traditional small mountain cattle produced little milk, so sheep milk was used for cheese. During these days of smaller private flocks, I have seen it made in the home. But before, cheese making required extra work and therefore became a communal activity. The wives left their ewes at the communal farm to be milked. All the milk was poured into a large cauldron; the cheese, produced by specialists, was shared in proportion to the number of ewes, usually 300-400 a family. This took place during a few weeks and the milk from, say, the last five days was left as payment to the shepherd and specialist for their heavy work. Georgians paid a lot, seven roubles a kilo, for tart cheeses from Daghestan. I was always looking out for unsalted, more edible alpine cheeses, but I was unable to find any because of the Georgians.

In Ginukh, however, they did make unsalted cheeses, which tasted like pecorino and mozzarella, in inside-out calf skins or stomach bags. In Tlyadal' they made a sheep cheese called *sik* in inside-out sheepskins where the lanolin in the wool, mixed with the natural oils in the skin, reacted with the bread-sized slices of cheese and its liquor to form a pungent golden cheese after six months.

ê

The most popular drink in Daghestan, as in Turkey or Azerbaijan – tea – was drunk from small pear-shaped glasses, filled to the brim and sweetened with sugar, cut from blocks. Temirkhan-the-Tycoon's mother said that if you skimmed the froth off tea, money would come your way. You could not drink cold water with or after hot water – only tea (or spirits). Herbs found in tea included mint, *chebrets* (another mint), caraway, adda and cloves. A sign of returning emigrants from Central Asia was the recent appearance of Kalmyk tea, in brick-sized blocks. It was mixed with one fifth extract of Georgian tea grounds and a little salt, then milk and butter were added before drinking from a five-inch bowl.

King Khosrows' dumplings

The favourite wine to the Daghestan palate, like the ancient Greek, was a 17 degree strong thick sweet red port-wine, probably the descendant of the noble wine exported to Asia Minor and Persia from the 12th century. However, I found preferable home-made three week old dry cherry wine in Muni; *injar*, dry full-bodied blossom-scented rosé in Yersi; home-made dry white in Novi Frig, (all about ten degrees strong); as well as sweet champagne and even beer from Derbent. The famed *buza*, a grey-beige fizzy cloudy sweet beer, also about

*Women moving wooden beehives near
Lower Inkhelo.*

ten degrees, was made from a fermented beige malty-tasting flour, described above. In Bezhta they were drinking the local tinny-tasting variant. A mere four glasses caused drunkedness. For 40 litres, five kilograms of sugar and two glasses of the fermenting agent were added to hand-warm spring water. The mixture was left in open glass jars to ferment for five days, when it was promptly drunk. Spirits were also home-made, tasting like ethanol, while a decent caramel brandy and vodka were made at the Derbent distillery.

Wine vinegar had its uses. A Lezgin woman living in Novi Frig was expert at making pickled preserves. Her front-door sized 600 litre barrels for pickling tomato, cucumber and Bulgar peppers, each contained 460kg of vegetable, 50kg of salt, costing five roubles a barrel, and 140kg of home-made wine vinegar. There were also acidic pickled mushrooms, garlic, carrots, green peppers and shredded cabbage in Makhachkala's Market No. 2.

All families preserve plums, apricots, cherries and berries in sugar, which are eaten by the teaspoonful with black tea at the end of a meal. During the Gorbachev anti-alcohol period, all sugar disappeared into bootleg liquor, so there was rationing and insufficient for these vital preserves. The lack of sugar was one reason why factory-produced juices and preserves were tasteless, like the apricot juice from Tlokh.

Urbech was a tonic brown paste, somewhat like Radio-Malt which was teaspooned into British schoolchildren during the 1950s. Apricot kernels were roasted on a huge iron tray in a communal oven in Khunzakh. They were then ground by millstone in the communal water turbine. *Urbech* was also be made from linen or hemp seeds or walnuts and the sweet version (called *ourba* 'walnut') was made by adding butter and sugar.

July apricots drying on roofs by the Avar-Koisu river near Sovietskoye.

Cannabis also grew everywhere as a weed. The leaves were not smoked, but the dried seeds, which had no special effect, were eaten, like sunflower seeds. Other exotic foods were used as natural medicines. For external effect, dried grass snake, crushed with honey, was eaten to get rid of skin rashes and yolk of egg with honey were spread on a wound so that it healed without a scar. Imam Shamil's diet was sheep's fat tail – *kurduq*, and roast corn *muku*, both strength-giving and a relief for rheumatism of wrists and ankles. Rich bear meat was eaten when you felt unwell and had no appetite, and cooked badger leg, which was very fatty, or St John's wort tea restored energy after an illness.

More specifically, hard pith of walnut was brewed and drunk for heart and sclerosis of the arteries; rowanberries were eaten for kidney problems. Two sorts of confusable unknown twigs which I bought in Makhachkala, were boiled in water and drunk to relieve respectively painful teeth and stomach-ache. Apricots followed by cold water, *kefir* – a tart yogurt, black dry-tasting 'bread berries' or tea from another unknown wood were all used for constipation, while blackcurrants or St John's wort prevented diarrhoea. When a travelling companion asked for remedies for constipation there was always confusion as to whether it was to promote or erase the problem. As all the privies were earth closets, it was clear that the local population all had diarrhoea – yellow through to bright orange – which explained the misunderstanding.

The idea of a village restaurant, where a stranger would be asked to pay for a meal, is virtually a slur on the tradition of hospitality, which, together with Socialism, might explain why such eateries were invariably so awful. The worst was lunch in the restaurant at Sovietskoye, where I left the barley soup with gristle (a dull version of Count Rumforsch's poor-house soup, circa 1800) and the *'bifstek'*, which turned out to be meatless beefburgers with cold floury macaroni. As the cutlery was black, I used my own one rouble twenty kopek knife. The signs of these restaurants were often tempting, such as that of the Karata Kafe Homeland Co-op, which grandly informs anyone desirous of a meal that opening times on their 24-hour clock are 11 to 22 with breaks between 15 and 18, but I always seemed to arrive during the breaks.

Despite having a guest who always interrupted meals to write notes and take pictures, the traditional hospitality of Daghestan flowed unrelenting. Once, every family in Daghestan had a lamp in their window in case a stranger needing help passed by at night. When a guest entered a mountain house, he was first offered the sweet water from their spring. Nowadays, he was also poured a strong drink. The toast made up of the letters *KhDSS!* (pronounced 'kha-de-es-es') covers you for the Lak *khinsebiana!*, *derkap!* in Dargin, *sakhli!* in Avar and *saou!* in Kumyk and Azeri. If guests were from the host's village, he bade them goodbye at his gate. When they were from another village, he escorted them to the boundary of his village. If the guest was an important foreigner, he was accompanied to the frontier of the region, or even Daghestan, in a motorcade.

But it was the food which proved overwhelming. My personal record was six feasts in an autumn day, starting in Derbent. Nasim Abdurakhmanovich Magomedov, the economic historian, had volunteered to accompany me, as he wanted to visit home. We arrived late and stayed at his brother's house, next to the carpet factory.

Derbent people have been waiting for centuries and so are very relaxed. "Tomorrow we might get some petrol," Nasim mused. I had only four days left of an already cut-back programme. Nasim collapsed in bed after his obligatory official drinking and snored and grunted all night, without choking or waking himself up. At six we were up to visit the Sunday market – at last I was going to see those carpets, nailed to the walls of Derbent. But first – "ah!" – a breakfast of pomegranates, bread, butter and fruit preserves with tea and, my salvation, filtered coffee. Then his brother proudly showed me his laden pomegranate tree, planted in the 1920s when the house was built. At half eight we reached the market along with a couple of thousand others.

After light shopping, we dropped into Nasim's widowed mother for a late breakfast of omelette, cheese, sour cream, bread, tea and sugar. We then went back there for a lunch of vineleaves stuffed with rice and meat, fresh chopped tomato, onion and herb salad in oil, small thin *khinkal* with crushed garlic and sour cream sauce and chunks of boiled mutton, served by three pretty girl helpers. The house, with tall ceilings and doors, had once belonged to an Armenian merchant, on a square built round the late 19th-century church which was now a museum. I didn't feel too hungry but the food was good.

We left our driver to change the punctured rear tyre and visited an antique collector, who mercifully did not offer us food. I found his clean white-painted outdoor lavatory, with an old school physics book, used down to the page on internal energy. I was growing uselessly agitated with Nasim's idea of staying to rest in Derbent, instead of leaving for the mountains. "But we have not seen the shrine of the Forty Martyrs!" He was right, it was fascinating. At 2.30 we returned to Nasim's sister-in-law. "As our hostess, she has to feed us before our journey," Nasim shrugged. Wonderful bread, soup with potatoes, pickled cucumbers, tomatoes and tea.

At about four, after photographing more of Nasim's numerous family, we discovered that our Dargin driver had been sleeping off his hangover and we had only seven litres of petrol. But we had no jerry-can and the petrol tank had not been repaired, as it was Sunday. Nasim had another friend who was director of a car mechanic co-operative. He too was delighted to have guests, especially one from Britain. Yes, he did have a jerry-can and wouldn't we stay for a meal? It was already prepared, it was already served, and would I take family photographs? Boiled cracked wheat, tasty roast and stewed lamb, rough young white wine, tea and bread.

We finally left Derbent at five and motored for two hours to a Sovkhoz farm

Dr Magomed Khalid acting as butcher in the village of Wachi.

near Kasimkent, where we stayed with a fat pretentious schoolmaster, who forced on us a huge bowl of slimy giant meat-filled raviolis, pickled tomatoes, bread with rough young white wine and tea. I was now only touching the glass to my lips as a toast – there must have been fifty that day. I politely apologised and left supper early to write my notes, which was taken as rudeness by our host – who, incidentally, was hardly ever in the room but was busy preparing food or alcohol, or maybe talking with his family, friends and neighbours. I had already turned down his invitations to visit his school, give a lecture and have my picture taken surrounded by ecstatic pupils. Instead, I promised him a real schoolmaster from Britain and vowed to do anything he wanted on our return from Akhti. As a last-ditch move to keep us, he said that there had been a landslide on the road to Rutul. We never went back.

I suspected that I was often unwittingly bad-mannered, so I asked Magomedkhan for some lessons. The 33 different Daghestan ethnic eating customs seemed to be more alike than different. They ate three regular meals a day, the largest for supper. At breakfast and supper, if no strangers were present, the whole family sat together at one table. In large families, the head and older sons might eat apart from the women and children, but in the same room. A meal began with washing hands in water, poured from a ewer or basin by the youngest daughter. The head man washed first, symbolically inviting the others to table. When a family gathered at table, the head recited a prayer, and was the first to take a piece of bread or *churek* with the thumb and third finger of his right hand and lifting the wooden spoon, from the near edge of the plate

Breakfast at the Krasni Most cafe, owned by Mr & Mrs Magomed Gapur. Here there are two types of unusually non-salted Dutch-style cheese, fried batter patties, 'urbech' (a Marmite – here made from ground roast melon pips, excluding the skin), and Georgian tea. There is a great need in Daghestan for food packing and preservation of its delicious natural produce.

to his mouth, without inclining his head, he tasted the soup or stewed cracked wheat *kasha*. (In Khuchni, I saw the baked grains crushed under a great stone, fastened to a three-metre long pivoted lever, called a *ding*, like Turkish bulgur is made.)

Manners were complicated. The choicest morsels were usually served to the head of the house, who gave small portions to the rest. The youngest finished first and the eldest last, taking care that all had had enough. I was surprised to find that holding back in eating was good manners, denoting rank and importance in men. Food could give satisfaction only if obtained through hard work. "Without food, there's no life, without work – no food," paraphrasing Lenin, and "Work, not meditation, provides bread" in Lezgin and the Lak "If you don't make your brains boil in summer, your pot won't boil in winter," emphasised their reputation for thinking.

Children were taught by endless adages, reflecting national stereotypes, that worthy people do not grab leftovers. The proud Avars say: "My granary is empty, but my heart is full of honour." But the Kumyk say that "a shameless man will eat even what is not put out for him," "a wolf, even when hungry, pretends to be full up," whereas "only a dog stays when his stomach rumbles." There is Avar machismo: "A real man does not overeat, even at home in front of his wife." Then there were physical reflections: "Although shame is on his face, his belly is pleased," of the Kumyk; or "Where there is bread, that is where his head is," or "a hungry man has no eyes," and asides like "hungry as a locust" in Avar, "greedy as a clothes moth" or a "bottomless barrel" in Lezgin.

A guest should only taste food when invited. But he was not to fill himself, and always quietly say a prayer of thanks. At meals it was customary to eat sufficient for physical need, finishing with a slight feeling of hunger. "When going to a wedding start off well-fed, for you will be starving before you return." The highlander's masochistic restraint in eating was eloquently described in Tolstoy's *Hadji-Murat*:

> The wife brought a small round table, on which stood tea, *pilichish*, pancakes with butter, cheese, churek, bread and honey. A girl brought a basin, jug and towels . . . although Hadji-Murat never ate more than cheese, he ate a little bread and cheese and, taking a small knife out of his pocket, spread honey on the bread. "Our honey is good. This year and every year there is honey: and lots and good," said the old man, pleased to see Hadji-Murat eating. "Thank you," said Hadji-Murat and left off eating. Eldar wanted to eat more, but he, like his *murshid*, moved away from the table and gave Hadji-Murat the basin and jug.

Guests were invited into the best room in the house, to sit before the host and the other males, and served the best dishes. Women and children did not sit at the table, but the hostess might join the men if she was repeatedly invited by the host and guests. The women brought the food upstairs from the kitchen and often the sons of the host placed it on the table. Food was quickly set out on the table, so that the men were not disturbed while eating. Although Muslims are not allowed to drink, when there were guests, the pre-Islamic habit survived, symbolically cementing kinship.

Until about 1900, the ritual alcoholic drink was the fermented millet ale *buza*, or other home-made beers. It was bad form to drink until merry and drunkenness was condemned by the community. The great *tur* ('ram') horn goblet, which had to be drunk to the bottom to endorse kinship, was no longer part of the table setting, but a glass or goblet did the job. Starting with the host, everyone had to drink to each guest, who had to return all the toasts, standing.

Nowadays everyone drinks every toast. Strict Muslim hosts drink water, but still make toasts. If a friend dropped in to greet the guest after everyone was already at table, he was introduced to the guest, but remained standing, while the host gave him a drink which he had to drain before formally greeting the family and guest. The guest also had to taste a little of each of the numerous dishes eating with his fingers and his dagger, with the help of a broken piece of bread. *Khinkals* were served with a pierced wooden or brass ladle and eaten with a carved wooden spoon, with its bowl set laterally, unlike European spoons. Broth was drunk from the bowl. My hosts often correctly picked out and cut up food for me.

Daghestan hospitality – Botlikh style: giant 'khinkal' dumplings, boiled mutton, 'chudu', butter covered ricotta and nettle-filled pancakes & garlic juice. It is good manners to eat a whole 'khinkal'.

It was impolite to mention the quantity of the food, or compliment a dish, which I found hard, or to ask for anything, implying discontent with what was served. The host constantly reminded the guest that he should not be shy and eat more. The guest never refused directly which was coarse, but answered, "Yes, everything that I could need is on the table." It was rude for the guest to eat more than others from a common dish. He had to take the food nearest him, unless it was the best apple, for example, when he declined it and it was then offered to an elder or a child. Dipping a bitten piece of bread into a common dish was not done. "If you lick it, then swallow it" goes one Avar saying. It was good manners to chew food thoroughly, not hurrying, but bad to stuff your mouth, blow on food to cool it, take large bites or eat with your mouth open. It was rude to be excessively jolly, joke constantly, laugh loudly or talk with undue animation, but worse to comment on another's manners. A cough or sneeze was covered by the hand while turning away the head. If the host invited local singers or a storyteller, the guest (or the host in the guest's name) would present a small gift in appreciation. After the meal, as a hint that it was time to leave the table, the host went to wash. A host was always ready to invite guests to his home to eat and drink, without loss of face, and often insisted on it. There was seldom panic on the arrival of a guest, as I can confirm, having once arrived in Khunzakh, unannounced, at one in the morning. Guests appeared every day, although many of the old customs have disappeared or are ignored as old-fashioned, excepting the taboos on unclean food.

King Khosrows' dumplings

The Daghestani interpretation of Islam prohibits eating pork, wild boar, the foal of an ass, cat, dog, wolf and fox. Eating horseflesh was rare, but only permitted if a horse was useless for riding, except for a complete taboo in western Daghestan among the Akhvakh, Karata, Dido, Bezhta. Also guests might only be given meat which had been killed in the Muslim way, with the animal's head facing south east to Mecca. Food was also banned if it had come by ill-gotten gains from stealing or cheating, or been prepared by women who had not completed ablutions after sex or were menstruating. It was unclean to eat walking in the streets, or in a crowded place, or if one was on horseback, lying down, standing up, next to a sickbed, in a hayloft or stable.

Eating provided an opportunity to state or strengthen loyalties to the clan or *tukhum*. Members of the village council were expected to behave generously to their countrymen. When a family killed a sheep or ox, all its relatives, neighbours and other counsellors had to be asked to supper, or else they risked being labelled a shameful family, the severest censure in Daghestan where community opinion or rumour drew the line between nobility and baseness. News of disgrace spread beyond the village and groups of people with bad reputations had to settle together, like Kadar, the Dargin Village of Thieves.

It was thought humiliating to eat at the same table with an intruder who violated the rules of honour and shame. So if a stranger, passing through, took advantage of shelter and food as a guest, but got drunk, the host would refuse to sit with him – though this was not what I found. Sitting together at table could also confirm that quarrelling relatives were reconciled. In contrast, if someone brusquely refused to have a meal with another, it was understood he was secretly offended. If a man heard bad words of a friend, he had only to say "I ate bread with him, in his home" for the argument to stop.

Table manners in Daghestan seemed to have more content than the form followed in western societies. This is because as life is based on subsistence agriculture, the Daghestanis are much closer to nature than our supermarket existence. In spite of all the hardship which currently afflicts Daghestan and the Caucasus, there is enough food produced in Daghestan for its inhabitants and refugees. That food may come bounteously from the plains, but – as it has always been – the fruits of the land are wrestled from the small quantity of soil found in the rocky man-made mountain terraces. Ironically, it is the same rock, so difficult for agriculture, which when used so skilfully in building gives the special feeling of homeland to the Daghestan mountain villages . . .

· 7 ·

Familiar surroundings . . .

Daghestan is mainly rock. Its masons and builders have always been well known outside its borders. Up to a certain altitude, forests cover the mountains, supplying timber for public buildings, homes and furniture. This woodwork complemented the stone buildings to form the familiar surroundings which preserved the identity of a village. The peoples of Daghestan have survived attritive earthquakes, the civil war and the war against the Red Army in the early 1920s, migration and Soviet attempts to move the villagers to the coastal towns in the 1960s and 1970s – all because of the enduring strength of the home and family. The largest village groups have over ten thousand inhabitants, the smallest under four hundred. However, Daghestan's turbulent history resulted in waves of emigration: in the 1740s, after Nadir Shah's invasion, from the 1800s to the 1870s, during the Caucasian-Russian Wars and before the Revolution, and many now live in Turkey, Jordan and Iraq.

One reason why life was hard were the natural barriers to travel. Transport has always been considered a problem in the mountains, carved up as they are by torrential rivers. Water has still to be more fully controlled for the benefit of people. These natural forces have determined the shape of villages, cascading down the mountain slopes, still numbering over 700 and home to two-thirds of the people. Since the mid-1980s a process of re-population has been taking place, confirmed by the new-village houses built next to many old villages. The politics of enforced poverty has reinforced loyalty to traditional spiritual structures, which must include shrines, mosques and homes. This feeling could only have been strengthened by the universal presence of tacky Soviet Realist statues, memorials and public buildings.

While there were a few asphalt roads on the plains and in the lowlands, which largely seemed serve only as links to roads outside Daghestan, most roads were bulldozed rocks or dirt, full of pot-holes. The most acute transport problems were in alpine villages like Bezhta, near the Georgian border, where the greatest variety of traditions also survived.

The effects of isolation has continued to the present. Bezhta has been visited

The village of Anchikh. Under inefficient collectivisation only 60 per cent of terraced land was cultivated.

Danukh village with man (woman)-made terraced fields over 2,000 metres high.

by few foreigners. Ethnologists Klaproth, Guldenstedt and the Frenchman Babst came last century, but apparently no one more recently. I sent the first letter to Britain from the post office. The postman said they received 20 letters a day during the summer and over 130 a day in the winter, when more men were away working. To reach Bezhta by public transport was difficult. The 20-seater helicopter service from Makhachkala was always overbooked. So were the helicopters and biplanes to the six other local airports in Daghestan. The helicopters also helped local shepherds move sheep about.

Buses from Makhachkala stopped a hundred kilometres from Bezhta at Sovietskoye. Locals thought that the new road, the Georgian-Daghestan highway, from there would bring 'civilisation', but the asphalt road stopped near Gotsatl', much further back. Asphalt had always been in short supply and had to be imported from Azerbaijan. A taxi to Bezhta from Sovietskoye cost 70 roubles, while a taxi from Makhachkala cost 150 roubles one way and a return fare had to be found, to avoid paying double. As the average monthly wage in a town was 160 roubles – more than in a village, the villagers were unlikely to be able to afford to travel often.

The new road, which the Georgians had stopped work on because they did not really want to be too close to Daghestan (there are still no direct airflights from Tbilisi to Makhachkala), unlike the Daghestanis, would really have opened the trade route to Georgia which was more prosperous, rather than to Daghestan. Georgians used to bring chickens to barter for local alpine potatoes, which were good enough to eat raw. They now traded salty hard sheep cheese at eight roubles a kilogram for Georgian 70 degree proof bootleg liquor at five roubles a litre. The local police lieutenant said that they only had

17 *militsia* in the whole region, so control was impossible. The nearest Georgian town was 56 kilometres away or eight hours by foot.

There were seven private cars in Bezhta and a few more motorbikes. A bike with a sidecar cost about 2000 roubles and they were very comfortable during the summer. But it snowed from September to May. After repeated collapses had claimed an unacceptable number of lives, traditional wooden road suspension bridges, upriver from Aguali, had been replaced by steel and concrete military bridges, but only since the 1970s. While little travel took place, the romance of speed was there. Small boys played 'cars' with rocks in the dust, while boys and girls 'rode the rapids' on inflated truck-tyre tubes three kilometres downriver from one end of the Bezhta village to the other.

In spite of these natural disadvantages, village economies worked before Communism, and have still not been entirely extinguished. Sixteenth-century Bezhta was a large village, benefitting from the excellent alpine pastures. In winter, food for the animals was stored in sunny parts of fields where the snow did not stay for long. In nearby Ginukh nowadays, hay was stored on the open-sided top floor of houses – different to other villages. Efficient use was once made of the land. The upper village was vacated in spring, which the people left to work on the farms lower down. If you were rich you could stay in the village all the time. Shepherds from surrounding regions led their flocks to graze in the hills.

About this time the village moved downhill for reasons of economy and defence and Bezhta linked with two other villages. The new, combined village further up the valley on the hill was then destroyed twice by the Russians during the late 19th century. Bezhta held out for three years against the Russians after Shamil's surrender in 1859 and like many other Dido villages which resisted, it was destroyed. So all the houses in Bezhta today were built after 1880. Nevertheless, it was difficult to destroy a village which was mainly built of stone, as it was hard work to dismantle stone walls. During the Caucasian Wars, there were records of villages being repeatedly destroyed every five years, which implied that they had been consistently rebuilt.

The current population of 2000 lived along the river, which joins the Avar-Koisu further down. Mountain villages may have originally been settled as a refuge from the incursions of new settlers further down the valleys and in the plains, but there had to be some economic basis for their survival. When I visited Bezhta, there was a village-owned, non-Party water mill for grinding flour. Women took turns on a roster looking after it for parts of the day and were paid for the flour that they ground. It took about ten minutes to grind a kilo. Nothing much happened there. There were only two footballs in Bezhta, and no facilities (unlike the new sports hall in Ginukh), so wrestling continued to be the main sport.

Bezhta was worse off than the rest of Daghestan – but not by much. The average annual earnings in Bezhta was 1000 roubles, about a fifth less than the rest of Daghestan. Because Bezhta was isolated, food was more expensive there

The communal water mill in Bezhta village, used for grinding alpine flour.

than in Makhachkala. For example, tomatoes cost two roubles a kilo in Bezhta compared to 50 kopeks in Makhachkala. In 1989 in Daghestan there were around 220,000 unemployed out of a male workforce of about 800,000, which was the reason that many had to go to Central Asia to work. Of the total population of two million, two-thirds lived in villages, where only a third of the workforce was employed all year, while some of the others had seasonal work.

෪

When the pot-holed road curled around yet another mountain bend, the first sight of a village was its tower, linked to its walls. Villages used to be protected by massive surrounding walls and a stone tower, visible to other towers which signalled the approach of attackers. In the North Caucasus, these towers were rectangular in plan, while in the south they were circular, because of near-eastern influence, giving better visibility for defence from the wild men who attacked – within living memory – from the mountains.

There was a difference between life in the three-room apartments in Makhachkala and the more spacious homes and gardens in mountain villages. City dwellers – there were six towns of between 50,000 and 350,000 inhabitants – all kept their family homes in the villages both by tradition and preference. In 1990 there was an explosion of private new building both in stone and mud-brick in the villages.

The flat rolled-earth roofs once gave a mountain village its typical layered look, like a chocolate Sacher-torte cascading down the mountain. But since the 1960s roofs were built pitched, covered in tin sheet, a replacement for corrugated metal and asbestos. These garish silver roofs have changed the look of villages. They were meant to be more waterproof than the old earth roofs, but after a few years rust had appeared and there was no protective paint.

Traditional architecture for mountain villages grouped houses together on a south-facing amphitheatre-shaped slope for defence, light and warmth. This bunching was also because the land – much of which was not used nowadays – was so precious. In such terraced villages, the flat roofs doubled as yards for the house above, while streets and paths ran inbetween or below irrigation ditches to save space. The upkeep of the roof was the responsibility of whoever used it. The two, or more rarely three, storey houses were entered through low doors to preserve warmth in the wind and snow of alpine winters. Animals were kept on the ground floor, while upstairs, behind the verandah, there was the guest room with the hearth, the great storage room – the *tsagour*, formed by a wooden wall with a central column and two small doors, and the bedroom for all the family.

The new stone houses made me think that the villages were growing, while the ruined old buildings gave the opposite impression. Some villages had been voluntarily depopulated. Most of the 120 families of Shali, a Lak village near Archi, moved to Makhachkala and Buinakst, leaving only 88 men. There were no non-agricultural jobs there and Zaid, the head of the village council, who was still a Communist, said that they needed 200 men – surprisingly not women – to work there. Rather than being short of labour, however, the impression was that they were just inefficient. Six shepherd's families had moved there from Archi and as Shali still has *tandir* ovens, they made the special bread for Archi for the festival of Uraza Bayram. As I looked curiously inside an old woman's spacious house and smiled as I recognised its familiar features, she asked me: "Are you laughing because we're so poor?"

ॐ

With all the delays, I was desperate to see more isolated villages. At five o'clock one afternoon, we set off up a valley to an isolated village in the Charadinskii rayon. The road stopped, cut by a swollen torrent, so Magomedkhan and I went on foot. When the bank ran out we jumped across the water or bounced off rocks in midstream, or slipped into the water. We climbed to catch a view that merely showed another bend, as the mists dropped over all nearby mountain tops, darkening the wet green scrub and black-grey slippery rocks, in diagonal layered slopes, which disappeared into the ragged stream. It felt empty and hopeless as we turned back into the bleak wetness through the wildly thrashing stretches of ruined road. We found our jeep at darkness and the lights did not work. Magomedkhan's mother was worried and had sent out the village jeep to meet us. Next day we heard that we had been misinformed – no one had lived there since the *kulaks* were deported in the thirties, it was a dead village.

While Bezhta was expanding slightly, Batlaich was shrinking. Batlaich is a village on the relatively more prosperous Khunzakh plain, 1700 metres high. The school there had only 200 pupils, down from 400, ten years before. The main local work was sheep breeding, which now needed fewer workers on the limited land available. At the school there were mainly military pictures, to encourage more boys to leave for a career in the army. In contrast, in the reviving village of Khiourukh, families had five children, who made up a third of the 2000 inhabitants. Local mayors had their own theories about the growth or decrease of their villages, but no general rules emerged. Villages near larger villages were vulnerable and the ethnic new towns set up in the plains, as part of the political war of attrition against the villages, known as "changing mountain people into fishermen," effectively bribed the villagers to move. When a small nationality had been persecuted, such as the people of Ginukh, the survivors were more tenacious.

The village of Archi was expanding, in spite of the inefficient local *kolkhoz* state farm run by Islam Abdullaev. Everyone worked in the ten linked hamlets where the total population had grown from 1000 to 1200 during the past ten years. There were 20,000 sheep and 700 cows, 7000 hectares of useable land and a further 5000 in the more distant valley. They could have doubled the area under cultivation.

Azeri and Mountain Jewish vendors at the millennia-old Sunday market outside the ancient walls of Derbent. They say you can buy anything here.

There were 40 state-owned horses plus 23 private horses. A good local horse was worth 1500 roubles, an old one, for transport only 550 roubles. The *kolkhoz* had a special fund for old people, invalids and babies and could also give help in money or produce, at the chief's discretion. All money granted to the village stayed with the *kolkhoz*. The state had a standard price programme, which accounted for about two-thirds of the annual produce. The rest was profit for the *kolkhoz*, not the village.

"What is the difference between real costs and standard prices?" I queried.

"Meat, including fat and bone but excluding transport – that is the raw live price – costs three roubles a kilo, but the standard price is two roubles and the market price is five roubles. There is another organisation which links the state markets and the *kolkhoz*."

I continued: "Who do you trade with?"

"Archi trades with Zakatal, the Avar region in Azerbaijan – there are ten trips a year over the mountains. We also trade through Kumukh with Gunib, Buinakst, Levashi, Makhachkala, Kislyar and Khasavyurt."

I prevaricated: "Why don't you get some trucks and drive the meat to Rostov or Moscow, where you could sell it for at least 18 roubles a kilo?"

Islam shrugged – at 45 he was not used to new ideas.

In 1936, ten poor families who complained about the *kolkhoz* in Archi were transported to Kirgizia and there are still 15 Archi families in Bishkek. Part of Magomedkhan's clan or *tukhum* house was sold by his father in 1987 for only 3000 roubles, when he needed the money. His father also rebuilt the small village mosque last year. Their family once provided the ruler of the area. The old house had four floors – the top for bedrooms, the next for people, the ground floor for sheep and the cellar for cattle. There was also a 5 by 3 metre prison, without windows, which could only be entered through a three foot high door or a smaller side door, probably for spying on the inmates.

Why did they want to live in such a hard place? It was their home. Their sacred rocks were here. We walked to Khilikh' village, four kilometres down the same side of the valley as Archi and up a spur. Stones marked the boundaries of fields, leaving a foot gap to avoid petty disputes at harvest time. Farther beyond the village, a far-off blockhead-shaped mountain appeared, as if it were stuck onto a nearer slope. This was their secret view of Bedekho, a sacred place for the Archi people. There were two more: the *Dartsa Maidan* or 'Meadow' where they were building a hunting lodge for tourists and the great stone on it, and there on one peak beyond Khilikh', monolithic posts and a lintel stood like Stonehenge, with a row of monolithic spikes on another. These stones were reputedly set up in antiquity by local astronomers to measure time.

ও

The walls of Derbent are another massive reminder of the power of the men who once lived there. Derbent by the Caspian Sea was recently confirmed to be the oldest settlement in the USSR, by the discovery of pottery sherds 5000 years old. Digging the road tunnel through Derbent in 1971 led to archeological discoveries. The cultural layers were ten metres deep, and easy to see, as Derbent was destroyed by fire many times. The earliest fire was during the ninth century BC, which was before the Scyths settled there. As well as Scyth arrow-heads, there were also Albani remains from the second century BC until the Sassanian Persians came.

In addition to the remains of Sassanian buildings covering 30 acres, archaeologists found seven-metre-wide earth walls beneath a layer of unusual unburnt-brick from the fifth century AD – the original walls of Derbent between the sea and the mountains. The walls may have been the third longest in the world after the Great Wall of China and Hadrian's Wall (excluding the circular walls of Constantinople and Samarra), built with the same purpose of protecting a settled society from the migrating hordes. All the old names of Derbent meant 'shut'.* The northern side was highly fortified against the nomads. The Egyptian Great Pyramid contained 2.5 million cubic metres of stone, only a little more than the walls of Derbent. The parallel walls were 350 metres apart, broadening to 400 at the sea, an impressive sight from afar. In old engravings, the walls were shown continuing hundreds of metres into the shallow sea, forming a safe harbour. The surviving intact walls were almost four kilometres long and up to 25 metres high. The fragmentary mountain walls were made of a skin of large rectangular stones, filled with rubble.

As well as the ancient city, several villages still had old buildings as a reminder of their history and villagers always pointed out the "first house." Recently – years after the rest of the USSR – the active or passive policy of destruction of buildings representing ways of life which were politically unacceptable to the Party was changed towards conservation. For instance, in Khunzakh, they have started to restore the old Khan's palace as a museum. This was not so in Gagatl, where the old Islamic law courts were in ruins, but the hive-shaped building, with a hole for placing the hand to be cut off as punishment, still stood. The great palace there, with arched courtyards and ashlar walls, dated 1275, or about 1870, was spared by the earthquakes in the 1970s.

In Daghestan I always felt the threatening presence of nature. There was an ironic contrast between the amount of water and the lack of drainage. As a Londoner, I thought in terms of urban rain which is discrete and runs away over smooth pavements. As a Cumbrian settler, I thought of steady drizzle and mist. But the prospect of my short, sodden, unmade Borders road was as nothing compared to the effect of rain on a mountain village. In Koubachi the main alleys were transformed into rivulets if there were stones beneath, or else lapping mud. Shoes became floating rafts sinking into the brown soup. Until I saw the effect of two days rain on these uncomplaining people, whose women

* e.g. Arabic *Bab al-Hadid* 'Gate of Iron'. The name 'Derbent' itself comes from the Persian *darband*, variously defined as 'the bar of a door; a barrier; a narrow and difficult pass through moutains; a road dangerous on account of bandits; etc. etc.' (F. Steingass, *Complete Persian-English Dictionary*).

carry their perpetual loads through the mire, it was hard to imagine life (without the fighting) in the trenches during the First World War. The custom of leaving your shoes in the outer porch when entering a house did not help them dry. In Urakhani, schoolgirls returning home washed the mud off their shoes in a water trough. In Kupa village, an old woman washed in a stream in middle of main road. Yet centuries ago there had been paved streets and stone and wood pipe drainage.

Like drainage, sanitation was almost non-existent. Clean outside squatters are traditional in Muslim lands. In the mountains of Daghestan villagers went far away alone to relieve themselves. Women and most men never used the common lavatories in the village. For example, in Karata there were two common lavatories for men and women, but only male strangers used them. In the state hotel in Botlikh there was a downstairs gents' with two ceramic bowls, side by side, set into a large block of cement covered in tiles, which flushed continually until the water ran dry, when it blocked.

Like most others, I climbed down the nearby gorge at night and squatted there. I think this lavatory was similar to a Moscow design. In 1983, I was in Moscow with an American rug collector, by the name of Dennis Dodds, who was caught short near Red Square. At that time he had no Russian, so he entered the ladies' on the ground floor of the Sviezda restaurant by mistake. All the doors were open with women crouching above the seatless ceramic bowls. He then located the gents' where the same thing was happening. Dennis rushed out shaken. I remembered this later in Daghestan, at the Pioneer camp near Majalis, where the twin-hole deluxe privy smelled of ammonia. In Kumukh, inside a warm inner chamber on the other side of the yard to the house, there was a wood rectangular orifice 18 by 9 inches wide with an M-shaped end. Wood shavings had been provided to scatter onto our droppings two feet below, as well as paper. In Koubachi, my *konak's** new house had a similar outside wooden board privy. But there the hole was eye-shaped, 9 inches long with its lids 6 inches apart, flanked by two half-inch thick foot-shaped planks, over a four foot plunge.

There was an ancient house in Koubachi on a steep incline where the wood privy was cantilevered over a 30 foot fall. It was probably built during a family blood-feud when it was impossible to venture out of the house safely. Most impressive was a wooden privy at the Aguali petrol station with its dramatic sweep down the gorge of the roaring Andi-Koisu river. In Bezhta, the wooden privy had collapsed on the tilt, which was disorienting, though the breeze it caused was invigorating. A high Daghestan Party politician invited me to feast with him and his family in his modest flat in Makhachkala. Beside the conventional bowl lavatory, I later found a very narrow roll of lavatory paper as well as a small chrome ewer filled with water, in the Muslim tradition.

---

* As explained earlier, a *konak* is your honorary kinsman host in a village. When you visit his village, you *must* stay with him or else commit a social offence.

Koubachi village terraced houses painted blue against the evil eye. One house's roof is the house above's terrace.

After the village founders had chosen an accessible, but not too unprotected location with adequate water supplies, they decided on the shape of the settlement. The ideal mountain village was built around a south-facing natural amphitheatre, such as Akhti. When Islam came, the mosque was sited in a commanding position, both overlooking and surrounded by the village houses – a solid symbol of its central spiritual presence. When the Communists came, the Party wished to take the spiritual initiative and erected concrete buildings for Socialist purposes. There must have been an ideal Socialist village design in a manual in Moscow. As the mosques had already occupied the best sites, they were sometimes demolished but more often converted to 'progressive' uses. Every village had a silver or golden painted statue of Lenin with his right arm outstretched in front of the massive Party headquarters, which were usually full of empty rooms. The most imposing statue group was in the centre of Gunib, where the statue of Lenin dwarfed busts of Orzhonikidze and Kirov, the bloody generals who repressed Daghestan in 1921. The Soviets had not forgotten that last century, Gunib was also the centre of Imam Shamil's resistance to the Tsarist Russians.

Next to the Party palace, there was often a Party portal, its design loosely modelled on the Neo-classical entrance to the Dynamo stadium built in Makhachkala in 1935, which was flanked by a pair of whitewashed cement figures of a Soviet boy and girl athlete. The village versions took on a life of their own, painted in vivid colours, such as the Karata portal crowned with concrete rams on the village square, where everyone was able to gaze in awe at the local agricultural production norms, etched on the walls flanking the gateway. The Batlaich portal was more orthodox, crowned by a whitewashed cement bust of Marx. There were often unkempt gardens of rememberance with the Party Board of Honour such as in Khriugh or Karata. The board was covered in folk-painting portraits of Revolutionary heroes, Second World War heroes and heroes of industry, blankly surveying the fruits of their sacrifice.

Nearby, forming an axis to the village, the Neo-classical Palaces of Culture – *Dom Kulturni* – looked ridiculous, like those in Tashpinar or Khiourukh, with their misproportioned porticos and squat columns, straining under pediments designed for some greater building. Sometimes they were built next to Islamic shrines, still covered in cloth streamers, as in Khiourukh. Tall phallic war memorials were erected in apparent competition to local shrines. In between these landmarks of Socialism, mosques had often been converted into cinemas as in Khunzakh, or similar 'clubs' as in Gotsatl' or Bezhta. Main regional villages, such as Botlikh and Kumukh were sometimes granted a Stalinist-style cinema, with a stepped facade topped with Elizabethan obelisks, a very distant reminder of the skyscrapers of Moscow. In this municipal jumble, main villages also had a restaurant. The most curious was in Botlikh, where behind a pebble facade, the internal restaurant wall decoration of champagne labels matched the tile design.

If I, as an outsider, felt the insult of this visual pollution among people who, until the Revolution had such a deep sense of original design, how would they have reacted if they had been free? When I asked them, the answer was always the same: "We have learnt to ignore these buildings and posters and slogans. They do not exist for us." But did they continue to see their buildings, textiles, carved stone and woodwork, metalwork, jewellery and arms and armour, or had too this habit of ignoring taken over?

A silver-painted concrete Lenin, now permanently dismantled, stretching his arm out (taking not giving) in front of the neo-classical 'Dom Kulturni' in the village of Tashpinar, 1990.

The new Soviet architecture failed to destroy the central structure of every village – the *godekan*. This was probably because it was invisible, often merely a log against a wall. It existed solely because of its function. Village men didn't sit indoors in *chaykhanis*, teahouses, drinking tea like the rest of Asia, instead they sat out in the cold *godekan*. To keep off the wind, a wide shed was sometimes built, with an open front and seating along the three inside walls, such as in Andi where the opening was separated from the square by an open arcade. In larger villages like Khunzakh, there was a *godekan* in every quarter.

In the past, it was wrongly considered by travellers and researchers that in the villages of Daghestan much free time was wasted in passive idleness.

G. G. Osmanov, the Daghestani socio-economic historian, writing in 1965, observed that: "Men working away from home would come back and spend the whole winter at home doing nothing." In fact, their immobility (like that of academics) was not at all what it seemed at first glance. Men often gathered at the *godekan* in their spare time to do light work in company, such as carving utensils, twisting rope or preparing sheepskins. At other times the revered old men sitting in the *godekan* would instruct the young in morals and customs, passing on legends and folk tales, or teach manual skills.

Games and entertainment were an important part of their rich culture and many of them took place at the *godekan*. Board games were popular – particularly among the Lezgins – where adults and children played together, especially in winter when men had more free time. The two players were always surrounded by eager advisors. Draughts boards were drawn on thick boards or carved on polished rocks with pebbles as pieces.* Many highland dances were also developed in the confined space of a flat roof which served as a *godekan* in particularly steep villages. I saw a wedding dance on a just such a roof near Archi.

The *godekan* was both the resting place for the revered elders and where all the village men gathered for meetings. In the correct sense of the word, views were democratically expressed and opinions exchanged on judicial and social community matters, as well as on individuals' problems. Solutions were reached by collective agreement. The *godekan* was an essential expression of the community and was highly respected. Strict etiquette was observed in seating, with the elders in the most important place in the centre, and the younger men along the sides. The juveniles were grouped on the edge and did not come forward unless invited to do so. In Ansalta, we sat down at the *godekan*, where Labazan, who was 55, explained that: "Men can sit on the *godekan* after the age of fourteen, but it is usual to wait until returning from the army. Younger children like to sit nearby to hear stories about the village. When old men pass by, young men stand up silently, waiting to be greeted."

I found that little had changed since 1867, when a Russian academic in the Gunib region observed that "all members of the *godekan* are well-ordered: they listen quietly and when they speak, it is to the point and diplomatically, till agreement is reached . . . this controlled conduct at a meeting is impressive to any admirer of order . . . it is a self discipline, not imposed in any way, and appears to be simply part of the highlander's character, the result of the ancient Daghestan quality of life: a practice acquired as self defence to maintain peace."

The most impressive building in the village was the mosque. Akhti museum was once a great mosque. In the wall by the door, there was a blue-glazed brick. The story was that the first mosque in Daghestan – presumably Derbent, built about 730 AD – had a solid mimbar, or raised pulpit, surfaced with blue glazed bricks from Mecca and every great mosque in Daghestan subsequently had one of these blocks built into its wall. When I drove past distant villages like Verkhnii Jengutai, I thought I saw silver missiles, ready to be launched, but they turned out to be the minarets of the new mosques.

Starting in 1988, there was a furious re-building of mosques in Daghestan, part of the silent war against the Communist Party. Only 27 had survived the 1928-38 destruction of 2000 mosques and 800 *medreses*. In 1988 permission had been given for the re-opening of another 17 only. In fact, we estimated about

---

* Such rocks could still be found in some old *godekans* in Maza, Gdum, Zrukh, Smugul, Ikhrek, Mykjrek; and in Fiy, the board was carved on a high rock, where in winter men would go up to play the game in the sun. Variations of draughts were called in Avar *chimkh*, Lezgin *tiama*, Rutul *kish*.

200 were being rebuilt, mainly in the north in the majority of Avar, Dargin and Andi villages. With the exception of Party members, many villagers have ignored the ban and were contributing their own money and equipment.

For instance, in Karakh village on the road from Botlikh to Khunzakh, where there are great spherical meteorites, they were restoring a not-so-old mosque, with inscribed stones dated 1235 and 1320 AH (1829 and 1917 AD). Young men were working on the site while the central part had been curtained off for prayer. A vernacular style was evolving, with neighbouring villagers noting each other's work and competing for better quality and faster progress. The new style involved the enthusiatic use of massive areas of beaten tin and carved wood inside the mosque, contrasting with the thick golden varnish on the great old wooden supporting columns.

To the south progress was more cautious. In Khiourukh, there were three disused mosques – one of which was used as a store. We were driven straight to another, the oldest, by people who quietly told us that they were believers. They contradicted the mayor, who was absent, saying that many local people wanted to re-open the mosque – our first evidence of such feeling in South Daghestan. The minaret tilted slightly because it had cracked when they bulldozed the road beneath, but the stone walls were upright, thanks to the two bands of carved wood built in to it, to stop earthquake damage.

It was best for the preservation of a disused mosque if it were used for storage as in Djuli, or making rugs, as in Ikra, but not so good if it were a metalwork factory, as the newer mosque with a Russian-style onion dome in Rutul. The saddest examples of dereliction were the older mosques. Perhaps the greatest mosque was built in the twelfth century in the now abandoned village of Kala-Koresh, near Koubachi. Its wooden doors, carved with facing lions and fragments of stucco with carved floreated kufic Arabic are in the Makhachkala Kraevedcheski museum, but the rest is in the open.

As another example, in Tsofkra Pervoy, where I saw 50 eagles circling in the sky, the ruined 14th-century mosque's square-section changing to round-section columns, covered in broken stucco, decorated with powerful archaic pagan horn-shapes, were open to the weather. In Rutul, the roof of the old mosque had caved in, exposing the once-lively carved and painted wooden columns. Outside, where the doorway had been, inscribed stones and wooden ceiling planks, painted with bright red, green, blue and yellow arabesques were left to rot, as was the carved wood mimbar pulpit. I talked to the children who had gathered round, about why they should preserve their heritage. They looked round, squinting at my strange burblings. The ruins I so admired were a reminder of their poverty and oppression.

As well as the columns, some mosques had other pre-Islamic features, like the zoomorphic rafter terminals of dragon neck and head shape, rising over the arcade along the front long side of the old mosque in Djuli in Tabassaran. This was similar to other finials on both sides of the surviving pagan shrine at Rekom, near Tsei in North Ossetia, where the sacrificed ram skulls were

The Krasni Most – the first privately-owned cafe in Daghestan, up the Avar-Koisu river.

stacked on shelves against the log cabin walls. The same many-headed motif also appeared on tapestry carpets, where it was called *ruk'zal*, 'house', in Avar. The corner-jointing of the shrine at Rekom employed a technique which also appeared frequently in Daghestan for wooden walls and even for free-standing columns. To save wood, logs were split into planks and to make a stronger joint to resist earthquakes, rectangular rebates were cut into both edges of the plank ends. This was more sophisticated than the Russian log-cabin corner joints of half-round recesses cut on only the underside of logs.

᠌᠌᠍ ᠌᠍

Just as the communal buildings reflected local styles which were often typical of an ethnic group, so did the family home. The house was the centre of the extended family, which from time to time became overcrowded and so split up. Earlier this century, such a new small family, having broken away from the large homestead, retained the patriarchal system and with it the division of labour between the sexes. The woman exchanged the many shared duties controlled by the 'eldest' in the extended family for even harder work. She now had to make by herself all the clothing for her family and the soft furnishing for the home from hide and wool, the readily available raw materials.

She may have gained self-confidence and respect from family and community, but the heavy load of work led to physical and nervous exhaustion. The wife's workload today confirmed the old saying that "the wife is the column of a house – the whole roof rests on her shoulders" (quoted earlier this century by the Avar poet Gamzat Tsadasa). The home was mystically protected by the column and the hearth.

Until nowadays, new buildings were protected by superstitious practices. The Hand of Fatima, a typical charm in several Islamic lands was stamped once or twice on the clay outside wall near the door to protect the house against evil spirits. A brass stamp in the form of a hand with engraved Arabic inscriptions and the forked magic Sword-Zulfugar has survived in the Kraevedcheski Museum (see page vi). Wooden rod talismans with verses from the Koran, written by the mullah, were placed on ceiling ledges to protect the home against *jinns* and *shaitans* – devils. Besoms or twig brooms inspired eerie Lezgin sayings about the security of the home and its occupants:

> *Don't step on a besom, or your house will be poor.*
> *He who steps over a broom on the threshold or is touched*
> *by even a twig will have a short life.*
> *Don't hit someone with a besom or he will die.*
> *Do not clean the house when the master has left on a journey until*
> *you know that he has crossed seven bridges, or else he will not return,*
> *having been thrown out like the dust.*

Like other popular symbols, the broom had quite opposite good effects too. For the Dargins it was a protection against the evil eye and the Avars presented a bride with a besom for fecundity, when she first entered the groom's house. I happened across two additional talismans. In Djuli in Tabassaran in 1986, there was a foot-long group of suspended cloth triangles (*tumar*), hung inside an empty new building to protect it from occupation by evil spirits. This is similar in shape and purpose to smaller versions, made of threaded beads, which hang from the driver's mirror in Turkish taxis. Then, there was widespread use of blue paint on inside and outside walls and doors and doorways to ward off the evil eye, which was popular, for example, in Koubachi.

The Socialist ban on all private building until 1988 may unwittingly have helped to conserve vernacular techniques and styles. Construction materials depended on local supplies of timber or conveniently sized stone. In Khilikh' three-storey traditional stone houses survived. The cellar was for cows. The ground floor was for sheep and humans in winter. The animals kept the place warm. The first floor was lived in by humans in summer.

Stone masons used to build ashlar stone houses, without mortar, like the old palace which survived the earthquake in Gagatl. Others used lime mortar to cement the stones together. In Koubachi local argillite walls were repaired with yellow stone from Derbent. To give an idea of present relative costs: in Novi Frig, near Kasimkent, one yellow Derbent stone 15 by 15 by 40 centimetres, cost one rouble, while cement cost five roubles a sack, both prices varying wildly elsewhere. There was a cement shortage as it had to be imported, because Daghestan had not been allowed to develop its own industry. Cheaper Samur river stones cost 40 roubles a truck-load, but they are round and slower to build with and they also require more cement.

In contrast, a three-storey village house in Bezhta was built with softer materials. Wattle or wattle-and-daub walls protected the ground floor, with boarding on the second and a verandah with lime-plastered walls on the third. Wattle, or woven branches, was mentioned in the old Nart giant legends in Ossetia and was used for all sorts of containers. Wattle for walls or doors were all woven at home, not in workshops.

With private restoration of houses permitted throughout the USSR and even in Daghestan, every other house was now a building site. In Derbent I stayed in a typical house under *remont*, where my host, who worked as a builder, was extending the verandah into the car-park sized yard. There seemed to be plenty of local bright yellow stone blocks, but little cement, bricks or wood. Mud bricks were easier to make and mud technology was well-developed in adobe-like new mud porches in Botlikh or chimneys in Akhti. There were funny building materials about. Old cast-iron Vienna Secession style bed-ends used as fencing in byres and fields alerted me to the decorative recycling of collected scrap-yard junk. The wall of old iron stoves in Gagatl vied with the wall capped with a cascade of squashed old buckets in Ginukh. On my first visit to Koubachi, I noticed that the footmat outside the restaurant was a car radiator core. Domestic cast-iron radiators were similarly used while old jeep and truck tyres were popular for steps up to the house. The most structural application was an upside-down saloon car body as a footbridge.

In older houses the roof logs and the roof were held up by a great wooden column with a capital, up to four metres long. Sixteenth and seventeenth century capitals were often shaped like great coiled horns, only to be compared with Aeolian stone examples from Ancient Greece. There were hundreds of

The author being presented with a 16th-century Chechen single family blood feud siege tower by the assistant minister of culture of Chechenia at Tazbichi near Itumkale, on the road to Dagesthan.

original shapes for both columns and capitals, of which one of the most striking was the tall triangular-shaped capitals covered in carved Celtic-style interlacing, made in Tabassaran during the last century. The design derived from a local mastery of the style, found in the main mosque doors from Tpig, which were carved about 1300. Only one great column was used in each house (with several in the larger mosques). After 70 years of totalitarian rule in Daghestan, it was amazing that the curse "May your column fall!" was still deeply offensive.

Sometimes the column was placed to one side of the main room in the centre of a wooden wall with doors on each side, leading to the storage area, called the *tsagour*. Over the course of the last century, the great column moved nearer the outside, as the central support of the verandah arcade. In every village, where the verandah faced a main street, for instance in Botlikh, great logs stuck out of the walls supporting cantilevered balconies, to save ground space.

House building was done quickly, to catch the good weather and so required help from the whole community, but the skilled work was done by journeymen. Among the Kvarshins, earlier this century, for example, relatives and friends helped lay foundations, plaster walls, and cover the roof with forest moss, which the young were sent to gather. Stone walls were built by men and plastering was done by women. Every passer-by considered it his duty to help out for at least an hour if he was not already busy. There was an unusual exception to the normal rules of hospitality for the professional builders. The master of the house was bound to offer his builders supper. But there was no ill-feeling when they repeatedly refused, lest it was taken as payment for their work.

Elegant architectural forms also appeared from agricultural products. Cow dung was moulded and slapped against walls to dry for fuel, called *kislyak*. The rounded bricks were then stacked in walls with the tallest ten foot high in Gagatl. To stand firm the base was two foot broad, and the wall tapered as it rose, forming swaying shapes. Walking up the hill, towards dozens of them made my eyes jump as I felt that I was approaching a gang of giant Narts guarding the village houses. The walls also acted as windbreaks, fencing and insulation. Even the haystacks varied from region to region in Daghestan. There were yurt tent-shaped ones, with central wooden supports and a wood ring on the top in Chavab, long pitched-roof-shaped stacks in the cemetery in Kuli and small, almost human nodding ricks, facing away from the wind near Urkarakh.

❧

The internal features of a mountain village house accounted for a far smaller proportion than the four-fifths of the total cost of a British home. Nevertheless, even today, the interior retained its individuality. As well as the great column, the threshold and hearth possessed strong symbolic power. They were complemented by a few articles of furniture, many of which were peculiar to Daghestan or the North Caucasus. I was never allowed to wander into the front gate or door of a house without first being invited, as this would be a reflection on the owner's hospitality. In contrast, the evident attention given to the large courtyard doorway in an otherwise blank surrounding wall expressed welcome as well as defence. Beside the doorways were carved stone inscriptions, dates, bosses, labyrinths, lion's heads and even Tamerlane's spots.

Doors were usually low in Daghestan to keep the heat in. Also, on average people there were shorter than people in Britain and more agile too. The family dwelling space was divided in two, usually the front half for the men, with firearms hanging by the door, and the back for women. The centre of family life was the hearth where all gathered after eating. In older houses, the hearth was to one side of the centre of the main room, later it moved to a chimney in the side wall to lessen the smoke in the room. This provided the opportunity of decorating the fire surround. In Gagatl there were still a few hearth walls covered with carved stucco fish-bone or horn motifs, like those which appear on rugs and felts, which were also related to the mosque columns in Tsofkra Pervoy. In Koubachi, they specialised in argillite stone fireplaces, with carved reliefs of floral arabesques and Arabic inscriptions on a painted background. Confusingly, they still made them in the 14th-century style. Another dire curse still encountered was "may your fire go out!"

Throughout the North Caucasus, every home possessed a wrought-iron hearth chain hanging down the chimney. Apart from the practical function of hooking up the cooking pot, the hearth chain had a central symbolic role for the family. If a stranger touched the hearth chain, he showed respect to the ancestors of the family and was given sanctuary by the family and became a kinsman, which cancelled all previous blood feuds. A bride also walked about the hearth chain three times on entering her new home – a sign that she had accepted her new family. The chain represented a microcosmic link between the fire and food, or prosperity of the family, and the heavens above, where the family ancestors lived. It was another variation of the universal cosmic pillar separating heaven and earth. Even recently when Ibraghim-my-Konak built his new house in Koubachi, he put in an old hearth and chain.

Next to the hearth there hung – right up to the present day – an extraordinary wooden object, of a design unknown elsewhere, although it was called *pastavyets* in Russian. It was a spoonbox in which were stored the wooden spoons for eating the traditional dumpling dish *khinkal* and its broth and the decoratively pierced wooden or brass ladle for filling up the bowls. The spoonboxes continued to be made until early this century and perhaps a hundred different forms survive.

In essence, the shaped back was higher than the box, which was divided into three or four sections. The visible surface of the back was shaped and carved or painted, or even inlaid with small framed mirrors. The cosmic decoration on the backs included round sun signs, facing pairs of sun-birds, pairs of horns or geometric circular and rectalinear shapes like those found on tombstones and other furniture. The front of the box was similarly decorated, but also with arcading. The smaller side sections of the older boxes were made from half-cylinders, carved from the solid wood and fixed with wooden pegs.

Other old forms of woodwork survived as well. I found a 19th-century small wooden chest near Khunzakh made of hutch construction, the earliest method of making furniture in Britain, which had not been employed there since the 14th century. All homes also had a great wooden chest for storing wheat, up to ten foot long. Their fronts were decorated like the spoon-boxes and sometimes with a carved banderole – a row of cigar-shaped tubes used to store a powder charge for a flintlock rifle, placed in a series of pockets across the chest of the traditional *cherkess* frock coat.

Like elsewhere in Asia, people lived at floor-level in private, but their guest room boasted a few pieces of furniture. Traditionally, meals took place on thick felts and carpets spread on the floor, with the family sitting on cushions or low tripod stools. Sometimes the head of the family and guests dined on low small tables. European style tables began to appear at the end of the 19th century. Of far older origin, the *takhta* was a deep divan for sitting or sleeping on, the centre of which also served as a table. I ate breakfast on one in Charah village.

In the mountains, the divan was developed into a high-backed wooden bench with massive uprights, shaped in curling waves, covered in flat relief floral carving. There were foot platforms en suite and the bench was covered with a stuffed mattress seat. Small wooden triangular stools and chairs continued to be popular and the most exciting was an Avar one from Oboda with a bifurcated back, like a pair of horns. Even nowadays, the guest room also contained traditional stacks of dowry bolsters, covered in silk, covered by white guaze, a painted tin dowry chest and a cabinet or shelves, filled with dowry ceramics or brass or bronze bowls and ewers.

In Koubachi, which has prospered as a centre of jewellery and arms since at least the 12th century, where couples usually marry within the village, the same dowry gifts move round and round, from generation to generation. Most houses have a few 16th and 17th century blue-and-white Persian bowls and 18th century 'Koubachi' wares, next to modern dishes with photograph transfers of cuddly animals.

The Avars also used curious one metre square frames, of joined batons of wood carved with arabesque foliage and arabic inscriptions on a painted background. The frames were hung horizontally from the ceiling for drying cheeses, herbs or meat. And of course, many homes had a carved wooden Koran stand. There was a strange Avar stand on four small solid wheels, dated 1147 AH (1738 AD) from Machada village. If further evidence of the originality of design in Daghestan homes were needed, the textiles described next are explosive.

· 8 ·

. . . and cosmic-domestic
textiles

I first got permission to visit Daghestan to study the unique flat-woven rugs. In addition I had another interest. In a book on Daghestani decorative arts, I had found a tantalising photograph of a silk embroidery which was unlike anything I had seen during 15 years study. After I arrived there I came across three more such laid-and-couched stitch embroideries in the museums and during the next four years, another ten which were patched and carefully preserved in people's homes – a sign that they had been cherished and reused. In the Eastern Museum stores in Moscow I saw 14 more. They were small enough to cover a cot, which suggested their probable use and would also explain their most exciting feature – a protective set of archaic designs, some of which were different from anything else which I had seen. It was like finding a Rosetta Stone.

They were all produced by one small ethnic group called the Kaitag, last counted as a separate people at under 15,000 in 1926 and whose language was related to Koubachi and Dargin, while their designs were closest to those found from 300 BC in the Altai mountain frozen tombs. The brightly coloured designs included rich combinations of sun-signs, sun-birds, sun-bursts, octagons, cosmic columns, horns, fantastic beasts like crabs, elks, reindeer, fat sword-fish, dragons, amoebae, masks and even a foetus. While many of these motifs occur in Daghestani wood and stonework, for example sun-signs on a tombstone from Assab village or on spoonboxes, the combinations were singular. For now, they must remain an unsolved mystery of an almost isolated artistic eruption in a small region. I have now seen a couple with garish chemical colours, proving that the tradition continued until at least late last century.

The earliest material for weaving was wood – wattle, mentioned along with esteemed felts in the Ossetic epic poems about Nart giants, who spread south to Daghestan as characters in anecdotes. Baskets, cots, wattle-and-mud walls and boat-shaped hay stores still survive. There was also evidence of an old tradition of woven reeds in the *chibta* rug, described below.

Rugs were made to keep the home walls warm, to cover raised platforms and special floors. They were decorated with bright colours and designs, many of which have only been found in particular areas of Daghestan. These designs were not random, they had an original meaning, perhaps long forgotten. Most Daghestan people I saw seemed entirely unaware of their rich heritage – they had been taught that it was old-fashioned or un-Soviet. But there did appear to be a lot of different designs about.

Although there were earlier settlers,* the barrier created by the Walls of Derbent appeared to coincide with areas of different techniques of textile production. Imagine a wedge shape coming up from the south with its point at Derbent. Above the wedge, the villagers made and still make flat tapestry woven *davaghins* and *dumi*, and felts – the *bourka* cape, *arbabash* cart covers, *istang* wall covers, masks and boots. Below the wedge, they wove and still weave *soumak* weft-faced brocades, piled rugs, and further to the south, kilim rugs, where slits marked the boundaries of different coloured wools.

The southern range of textiles were still sold at the Sunday market on the outside of the northern walls of Derbent. The rugs had loops stitched to their edges, and were nailed to the walls and two of the towers, forming a river of red wool – though unfortunately a chemical red, not the beautiful old madder root red described below. The market has

Khadijat Gasanalieva Gasanguseinov spinning wool at home in Shara, her Lak village.

been held there since at least the 12th century, outside the city limits to avoid paying city trade taxes. That October Sunday in 1988, a couple of hundred *soumaks* and piled-rugs were for sale from about 300 roubles. Whole families came to examine the rugs, pulling them around and arguing with the old women from the villages where they had been made. Other women were selling sackfuls of unspun lustrous wool, heavy with lanolin oil, for knitting. By the 12th-century North Gate, through which more families emerged looking

---

* "The existence of aboriginal Caucasian languages and archaeological finds show that there were several mountain settlements before the Walls were built" (J. Baddeley, *Rugged Flanks of the Caucasus*) – and much subsequent evidence.

ready to buy anything, there were also cars, motorbikes, cannibalised spares, bicycles, and clothes.

The market was run by Azeris and Tat Jews. Old ladies, with gold-capped front teeth glinting in the sun, smiled and cackled: "In Derbent you can find everything." Even smart ladies' shoes from Yugoslavia were available at 200 roubles a pair. On both sides of the road verge running along the wall, more old women were crouched, selling second-hand clothes. I bought an old tinned copper ewer with teardrop-shaped stamped blazons inscribed in Arabic. The old man started at 30 roubles, while I looked away, grimaced and opened at ten, so we agreed at 20.

*

In the northern Avar, Dargin and Kumyk regions, the home wall covering was traditionally a *dumi* or *davaghin* rug, about 4.50 by 1.50 metres, hung horizontally on cloth or leather loops. This warm stiff woollen tapestry was made thicker by the doubled warps. They were often woven during the winter by young girls and the finished result was shown to the village at the *godekan* – the men's meeting place – where the desirability of the bride was accordingly assessed. It seemed that the *davaghin* had three borders and the *dumi* one, but no one really knew the difference implied by the two names. These rugs used much wool dyed with indigo blue, which was the only imported dyestuff and therefore exotic, for the background. The Persian word *dabag* means 'tanner' or 'dyer', which could be the derivation of the name *davaghin* for the largely blue rug.

The second most popular colour was red from the madder root dye. Madder still grows wild on the banks of the Sulak river, and it was a valuable commodity cultivated near Derbent from the 13th to 19th centuries – before the introduction of cheaper chemical dyes. The *davaghin* was often decorated with the *ruk'zal* design. I examined one such rug which was dated 1133 AH or 1720-1 AD, the earliest known. The motif was possibly derived from the form of the surviving ram-cult shrine at Rekom in nearby North Ossetia, which was an arched roof wood building with zoomorphic head gable terminals, similar to one side of an old mosque in Djuli in Tabassaran. There was another undeciphered design known only on six *dumi* from Butsrah village, which was reminiscent of either a Chechen tower, a man and woman dancing or a dragon and phoenix in combat (see photo on page 158). As yet, no one knows the derivation of the word *dumi*. One proposed link with an Kumyk word meaning 'story-teller', who was supposed to have sat on the rug, seemed unlikely.

Today, in modern and old houses, treasured machine-made piled rugs were also hung on the walls, a background for the shrine of family photographs, as in one exquisite bedroom in Arguani mountain village with dowry pillows displayed on the bed, as well as china and metal ewers and pots in the plastic laminated dresser.

Rolling felt to make 'bourka' capes at the factory in Rakhata village. They roll a sandwich of long-haired and short-haired felt for half an hour. It is hard work.

Textiles also provided high-status insulation for covered carts. There were felt *arbabashs* and striped kilims, called *palas*. The *arbabash*, or 'cart-cover' in Turkish, was a standard three and a half by one and a half metres. Turkic Kumyks and Nogais used carts on lowland roads, while donkeys were used on the steeper mountain tracks. The vegetal designs were cut out of different coloured felts and sewn together like a mosaic. The joins were then covered by a sewn-down narrow band of white cloth. Two-coloured *arbabashs* were often made in pairs to use up all the dyed felt. Similar felts with more robust animal horn designs, called *istang*, had the same purpose for the Chechens as the *dumi*.

Tall siege towers, rather like those in Bologna, dating from the 15th century are found in southern Chechenia and north Daghestan. The *istang* felts were hung horizontally in the man's top room of Chechen siege towers. I bought one of these felts from Khunzakh, after – I was told – it had been turned down by the museum people, who said that it was not "theirs." There were also two five metre long *dumi*, again from Khunzakh, which copied the felt *istang* designs. On top of his siege tower, the man's display also included his *shashka* sword and his *pandur*, which he strummed when he sang. The towers were used as refuge for a single family from another family during blood feuds. Imam Shamil, who led Daghestan, which included Chechenia before the Revolution, in the independence war against the Russians from 1834-1859, knew of a feud which had lasted over 300 years.

The towers had to be well protected. The front door was three metres above the ground and there was no internal stairway to the next floor, as retractable ladders were used for additional security. In 1923 the Soviets abolished the wasteful blood feud so the towers were abandoned today – though recently the blood feud has reappeared in Chechenia. In 1986, I was presented with one of these towers in the hamlet of Tazbichi, near Itum Kale in south Chechenia, by the deputy minister of Culture. It was a new experience to draft an appropriate thank-you letter.

There were other small Daghestani felts with the designs embroidered or rolled into their surface, like the felts of Beyşehir in Anatolia. Their disjointed designs were a crude imitation of some of those found in the Kaitag embroideries. The Kumyk prayer mats from Sultanyangiyurt village, were about two by one metres in size. The natural white or brown felts were embroidered in wool with outlines of crescent, ewer, or microcosmic signs. Similar engravings also appeared on contemporary tombstones. Other white ground mats were made in homes in Bezhta, decorated with large central whorls in coloured rolled-in felt. These must have represented merely a fraction of the felts which I failed to find.

Weaving a 'dumi' using the weaver's left hand as a heddle.

ะ๑

There were different villages with specialists in metal, wood, stone, hide or ceramics, as well as larger centres of carpet weaving and workshops for jewellery and weapons. Around 1900 the male workers had begun to demand higher wages and many left for building jobs in towns, or work in the fishing or oil industry. Between 1913 and 1915 there were 100,000 who left, mainly from the highlands, which presumably included those who were mobilized for war. By 1928 the Party had banned all private industry and crafts on pain of severe punishment, and Party propaganda put out that: "Crafts and home industry grew into successful co-operatives in villages in the highlands, and developed into their largest trade. This was against a background of the shortage of land for agricultural work and a tradition of flexible labour. Those with less ability worked on the farm, while those with a talent for craft joined the workshop, taking time off in summer for harvesting. This combination ensured good earnings, with a buoyant demand for craft goods from their rich neighbouring republics."

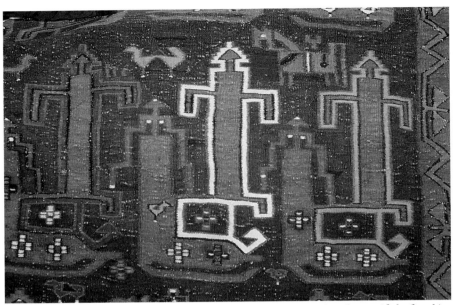

A Kumyk 'dumi' tapestry woven carpet (19th century) with an animal combat motif also found in a 13-14th-century Azerbaijan carpet in the Kirchheim Collection ('Orient Stars', London 1993).

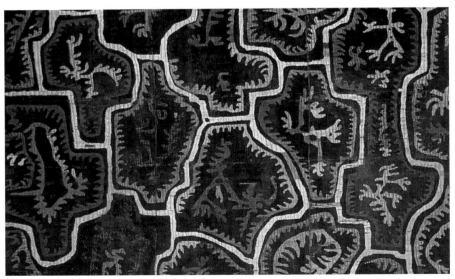

An unusually large Kaitag silk embroidery (1.30m high). The pregant elk (?) in the bottom left is similar to ancient rock drawing such as are found in Gobustan in neighbouring Azerbaijan. The figure at the top right is similar to a 14th-century carved stone masked creature built into a wall in Koubachi. This shows the ever-present mixture of cultures resulting from Daghestan's turbulent history. Extraordinarily, Kaitag embroideries coming from a such a small area seem to have greater variety of designs than any other artistic eruption in the world.

18th-century Kaitag silk embroidery on cotton patchwork. A talismanic cover which was probably used to conceal the face of a dead person, showing a symbolic route to the next world in the mirror image of the microcosmic design with 'axis mundi' separating the primal mound from an umbrella-like heaven, also linked with a snake-like lightning bolt.

Late 19th-century Kaitag embroidery with analine chemical lilac dye, boasting sun signs similar to those carved on tombstones in Digbalik village near Koubachi.

An Avar 'davaghin' tapestry-woven carpet (19th-century) with a 1.5m great horned design found in Chechen felt mosaic 'istangs'.

I seemed to see more vertical looms kept on the verandahs than weavers, but I found several women who still wove unpiled rugs at home, and they were not all old. Of the many weavers I met, four were outstanding. In Akhalchi, Zubazhat Magomedovna was weaving a beautiful white ground *dumi* (see photo on page 157). She had worked for ten years in the rug workshop in Batlaich, where I had previously seen her girl-pupils' unfinished kilims in their school. In Tlyadal', the accountant's wife had woven two great kilims with stunning 'Lezgin star' designs and colours. In Khilikh', a very old woman and her 100-year-old brother showed me her narrow backstrap loom (see photo on page 80) and her striped bags which complemented the brightly coloured appliqué swaddling bands of her ten children and their talisman-filled cradle covers. Then in Kuli, a Lak woman master-weaver called Miaset had even started a private tapestry atelier with her neighbours.

In contrast, few piled rugs were now woven at home. Since chemical dyes were introduced in 1865, carpets became cheaper to make and merchants standardised formerly exciting designs into drawn cartoons, putting a new interpretation on the weaver's memory. This continued in the Derbent and village carpet factories. When the factory in Khuchni village recently had to make kitsch 'Bugs-Bunny' rugs, there was almost a strike by the women who were angry at being forced to demean their art. Later, I was specially introduced to a rug designer who looked and sounded like a local version of the virago Dame Edna Everidge, as she proudly explained to me how she had designed the 'Bugs Bunny'.

Since the 1860s, oriental rugs from workshops have the boring look of flock

Habib and Patimat Ismailov, school teachers in Gapshima village, who gathered Kaitag customs on the use of embroideries. Habib's features are similar to those of the bronze on page 108. Patimat recites Shakespeare in French.

wallpaper, British pub floor-covering or patterned table mats. In the Derbent carpet factory, women wove piled rugs, from squared paper cartoon designs, drawn and coloured by designers from the Art Institute in Makhachkala. They let me photograph their archive, which included few unusual rugs. It was only recently that they had decided to search out and faithfully copy old designs. This was too late to improve standards, as most of the surviving piled rugs would have been made in similar workshops and used designs chosen by the merchants. Flat rugs were spared this fate as they were not valued by the world market until the last ten years, so they survived as home production and the merchants, or later the State, did not get near enough to weaken their designs.

As late as 1987, Daghestan flat rugs were barely recognised as being of any particular value locally. I invited the Director of the Arts Museum in Makhachkala to listen to my talk about their flatweaves at the International Carpet Conference in Vienna in 1987. She sat in shock with her mouth open when 600 people came to listen and as a result, she told the government – several of whom were her kinsmen – that they should start up a museum. They have bought a few hundred flat-weaves since then and I often dropped by to look over their new aquisitions, to help advise which were chemical or natural dyes.

. . . and cosmic-domestic textiles

The exception to the general decline in standards of weaving and designs were the beautiful *soumak* weft-brocade rugs, woven in over twenty villages in the Lezgin region south of the Walls. In neighbouring Ikra and Kabir villages, near the Samur river, women, mothers with babies and girls wove the long-shaggy backed *soumaks* using classical Anatolian designs, whose origin or transfer there was not understood by anyone I asked. They wove from memory, without looking at the cartoons. Anyway, the shaggy side of the *soumak* faced the weaver so she could not see the result of her work while she was weaving. In fact, Kasimkent was the old *soumak* weaving centre and Kabir was known for its piled rugs.

Idayat Ahmedovich Kakhrimanov was a manager of the Ikra manufactory in the old mosque. I followed him home to see what his family's tastes were. It was refreshing to see that over his wife's dressing table there was a painting of a legendary princess, who had just released a bird to her lover across the river where kine were drinking, while in the living room there were painted geometric stars covering the ceiling. There were also some unusual *soumaks* woven by Idyat's wife's mother, and his wife's octagonal piled saddle rug. There were certainly interesting 19th-century examples in their homes, but one of their most popular designs – the star medallion which appeared on a rug in a Crivelli painting, was of 15th-century Turkic origin and the 'darts' between the star medallions were only found on 16th-century Damascus rugs.

Idayat gave me the statistic that "in Ikra the *soumak* factory in the old stone and wooden mosque produced 4000 square metres last year." Mrs Asiat Tarikova Emirkhanovna, the director of the Kabir factory added: "Our weavers produced about two and a half square metres a month and the co-op sold it for 83 roubles a square metre." Asiat also designed the Kabir *soumaks*, assuring me that she was "continuing the tradition." There was a notice board where old designs were pinned up. Many looms were not in use, but that could have been because other women were working in the fields after the harvest. These *soumaks* sold for about 300 roubles in village shops, such as Majalis, and at the Sunday market in Derbent.

I could never make up my mind if the unusual technique of the *chibta* rug was a new invention or part of an ancient tradition. It was made of distinct woven areas of reeds and wool. In a strange yet attractive way, the background of thin reeds was woven in *soumak* technique, whereas the design was in tapestry-woven wool. This must have created tensioning difficulties. The three metre long *chibtas* were only woven in Urma, by Avar women, earlier this century. When I met the retired lady ex-museum director who was responsible for the craft revival she confirmed that the technique was indeed old, but unfortunately I have never seen the old prototype. Still, it was very unlikely that a such a complicated technique could have come from nowhere.

It was frustrating to note the poor quality of the chemical dyes in Daghestan especially the reds, when Derbent was famed for centuries for its exports of dried madder roots for dyeing wool red (see my forthcoming book *Madder Red*).

In Makhachkala market No. 2, I bought wild madder roots, which the old lady vendor said grew in profusion along the banks of the Sulak river. Madder roots are one of the main sources of natural dyes for wool, producing red, brown, violet, pink and orange colours, depending on the mordant in which the wool was stewed before dyeing. The mordant for the unusual dark red wool in *dumi* and *davaghin* rugs was rock salt.

The prosperity of Derbent was partly due to the commercial growing of the madder plant by the Tat, Iranian-speaking Jews who settled on the plain between the sea and the mountains to the south of the ancient city. Madder was planted on top of half-metre castellated chanels to encourage root growth. The leafy plant took about three years to grow strong roots, the thickest of which (c. ½") were then cut off and dried. It was a tasty green plant for sheep and goats, so careful fencing was required. The dried roots could be kept for a long time and were crushed and boiled in water to release their dye. A large order for wine from Hungary in the 18th century led to much of the madder being replaced with vines – a bad business swop.

Even though Daghestan is filled with herds of sheep, their rich, glossy fleeces catching the sunlight, the wool in modern rugs was dull, flat and listless, like the negative version of an advertisement for hair shampoo. The Macmillan *Encyclopaedia Sovietica* records a strange legacy of the Hitler-Stalin pact in Daghestan, that in 1938 Wurtemburg rams were introduced to Daghestan. Gunib sheep crossed with Wurtemburg gave good wool, especially when they grazed at 1000 metres. On a graph where quantity was plotted against thickness of wool, the southern Lezgin wools occupied a narrower range than other non-Daghestan wools, so it was better for twisting than the more mixed thickness of the drier Central Asian wools.

Because of the Party dogma of centralisation, these good local wools were sent to Moscow to be chemically washed and dyed and were returned lifeless, like the dyed bales of wool for *soumaks* which I saw in Ikra in 1986. In 1990 I visited a ghastly craft shop in Makhachkala, where they proudly told me that they were importing Australian wool which had been dyed in Britain. That was dull too.

Outside the state system, however, wools were still handspun in Daghestan. In Koubachi where they knitted socks but did not weave, the old women still used a local design for an arm extension for spinning wool (usually looped over a horizontal broken bottle neck, fixed at the top). It was made of a carved stone base socket to hold the wooden surface-carved painted pole. There were other variants in Dargin villages, and several Turkish-style designs for other spinners throughout Daghestan.

We often passed – or rather were held up by – several large herds of sheep on the road in the morning or evening in the charge of a couple of grizzled shepherds and some boys. The shepherds, who travelled up to 500 kilometres with their state farm flocks to winter in Kizlyar or Khasavyurt, often spoke more languages than the villagers. The village children were devoted to these wild, gentle and free men. They spread the unofficial news as they stopped off from

'Pamiyat Sluzhba' – or a conscript's scrap book covered in Red Army coat felt with bullet binders, plaques of tanks and a fist punching through a wall where each brick represents a day of service. Daghestani soldiers were kept 50km apart from each other because the Russians were afraid they would form dangerous organisations.

village to village. They kept to the old shepherd routes, some of which ignored more recent borders, like the trail over the mountains to Azerbaijan, from Archi to Zakatal. Their sheep were associated with good luck as when they put a ram's pelt on the threshold before the bride entered her groom's house.

In Daghestan, my obvious interest in wool, silk or textiles was a constant delight to the villagers, who had been officially told to ignore their most loved possessions for so long. It was as if the old women had been waiting for me to pass by to laugh at the strange places their carpets ended up in. *Soumaks* were found in guest rooms in Koubachi village as soft sleeping palettes. In Novi Frig near Kasimkent, a striped *palas* flatwoven rug was used outdoors to keep a horticultural cloche warm. A more frequent sight in the past was in Richa, where a woman was tossing grain on to a striped *palas* rug, similar to the Anatolian habit, photographed in 1968 which still survives in some villages – they sort the grain sitting out of doors on the flat-woven rug. In Ginukh, they plaited rope from wool and in Tlyadal' another *palas* was used as the lavatory door. In Akhalchi I found my rarest rug – used for crouching on while milking in the cowshed.

Looking for rugs was an excellent way of getting villagers to show off their homes. Even when there were none, the reason for their absence sometimes threw a vivid light on local history. One spring, we picnicked at dusk on the edge of the moving sand-dune overlooking the rich flood-plains which were once part of Kumtorkala, noted for its flat-woven rugs. Yusuf, our host the mayor, made rippling movements with his hands to show how a recent earthquake – nine on the Richter scale – had moved its devastating way across the landscape. When we returned to see his spacious new house in Korkmascala, I wanted to see his *dumi* flat-weaves and he meekly replied that they had all been sucked into the earth with his old destroyed home.

Another time I also ran out of luck. Jon Thompson my old friend and teacher about textiles, had visited the mosque in Gubden in 1987 and found an extensive collection of old *davaghin* rugs, which he photographed. Unfortunately, he lost his roll of film. I returned there the following year, ready to take more photographs. Close to Gubden, surrounded by menacing grey yellow clouds, at last I saw the distant minaret. A steep climb through the old town up the hill led to a dead-end. A minute old crone, who could have been the double of Alice's White Queen, peeped

The Charodin tightrope walker at Khunzakh wearing a blue and red velvet talismanic gilet to prevent falling off his rope.

through her doorway under a sign saying "War veterans live here" and pointed us up the final climb. But the mosque had disappeared. It was now a building site: except for the minaret, all the old mosque had been demolished to rebuild a glorious carved stone structure, the first new Dargin mosque since the Revolution. The rugs, the watchman said, were distributed among the homes of Gubden to be returned when the mosque re-opened next year. Next to the mosque, in the shed with the mimbar pulpit on its side, there were just two old fragments, on which the site guardian slept.

Then there were the frustrations of searching for a rug which was not valued by the locals on the previous visit but had subsequently disappeared. Temirkhan-the-Businessman had bought a new Vsykhod truck, with a bus body on the back and with Ramazan-the-Librarian and his two daughters we drove off to Koubachi to give my *konak* Ibraghim two red Scottish tartan woollen cloths in exchange for masks, which never appeared. We stopped by the road to buy fruit. A woman was selling melons piled high on a *davaghin* fragment with a unique design based on the sun-burst patterns in Karabagh rugs. She did not want to sell it because she would have to move the melons, but she would ask her mother. When Ramazan returned a week later with a rug to swap, she was no longer there as she had sold all her melons.

There were occasional consolations. I discovered another *davaghin* like my unusual "trees with dancing figures" example, underneath three layers of rugs upstairs in the Botlikh mosque. It, too, inexplicably had main borders of differing widths on each side which were only found in Daghestan on this particular design. Only once was it possible to arrange a few days free to go carpet hunting for the museum with Kamil from Khunzakh. In Tanusi village, there was one *dumi* and one half *davaghin* with natural dyes. Further along that road in Atsal-Lukh village there were none. But next door, in Akhalchi, I found an exciting half *davaghin* with a 12th-century Seljuk-style border, its centre filled with diagonal palmettes with no colour repeats. It was wet and partly covered in mud and cow dung. Next day we went to Butsarah up high in a parallel valley in the direction of Gotsatl'. One beautiful *dumi* had been earmarked as a gift to the mosque by the old woman owner. But we found another. Yet another with a large cross design had a faded chemical pink. In Oboda there was a small flatweave with a dramatic new design like a 17th-century Turkish village leopard skin rug, but with that same pink. Night fell and it got too dark to see the rugs by yellow lightbulb and we had to return.

Detail of masked horsemen on an 18th-century Kaitag embroidery.

· 9 ·

Capes, masks & costumes

Costume is a form of display or disguise, or sometimes both, even when its design lies outside the control of the people who wear it, such as football gear or prison or army uniform. People use costume both to conceal their individuality and to stress it, and so it becomes a measure of their identity. In Daghestan, and also in the USSR, costume was seldom purely functional. The cut, the cloth, or the patterning and other embellishments picked out sexual status, nationality and class. Dressing-up is one of the few non-practical and pleasurable human activities that starts at birth, but continues through puberty and adult life.

This is not the case for children's games, where their playtime roles are later suppressed or redirected to more severe adult activities. Soviet-thinking academics have dismissed children's games as being the dying shivers of a former civilisation, but I follow the Jesuit regard for children's education and think that their games are a conduit for passing cultural values from generation to generation. For Daghestanis, in addition to the influence of games on childhood and costume throughout life, the felt mask and cape were symbols for the time of manhood – or was it a performance where, unlike the emperor's clothes, when reality intruded, the fantasy survived?

Even recently, when as much as a third of the population of Daghestan has moved into urban life, women seldom left their villages and so retained many of their traditional ethnic styles of dress, while men travelled more and so dressed uniformly. However, when writing the captions for the costumes in the 'Daghestan Today' exhibition at the Aga Khan's Zamana Gallery in London, my colleagues at the Kraevedcheskii Museum in Makhachkala had debates as to which of the women's clothes on show really belonged to which ethnic groups.

In the Daghestan Academy of Science's private study film 'Women's Traditional Costume in Daghestan' (1983), while the original dresses came from dowry boxes in the village houses, some were admitted to have been made up of different fragments – so little had survived. The Kumyk plainswomen's costume, at least, was easier to identify than the mountain-dwellers' dresses and pants.

Lavish costume jewellery was an essential complement to costume in all

Daghestan, and was usually made by local silversmiths. Women wore a lot of jewellery, as well as their golden front teeth, flashing as they smiled. An extensive variety of rings, bracelets, earrings and belts were made of silver, niello, granulated or gilt, and set with coral, other semi-precious stones, glass or paste. Necklaces, pendants, bibs and aprons were also made of medallions and coins. In Balkhar, the front of a dress was almost entirely covered in coins, medallions and ornamental figures and, in old film footage, there was a Lak wedding-dress, completely covered in silver coins.

Cataloguing the jewellery also posed problems. For commercial reasons, over the centuries, centres like Koubachi and the Lak Kazikumukh had produced jewellery for the other ethnic groups of Daghestan in their respective styles. There has been a continuing tradition of silversmiths work especially in Koubachi and Gotsatl' villages. Much decoration was niello, which is rarely made successfully in Europe. Today this delicate work was usually done by women. A mixture of exact proportions of powdered silver and other metals was placed into an area of hollowed-out silver and covered with a greasy flax to prevent oxidization. The object was then rapidly turned over a gentle yellow flame to fuse the amalgam to the base. It was difficult to get an unpitted finish to the niello, which showed up clearly when the surface was burnished.

ào

Mountain women wore a long dress, where the fullness was often tucked into a bodice. Under the dress, they often wore long pants which came down to their feet. Some of the pants were baggy and others tight-fitting at the calves, almost like men's. In the mountain villages the pants were narrow. Around the waist, they wore either a woven sash or leather belt decorated with coins or medallions. In some villages women wore an overdress on top of their long tunic. Some were open down the front, with wide sleeves stitched to the elbow and then loose to the wrist; others were open only at the bodice, with sleeves sewn down to the wrist; while the more extravagant had tunic and overdress in different silks and decoration down the front, around the hem and the sleeves of metallic golden thread lace or embroidery. The same style of garments were used in winter, but made of darker fabrics and quilted for warmth.

Last century, patterned Russian silk brocades were fashionable, unlike today's cheap synthetics. Bright colours were popular, with black for mourning. The main differences in dress were between the plains or southern women, who wore two layers of dress, and the northern or high-mountain women, who wore trousers under their dress and tunic, probably because it was colder. Sparkling Kumyk women wore silk dresses edged in black lace, with military-style breast buttons and braid, in the French fashion, crowned with a white lace headscarf, garnished with silver gilt belts. Lezgins dressed in over- and under-tunics, with a headscarf and jewellery from Koubachi in Lezgin style. The Lak women wore an over-dress with short sleeves, an under-dress open down the front with long sleeves, an optional expensive St Petersburg headscarf, and a gilt pectoral and belt. Avar women were clothed in trousers under two long dresses, the outer with shorter sleeves. Their typical adornment was a breast brooch of silver and niello, with silver rouble pendants and headscarf and under-scarf. Archi and Bezhta women wore trousers too and the latter still wore their skirts tucked inside their belts. Dargin women favoured white head-scarves and sometimes all-white clothes.

Young girls show their hair in public – the longer, the more beautiful – while older girls and married women even today hid theirs in a snood (see page 104) or under a head covering. The design and cut of snoods varied greatly from nationality to nationality. An Avar woman in traditional costume walking alone near Sovietskoye would not take off her green headscarf to show her head jewellery, saying that her husband would not approve. They also used the back flap of a headress as a sunshield for their eyes. Another woman in stunning Avar traditional dress hid her face at Sovietskoye market amid cackles, as she did not wish to be photographed. Why was she so shy if she was wearing such noticable clothes and jewellery? She was probably merely showing off to her community that her husband was a well-off and traditional man.

Ethnic styles also abounded in the head-dresses of highland women. There were several differing close-fitting caps adorned with silver jewellery. Some head-dresses were of crown-like shapes, some were four-cornered, while the most striking was the Alice's Red Queen hat, padded with wool from Andi and Botlikh. Most archaic, with its long braided sides and a padded spherical hat, the Ginukh model appeared to derive from the ancient Cretan, as did their bull-dancing. But nature was best. Near Koubachi, two girls went to the trees to pick mistletoe, which they wove into their hair as a festive decoration. The head-dresses were covered by kerchiefs, scarves or long lengths of fine fabric. They were lavishly decorated with coins, beads or fine gold braid across the forehead, or silver niello discs on the temples. In Koubachi, Ibraghim-my-Konak's wife instantly let me know which design she preferred of the Scottish tartan shawls I had brought. It was the most colourful.

Outer garments varied with the climate. There were long sheepskin cloaks with false sleeves for carrying things, waist-length capes as well as short padded and quilted jackets. Earlier this century, among the Kvarshin, a housewife had only to mention to relatives and friends that she had invited a master cutter to cut out a new *shuba* sheep-skin overcoat and a dozen women would gather in her house that evening to help sew the garment. During the party, the hostess served some light refreshments and the *shuba* was finished. Only the cutter was recompensed. Many designs of *shuba* were still to be found in homes. I was given one, which was heavy and unfortunately tasty for the British lower-altitude moth.

Footwear was mainly homemade. For indoors there were colourful knitted socks and stockings, soft shoes and slippers in Moroccan style, and embroidered felt slippers. For the mud and the wet outdoors, women wore felt quilted boots and leather over-shoes. Contemporary women's boots from Archi

Uslipat Abakarova, at over 70, a Bagulaal Avar from Kapucha. She was the greatest interpreter of Daghestani dance, flanked by pupils in different Avar costumes. She danced right up to her death. (Photo: Alla Ulanova)

Bezhta grandmother and granddaughter.

Patimat Magomedkhan wearing the Archi traditional costume still worn by women working in the fields.

village had felt uppers, faced with leather. The felt sides and sole were reinforced by stitching in close lines, looking like a corduroy. The felt joins were covered with coloured wool, couched with metal-wrapped threads. Archaic upward-pointed toes prevented splashing with mud from the unpaved roads during the long rainy weather. In Bezhta knitted calf-length socks with felt soles were worn outdoors. Traditional footwear has been largely replaced, but some survived in the villages.

Well into the 1900s, clothing in Daghestan was made from cloth woven locally in villages. There was an old-established spinning and weaving trade, mentioned by medieval Arab and Turkish writers. Sheep farming developed to keep up with demand. Autumn wool was considered the best and plucked out by hand. The highest quality was camel wool, imported from Transcaucasia to the south and Central Asia to the north east. Cotton from the plains was in good supply and there were also silk centres there, such as Gubden, which still looks prosperous. Velvet, brocade, satin, taffeta and muslin came from Europe and the East. In addition, gilt, silver and silk threads from India, China, Iran and Central Asia were used for intricate embroidery of richer garments. Derbent was the market centre from at least the twelfth century, and their boast was still that again "in Derbent a man can buy anything."

❧

Moscow dogmatism exaggerated the role of the Daghestani class structure. Sovietised authors wrote that "before the Revolution, the average highlander had a scanty wardrobe. In a poor family, a man might have only one change of clothes and often a father and son had to share one smart outfit to attend public functions. Often, young girls going to a wedding had to borrow a scarf or dress from a relative or friend and jewellery, even from their own village, was beyond their reach." This was perhaps true only after the several wars. "During the Civil War, women had resorted to spinning, weaving and making quilted jackets, footwear, and trousers mainly to clothe their men, but also themselves. The Soviet Government understood their hardship, and as soon as Daghestan became an Autonomous Republic in 1921, after the victory of the Red Army, they began sending in supplies. But manufactured clothing arrived slowly and by 1927 only half the children had winter coats and 35 per cent of women and nine per cent of men had none."*

Soviet-induced poverty assisted the transition to contemporary clothing which was quicker and easier for men where war, revolution and mobilisation forced changes. But it was slower for women, who married within their remote community and seldom left it, even till 1931. The Civil War and the war aginst the Red Army caused great destruction, followed by economic breakdown,

* Ethnographer and costume specialist S. Sh. Gadjieva, quoted in *Contemporary Culture and Life of People in Daghestan.*

which cut off most supplies, including textiles. Men often wore their military breeches, kept from service. Today, men wore track-suits or jackets – Bezhta village men pull back their jacket collars over their shoulders when feeling hot – and trousers. Children wore old-style Russian school clothes or tracksuits for boys, while in the villages women went about in simplified traditional dress. Outside Koubachi, there was a changing-hut where the bus stopped, going to or coming from Derbent, where women changed from traditional to modern dress. Family groups were confusingly dressed both in traditional and Soviet-style dress, like the people I saw in Bezhta.

As herdsmen, traders or fighters, much of men's lives were spent moving about, so all over Daghestan men's clothes had become uniform by the eighteenth century. They wore a tunic-like shirt and full plain trousers. Over the shirt, a quilted waisted jacket, the *beshmet*, with long sleeves and a narrow stiff collar was embroidered on the breast- and side-pockets. The jacket flared at the knee, shaped by wedges sewn in below the waist with a three metre hem. This jacket was considered a light outer garment which a highlander could wear at home, out on the street or to work in the fields, and was made from rough homespun to satin, taffeta, or silk.

For social occasions, in public or simply in cold weather, over this jacket men wore the all-Caucasian *cherkess* or Circassian coat, made mainly from homespun materials. It was similar to the jacket but wider and longer – both below the knees and with wide sleeves, of finger tip length, to be turned up for convenience – with a V-neckline and two breast-pockets, each sewn into small sections for a banderole. The hem, sleeves and pockets were finished off with a braid of silk and golden thread.

An important outer garment was the sheepskin *shuba* which in winter was worn over the *beshmet* and sometimes even over the *cherkess*. The style was like the women's, only the sleeves and the coats were longer. The coats varied according to the climate and the man's wealth – the finer were of white lamb-skin or furs from Russia.

A hat was essential to the identity of the Daghestan mountain man. He would gladly give away anything that was his, except his hat or his *kinjal* dagger. I was told not to offer to buy men's hats, when I caught a glimpse of an elongated bell shaped black felt shepherd's hat, carried upside down, filled with food, moving along the road to Aguali. *Karakul* pelts were from aborted lambs and so the wool was soft, full of shiny lanolin and tightly curled. Two *karakul* hats cost 400 and 300 roubles in Makhachkala market Number Two, because the golden colour was rarer than the silver. Modern fashion was either a Russian brushed felt hat, a local raked trilby or most popular – the *aerodrom*. This distinctive wide-peaked cap has become the modern equivalent of the Ottoman fez (which until recently was banned in Turkey to discourage Ottoman revivalism), as the man's hat in Daghestan and some other Caucasian republics. When I wore one in Moscow, people stared.

To go with his hat, the older man would treasure his walking-stick, of cornel

A long false-sleeved 'tsuba' sheepskin coat in Batlaich vilage.

or apricot wood decorated with flat metal discs and ribbon, which was clipped and hammered into the shaft, invented in Untsukul late last century. Nowadays men villagers wear rubber boots or army boots, but until the 1950s it was possible to see archaic Scythian-style over-shoes with upturned-toes or short-haired leather moccasins, which were both worn with leather gaiters.

Before the Soviets came, when the Daghestan highlander went looking for loot or to war, he wore his *djigit* dress. The distant glimpse of a black cape on horseback must have induced the same terror as the fluttering pennant of a Japanese samurai. The *djigit* wore his armoury. His hand rested lightly on his *kinjal* dagger and sheath, usually decorated with silver gilt and niello. Ocassionally the dagger had a carved ivory hilt and the sheath was damascened in gold with carved ivory plaques. The sheath hung from a narrow leather belt decorated with niello and silver studs or slides, like medieval European belts. On the other side hung his sword, the *shashka* in its sheath. An expensive example would have a steel blade damascened in gold and a leather-covered sheath with silver gilt and niello mounts. His firepower was a pair of exotic flintlock pistols and a miquelet rifle (named after its North African lock mechanism, of Spanish origin – showing how international the arms trade was), its lock damascened in gold, with silver gilt and niello mounts. The more important the man, the richer his accoutrements. Under his weapons, his black wool-cloth *cherkess* coat with a woollen cloth *bashlik* hood, worn in cold weather, were standard dress for over two hundred years until the 1930s. The 16 cigar-shaped pockets across the chest were filled with decorative *gazeri*, or charges from a bandoleer, wood tubes with silver and niello caps. Always ready to ride, he wore black breeches, narrowing at the knees, kept tight with a loop under the instep, covered with his tall black soft leather boots, which would rest on stirrups of iron, damascened in gold. His saddle was also decorated, the woollen-cloth cover embroidered with laid and couched gilt-wrapped thread. They often, however, spurned stirrups and rode bareback.

Male and female participants in the Khunzakh and Shamilkala festivals certainly enjoyed dressing up in traditional costume. The men and boys always dressed as *djigits*, and the important ones as Shamil or Haji-Murat. In another festival at Akhti, a torch parade started the spring festivities at dusk. We, the 'important' people, sat on the podium under the statue of Lenin and a slogan, saying "the Party is the mind, honour and conscience of our epoque." In front of a giant cardboard toothed-wheel, representing the absence of industry, the white-robed queen of the festival recited a Lezgin poem to the crowd while the organiser sat to one side, resplendent in his white *bourka*. A husband and wife in costume, performed an arguing dance, followed by a satirical song from a horned clown and girls in long pink dresses, playing tambourines. The finale was a costume pastiche of all Soviet nations, with the Ukranian, as usual – so I was told – playing the fool.

Costume was also a feature of a Caucasian 'national' identity at all the great circuses, as in Odessa. "Riding bare-back at the gallop, the four famous

Caucasians – the Tuganov brothers – in tight blue *cherkess* coats, scarlet hoods blazing from their shoulders, their cocked hats shot with gold. Rifles were slung over their backs and daggers jangled in their belts. To piercing whistles, one danced the *lezginka* on the back of his horse, another did flips in the air, the third spun on his saddle, the fourth lunged from side to side of his horse. Now all four leapt on to one horse – one around its neck, another under its belly, two on its flanks, next to the flashing hooves. They suddenly let go, but hung by their feet, and then they started shooting." Back in Daghestan, during festivities, at night, all men who had firearms went out shooting to frighten off evil spirits. My host started shooting once when I was at supper in Untsukul. I didn't know what was going on.

As soon as they could walk, the children began role-playing games, encouraged by the lullabies which sent them to sleep. The games which I saw were segregated, with the boys playing outdoors while the girls stayed at home with their mothers or started working quite young. Boys enjoyed fighting, dancing, playing music and singing, while girls played brides and also danced and sang. They seemed very unregimented and Daghestan children exhibited a healthy tendency towards anarchy with impossible reserves of energy. This contrasted with what was written about children's games like 'little *siskin*, the song-bird', 'cranes', 'blind bear' or 'blind-man's-buff', 'cock fight', 'geese & swans' and 'cat & mouse' which were allegedly thought by the Lezgins, for one, to help develop mental and physical curiosity, agility and speed.

I was told that it was not describing Soviet Pioneer youth-camp ideals but local traditions when they wrote that: "Games played by adolescents were often aimed at developing courage, stamina and team spirit, submitting to collective rather than personal interests, which stimulated the will to win. At the same time, roughness and disrespect for the opposition was not allowed."* I was assured that the universal games, such as tag, hide and seek and the more complicated 'horse', were old Daghestani and not recent Soviet games.

The Pioneers were founded in 1922 as a Communist children's movement, with the slogan "Always ready!" on the lips of the millions of seven- to 15-year-olds who were said to go to camp freely every summer. The youngest, who were most receptive to indoctrination, joined the junior part of the organisation, called the 'Octobrists', after the month of the 1917 Russian Revolution (perhaps a political pun on the Decembrists). In Daghestan, there were scruffy-looking Pioneer camps near many of the chief regional towns. They were the hatching grounds, where one in ten were picked as youth leaders for the Komsomol – the Union of Communist Youth – and on to the higher echelons of the Communist movement. It was odd that Soviet Youth leaders were often rather old.

These camps encouraged Soviet team games. However, variations of tag

---

* M. Z. Magomedov, a local sports historian writing about 'Popular games of the Lezgi as a method of educating the young', in *Community Life of Daghestani People: 19th to Early 20th centuries*.

The Daghestan Boys' National Dance Group in full 'djigit' costume at the First Avar Festival in July 1989, in Khunzakh. They dance on toe-point without blocks.

were played all over Daghestan. The world-wide standard game was: the players drew lots to decide who was 'it'. 'It' counted to an agreed number and then tried to touch another player as he ran away. When he succeeded, they changed places. Variations included that a player couldn't be tagged if he flung himself on the ground, with outstretched legs and hands touching his toes or if he froze on one leg, holding the other with both hands behind his back. Also there were 'safe' places such as a tree, stone or circle, drawn on the ground. In a noisier tag, girls ran around two 'its' in the middle – one girl was sitting while the other stood, with one hand on the sitter's head. With her other free hand, she tried to protect the seated girl from being clouted by tagging the attacker, who then had to sit with her own protector at her side.

Tag was also played by throwing a ball to hit the victim, as in *tochka-tochka* or 'stop!'. Half a dozen players stood around the one who threw a ball in the air and called out the name of whoever had to catch it, who in turn had to throw it at one of the rest as they ran away. But, if he caught it, he shouted "stop!" and everyone had to freeze, whereupon he calmly aimed at the closest, who was then out. Catching the ball allowed him to choose to throw the ball up again and call out the name of someone who was running away to avoid the ball and who then lost a point if he couldn't get back in time to catch it. 'Wolf is coming' was another old version of tag. On a flat surface, a path was marked about a metre wide, with zig-zags. Inside the corridor were two wolves guarding it. The rest of the players were hares who had to jump over the corridor. If a hare was touched by a wolf, he was out. There were popular tag board games too, including 'wolf and goat' in Rutul and Tsakhur regions and 'bear and sheep' elsewhere.

Hide and seek was usually played at dusk by boys and girls, but more often only boys. One stood blindfolded at a tree or a wall, counting to some agreed number, while others hid – behind houses, heaps of clothing, or in chests. Some even disguised themselves as women and mingled in with them. When the hunter spotted a player, he called out his name. If he was right, they both ran back to base. When he had found all the players, he changed places with the first player whom he had beaten racing.

The following games seemed more suited to the mountain village mentality. 'Horse' was an old Azerbaijan game and spread to several villages in the southern Akhti region, such as Mikrakh, Usukhyaii and Lutkun. It was also played in Cork in Ireland. Some 20 players divided into two teams. They formed two circles about ten metres apart. A player from one team threw a ball high into the other circle. If an opponent caught it, he got a point, otherwise, the thrower got one. When a player had five points, he chose a 'horse' from the other side and rode him piggy-back to his own circle, where he continued playing mounted. The aim was to turn all the opposition into 'horses'. But, so that a 'horse' had a chance, there was an extra rule. If a 'horse' caught a ball, which was difficult, as his rider was clearly higher up and his hands were free, then he changed places and rode him back to his own team. A cunning move was to choose a 'horse', who had already scored three points or was the strongest to weaken the opposition. In Bezhta, three little girls played a simplified version – one was the 'donkey', one the 'rider', while the third ran up to push her off and take her place.

A popular game in Tabassaran was 'blow the fire', played late at night, during the spring celebrations. A large threaded needle was stuck into the ceiling beam. The long twine was knotted to another needle, on which a lump of hot coal was spiked. The players sat on the floor in a circle facing the swinging hot coal. They had to blow to keep it coming in their direction, but were not allowed to dodge it or they were out. When the coal cooled, it was replaced by a new hot one. This game may have originated from a Zoroastrian ritual where the magic powers of fire included fertility, purification and protection.

Every village had a regular place for relaxation, music and dance. While men showed off their skills on horseback, girls often played games. But occasionally, in accounts of Soviet scholars, there are glimpses of something quite different. "During spring celebrations in Tabassaran, all sorts of games, tricks and jokes were accepted as fun. Some games of youths were frankly erotic in meaning."

More than just playing 'brides', which I saw, weddings were re-enacted in detail by teenagers as a winter game, at least until recently. The Khvarshin and

Magomedkhan Magomedkhanov and his sister Patimat, and her son Muheddin sheltering under his 'bourka', looking towards the pass to Azerbaijan uphill from Archi.

Tindi had four Fridays set aside for pure entertainment popularly called the 'Middle of Something'. There was a day for teenagers. On the second Friday of the mid-winter month, separate parties were organised for youths and girls. Occasionally, with the mother's permission, some youths were admitted to the girls' dinner, where a favourite game was re-enacting a wedding, where even the bride's dress had been prepared in advance.

During the winter there were similar performances of wedding rituals with stuffed-cloth dolls. Their faces were painted and they were precisely dressed. The boys sometimes also carved wooden marionettes, which could also dance to the music. The doll was sometimes human. The Avars from Kazbekskii rayon liked a giant bride mummer, entirely covered in a white cloth, with a silver head-band. Underneath, the mummer either held a round dish or put it on top of a ewer on his head. Puppets played other characters, for example in rain ceremonies. At New Year, youngsters would make the rounds with songs of praise to Allah and Spring, carrying a small tree (or large branch) on which to hang presents decorated with ribbons. The tree was sometimes topped (in Kara-Shura) with a carved wooden bird whose head could be nodded by a string in sarcastic disapproval of mean gifts.

Long ago men devised ways of dressing themselves as totems of macho or animal cults, perhaps in competition with the overwhelming presence of the mountains. Treasured felts were frequently mentioned in the ancient epics about Nart giants, which spread from Iran to Ossetia, and then south to Daghestan, where Narts only appeared in folk-tales. The following two occurences are typical. In the first story the two wives of a giant Nart are working on a *nymat* (Iron* for 'felt') for their husband, which was made of a hundred fleeces – compared with six fleeces for a real man. In the second, a more grisly furry coat of the Nart epic hero Soslan Kartsa was made of the beard-skins of the men whom he had slain. Two traditional felts were designed for display and disguise – the *bourka* cape and the ritual mask. They had nothing whatever to do with Communism, instead they were derived from pre-Islamic pagan ritual dress.

The *bourka* is a shaggy full-length cape with wide square shoulders, the traditional all-purpose mountaineer's garment – a symbol of Daghestan. Even today, men, like their ancestors, asked to be photographed in their *bourka* and *papakha* sheep-skin hat. In the second century AD, Ptolemy recorded that the Alans, a tribe which occupied the Caucasus, wore black woolly cloaks. The next mention was in the seventh century, when Movses Khorenats'i (uncorroborated by Faustus of Byzantium [Book III:vii], whom he usually plagiarised), noted that "the giant leader of a savage group of Caucasian mountain-men, invading Armenia from the north-east, was covered in spear-proof felt armour," which reminded me of a legendary Nart.

Shamil's armed followers demonstrated that the cape was also reasonably shotproof. A good *bourka* always stood up on its own. The black capes could still be seen folded, tied to the saddle of a shepherd's horse, or sheltering goods or lambs in their camps, or on a mountain village bed. The three-inch-long hairs stopped water gathering and penetrating the felt, so a mountain-man could roll up in his *bourka* and sleep in the open, as I once tried on a chilly verandah in Untsukul.

The felt cape was endowed with wide-ranging significance and was almost accorded the status of a supernatural relative. White *bourkas* were used for festive wear, with black for everyday. A *bourka* was considered the highest present, expressing kinship. Standing under the *bourka* with someone was a further sign of kinship and protection. They were only made full-sized, for men not boys. Magomedkhan once posed for a picture with his little nephew, whose head was looking out from the *bourka*, where he was completely safe, like Oscar's father in 'The Tin Drum', hiding under his future mother's skirts.

In disputes, the felt also had its role in a blood-feud. When men fought a duel with *kinjals* or daggers, they stood on a couple of capes and the one who was

---

* One of the two Ossete dialects.

forced off lost. The final job of the black *bourka* was as a cover for the shrouded corpse – male or female – when it was carried on a stretcher to the grave.

To stop a knife fight, a friend would put a *bourka* between the fighters. The cape similarly appeared in folklore as a substitute for the hero as victim, enabling him to escape. Once there lived a hunter. Before he went off hunting, he said to his wife: "Do you see that fire? Don't throw any raw liver on it!" His wife obeyed him, but after a while she thought: "What will happen if I do?" So she threw it on and the fire hissed and went out. "Aaah," she thought, "so that's why my husband told me not to." As there were no matches in those days, she left her house and looked far and wide for another fire to rekindle her own, and at last she saw a distant light. She went up to it and there stood the one-eyed cyclops demon – the *valuch-tush*. She was afraid and wanted to run away, but he stopped her and took her into his cave, and hospitably cooked some meat for her. While she was too frightened to eat, he ate his meal and fell asleep across the entrance, so she could not escape.

Possibly the earliest representations of the 'bourka', a square-shouldered hairy felt cape, taken from S. A. Pletneva ('Kazary', Moscow NAUKA, 1986), as a Khazar idol featuring a man in a 'bourka' – stone figurine in the State Hermitage Museum, St Petersburg. Pletneva calls this an "idol wearing a 'bourka'." Movses Khorenats'i, the seventh-century historian of the Armenians, mentions a raid by mountain men whose leader wears spear-proof felt armour (tr. R.W. Thompson, Harvard, 1978, p262, 'History of the Armenians', III:9).

In the meantime, her husband returned to find his fire out and his wife gone, so he set off to find her. He reached the cave and saw the demon dozing and, inside, his wife. He signalled her to come out and when she saw that it was her husband, she became brave enough to step over the demon and run off. When they returned home, the hunter ws angry with her, saying: "You got us into trouble, and now the *valuch-tush* will return for sure and get us both." But she replied: "Listen, let's close the shutters on the window – let's get a dog." The husband smiled and asked: "What are shutters or dogs compared to a *valuch-tush*?" All the same, he put up a tree-trunk in his yard, with a sabre sticking out from it, point-first, and covered them with his wide-shouldered *bourka*. He hid in a nearby tree with his gun, waiting for the cyclops to come.

And indeed, night brought the demon. He took the cape for the man, jumped on it and stabbed himself instead. Next, the hunter shot him and wounded him again, as he ran off. The following day, the tracker set off to see what had become of the demon. He found the *valuch-tush* dead in his cave, and a one-eyed child and a woman. He asked the woman: "Who on earth are you?" She replied: "I'm just a woman – five years ago I was taken off by the demon, and we had a child." The hunter killed the child, as it was cursed with one eye, and took the woman back to her village where her relatives welcomed her home.

I had been told that the craft of making *bourkas* had died out. It had been more like attempted murder. But in spite of the Stalinist Party prohibition of all private production from 1929, I accidentally found that *bourkas* were still made by a few families in Gagatl village, next to Andi. The 19-year-old girl I met took a day to make a cape which sold for 90-110 roubles. But a complete lined and embroidered luxury model sells for 300. I told her to put up the price.

The dust from the wool made it unpleasant work, usually during winter when the village was snowed up. Four kilograms of wool was used in a garment. The wool was first carded by hand to clean off the brambles and droppings, using a vertical steel spiked comb, mounted on a wooden triangle. The natural coloured dark brown-black wool was then teased out with a gut-stringed bow. The wool was laid out to shape on a large coarse black blanket, called *palars*, by 4-6 women who beat it crouched over on their knees with the backs of their forearms and elbows at a kind of party where rhythmic songs were sung accompanied by the drums, *pandur* and balalaika (I have tape-recordings of felt-making songs).

The felt was repeatedly wetted and rolled on a two by one metre bumpy wattle frame, called *ch'um*. Beside the storage chest where the willow-bark for dyeing was kept, her grandmother stirred the black dye vat where a couple of bourkas were simmering overnight, on the cow-dung fire, directly supplied by the cows who spent the winter in the adjoining byre. Each *bourka* uses up 2kg of dye and 100g of ferrum sulphate mordant, which they buy in plastic one kilo bags. The felt was next washed in a pool at the edge of the village. It was then brought back home and shaken out by two women on the rolled-earth verandah and laid out to dry. A fistful of stiff linen stems was used to brush out the hair on the *bourka*. Their calf was sniffing at a packet of cow-bone glue powder, which was dissolved in water and stippled over the cape, to make sure the long hairs did not work loose.

The roofs and clothes-lines were covered in drying felts. The Gagatl *bourkas* have rounded shoulders, popular in north Daghestan, unlike the pointed shouldered version made by the factory which they call *kabardin* – I have seen both worn. Gagatl *bourkas* really did stand up on their own. Afterwards, home-made capes were often embroidered on the inside, at the bottom.

It was similar among the neighbouring Kvarshin, a people one thousand strong, who were transported down the mountains, north to Vedeno in 1944 (see the Ginukh genocide, page 254). Sheep-shearing took place twice a year,

North Caucasian mounted masked hunting society, note the raised Mauser pistol. The horned mask is found on both sides of the Great Caucasian Mountains – one more example of a common Mountain (as opposed to Plains) culture.
(From E.N. Studenetskaya's 'Maski Narodov Severnogo Kavkaza').

producing spring wool and better quality autumn wool. Both wools were used to make a felt hairy woollen blanket, *tsakh'a ala*. I saw one of these in Archi, which looked like an unstitched cape. Making a blanket or felt was communal women's work, for the autumn wool had to be combed, rolled by hand, washed and spread out to dry. The barter for one such blanket was a cow in calf. A specialist helped prepare the finest cloth, called *enu*, which, it was said, could pass through a ring, and extra men's help was needed for the drying.

Bourkas were reputed to have first been made in Andi, where I met the last old woman who knew the secret of making an especially silky long-haired cape. But today, except for Gagatl, they were made by women at the factory in Rakhata, an Avar village, near Botlikh, not far from Andi. The male technical director believed his method was traditional, except that they used machine-carded short wool, but there were further differences from the home method. Long white autumn wool was collected from Akvakh, Gumbet, Tsumada and Botlikh flocks. After the long wool was traditionally hand-carded, it was taken to the felting room. The long wool was first teased with a strung bow and laid in the shape of a cope, on a linen cloth, on the floor, where it was wetted. A second layer of short wool was laid on top, wetted, and then rolled up by two women workers. For half an hour they repeatedly lifted the roll onto the table, unrolled it, combed the long hairs, wetted, re-rolled and pounded it on the floor. It was hard physical work.

Then the felt was dyed black in traditional boiled willow-bark, from the forests of Chechenia to the north. Afterwards, the cope was immersed in a water bath outdoors, taken out after a few minutes and held, dripping, by a ring of women, who beat it with sticks. The felt was laid on the ground where the hair was steel-wire brushed. It was then dried, sprinkled with cowgum for waterproofing, and further dried in the yard. The felt became a *bourka* when the shoulders were stitched into a square shape. Donkeys took the folded capes for a last wash in the river and they were finally dried outdoors. As a finish, grey cloth linings were machined-in and black leather piping and two small red triangular tabs were sewn on the lapels. The whole process took about a day and a half.

They hoped to make 16,000 *bourkas* (and *arbabash* felt carpets) a year, which were all bought locally, retailing in Daghestan for up to 300 roubles. One family might own two or three. The official average monthly wage was 150 roubles. The hairy felt was also cut up for linings for the inside of boots for Siberia made in Kuban. Also pilots wear *unty* gaiters with fur on the outside and felt on the inside.

à.

With the fear-inspiring uniforms of power underlining the totalitarian Soviet state, the mere existence of independent societies was forbidden, let alone the secrecy implicit in the masked activities in Daghestan. Nevertheless in the 1970s, one scholar had the courage to write about the North Caucasus that: "Masks are known to everyone – they are worn in festive perfor-mances, New Year carnivals and street

'Rider' mask from Koubachi village, dated 1986, made from Red Army greatcoat felt with white star (Socialist?) and tin nose and beard, reminiscent of Qajar Persian iron mask armour.

processions. But masks have not always been related to joyous occasions. Sorcerers, as resurrected ancestors wore masks to terrify, and warriors wore masks to protect their faces and scare the enemy. But mostly masks were used in rites to ensure fertility of the land, living creatures and man. And even if, in reality, the mask did not possess the magic powers invested in it by the believer, it still created enjoyment, happiness and hope."*

* The late Dr E. N. Studenetskaya, writing in her fascinating illustrated booklet on masks 'Maski Narodov Severnogo Kavkaza' (Leningrad, 1980). The study, entitled *Prospekt*, is frustratingly brief, which is ironic because she had written massive volumes of valuable unpublished material about all the Caucasian objects in the extensive collections of the St Petersburg Ethnographic Museum.

But Caucasian masks were virtually unknown, so I tried to track them down. I was first alerted by the astonishing photographs in E. Schilling's book about Koubachi. During subsequent visits, I photographed three masks there, one was dated 1986, and I have been kindly given three more, including ones from Gapshima and Khudut. I was shown the eight (and a hobby-horse), which had been collected by Schilling from 1925 to 1944 and eight more from the rest of the North Caucasus in the Leningrad Ethnographic museum. A photograph of a posse of seven masked Kabardian horsemen – two brandishing Mauser pistols, two more pictures of groups of horned masked men with a ram, from Ikalto in Georgia and others of different bear mask and goat mask festivals gave an impressive idea of their use.

'Cruel Khan' with 'aksakal' mask – Koubachi village.

A 14th-century carved stone relief in a wall in Koubachi seemed to portray a man with a mythical *simurgh* bird mask and a serpent wrapped around his waist, running on bird-clawed feet. I have seen six iron masks of male faces with moustaches and beards, wearing helmets, usually with plumes. The oldest (now in the State Hermitage Museum in Leningrad), from the tenth century, was found in the southern Russian steppes. The other steel masks were dated from the 12th (in the Royal Armouries, Moscow), 16th (in the Daghestan Kraevedcheski Museum, Makhachkala), to the 18th centuries (in the Tower of London).[*]

These examples can only represent a fraction of the tradition which was widespread in the mountains of the North Caucasus. For example, there exists

[*] Other masks: S. A. Luguev, of the Daghestan Academy, suggested photos of Shaitli masks from Yuri Karpov of the Leningrad Ethnographic Institute; Paruk Debirov's drawings of Itsari devil mask, goat mask, goat rider and Itsari wedding mask dance horseman (in the author's archive); Wagidat Shamadaeva's list of Daghestan masks and drawing of the tall bride; in Magomedkhan's wife Rasiat's Khudut village, Dargin, there is also a sack mask that I have not seen.

Masked scarecrow from Kamna near Chokh, on the Avar-Koisu river.

a Dargin mask which is almost identical to two others from Karachai, far over the mountains to the north-west.

As felt helmet masks survived in the same village, Koubachi, where the steel helmet masks were made, they seemed to be related to the tradition of 'scare armour'. There were other more ancient local precedents. An early example was Hercules' terrifying lion-head helmet, which also had the magical effect of transferring the power of the lion to the wearer. He was a legendary father of the Scyths, whose arrowheads have been found widely in Daghestan. Rustam, the hero of the Iranian legends, also wore the same head-dress, and the Sassanian Persians ruled Derbent until the Arab invasions during the seventh century. The plumed masks possibly also derived from an ancient re-enactment of the Iranian Zoroastrian creation myth. An ancient Daghestan bronze in the Moscow Oriental museum also had a broken plume or plant growing out of the top of the two-sided head of a male and female body. These attributes were confirmed in the Zoroastrian scripture account of the creation.*

Up to the present, in Koubachi, the nearby Itsari and Tsunda (the latter used masks, but the ceremonies are not yet known) villages, on the second afternoon of the three day wedding, young male friends of the groom interrupted the feasting with a ritual performance in masks and costumes. The Cruel Khan (or Shah) kidnapped the Bride – played by a boy – who was rescued by the Rider after a battle in the presence of the *Shaitan* (Devil) or the Khan's servant, sometimes dressed as an Arab with his face and hands blackened with soot. The Cruel Khan sometimes wore the steel mask. However, in 1986, a boy dressed up as the Cruel Khan in an *aksakal* felt mask, steel mail, white Red Army long-johns (an in-joke) and a huge white hood with a red tassle and a painted inscription in the Koubachi language. He carried a whip and a binocular case, which was probably a begging bowl. The Cruel Khan was surrounded by his women played by young men. The climax was the appearance of the warriors in gruesome painted masks who tried to abduct the women. A battle followed in which the Cruel Khan was always defeated.

In another such fight, there were half a dozen warriors against 20 ruffians. It sounded like the English 18th-century game of village football, except that the brides took the place of the ball. Another sort of conflict performance at weddings occurred in the Rutul and Lak regions (Arakul village) in the hunt of a mummer, masked as a *tur* goat. Sometimes a character with a hobby-horse, covered in a plastic cloth, was the narrator (the Leningrad Ethnographic Museum notes called it a 'sham-horse', which meant 'minstrel' according to Dr

---

* *The Greater Bundahsn: An Encyclopaedia of Zoroastrianism*, Ms TD 2, Chapter 1, p101, c.800 AD, translated from the Armenian by Prof Sir H Bailey: It was forty years in the ground. At the end of the forty years it grew out in the form of a *repas*, a red plant like rhubarb, with one stalk and fifteen leaves. Marte, the male, and Martane, the female, grew out so that their hands were placed back to their ears (like many figurine bronzes from Daghestan of the Zoroastrian period). They were joined one to the other of the same stature of the same form. And in the middle of them appeared the *gdh* – perhaps meaning good fortune – of which mankind was created.

The rams of Kazi-Kumukh (Archi shepherd in transit).

Alla Umakhanova, researching dance symbolism in Daghestan). Avars and Laks also liked a pantomime wedding-horse, which in the south the Rutuls and Tsakhurs turned into a camel.

Schilling wrote that the Koubachi customs had died out before the 1920s. But during the 1950s masked buffoons took part in all the celebrations in Koubachi, including *gulala*, celebrating the last three days of bachelorhood. They wore mail and agressive painted felt masks, a reminder of the warlike Union of Men. At weddings, the masked buffoons usually carried a cradle, in which they tried to put a little boy, to ensure a male first-born.

My Rider mask was a painted white felt, stiffened by a patchwork of diagonal close-stitched cloth inside, like 18th-century Mughal Indian battle helmets. The sides were decorated with a chessboard design, in which there were cut-out ears, and the high forehead with a pink star. A red paint stripe on the forehead was once a symbol of beauty and may have derived from an ancient custom of tattooing, which survived in Kazi-Kumukh and the southern Samur districts until early this century. Only the fastening threads remained of the beard and moustache.

The black felt devil or ram mask from the nearby Dargin village of Khudut had joined stuffed horns like a hold-all bag-handle. The eyes and ear-holes were surrounded by a stitched band of red cloth, setting off the white sheepskin beard and the dark horse-hair moustache and eyebrows. The sweaty plastic-foam inside lining indicated recent use.

Another masked character whose role had become confused, was called *aksakal*, meaning 'white beard' or 'elder' in Turkish. The *aksakal* in Daghestan seemed to be the same as the *azhegafa* or billy-goat mask in Kabardia, in the North West Caucasus. My mask was made from a Red Army greatcoat (recognisable from the black metal clip inside the front flap), and decorated with white-painted lines, a white wool sheepskin beard, brown goat-hair moustache and eyebrows, with cut-out ears and a white horse-tail plume.

In Koubachi at Bayram, at the end of Ramadan, children, like Ibraghim-my-Konak's nine-year-old son, competitively collected walnuts and sweets from house to house. Earlier this century, Kumyk children and teenagers also celebrated by dressing up, painting their faces or wearing masks, going from home to home and performing antics in disguised voices, for which they were rewarded by presents. One night Niamh was sitting in the mayor of Koubachi's home, when four masked young men burst in, shrieking and ullulating. They leapt into the main room, pelting everyone with walnuts, while the women of the house cowered in the corner.

It was explained later – not by the villagers – that the walnuts represented fertility and should be thrown at women. Everyone was screaming with excitement. The men of the house tried, but failed, to grab the intruders' masks to reveal who they were. They were wearing cylindrical tall grey felt masks, slightly tapering down from the top, without plumes, but with beards and eyebrows. The terrifying masks were painted with slanted white or orange stripes. One also sported short triangular felt horns. Another wore steel mail, and they all wore baggy white Red Army long-underwear. Their loose shirts were held in with belts. One had a bag full of nuts slung on his belt and the others had them over their shoulders. After five minutes they left. Half an hour later, as Niamh was preparing to drive to another new part of the village for the night, with whooping and screeching they 'attacked' her car, bouncing the yellow Volga and trying to turn it over. They mimicked the driver when he offered them cigarettes. One took his mask off when he was trying to get the window open, revealing a handsome, clean-shaven face. When the driver wound down the window to push them off, they threw in more nuts and tried to grab Niamh and the others who were all laughing. They then went off to surprise another house.

At the Lak First Furrow spring festival, a wolf with a black face chased a ram, which was cheered on by the crowd, according to Wagidat Shamadaeva, who saw it in the village of Gundi. Other animal costumes and masks were probably connected with fertility festivals, such as the Lak ram and cockerel and the Dargin bull and ram. In festivals in Daghestan and Chechenia, masked mummers accompanied the popular tightrope walkers. Usually dressed as a bear, wolf or devil, they entertained the audience, while the tightrope walker took a rest. The mummers also collected payment for the performance, teasing and bullying the audience to give more. In Ossetia mummers also appeared on New Year and at weddings, as bears or monkeys.

Two different *aksakal* masks survive. One is entirely a white sheep fleece with a red nose, eyes and mouth and sprouting two barber's-pole hornlets, the other a white felt triangular face with a pointed moustache and beard. Masked mummers also danced around the sanctuary of St George on his name-day in the Ossetian mountain village of Dzgvis, where the pagan religion had adopted some Christian saints.

Earlier this century, different masks were used for a variety of occasions by several of the other peoples in the North Caucasus. For example, the survival of the Karachai and Balkar mountain cattle-rearers depended on haymaking for winter fodder. Every group of haymakers chose a strong and clever lad whom they called *aksakal* – 'whitebeard' – or *teke* – ram. Wearing a weird mask, like my Dargin devil or ram, he was armed with a felt whip and a wooden hay-fork. He would demand 'tribute' from every passer-by, be they his own brother, a peasant, an official or a prince. His haul included delicacies, cattle or money for the evening's festivities. After work, he entertained the harvesters. Whenever he met another *teke*, they had a fight and the victor, representing the harvest, assured his own people of abundant hay. But at other times, he set an example by his own work, as well as watching over discipline and keeping work standards high.

Pagan cults of the death and resurrection of the god of fertility were common to agrarian peoples worldwide. With the Kabardians, Cherkess and Adyghes in particular, the *azhegafa*, or ram, played an important role in the festival of the First Furrow. With his band, he went around all the homes of the village, performing his 'death and resurrection' for a reward or ransom paid by the owner of the house, as in the photographs in the village of Ikalto in Georgia. The resurrection of the ram symbolised growth of grain from freshly seeded once-abandoned soil.

In the Caucasus, over the centuries, masked rituals sometimes degenerated into masked amusements, which in turn evolved into satirical performances. Before the Revolution, mummers derided unfair judges, greedy mullahs, Tsarist generals or police officials, like the Ottoman *karagöz* shadow-puppets. Their jokes were often socially or politically unacceptable, so their masks kept them out of trouble. The double identities which had to be adopted during the Soviet period to cope with the hypocrisy of reconciling Party dogma and traditional honour made masks unnecessary, and so they became an invisible part of the satire of everyday life.

· 10 ·

Fighting dogs &
magic beasts

A part the from the kitsch animals found outside Happy Eater roadside cafes and in Donald Duck movies, the role of the animal as symbol has largely disappeared in modern industrial society. This has been our loss as the acres of faceless municipal buildings eloquently testify, in contrast to Daghestan mountain society where animal cults somehow survived in a large variety of forms.

It's a two-way business – people have assigned human attributes to selected animals and people believed that some of their own qualities derived from animals. These acts of sympathetic magic evolved to explain some of the oldest human mysteries, such as the evolution of a small ethnic group and continue until today to express the aspirations of repressed peoples. Three background pressures remain constant – the great mountains, surging from the centre of the earth; the secrecy of deep woods, where wild animals still roam; and the remorseless roar of the rivers cutting into ravines, a reminder of the merciless seasons.

Selected myths, folktales and reality tell the story of the origin, transference and survival of cults of animal conflict. Legends and folktales of the origin of ethnic groups speak of progeny from the union of animals and women. The earliest known example of a pregnant woman with a goat as father is portrayed in a mesolithic rock drawing at Cinna-Khitta. More rarely today, bull dancing and bull fights survive. Men wearing animal masks collect joke scare-money in village festivals. Village cock fighting is regarded as a boy's sport in preparation for the more adult fights between giant dogs which have now, like many people, often migrated from the villages to the towns.

Everywhere, a pair of horns is displayed at the symbolic entrance to the home. While 'Pancratin', an elixir of life made from ground deer horn, is sold for a fortune – 3000 roubles a kilo (with caviar at only 60). Today, the excess of hunting by outsiders of the great horned *tur*, a Daghestan magus, has caused the founding of a Green party. The ram is the current emblem of Daghestan, seen on flags, badges and so on, symbol of virility and fertility. The ram reappears in his paternal role in contemporary festivals, for example both in the village of Akhi (or Kostik) from a Daghestan tourism brochure and at a wedding I attended in Shovkra, a Lak village, in July 1988, where the usher grasped not only the usual decorated baton, but a brown-glazed ram's head, whose knuckle I had already been offered as honoured guest.

Legends indicate that bears are also archetypal ancestors in Daghestan. The following stories show how the legendary role of bestiality is linked with the forces of nature. There are many ancient and recent folktales of relations between men or women and bears of the opposite sex. Late last century, bestiality was punished by a mere fine, or considered a good joke, as is reflected in this 19th-century story: The imam of a (nameless) village had died, so the Council of Elders gathered to choose his successor. A very old man, known to be a joker, interrupted the speeches, suggesting that the new imam should be a man who had not had sexual intercourse with a donkey, so would all those in that condition step forward. But no one moved.

Bears shared many customs and attributes of Daghestan mountaineers, although some similar stories occurring in Russia show the universality of bear folklore. Bears kidnapped their brides, like mountain men. The Narts, as mentioned elsewhere, are mythical giants, leading characters in the ancient Iranian epic which passed to the Sassanians, who ruled Daghestan before the Arab invasion in the seventh century, and to the nearby Ossetes, who both spoke related Iranian languages. For this reason, the Narts reappear later in non-Iranian Daghestan folklore, as in this story:

A family of giant Nart brothers, who lived in a far off wood, had a sister. One day they returned from hunting with a female bear they had killed and found that their sister was not at home. For seven days and seven nights they searched for her, covering their own two mountains and even three more distant, but they could not find her. The Nart brothers had given up all hope when one night they heard a female whisper: "Your sister has been carried off by a bear who is the husband of the bear you killed. She is living with him in the black cave."

The Narts went to the cave and kept watch at the entrance. The youngest was on duty one night, when he noticed a bear leaving the cave. He was about to kill it when the bear cried out in his sister's voice: "I am your sister! The bear has turned me into a bear and I have given birth to his son. When he is 40 days old, you must burn the pelt of the bear you killed." Her brothers did as she had said and on that very night the sister and her son returned home, changed back again, the baby Nart carrying his dead father bear on his shoulders.

There is also a Muslim adaptation of the pagan legend of the half-bear, half-human creature. A mountain called Gebyekkhala is covered by a wood where a large stone has a great hoof-print, reputedly made by the winged horse Buraq which bore the Prophet Muhammad up to heaven. This stone was thought sacred by barren women who prayed on it for Muhammad to grant them children. The stone was protected by a bear for whom the women left offerings. Once the bear carried away a woman who was praying there and people gathering firewood heard her cries. Some years later their young son appeared near the stone. Above the waist he looked human, but below he was covered in thick bear fur. The 'boy' would arrive there in the evening and wail like a bear throughout the night, scaring people away. One of their descendants added: "When I was a child I was forbidden to go there as my family were afraid that the bear might take me too."*

There are also tales of female bear sirens – perhaps recalling traditions of local Amazons. The Kumyk legend of Sultanbek and the bear says that during a snow-storm Sultanbek trips and falls into the lair of a female bear who is hibernating and becomes her 'husband'. The bear often goes off and returns tired and wet, but never tells him where she has been or what she has done. After some time the bear lets him go. When he returns home, he tells his family the story, and they take the bear a bull as a gift.

Bear potency seemed to be admired and to be transferable to humans too. In the village of Almak, Kazbekovskii rayon, old men say that formerly childless parents pierced the fangs of a bear and hung them by threads across a cradle, and when they had a child, placed them under its pillow. Later the fangs would be passed on to another such couple.

In fairness, there are also stories of romantic, faithful, gentle and decently paternal bears – again reflecting different mountaineers' ideals. In contrast to present practice where young people cannot show any affection towards each other in public, in the village of Urchukh, Sovietskii rayon, a bear fell in love with a woman and came to the village every night to see her. In the village of Bashlikent, Kayakentskii rayon, a woman called Nukhye lived for a long time with a bear in a wood. When the woman died the bear was distraught. Villagers ran to see the bear wailing and ripping bark from the trees. In the village of Apshi, Buinakstii rayon, a bear kidnapped a woman. When they had a child, the bear went to the village to fetch a cradle.

Like people, bears could also be platonic and nice, as Kusum Omarova aged 82, from Machada, Sovietskii rayon, remembered: "Once I was up a tree, picking pears in the wood, when I noticed a bear down below scooping some pears, which I had dropped, into my basket. I fainted in fear and fell from the tree. When I awoke the bear had carried me and the basket back to my village." There are real bears about as well, which keep the legends alive. Alla Umakhanova from the Filial of the Academy of Sciences said that she saw a bear two metres high in Amsar village near Rutul in July 1987. It was about a hundred metres away. The villagers wanted to kill the bear because it had eaten two cows, but they were not allowed to, as bear hunting had been forbidden for the past ten years. In Kala, Tsuntinskii rayon, in July 1987, she also saw a mother and cubs walking far in the mountains, on the other side of the Samur

---

* She was an old lady, Mrs Chakar Isakova, born in 1873, who told my friend and collaborator Dr Abdurakhman Abdurakhmanovich in 1968 when he was collecting folktales in her village, Almak, in Kazbekovskii rayon. Abdurakhman (an Avar) has always worked with the twinkling humourous Abdulhakim Magomedovich (a Kumyk) who was exceptionally made a full professor of folklore – a truly civilised appointment.

The 'dancing bear' at Dargin weddings and festivals – ?Kisha village.
(Photo: Alla Ulanova)

Three Laki sheikhs buried near Mukhar village.

river and later swimming in the river. In Kaitagskii rayon they say there are bears too.

&

The Avar national shrine in Zakatal (now in northern Azerbaijan) was by tradition a plain wooden hut. Like the shrine of the Ossetes at Rekom, or another Avar shrine in Kheleturi, near Botlikh, the walls would have been covered with the horns of sacrificed *turs* and buck-deer. Sacrifice was linked with hunting in earlier societies. An uneasy domination over the animal world was locally symbolised by the occasional submission of the wild bear and more convenient sacrifice of the domesticated bull or ram. The meat of a sacrifice was boiled and the smells were supposed to please the gods, while the flesh was eaten by the participants and their families.

Another survival of sacrificial customs also appears in the village of Balkar, where a small boy gently holds up a bull skull, decorated with a branded sun-sign. This reminds me of another bull story about the late 19th-century traditional method of driving illness away from Inch'kho village, as told by an old villager: "When I was about ten or eleven years old, I remember that many people in our village were struck down by a terrible illness. I don't know what kind of a disease it was, but it mowed people down like a scythe cutting grass. In order to drive it out, the villagers slaughtered a bull and put drops of its blood on the forehead and cheeks of children and adults (so joining in kinship with the bull). They dug a big pit at a crossroads on the edge of the village and set cooking pots upon it.

"The meat was cooked with maize and beans to make a ritual dish called *muk*, which was distributed to the villagers. They then dragged the bull's hide (where they believed the illness was concealed) behind them, stopping for a long time at every crossroads (to let the illness escape). The villagers, especially the children, threw small round pebbles from the river at the pelt. Then they made several circuits of the village with the hide, after which they ceremoniously buried it together with the bones in a hole, specially dug outside the village. Before filling the pit with earth, they threw in oak branches and herbs. All this was accompanied by prayers in Avar and Arabic (bringing the pagan ceremony into the Muslim world), recited by men wearing the shepherds' sheepskin hat, or *papakha*, unusually inside-out. They trampled the earth on top of the grave, while reciting incantations, such as 'May the sun and moon show the way, may the wind drive the illness away'. Finally, they set light to a tuft of the bull's eyebrows on the mound."

Symbolic burial was not confined to bulls. In both highland and foothill villages of Itsari, Ashali, Kvanada and others, there was a ceremony surviving to the 19th century where frogs and snakes were caught for a similar burial in order to stop prolonged rain.

The First Furrow festival is one of the most ancient fertility rites in the world and naturally features bulls and/or a pair of oxen pulling a hand plough. In Ginukh, where just 400 people speak their own language, they place doughnut-shaped breads on the horns of a bull and boys try to lift them off. This may well echo Cretan or Ancient Greek bull dancing, described by Mary Renault, as Jason and his Argonauts certainly reached Georgia, just over the mountains from Ginukh. Another example of bull adornment occurs in Kundi village where the 'sower', who is master of the festival, decorates the bull's horns with red and white ribbons and then leads the bull pulling the plough. He wears a hide coat turned inside out and sprays water on all the participants of the festival.

As the bull is man's partner in making the land fertile, it was inevitably considered a sexual rival to man who had to be ritually fought and defeated. When Maimakhan Aglarov, an Andi, saw bullfighting as a boy in Zilo and Ashali (his own) villages in Botlikhskii rayon, a man called Hizri, who was about 50, overcame a bull, catching his horns and pushing up his chin. In Khunzakh they also have bull-fights at the same time as dog-fights. The director of the Bezhta village art school, near Ginukh, is also interested in local customs – they all are. He said that at their festival there is bull-fighting and sheepdog-fighting, organised each year by different Communist Party agencies – the Kolkhoz, the Otdel Kultury of the Obkom or the Lezkhoz. There are five fights a year at other local festivals. (He also spoke of Kurban Ibraghimov, whose dog, named Almaz ['Diamond'], a 40kg black dapple Caucasian 'sheepdog', was a champion dog – as can be seen below, I eventually met both of them, but as it turned out Kurban didn't own Almaz).

The other side of the coin to animals taking on human roles is humans taking on animal roles. As well as the satirical irony of a local version of Orwell's *Animal Farm*, genuine paganism must have posed a bureaucratic puzzle to the Soviet system with their own stuffy anti-religious atheist activists. While officials ignored this cult, attempting to dismiss it as a local joke, Soviet academics studying Daghestan rarely acknowledged the power of humour. This activity is transformed into a ritual, which is extended beyond the individual identity of the mummer, by the wearing of masks. This adds the animal dimension to what I have said previously about masks (pages 184-190).

The earliest example is from a 14th-century worn carved stone relief from Koubachi village, which appears to portray a man, rushing on clawed bird-like feet, wearing a *simurgh*-bird head mask with long feathers streaming behind. The wavy serpent coiled in submission around his waist reproduces the other partner in this Zoroastrian cosmic conflict. This was the religion of the Sassanians, whose Iranian emperor, Khosrows, built the walls of Derbent, just a day's ride from Koubachi, down to the Caspian sea.

As often happens with other popular symbols, over the years, rams and devils became confused in contemporary masks of striking, ancient majesty. In August 1990, Raziyat Magomedkhanova gave me a felt devil mask, as she called it, from her Dargin village of Khudut, in Dakhadaevskii rayon (near Koubachi). In

Dargin it is called *k'archi*, the joker, when three or four masked mummers perform at festivals such as the First of May. They also gather money for tightrope walkers and other performers. This is a scary mask, with its carry-bag handle of joined horns, stitched rims of red cloth around eyes and earholes, and sheep or goat hair beard, moustache and eyebrows.

There are similar *asegafa* or dancing goat masks of the Turkic Karachais and Circassian Kabardians, living on the distant north-west slopes of the Great Caucasian mountains. There is also a photograph of a Dargin giant bear mask too, seen by dance historian Alla Umakhanova in 1983, worn by a jester at weddings and festivals. A colleague and researcher Wagidat Shamadaeva, from the Makhachkala Fine Arts Museum, was visiting Kundi, Lakskii rayon, on March 20, 1987, for the festival of the First Furrow. In one game there, a wolf in a flesh-coloured or black mask chases a sheep, also in a mask. Everyone wants the sheep to win and protects him. But the wolf keeps on attacking and all the action is directed towards saving the sheep. They run about and do somersaults. The wolf and sheep have little hanging bags containing flour or pepper which they threaten to sprinkle over the audience, unless they are paid a forfeit, after a haggle, of one to three roubles. The wolf stands aside from the crowd, holding everyone in contempt and making obscene and rude comments at them.

The first known dancing on point, or toe-dancing, is connected with ritual goat impersonation in ancient Georgian masquerades, called *berikaoba*, recorded in an engraving by S. Orbeliani, an anthropological researcher and artist, based on a fable, which depicts one of the masked characters dressed as a billygoat who is trying, according to the 20th-century anthropologist E. Gvaramadze, to jump up on the hooves tied to his feet. From nearby Gigatl village in Daghestan, there is also a small bronze sexless figurine, with curved goat horns on its head, standing on footless legs, perhaps even on point, in contrast to the feet of all others known from that region, dated about the tenth century. Across in north-west Georgia, the Svans performed the ancient totemic dance *tsekva*, too, where the dancers stand on toes as if on hooves, as in other Caucasian mountain dances where mummers wear masks of wild and domestic animals. (Gvaramadze was probably of Svan origin, writing about his own culture. The Svans are a mountain ethnic group, who have been unwillingly assimilated by the Georgians. So it would be understandable for him to stress both the great antiquity and uniqueness of his people compared to all other nearby indigenous ethnic groups).

In the Dargin village of Itsari, to this day they perform an original masquerade, called *shakha*, with some 25 participants dressed as goats and ponies, where the principal character is a goat who dances at great length, but without toe-dancing. In the same village there is another goat dance in which a couple, man and woman, clearly imitate the animal, lifting knees up high at each step, as well as the Cossack crouching-kicking dance, *prisiadka*, and toe-dancing. What there is today can only be a distant memory of the old dances.

However, real animals are a threat and need to be hunted. Magomed Debirov, an Avar who is writing a manual of folk medicine, which has given him the chance to find out about local customs, says that in his village, Machada in Sovietskii rayon, there is one exceptionally wily and fast hunting dog who frequently catches wild mountain sheep and *tur*. The hunt starts as early as possible. Two hunters and a dog (up to nine dogs in Archi) have evolved a special hunting system to suit the locality. If the dogs bring back nothing, they are sometimes trained to do better by getting no food for up to three days. During the late 19th century Russian colonialists and other European gentlemen would come to the Caucasian mountains just to hunt *tur* for their magnificent horns. The recent appearance of an outsized hunting lodge in an unspoiled alpine location, exclusively for the use of outsiders hunting *turs*, stimulated the creation of a Daghestan Green party (see Botlikh), as I have mentioned. Outsiders also hunt wild pigs, but the locals only shoot them as pests which come at night to steal potatoes, and would never think of eating the meat.

Solemn dance at a Koubachi wedding.

Somewhere between the archaic and the real worlds is a broad place where folktales are endlessly passed on. There are many animal characters in folktales from Daghestan and North Caucasus that conform to Jacob Grimm's observation that man automatically endowed animals (as well as inanimate objects) with human characteristics – such as Raynard the Fox. Several of the ethnic groups in Daghestan and North Caucasus tell their own variants of folkstories which share common origins – but often have a different sting in the tail.

This also seems to be true for many other aspects of their cultures. In many stories, a submissive animal, treated with reverence, always lost out in the end, and gradually became a figure of ridicule, deserving exploitation. The objects of satire in many tales appear to be religious leaders, such as the Mullah, Imam, or

Hadji. The moral: Don't believe the Hadji, don't let him deceive you. Representation of negative qualities of the ruling classes in animal stories shows people understood and believed in their own strength in the event of a struggle against social injustice.

For instance, in the tale of the wolf and the goat in Lezgin, doubt is expressed about the existence of justice in those possessing strength. This comes up in the dialogue between the wolf and the goat over water in a spring which has been muddied and ruined, supposedly by the goat or his relatives. Despite Soviet propaganda against religion and the old ruling classes, Daghestan has an older tradition of free villages and an anarchic attitude towards authority. As in Europe, the unruly fox is favourite of all the animals as the main character. In many stories he appears almost like a mythological hero, endowed with magical powers, as in the following tale of bear, the wolf and the fox: The fox persuades the bear that in winter he should be eaten by her, in return she will restore him in spring and give him 28 sheep, enough for a tasty month's diet. The bear agrees and is eaten by the fox and the wolf. In the variant tale of the camel, the fox, the bear and the wolf, the fox persuades the camel that she will revive him and give him barley the following year.

In these stories, animals believe in the magical powers of the fox, but in later interpretations the irony becomes clear, as does the stupidity of other animals. The fox is agile, bright and brave, so eases out of awkward situations and wins out over the stronger animals, such as wolves, bears, leopards and lions. The fox stands for people who are swift to recognise social injustice. So, in a struggle with her stronger enemies the fox is sure to win, whereas weaker opponents always triumph over her. The fox is crafty, not only fooling animals but people as well.

In a tale called 'Winter is ahead, I will still catch up with it', the fox is on her way to see the wolf and meets some girls who surround her and ask her to dance the *lezginka*. The fox agrees but insists she must be dressed for the part and they adorn her with all their kerchiefs, rings, bracelets, earrings and belts. The fox dances and asking the girls to make a bigger circle, slips out and runs away to the stream where the wolf has been fishing with his tail. On seeing the fox so smartly dressed, he gladly exchanges his catch for the stolen finery.

Naturally, folklore passes into language and sayings originate from animal stories, for example "he has a fox's walk," and "a serpent whispers but a fox talks." Daghestanis consider that the craftiness of a fox lies not in her head but in her tail, and so boast "if you're a fox, then I'm the fox's tail."

In contrast to the fox, the wolf takes on the image of a strong, hard, extremely stupid and greedy man. The wolf stands for an oppressor resorting not to intellect, but to brute force. The wolf is always fooled and disgraced by the fox. Many stories throughout the Caucasus have the wolf as the main character with the tale of the fox and the mule in Lezgin, the fox and the badger in Kumyk, the lion and the fox, or the quail and the old goat in Adyghe, the wiseman in Tabassaran, the woodpecker & the hunter and the wild boar in

Avar, the fox and the rooster or the badger in Ingush, the badger and the bear in Ossete, and the calf in Azeri.

Dogs today are playfully called *volkadav* 'wolfish'. But unlike dogs in European stories, dogs have more important things to do than chase cats, which are well-loved in Daghestan. So stories about war between cats and mice are widespread, for instance the tale of the aged cat in Ossete, the old cat and mouse in Adyghe, the repentant cat in both Avar and Kumyk and the cat and mouse in Lak. But the 40-odd North Caucasus and Daghestan peoples have different preferences of content or form – the Avars like tales about mice; in Kumyk stories, prose is combined with songs; Lezgin tales favour proverbs and dialogues; the Nogai, a Turkic people from the plains, like ancient motifs in their stories; whereas for Daghestan mountain dwellers, animal satire reveals more about daily life.

Dogs are kept not only for enjoyment but to test their abilities. Fighting dogs are different from hunting dogs. Emil Salmanov, an Azeri who came on my first trips, said that there were four breeds of fighting dog: shepherd or *chaban*, guard-dogs, borzoi and the great Caucasian *ovcherk* or mastiff. Over several visits, I tracked down each of the beasts. Daghestan and North Caucasian dog fights are a ritual activity, where giant dogs fight according to complex rules. The onlooker appears to feel that he or she is witnessing a majestic event, where the fight takes on a meaning greater than its reality, becoming an expression of hope. This may explain a part of the passions aroused in a numbing totalitarian society.

A chance meeting with a yellow dog, lying on a dust street in Karata, a mountain village where I had found out some of their lore, in turn led to a meeting with the mercifully chained-up champion near Buinakst. The champion's owner put me onto a doctor working in Market No. 2 in Makhachkala, who enlightened me on a few more points, giving me sufficient knowledge to appreciate a real dog-fight, if I could find one. The yellow fighting-dog-to-be of Karata village was owned by one Omar Pakhruddinov. He kept him in a stable or shed or under his house, because dogs get cramps in kennels.

"In three months time, next December," explained the proud owner, "he will be two years old and ready to fight, when he will receive his name. He already weighs 50 kilos and eats two kilos of meat a meal – four kilos a day, as well as bread and margarine and soup, but no salt."

Fighting dogs have a special morning training regime including a six kilometres run beside a car. Their fangs are reputedly sharpened, but no owner knew of this actually happening because, they said, it would rot the teeth. Breeding counts – last year at Buinakst, Omar's dog's uncle, a dog from Baku called Borsig, weighing 76 kilos, retained his title of champion of the area from Karachai in the north to Baku in the south, for the 18th time during the last three years. Soon a letter came from Karachai challenging him for a purse of 2000 roubles. His owner replied, upping the stake to 3000 roubles, but then the challengers got cold feet and made no reply. If you have a good dog, you keep him for big fights.

Dogs can fought up to 20 times a year. The owners can wager a Jiguli car on the result of a dog fight – when two men bet, they shake hands and a third clasps their hands on top. Everyone bets. Over a thousand people come to watch fights, including wives, and as many as 150 cars are regularly parked in front of the hospital near Buinakst, which I was to visit later on. The next fight was on October 28, one of the ten meets held each year.

Dogs know they are to fight when their collar is removed. They fight one round till the finish, but the fights rarely ends in death as the losers simply run

away. They retire at seven years old and are then kept as pets and live to an age of about 13. Interestingly, they lie outside the Islamic tradition against dogs, and a great fighter would receive an Islamic burial wrapped in a white shroud. The owners – an eccentric Runyanesque bunch allowed to flourish between the layers of 'Soviet' society and often leading double lives – had a catechism which included intoning the legendary trainers Bahadur, Ahmad and Ishak, who owned great dogs with names like Galbats ('Lion') or Chari ('Mixed Colour'). Rumours abound – the world champion weightlifter from Donets wanted to buy the champion dog in Buinakst for 2000 roubles

Seventy-five kilo 'Borsoi', the Caucasian champion fighter.

(old value), but his owner would not sell. In comparison, a good donkey costs 200 roubles. By some code of honour, if you sell a dog you can only use the money (perhaps because it is considered unclean) to buy underwear for your wife.

On the trail of an evidently both organised and lively social network, I went to see a man about a dog. The owner in Karata had spoken of the great champion in Buinakst. When we drove back through there, people who looked like dog-fighting types had never heard of man or dog, so we thought that he had made it all up. Back at the Daghestan Academy of Sciences, Magomed Debirov told me of yet another owner called Gadjimagomedov Abdulla (they always gave the first name last) who lived in Proletariat Street in Buinakst.

We got approval from the deputy director of the Institute to go back to Buinakst, but there was no vehicle. I wanted to go by bus for the experience – there is little climbing and an asphalt road, but that was unsuitable for an important guest. A junior minister whom I knew eventually lent his red car with a moustachioed driver wearing a very wide *aerodrom* peaked cap, who helped us blend in with the background. We left at nine and reached Proletariat Street at ten.

The first three people we asked knew everyone in the street which was very long, but had, as usual, never heard of Abdulla or dog fighting. This temporary blindness is common, born from a wariness of strangers in a hostile totalitarian regime. But one man there happened to have a friend who had just arrived. He mentioned there was a cobbler in the market who had a dog. The second cobbler we tried was the one. The diminutive, wiry, ancient-looking Kurban Abdurahmanovich Kundilayevich, a Dargin, took us to his home in Gogolieva Street to see his dog, Tsigan. We met his son outside the yard doors and waited with him, thankfully, while his father took the beast from its reinforced concrete steel grid house to chain it up in the back yard.

Tsigan is a five-year-old black *Kavkaskaya ovcherka*, weighing in at 55 kilos and unbeaten in 50 fights (an exaggeration if he only fights six times a year as his owner also said) in Azerbaijan as well as Daghestan. He eats bread and soup and trains every day by running ten kilometres in an hour beside the car every day. Tsigan, which means 'gipsy' in Russian, is the champion of Buinakst and already has two litters in Azerbaijani villages near Baku. He will retire when he is eight years old. I recorded Tsigan's terrifying bark while he was being encouraged to go for me so I could take ferocious pictures. Kurban has been in dog fighting for five years as a hobby. There are about 50 fighting dogs in Buinakst, although this was probably another exaggeration.

Fights are arranged privately before the meet and although there is no weight category, the owners want a good match. Meetings take place on public holidays, usually with ten fights. The dogs usually fight in a ring ten metres across, but are obviously uncontrollable until the owners drag them apart. There is little sparring. While some fights last two minutes, the longest I saw, a draw, took 42 minutes. But dogs are rarely killed, as the loser starts whining and runs away. The owners do it for sport, so there is no prize money or betting – or so I was told.

As a bribe, I gave Kurban a cheap gold-plated miniature chain for the dog and asked him to show us some more dogs. We drove to Mayakovskii Street, where the wife of his Dargin friend, Saituddin Magomedov, showed us Galbats. At two and a half years old he had won all his 20 fights. He weighed 55 kilos and ate two kilos of meat a day. His father came from Azerbaijan and his mother from Kutan village near Buinakst. To photograph him near his

Dog wrestling in Makhachkala. T'iduk vs Keda. In the background is a young dog learning the rules. It is a family event, and the dogs are far too valuable to be killed, and the winner stops when the loser has lost the taste for the fight.

doghouse, I squeezed past one side of the yard to avoid attack, while he was barely restrained by a steel chain.

Because their owners were of the same clan, Galbats ('Lion' in Avar) would never fight Tsigan. Emil was telling Kurban that we had really come to see the champion dog that we had heard about. It was becoming clear that he wanted us to think that his dog was the best, even if it meant not seeing the real champion. He took us to another friend's wife, whose three-year-old fluffy sheepdog, Kaplan, had, he assured us, won five fights, while his father had been champion of all Daghestan. We left quickly and drove to another house up a bumpy hill near the edge of town. Kurban got out and looked through the dog-level hole in the main gate. Nothing. He disappeared next door for five minutes, where he found the mother of the champion dog owner, who said he was working near Buinakst on a *kolkhoz*.

As we drove five kilometres along mud roads into the country, Kurban said he had only been bitten once by a dog, on his finger, as he separated two who were fighting. At the *kolkhoz* he talked to some people. Our man was down the road. We came to a shack straight out of the Wild West and Kurban got out of the car gingerly. He made odd aspirated dog noises, while poking through the shack walls with a long thin stick taken from one of the piles of junk, while we stayed in the car. Apart from three kittens playing in the sun, there was nothing again.

Back past the *kolkhoz* and down a side road past the hospital. A brief enquiry at the gate of a house in Lomonosov Street revealed that yes, there was a dog here. Streets are inappropriately almost always named first after Russian Communist heroes and then other famous Russians. Lomonosov was the 18th-century creator of the Imperial Academy of Sciences. We brushed past a glossy Asiatic fighting cock (*petukh* in Russian) which the owner Mikhtar Ismailov, a tall, spare Avar, fiftyish, said was for children's play fights. The force of authority through successful experience sounded in his voice.

However, Djavatkhan Magomedkhanov would disagree, as he owns Rex, the champion cock from Karata. Rex had beaten all comers from Karata, Tliarata, Botlikh and Khunzakh villages and had fought four times in a single day. But perhaps Mikhtar was right. At a cock fight, put on for me, in July 1989 at Khunzakh and at another at the 1990 First Furrow festival in Akhti, where boys put two magnificent black English fighting cocks in the ring, none of the cocks fought with much enthusiasm.

In addition to cocks, Mikhtar has had dogs for eight years. Borzoi, Mikhtar's black five-year-old, is the champion of the North Caucasus. With clipped-back ears, leaning forward with menace in every 75 of his kilograms, he is winner of 25 fights. The longest, his first, lasted ten minutes while he was learning. Mikhtar had been offered and refused 5000 roubles for the monster. Borzoi had survived an illness at eight months and been given to Mikhtar by a relative a year and a half ago. His other dog, Gavri, white, four years old and weighing 60 kilos, had only fought three times, but looked serious.

Mikhtar led them singly from their separate compounds on steel chains and tied the dogs to trees some distance apart and well away from us. Over an omelette, bread, butter, cheese, pickled tomatoes and tea, Mikhtar opened his heart to us and his wife revealed that the dogs eat eggs, *kasha* (Russian-style buckwheat porridge), milk, bread as well as the dried hind-quarter of a cow lying outside. But they do not like herbs, fruit or vegetables. Borzoi, in addition, did not eat pork. For training he ran about the nearby heath covering a modest three kilometres a day, looking over the field where his local victories were won.

Matches were arranged by word of mouth. The vet checked the dog's health quarterly but not especially before a fight, nor was the diet changed then. All this time Kurban was angling to match Tsigan against Borzoi but Mikhtar was not interested in fighting a local dog from Buinakst and muttered that anyway the dogs would not fight each other. I was not sure about that. I photographed his pictures of fights, taken by Chechens in March 1984 and May 1987 in Buinakst, and in February 1987 in Glav Sulak near Babayurt, 30 kilometres from Makhachkala, confirming that the sport was widespread. The next fight was on November 7. Mikhtar knew Rasul Gamzatov, the national poet (but then, everybody does) and had heard of the Abdulla, whom I was never to meet. We might also like to look up a doctor in or about the Makhachkala bazaar called Mutamehmet (he wasn't), who also has a dog.

Fighting dogs & magic beasts

A few days later, in the market, the doctor, who unlike his father, had liked dogs since he was a boy, led me from his tiled laboratory to a more comfortable seat in his friend's men's *aerodrom* flat hat shop. His friend was a war veteran who spoke a little English. His love of dogs had been fired by reading what he thought was "Gound of the Baskrevils by Sirr Artur Konan Doyles." He confided that he did not have a dog just now.

He knew the words "dooog" and "gound" but not "mastiff," which is in the Russian dictionary. He thought that Winston Churchill's bulldog was a "fighting gound," weighing at least 60 kilos, and directly related to Baskrevils . . .

&.

It felt it was October 23rd 1989 during my dawn hangover caused by too much brandy at a Makhachkala wedding. With pain, I remembered making an appointment yesterday in Market No. 2 with Utugmama Nadjmuttimis, the half-Jewish, half-Dargin food safety doctor to see his dog at seven on Sunday morning, walking in Lenin's Konsomol Park, where the First Secretary of Daghestan lived. After a bus ride, I staggered to the Spartak Sports Stadium and noticed I was entirely alone. Ten minutes later I stopped a senior jogger in the chill sunlight who said he had seen a dog, so we walked together into the bushes and found Aslan, the 76 kilos golden dog.

Aslan, which means 'lion' in Turkish, was two and a half years old and had won all his six fights, the first lasted longest at about 15 minutes. Aslan kept trying to eat my arm, but was frustrated by some nifty lead work from his owner. If he keeps winning, he will fight once a month, but if he loses, he leaves off fighting for a year to forget about losing. He was going to fight Borzoi in Buinakst, maybe in December. Utugmama had bought Aslan when he was a four kilo puppy. Once Utugmama was dead drunk at his brother's son's wedding and fell over and could not get up. When his brother tried to lift him, the dog attacked his brother.

I was becoming curious to see a fight. It was confusing for me that all the dogs I met were champions. It was also clear that the owners were using my visits to set up fights. The 26th of October 1989 – my last day in Makhachkala – was busy, but I had at last been promised a fight. Hadji Gamzatov, director of the Academy of Sciences History, Language and Literature Institute gave me his inlaid walking stick in case I was attacked by a fighting dog – the word had got around. I ended a fast talk to teenagers at the Ped-Institut after 20 minutes at 2.45, simply to leave for the outskirts of Makhachkala to watch the fight.

After a winding and bumpy drive off the asphalt road, I was puzzled to find that Tarzan, Daniel-the-Historian's brother's dog, weighing in at 45 kilos, seemed to like people. Worse, it gradually became clear that no other dog had turned up and there was to be no fight. While I was trying to leave, suddenly a feast of giant *khinkal* dumplings, boiled mutton, herbs, garlic and vodka was

Cock fighting at the Novruz festival in Akhti. They were English fighting cocks.

produced. It was the usual consolation for any disappointment.

Waakh-baba! means 'cor blimey!' in Avar. At last, March 20, 1990, a dog fight on a dusty lot in the outskirts of Makhachkala, once more organised by Daniel's brother. And this time the rumours were true. Daniel, the historian from Karata, was slightly drunk when we turned up a little late at the dog fight. His brother's black dog Kanda, at 42 kilos, had just won his bout against the walnut Kazbek from Buinakst, at 50 kilos, so we received a warm welcome. In the second fight, my first, Keda, a black grey Avar dog (dogs, too, could belong to different Daghestan nations if they obeyed orders in the local language), won against T'iduk, meaning 'bear' in Avar, who was brown. Both weighed 50 to 60 kilos.

Keda stood under the football goalposts before the fight as T'iduk waited for him in the crowd. Keda saw him and dragged his owner across the ring. Raring to go, they were held back from behind by their owners until they leapt at each other at the start. Edging round for position, they grappled one way and changed around, up on hind legs, paws and jaws over and under – chasing tails or going for the vitals is out – until the throw, a quick pin and submission by bearing of teeth. In triumph, the winner was taken away.

Five minutes later another brown dog, Baikal from the village of Khushet, was waiting for the next fight at the side of the ring looking down his white nose, but twice there were no other dogs who came forward, so Daniel, snarling, said he would fight the dog himself, and was held back, heaving, by his laughing friends. Other dogs soon appeared for the third fight, but I lost their names – no one knew, even Ramazan Khappoulaev, who had been distracted from taking notes for me by his chatting friends.

After the first fight ended, the crowd's attention moved on. A three-month-old puppy had been brought along to watch the fights and learn the rules, creating a rustle of admiration from the crowd, mainly boys and men but with two groups of schoolgirls. I was in the ring which was controlled by Kurban, the cobbler from Buinakst, beating the ground hard with a stick around the edge to keep the crowd back. The crowd were enthusiastic and threw pebbles at me three times when, crouching low, I paused too long to take pictures. In the fourth bout Kandal, a white from Makhachkala, refused to fight the 45 kilo Kanda, owned by Imanshapi from Kaspiskii rayon. Kandal, black with a docked tail, was then acknowledged by Almaz, a brown from Makhachkala. The last fight was long and close.

The dogs jostled on all fours for minutes before they rose, locked together on their hind legs three times. The crowd went silent, then got carried away and shouting, closed in on the ring, pushing to get a better view. I took my eye from my camera to find that the distancing effect of the lens had prevented me seeing that I was getting crushed into the dogs. In the rising dust, I took my last pictures, holding the camera over my head and twisted away. Kanda was defiant even after losing. Men were strutting proudly and boasting. When all the fights had ended, an argument began over the result of Daniel's brother's dog's fight. The loser claimed that his dog had lost unfairly, as he had been pulled off the other too soon and never submitted early in a fight. The owner was a tough looking, wiry character over 6' 4" tall. After some technical discussion, he told Daniel that he would "fuck him and his dog." Daniel drew himself up to his full 5' 3", thrust his paunch forward, growled and retorted, "I fuck you too!" Then, turning aside to the crowd, he demanded, "What kind of a man fucks dogs?" – before being carried off by four supporters to avoid a dangerous scuffle. Spectators suddenly climbed trees like goats to get a better view of the aroused giant and his dog restrained by the crowd.

Following press protests this year, meets are no longer 'official' though not illegal – as though they ever really were official. "If boxing is allowed, why not animals?" is the enthusiasts' response. However, dogs can, and do, choose not to fight by wagging their tails when presented to an opponent across the ring. They have been trained from when they were puppies in the rules, which are somewhat like those of Cumberland wrestling. They stop fighting on submission, which is signalled when one dog bares his teeth. They have their ears clipped when young, so there is little blood in the sprays of sweat as they clash. The attraction – and it was spellbinding – of the fights, was in witnessing a mythic struggle, where, in spite or maybe because of the sordid background, dogs wrestled with teeth and grappling paws like heroes.

· 11 ·

The society of godless zealots

I was counting mosques. Cinemas, clubs, storerooms, lathe workshops, carpet factories, museums and roofless ruins were all turning back into mosques. Whenever I saw a mosque being rebuilt, I would stop and ask what was happening in neighbouring villages. Because the Andi were specialists, they rebuilt other peoples' mosques and could tell about other regions. As soon as a new tin roof was on, matting, rugs and curtains spread in the middle of the building site, like spiritual ivy. There were 2000 mosques in Daghestan in 1928, when ten years of destruction began, leaving 17, so that the Party could claim to tolerate Islam. (There were over 800 villages and each village had one or two, with more in the larger settlements.)

The mosque is not an essential part of Islam, unlike the Christian church, and prayer can take place at home, so the mosque had current importance as the sign of a national movement against the Russians. Gagatl claimed to have re-opened the first in 1988. The rest of north Daghestan followed the Andi example: the Avars, the Dargins and the Kumyks. For instance, Gotsatl' Klub was an ex-mosque with a cinema screen and walls covered with slogans. An anti-religious cartoon showed a mullah holding up a Koran with the slogan "You can't block out the sunlight (of Socialism)" in Russian but not Avar, paraphrasing Auden's "There stood the church, blotting out the sun." Again, in Khunzakh, the *kino* sign from the roof lay against the wall, while the projector holes were blocked off and the tall arched windows re-opened.

Work on the mosques was enthusiastic. On the outside walls, plaques in Arabic commemorated recent re-openings. An eagle perched on a telegraph pole below one of the highest villages in Daghestan, Kheleturi. Even there, they were rebuilding the ruined mosque and ritual washroom. In the fields too, shepherds' miniature mosques were appearing. The south was more cautious, with the Laks re-opening six. Only a tenth of the young Laks were religious, in comparison with two-thirds of the middle and older generations. This was partly because over half the Laks lived in towns. The Lezgins, Tabassarans and Azeris were only at the planning stage in 1990. But local politics still impeded progress. In theory, if you are a powerful Party leader and you want to keep your career strong, you block mosque rebuilding by turning local people against each other.

Daghestani resistance to Russian and Communist rule from 1800 onwards was the most ferocious that the Russians ever met and was focused through Islam and especially Imam Shamil who led the irrepressible struggle from 1831 to 1859.

This was the background to the current political significance of Islam as the unifying factor in a Daghestan independence movement. The Communist Party's monumental lack of practical achievement made it ever vigilant of alternative ideologies. For many years it had waged war against local culture, especially the Islamic bedrock of Daghestan, through the atheistic Society of Godless Zealots. This Party organisation was staffed by native Daghestanis with obviously Islamic names like Ismailov and Muslimov. In the USSR Supreme Soviet, KGB chief Kuryukov in his post-perestroika maiden speech, after he was 'elected' a deputy, signalled the end of the open period: "The growth of nationalist movements and fundamentalist Islam are dangerous to the Soviet state."

The only point on which state and religion agreed was that Islam was incompatible with Communism. A fundamentalist Sunni Islam, Wahhabi, which supports the local Sufi mysticism (described below) has recently appeared in the USSR, mainly in the North Caucasus. While more political than religious, Wahhabi is definitely not connected to Persian Shi'i fundamentalism – as Gorbachev mistakenly thought.*

و

Magomedkhan and I were at the schoolteacher's house in a village near Khunzakh in 1990 at the height of glasnost. But little openness had reached Daghestan. We were talking about the Islamic revival and wanted to check some fact, so he produced his main reference book. It was the *Atheist's Dictionary of Islam*, published in Russian in Moscow in 1988. Unlike later anti-Daghestan Soviet propaganda, a Russian historian, M. N. Pokrovsky, wrote in 1924 that "Daghestan supplied the whole Eastern Caucasus with scholars of Arabic, reciters, mullahs (teachers) and *qadis* (judges of Islamic law)."

But by 1928 the 800 religious schools were under destruction. Soviet suppression was both physical and literary, including rewriting history. After Shamil, "from 1864 to 1897, schools were run by ignorant mullahs, some of whom could barely read, and who taught in ungrammatical Arabic, a language the children couldn't understand."† Besides the fee for each student, the mullah

---

* It is also unrelated to the late 18th-century Saudi revivalist movement, named after Muhammad 'Abd al-Wahhab, which aimed to go back to the roots of Islam and was accordingly opposed to Sufism.
† A. Omarov, a more 'correct' late 19th-century Russian historian quoted by S. Gadjieva in *Family and Marriage in Daghestan in the XIX-XX centuries.*

required periodic produce or invitations to dinner. When the mullah was leaving, he usually showed "his index finger, around which was tied a piece of thick woollen yarn." This meant the family had to send the teacher generous amounts of food and drink. Over the whole of Daghestan there were 84 Russian schools of which 53 were in villages. Literacy was barely ten per cent. Even Lezginka, the national dance group, performed an anti-Islam dance, choreographed in the 1960s, called *Medresi*, where a buffoon mullah beat his unruly pupils who mocked him. In the programme, the photograph of this dance was strangely superposed over the old city of Baku. The theatre was full and the children loved it.

I felt ashamed for them. The Soviet schools taught that their religion was bad. When a friend's 60-year-old mother was younger, her children stopped her praying because they were embarrassed that she was so outdated, especially as she was a school teacher. Now she prays five times a day at home. The village of Tanusi, high up the hill beyond Khunzakh airport, had a mosque with a stone inscription dated 1094 AH (1680 AD). Inside in the dark, two old men were teaching Arabic to six boys – the first working *medrese* religious school which Magomedkhan or I had seen in Daghestan. The Society of Godless Zealots had sent waves of lecturers to the villages to spread the word of atheism. The villagers ignored them. Even the village libraries of Daghestan have sections filled with hundreds of unread small-edition (one to two thousand copies) atheist books, which continued to be published locally until at least 1985.*

I emphasise again that Daghestani resistance to Russian and Communist rule was the most ferocious and long-lasting which the conquerors of that great empire ever faced, so it was hardly surprising that the Russians were chronically scared. As a consequence they tried to crush its spiritual root and strength, the mystical Sufi Islamic brotherhood. Ever since the end of the 18th century, since the first jihad led by the Naqshbandi Sufi Sheikh Mansur against the Russian advance in the North Caucasus, the religious and political life of Daghestan has been dominated by the Sufi *tariqat*, to the extent that in Russian histories the 'Murid movement' is equated to resistance to Russian conquest. This insubordination culminated in independence for Daghestan, grasped by Imam Shamil from 1845 to 1859 and reappeared in the war against the Red Army in 1920 and in subsequent uprisings. Until the late 1970s the consensus among Daghestani anti-religious experts was that the Sufi way of belief, the *tariqat*, survived only in unimportant splinter groups. Since glasnost, an unexpectedly large number of believers have made themselves known, which has made the experts revise their view of what they considered their previous success.

Two main Sufi groups are currently active (and interlinked) in Daghestan and Chechen-Ingushetia: the prestigious Naqshbandis and the Qadiris. Both

---

* *Musul'manskii Konfessionalizm v proshlom i nastoiashchem*, N. M. Vagabov, Makhachkala, 1985; and the *Biulleten' Ateista*, vyp. no. 3, Makhachkala, 1979.

The recently restored old mosque at Gapshima village. The 2000 mosques of Daghestan were reduced to 17 through Soviet policy from 1928-38 and since perestroika over a thousand have been restored, paid for by local subscription.

men and women are born Sufis – it is an automatic inheritance. It was surprising that women were included in this religious elite, in view of the many other sexual inequalities. I met one young Chechen who was uncertain which movement he belonged to, as his mother was Qadiri and his father Naqshbandi, which showed that the groups intermarry.

Sufism here can be compared to the 19th-century Mafia in Sicily, where the resistance to the foreign oppressors was carried on by economic co-operation as well as political honour and violent reprisal. Resurrected by a succession of local teachers, the number of brotherhoods or *murid* groups following different teachers – who might be living or dead – reflected the strength of the Sufi movement under extended persecution in such a mountainous country, rather than any ideological fragmentation.

The Qadiris are made up of both the traditional followers of Kunta Haji, active since the 1850s, and the more recent brotherhood of Vis Haji, founded in Kazakhstan in the 1950s by deported Chechens, and which has now returned to the north of Daghestan. They practise the loud *zikr* chant, which has recently been televised in Chechen-Ingushetia. I saw a video film of the Kunta-Haji rite and I had been given a private tape-recording which lasted two hours. Both show parts of a Chechen *zikr*.

The hypnotic male chanting, swaying from a single voice to the roar of the whole company was like the sea. Only this was no normal sea: it may have begun there but soon it changed into the waters of the Old Testament Creation and moved about the firmament. It felt dangerous to hear that primal music which could stir the forgotten roots of humanity, releasing unknown powers. The chant took everything along on its path or *tariqat* towards the mystic experience where man communicated directly with God. I was told not to listen to it alone. The only equivalent might be the opposite effect of the Dionysiac chants, releasing their pagan murderous energy among the group of possessed women, described in the Ancient Greek play, the Bacchae by Euripides.

The *zikr* varied from day to day or from brotherhood to brotherhood, and could be composed of mystical poetry, prayers from the Koran or repetition of names of God. It was recited in addition to the five daily prayers of a practising Muslim. The loud *zikr* was normally chanted in a group, but could also be said individually. It took about an hour, but some Sufis continued all their waking time. The *zikr* film which I saw showed a large crowd with one group of women, surrounding the participants. After prolonged solemn chanting by the men standing in a stationary ring, they swayed slightly and juddered apparently uncoordinatedly from foot to foot and began their extraordinary movement. Each man stretched his left hand straight down, with the palm horizontal and open. He raised his right hand above his head and brought it down to clap against his left which he did not move. At the same moment his right knee jerked up and stomped back on the ground and so the circular movement began, repeated again and again to a new loud rhythmic beat (see photo on page 286). They seemed possessed. I was told that women also performed this *zikr*.

The Qadiri leadership was always kept in one family. In contrast, the leaders of the Naqshbandis were selected on merit and so the order was more intellectual, with three significant branches, identified by their leaders. The Naqshbandis also have the eternal honour of having fought the Russians continually for 200 years, from the very start of colonisation. The Naqshbandis practised the silent *zikr* usually on their own, which was obviously safer than the loud group *zikr* during times of persecution.

The society of godless zealots

The first branch are the followers of the Avar Sheikh Hasan of Kakhib, which spread throughout the mountains of Avaristan during the second half of the 19th century. Second was the brotherhood of the Dargin Sheikh Ali of Akusha, thought to have been executed in 1930. They flourished both near Akusha and in the coastal industrial centres. Third, the followers of the Amay group, which was founded in the 1920s. They took part and were crushed in the anti-Soviet uprisings from 1926 to 1936, which began in the mountains. The brotherhood was resurrected in the 1950s, then liquidated by the Soviets, but they reappeared in the 1980s in the lowlands of north-east Daghestan. Other *murid* groups have been reported in south Daghestan.* There are some Shi'is in Daghestan, descended from the Persians in Derbent, the Azeris and some Lezgins under the influence of Azerbaijan in the south. They have their own ceremonies, the most popular of which is the violent mourning festival for the martyr Hassan Ali, *Muharram*, locally known as the *Shahsei-Vakhsei* ceremony, after the name of a chant, took place both in Buinakst and in Derbent, by the Magal quarter mosque. Paruk Debirov, the art historian, now in his seventies, remembered watching it as a boy and hearing the men groan "Shah Hassan! Hassan Ali!" while whipping themselves on alternate sides of their backs with a steel chain. The festival currently took place annually in Derbent and nearby Azeri villages, including Jalgan with 300 houses and Arablinka with 200. Miskinji was the only Lezgin village with 200 homes. With the stand-off against Soviet troops in Azerbaijan and the 1990 invasion of Baku creating hundreds of martyrs, this festival is likely to become more popular in southern Daghestan.

❧

We were driving away from the festival at Khunzakh, when our bus suddenly stopped. There was silence as everyone remained seated. At a silent signal everyone moved their hands forward, palms up as if holding a baby, inclined their heads and began to pray without a sound. It continued for two minutes. We had stopped at a holy sheikh's shrine, whose spirit was supposed to have caused a recent car crash, killing the driver and his mistress on their way to a tryst. Later we stopped at Tlokh by the Andi-Koisu river and the driver and passengers got out and went to the river to say their evening prayers.

Because of industrialisation and migration from the villages, Sufi groups have been forming in the towns, where the corruption of the Party unwittingly provided a focus and encouraged opposition from their higher moral ground. "Today [1989] an honest mullah is better than a bad Communist."† This view had been backed up by the population, including Party officials, who were now openly practising religious rites.

* Brotherhoods like these also disappear and reappear as they pass through the male and female branches of the familes.
† T. Aliev, writing in *Sovetskii Daghestan* (1989, no. 3, pp 26-27) – a surprising place to find this sort of statement..

The ruins of Kalakoreish mosque (tenth century) the former capital of the Kaitags and burial place of their rulers.

The aims of the new Shamil Foundation were recently set out on a poster in the front hall of the humanities institute of the Filial of the Academy of Sciences, and a moderate first issue of *Islamiskii Novosti* ('Islamic News') appeared in 1991. The Daghestani Communists explained their "split ideology" by saying that their ancestors had observed these customs, and they could not abandon them. Did this also imply that there would be a return to pagan horse burials? Not as far as I knew. Even the Secretary of the Daghestani ASSR OBKOM,* Mrs Patimat Churlanova (rumoured to be a hardliner), who greeted me with smiles from the back of her black limousine, admitted in print that "the national and religious are so tightly interwoven that it is difficult to separate them," and that "that the observance of national customs are an obstacle to Soviet internationalism."

There was talk too of a return to the *shari'at* or Islamic law, with its disturbing implications of capital punishment, unequal rights for women and cutting off hands as punishment. The ruins of the *shari'at* court in Gagatl and the Igralib village column both exhibit holes formerly used to support the arm of a thief while his hand was being cut off.

Pilgrimage is more important to the mystical than to other versions of Islam, becoming a physical manifestation of following the path or *tariqat*. In Daghestan, the choice of new shrines appeared to have been deliberately political, commemorating resistance against Russian and Communist

---

* The *oblast-komite* – the powerful Communist regional central committee.

conquests. In 1990, for the first time since the 1920s, 200 Daghestanis went on the hajj to Mecca, and the Saudis paid for everything out of respect for Shamil, according to Daghestanis. Previously only six a year had been allowed to go to Mecca by the Party. Because Saudi Arabia did not acknowledge Soviet passports, the pilgrims went through Syria or Jordan, where the mainly Chechen emigrants had arranged for them to collect Syrian or Jordanian passports.

Two stories tell of ordinary people visiting shrines in Daghestan. In the back of a truck, bumping away from Gagatl, we talked to Mrs Ramazanova, a middle-aged religious woman who led the prayers whenever we passed a graveyard. They opened their hands pretending to read. Four young girls with us were embarrassed and giggled until they were cowed by the woman. The previous Sunday, she had been on a pilgrimage to a holy stone, surrounded by trees with votive ribbons, high up the mountain on the far side of the valley. It was her first visit and she found it moving. It was just as in Archi, where the *debir* had given me and Magomedkhan's little sister magic earth from the tomb of Sheikh Mamma-Debir, who shared the same mystic teacher as Shamil – Jemalladdin from Kazikumukh – and, in his time, became likewise a great teacher of the *tariqat*. (The imam, who originally led the prayers in the mosque and later was in charge of the mosque, was called the *debir* in Archi after the 12th-century saint, who brought Islam from Kazikumukh.) The current *debir* gave me magic earth from his tomb, wrapped in a kerchief. Magomedkhan's sister was allowed to try on his woollen coat and hold his walking stick, wound with many-coloured ribbons which were kept inside the stone shrine.

Shrine visiting and upkeep continued secretly throughout the 60 years of religious persecution. The cloth streamers tied to sacred trees or sticks wedged into the walls of the shrine provided a silent declaration of remembrance. Recently pilgrimage has become more visible and more popular. It was now also possible to complain openly of anti-religious Party activity. When Magomedkhan and I met the First Secretary of the Akhti region, Magomedkhan did not wait to be spoken to. He repeated three grievances that the open-mouthed First Secretary had ignored, which many people considered a disgrace. Firstly, they had not removed the poster of the Russian girl discus-thrower in briefs, which was an insult to Daghestan women. A resigned smile came in reply. Secondly, they had not removed the outdoor privy, which they had built next to an old cemetery and the tomb of a holy man. Silence. Thirdly, they had not removed the words *SLAVA KPSS* – "Glory to the Communist Party" – from the walls of the great mosque in Akhti. The First Secretary limply protested that the giant letters stood out from the walls and were not fixed directly to them.

The clergy in Daghestan were also changing. For example there was a new imam in Botlikh, one of the 17 unclosed (and therefore token) mosques, Ruslan Choupalayev, 30, an Andi. I could not meet Magomed Habib, about 50, because he was ill in bed. He was a good man, originally from Botlikh, so he knew everyone and was more popular than the previous imam, who moved to be the assistant in Khasavyurt. Magomed was known as a saver of marriages. If a couple wanted to divorce, they talked to him first and often changed their minds. He encouraged people to be hospitable, frank and law-abiding. Of more immediate relevance, he said that it was alright to rebuild mosques.

ॐ

There had been religious demonstrations for the first time since the Revolution. The Daghestan government had attempted to stop mosques being restored by withholding permission both to rebuild and to open. In official meetings, imams said that it did not mean anything if mosques were opened or not, what mattered was that you believed. Two Islamic demonstrations in May 1989 and February 1990 led to the dismissal of the Communist-backed religious leadership and the traditional election of a mufti – originally an authority on Islamic law, elected by his peers – of Daghestan. They also demanded that Arabic be taught in schools, as a foreign language and – a political point – that corruption among Soviet officials should be stopped. One of the recurrent slogans was "War on the repression of the North Caucasian Peoples."

The demonstrations, each a thousand strong in Revolution Square in front of the Communist Party headquarters in Makhachkala, the capital, achieved their limited demands using traditional techniques. When they had no answer after five hours, they said simply: "If you ignore us, next week we'll be joined by our brothers from the mountains." The sight of a disciplined mass of grim bearded men in silver and golden lambskin hats chanting and swaying in complete unison must have made the threat credible and terrifying. The president of Daghestan, Magomedali Magomedov, a tough mountain man, agreed to their demands. At another demonstration in Kizil-Yurt in June 1989, the believers demanded to be given government land designated for official uses, such as Palaces of Culture, on which to build mosques. In contrast to the political elections, if, through inexperience, the elections for a new mufti were confused, they were considered to be fair.

They succeeded in splitting the old Communist-controlled North Caucasian Islamic Board into three muftiates, one of which covers only Daghestan, and the others Chechen-Ingushetia and Kabardia. They gained a site for a central mosque in Makhachkala and freedom for religious worship (some time after it had been granted in Moscow) and permission for five believers to make the pilgrimage to Mecca each year, which was immediately exceeded. It was now permitted to import a limited number of Korans. The Saudis have paid for 30,000 Arabic Korans for the USSR. However the local people all wanted Russian-Arabic Korans, which were virtually only obtainable from the Ahmadiyya Muslims in Britain. Since then, the Koran has been translated from Arabic into Avar (though not yet published) and it was said that Arabic Korans are being printed in Moscow. There was a great demand for Korans and many people were learning Arabic.

The job of mufti as the regional religious representative was introduced during the Soviet period. The nomination had to be approved by the Party. Before then, it was customary to elect a mufti in Central Asia, but not Daghestan, where there were imams for all the main mosques, elected by common consent. The most important was the *qadi* (a kind of judge) in Akusha who could appoint the *shamkhal* or regional ruler. There were now more than thirty imams and the *zikr* ceremony was practised outdoors in Makhachkala.

The election was confused as they had no experience and were uncertain of procedure. There were two factions, if that word does not imply too much order. There were groups with leaders and there were unorganised groups (which were probably Naqshbandi). Some groups were made up of members who turned to religion because they were oppressed by the system. Others expressed dangerous conflicts between believers and political people, which could lead to extremism. The state department of religious affairs did not like the mufti to be part of a group. This was naive of them, for the mufti could belong to the Naqshbandi without belonging to a group.

The election organisers agreed to have one voting representative for each 500 believers. But the problem, after all this time under atheism, was to decide who was a believer. In the villages public meetings must have taken place where believers declared themselves and past anti-religious acts were summarily judged by a council of local and outside religious leaders. In Daghestan everyone knew about everyone else. About 500 representatives argued for three days. They voted by raising a single finger in contrast to the Soviet way with the whole hand.

Traditionally, they gathered seated inside the mosque or standing outside. This time they voted in the *klub* which was full, so some had to stand. It was difficult and uncomfortable to enter because of identity checks by religious leaders at the door. The first candidate was from a *medrese* in Jordan. The second was the father of a researcher at the Filial. Although he was a good Arabic scholar, he was considered too old for the work. The new mufti of Daghestan was Bagaudin Isaev, the Kumyk imam of Makhachkala, aged about 60. He was an ex-state-worker and was considered to be a clean man, a realist and a deep believer. Also, more importantly, Bagaudin did not belong to a group.

Magomedkhan made the comment: "For the Muslims of Daghestan and indeed in the whole USSR, freedom came unexpectedly and more rapidly than they imagined. This caught them unprepared and unorganised and explains why it took so long to elect a mufti. Specifically, due to inexperience, the voting procedure was poorly organised and evolved slowly, also private interests initially confused the issues, which delayed achieving the necessary 51 per cent majority and in the ensuing confusion, the loudest voices often won. This was understandable because, for at least 50 years 'unclean' people were involved in the official religion with non-altruistic aims. The religion was effectively closed down to the religious: if something is closed, it is not known, if something is not known, it is possible to make mistakes." There was even an article about the elections in the local (Communist, of course) Avar Gazette.

These were internal problems which are continuing and until they have been solved there was little energy left to devote towards integration with the rest of the Islamic world. After Iraq invaded Kuwait, there was a demonstration by the religious faction in Makhachkala condemning Iraq. Subsequently, there was a tendency to support Iraq. The reason was similar to Azerbaijan, where because of their hatred of the Russians, the enemy of the USSR, who supported the United Nations resolution against Iraq, must be their friend.

The focus of the movement was the spiritual resurrection of Imam Shamil, the religious liberator of Daghestan from 1845 to 1859. Beside a great dam, an ugly new town had recently been built, housing the 5000 workers constructing the hydro-electric plant at where the Avar-Koisu and Andi-Koisu rivers joined to form the Samur river. The project may have been running years late because of a lack of concrete, but the village was gloriously named Svetagorsk, Russian for 'Light of the Mountains'. On August 10th 1990, I was advised to be driven there to witness the official name changing to Shamilkala, or 'Fortress of Shamil' – the first village, square or even street to be so renamed. It was also the first Islamic festival in Daghestan since the Revolution.

While many hearts were beating with pride in the demonstration of the survival of an oppressed people, others were sinking with the realisation of its form, which was identical to a totalitarian demonstration, with Shamil replacing Stalin as a cult personality. Two thousand people paraded into the football stadium, holding up posters with Russian and Arabic slogans: "Shamil was a great democrat – Marx." "Love freedom like your own mother, and life will be for ever beautiful – Shamil." "People of Shamilkala! be worthy of the glorious name of our hero." "Shamil, the recognised genius of the Muslim world . . . we support peace in our community."

The top balcony of the stadium was reserved for religious people, facing the speech-givers. The Party Secretary read his speech in Russian. Three old-style cannon fired blanks, producing clouds of white smoke against the mountains, behind the cloth bunting, with the slogan "Generations to come will praise his memory, perhaps not as a prophet and imam, but as a freedom fighter" – a quote from a French contemporary of Shamil, Zakkon. As local policemen joined in with the armed costumed performers, Imam Magomed Gadjiev from nearby Gimri, Shamil's birthplace, ranted at the crowd in Avar without notes. As well as a woman poet, related to the Gamzatov clan, another woman gave an extraordinary speech in Avar about the importance of Shamil's women and a famous Avar singer sang her songs. There was a mounted parade of ten Russian hussars and *djigits* with green flags, with a mock charge, after which the actor playing Shamil turgidly mumbled from his notes into a microphone at the crowd, from horseback. Village girls and women appeared in lilac satin dresses and danced with all the officials and performers. Next, men and women formed separate lines and prayed on the football pitch. This was also the first time public prayers had been seen in Daghestan since the war in 1920.

The bizarre finale was a football match between the local team and an American schoolboy eleven from Spokane, Washington, which was twinned with Makhachkala. A Daghestan emigrant to America after the Second World War was reputed to have founded this unlikely link, and the soccer schoolboys were on an exchange visit to Daghestan as one of several two-week exchanges organised by the Spokane-Makhachkala friendship society. The schoolboys, unsurprisingly, lost against the local men. As we had been away feasting on ram during the match, we met the American redneck youths, aged 16-17, beside the dammed lake waiting for the long boat ride back. I had not believed that they were Americans until I heard the strange language they were speaking. As their bossy Daghestani Soviet woman minder ordered them about, I sat down and introduced myself to an exhausted young man called Chuck. "Geez, the food's awful. We just stopped eating in Daghestan. Ugh. I wanna hamburger. All we wanna do is get back home. Everything's awful in Daghestan. I dunno why we had to come here anyway. Yeah, we won one game in Makhachkala and lost another. Why are you here anyway? What do you wanna find out about these people? God, that's the worst job I can think of. And you like it?!"

Cement giant Socio-Realist statue of Slav sporting virility outside the Dynamo Stadium wrestling school in Makhachkala.

There is an inherent instability in the religious revival, where all possible results seem to be equally unpleasant. Even the 'common market' agreement with three other north Caucasian Muslim autonomous republics – Chechen-Ingushetia, Kabardino-Balkaria and North Ossetia – seems dependent on the survival of Yeltsin's independent approach, as night falls on the Gorbachev years of hope. A violent outcome can only be avoided if a moderation appears which neither the Soviet authorities nor other Islamic movements have been able to achieve.

Their hopelessness reminded me of my own rite of passage. At two one rainy August morning, I awoke and stepped into the grey-black along the veranda and downstairs in the large old town house, where we guests, to find the lavatory. For modesty, I had put on my cream-coloured trousers and for comfort, my black Italian sandals. Unusually, the toilet was inside the house, on the ground floor next to the cattle byre. It was of a sophisticated design. The light revealed a wooden floor with a nine-inch step at one end of the room – the lavatory. The 'tread' was made of two planks set into the walls, with a central eye-shaped hole in between. It was cool and peaceful after the exhaustion of the 14-hour journey of the previous day.

We had been turned back on the way to Bezhta, as freak August rains washed gravel and rock landslides over the vanishing roads into the river gorge. The gravel was moving and it was scary. A jeep could have been cut off between two falls. The small room with white walls was cosy and warm. So I dropped my trousers round my ankles and gingerly stepped up onto the boards to ease my 16-stone frame into the traditional crouching posture. My second foot never came to rest on the plank. There was a crack like a gunshot as the front plank broke in its weakened middle, the step came away from the wall into a diagonal position and I found myself standing up to my knees in vitriol and excrement. I leapt out, rushed outside to wash myself in the dark and plunged my hands into a bucket which was filled with grease. I relaxed and started laughing silently at the symbolic end of my apprenticeship in Daghestan. What was the correct behaviour for a guest in this situation? I woke no one, but left the light on as a warning. Next morning as I quietly rewashed those once-cream trousers again and again and again, the old lady, her friend and her granddaughter cryptically smiled.

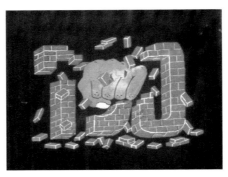

Back cover of 'Pamiyat-Sluzhba' – punching through the wall of 730 days of conscription (see page 165).

· 12 ·

The secret garden of Botlikh

Where was the Party in the new web of religion, independence, and nationalism? Of course, it had not disappeared at all. During the four years to 1991, the cult of Shamil had become noticeable throughout Daghestan. This was against a background where the best reference book on Islam is the 1988 *Islam Slovar' Ateista* ('Atheist Dictionary of Islam'). As well as unpleasant anti-religious posters in village *klubs* (Communist centres), there were still sections in every village library filled with crude anti-Islamic atheist booklets. Much of the atheistic literature was directed against the veneration of shrines. Yet since 1980 visiting shrines has become more popular, especially those connected with the Caucasian War and later wars and uprisings against the Soviets. In addition, historic places have become shrines, such as Shamil's escape cave in the cliff-face near Gunib, or the satisfyingly massive ruins of the Russian fort at Priablizhenski.

The Communist Party's monumental lack of practical achievement contrasted with the energy it directed towards its own survival, most recently in subverting the elections. The Party was a colossal, blind omnivore, carelessly crushing Daghestan. Exploring this labyrinthine system, with its contradicting symbolic signposts, spread a confusion of the soul. The weight of oppression exaggerated any signs of non-conformity into signs of freedom. For instance, in Bezhta, a roof ridge illogically sported ram's horns, a tin red star and a television aerial, while a cut-metal Moscow Kremlin similarly decorated a house in Charah and a bridge near Muni was crowned with a tin spaceship and star. Every village, like Karata, displayed painted portraits of male and female official local heroes behind grandiose portals: "We are proud of these names 1917-1987" – glossing over the war against the Red Army in 1920, the uprisings from 1926 to 1936 and the 1950s purges, when villagers were summoned at night to go to Makhachkala, never to be seen again.

Further long-reaching crimes were committed during the first-ever elections in 1990. By chance, I happened to be the only foreign observer of what were more like elections in Britain during the 18th century than what was termed 'democratic' today, though perhaps it was fairer to compare them to similar elections in Afghanistan or Rumania. Elected deputies stood to gain patronage for jobs and a strengthening of local clan or *tukhum* power. The Communist Party and its tribal power-base clumsily orchestrated the charade. Only 15 out of 158 new republic deputies were not Party members. So ten per cent of the elected deputies represented over 90 per cent of the population.

In fact, during the Brezhnev period, Vestnik Statistiki gave party membership at only 60-70,000 in Daghestan, i.e. about five per cent. This may seem a low figure as many wanted to join the Party for the privileged employment it granted rather than for idealistic reasons. So the Party actually strove to keep *down* numbers, apart from the occasional *chiska* recruitment drive such as at the start of the Great Patriotic War (World War II). While it may have been possible to expose some of the electoral malpractices throughout the USSR under glasnost, in reality nothing was done to put things right.

After recent events in the Baltic states, Azerbaijan, Armenia, Georgia, Uzbekistan, Moscow and Leningrad, it seemed that the disintegration of the Soviet Union was due to a mixture of economic breakdown emphasising internal ethnic conflicts. This had been overlooked by Western Soviet historians, who thought in terms of an ideological struggle. Daghestan ASSR, a small closed 'Autonomous Republic', in reality under Moscow's orders, was unique in the Soviet Union in having 33 indigenous ethnic minorities, and so elegantly reflected the tribal unities and divisions within the USSR today. If Yeltsin had declared an independent Russian Federation (RSFSR), he would have set an example for all the 'autonomous' republics inside the RSFSR, like Daghestan, to follow. The hollow Republic of Daghestan was duly created.

"One day high in the mountains of Daghestan, Mulla Nasruddin's donkey was getting thin after 70 years of glorious Soviet rule. He was glad to find a pile of paper to chew. After sniffing at it to make sure that it was not the lost *spravochnik* – the charter excusing donkeys from all further carrying work – he noticed that it was a pile of voting slips from Makhachkala . . ." Reality had swiftly passed into folklore.

ຂ๑

In the first 'democratic' election for at least 70 years, three elections took place at the same time. Nomination of candidates (without residence qualification) for Daghestan or RSFSR required 300 signatures, while local candidates needed 60. They could only stand where the Communist Party allowed them. As several candidates were ignorant of the voting rules, the Communist Party arranged for all 41 First Secretaries of Raikom and Gorkom (the regional and town committees of the Communist Party) to be elected virtually unopposed. Such as a certain Mr Resulski, Second Secretary of the Obkom (sub-regional committee of the Communist Party), who lived in Kaspiskii rayon but was elected unopposed in the distant Kislyarskii rayon, where he was unknown. The Kirovskii rayon in the capital Makhachkala had three unopposed candidates in 13 seats.

The secret garden of Botlikh

Canvassing was dreary. Each candidate was given a small poster with a black and white photo which looked just like the posters for criminals or missing people at the local airport. Registration lists were published with each candidate's name, date of birth, statement of membership of the Communist Party (where applicable), job and home address. Most regions had two to four candidates. On March 3, election eve, one of the local Party papers – Komsomolets Daghestana – published *Elections-90* where, in random order, candidates were given between a quarter and half a double-A4 size page, including a passport photograph, biographical details, a vague statement about perestroika and a signed or unsigned interview. Candidates also could distribute a six by eight inch copied leaflet with a passport-sized black and white photograph, stating their policy.

Only the Communist Party had funds or means to call public meetings and were given prime evening time on television, while opposition candidates only got afternoon time when people were out at work. The embryonic opposition reflected complete unfamiliarity with any form of democracy. Only one non-Party samizdat paper appeared: *Impul's*, No. 3, February 1990. It was a double-sided computer-printed broadsheet, recommending 30 candidates standing for 'Klub Perestroika' – now the Social Democratic Party of Daghestan. It summarised their policy and listed the names of the authors who were from the Filial of the Academy of Sciences (where, unlike at the Communist Party, there is an acute paper shortage). There was also an account of a local Pravda smear campaign against a procurator who had exposed courtroom corruption since 1984.

The new Daghestan Peoples Front has been far weaker than that of its Caucasian neighbours. Because of the complicated local tribal honour system, and the imperial way that the Communist Party had set local minority interests against each other, the Front had not gained respect. It was reputed to be composed of people who had been beaten by the Apparatus, and no Communists had been won over. At noon on March 26, 1990 only 500 (in addition to the numerous KGB) had attended a meeting outside the Kumyk theatre in Makhachkala.

After the first round on March 4, the contesting candidates were reduced to two for the final round on March 18. I then witnessed what I understand was not an isolated incident of ballot-rigging by the Communist Party. In Makhachkala, the capital with a population of 350,000 and 70 deputies, there was a close result in Gorkovskii okrug No. 35 constituency. Magomed Gabidullah, about 45 years old, director of the Institute of Schools and supported by the Communist Party beat Ramazan Khappolaev, also about 45, director of the national library and a TV personality, by 1616 to 1510 votes, after a two-and-a-half hour count. This remarkably reversed the primary result where Ramazan had soundly beaten him and two other rivals.

The election procedures were as follows: All constituencies consisted of 4–5,000 voters who each received an invitation, filled in by hand with their name, address, list number and polling station from the Divisional Election Committee [*Uchastkovaya Izbiratel'naya Komissiya*]. Any time after the doors opened at 6am a voter could walk in past officials standing inside the door of a school or similar institute, and approach election officials sitting behind tables with lists of voters to find out if he was registered to vote there. If not, he showed his passport and was registered at the discretion of the election commission. Everyone over the age of 18 on March 4 was then given three voting slips, a different coloured one for each election, called *blanki*. He entered the red cloth-covered booth to cross out the names of the candidate(s) he did not support on each slip, unlike in Britain where voters put an 'X' against their choice. Also unlike in Britain, the slips bore no numbers or other form of identification to control the number issued or link a slip with a particular vote. The voter then placed his folded votes in the sealed ballot box, decorated with the emblem of the Communist Party, watched by two official observers. A voter who showed one passport should legally be given only one set of three blanks, but if they were known Party supporters or replied positively to discrete questions from the officials, they were allegedly given blanks for their entire family. In contrast, Mr Abdurakhman Amaev, about 50 and a supporter of Ramazan, was surprised when he went to vote at about noon. He asked for his blanks but was shown a tick against his name and told that he and his wife had already voted. When he questioned this, he was sent to the chief of the local election committee, who apologised and wrote their names on the extra list, so they appeared on two lists. He was then given two packets of *blankis*. One packet only contained two, instead of three – and the missing one was Ramazan's. He questioned this and was again told that the committee had been mistaken and given the extra voting slip. It was thought that when old people came to vote they were also given two rather than three blanks, as they would not be aware of what was going on. Ballot boxes were also transported to hospitals and old people's homes, where the names on the slips were sometimes crossed out by officials on behalf of the infirm. It was also unclear how constituencies were allocated to soldiers.

At both the almost inactive polling rooms I visited during late morning – the school in Marx Street for Borough No. 10, named 'K. Marx', and the History, Literature and Language Institute of the Filial of the Academy of Sciences – the officials refused to let me photograph the voting slips. All spoiled papers were supposed to be returned to the central election committee, to prevent forgery or multiple voting. This did not work in one constituency in Buinakst, where it was reported on Daghestan television on March 6th that there were 160 more votes cast than there were voters when the First Secretary of the Gorkom (town Committee of the Communist Party) was "elected." There was no recount.

On March 19th Ramazan was telephoned by an anonymous caller who said that if he looked under a cement bag in a store room, down the stairs behind the voting room in School No. 1, he would find some unmarked slips. There were 66 unmarked green slips and 11 white for the two other elections – but there were no blue slips for Ramazan's election. This appeared to indicate rigged voting, with the extra blue slips filled in to swing the vote against Ramazan, especially as in one polling centre, where Ramazan had won by 340 votes in the first round, he mysteriously lost in the second. Counting was done locally under the supervision of the election committees, who had been appointed by the Communist Party, as had the officers of the supervisory committee, who allegedly interfered with all aspects of the elections. Membership of the election committees did not reflect the 33, often rival, nationalities, or simply did not include 'unconnected' people.

The 'loser' (left) and the 'winner' (centre) in the rigged local election of 1990 in Makhachkala.

The count involved a list where the results from about six ballot boxes were written: votes for candidate A, votes for candidate B, number of spoiled papers and number absent, which should have tallied with the number of unused voting slips. The list had to be countersigned by the local election committee – which it was – but Ramazan and others saw numbers were written in pencil, which had been changed in pen later. The total of unused voting slips had been changed from 571 in pencil to 538 in ink. When he asked for a recount of this figure, the committee recounted 572 – another mistake – but refused requests for another recount, declaring that they had no time.

This haphazard attitude also affected the way the results were presented. An alphabetical list of first round winners and runners-up elected on March 4th was published in *Daghestanskaya Pravda* ('Daghestan Truth') on March 13th and the results of the second vote on March 18th were published there on March 27th.

Day seven of the first Muslim women's hunger strike at the foot of Lenin's statue in Revolution Square, Makhachkala. They were protesting about recently missing relatives feared killed. The result was that the nominated Justice Minister was not promoted. But no one was charged with the murders. (December 1991)

Neither results gave the numbers of votes for the different candidates, the turnout (later estimated at 60 to 70 per cent), the size of the constituency or the number of spoiled votes. The results were simply lists of the winners.

The complaints procedure did not work. Ramazan submitted evidence of these irregularities to the head of the local election supervisory committee (there were town and regional committees), an upright chemistry professor, who promptly came round at about four, listened to the story and said that, following the rules for complaints, at ten next morning the over-supervisory committee would decide if a recount or re-election was needed. It had been rumoured in the town that the head of that committee, the powerful Secretary of the Agricultural Party Committee was also the official representative of the Raikom. He had also been elected a deputy of the Makhachkala Gorsoviet after only the primary election. Several of his colleagues were on the committee – all known to support Ramazan's rival. The Secretary was reported to have said that he did not wish to pursue the matter.

On the day after the elections, I accompanied Ramazan when he went to congratulate the successful candidate who was initially nervous and kept repeating that "all is forgotten." Indeed he and Ramazan will need to work together. He is a better man than his supporters and promotes minority languages in Daghestan, ironically, like Ramazan, he is the only cultural representative out of all the deputies. Meanwhile unsuccessful candidates and their supporters now have five years to reflect on the difference between electoral theory and practice.

Five months before, in a real contest with four candidates, Nurmagomed Kuramagomedov was elected mayor of the newly established soviet or council of Khunzakh, the regional centre with a population of 8000. He was not a member of the Party, but a keen engineer who did not sleep all night when I brought him books on European tools and D.I.Y., a new concept in Daghestan. Since the election the new soviet had received not a kopek from the Communist Party, who used to run Khunzakh, and so they were powerless to carry out any new projects, like putting in drainage to stop the river flooding a main street whenever it rained. I suggested that Nurmagomed requisition all Party property, but he expressed his fears and said he thought that only Yeltsin could change things and that it would take three years.

The pettiness was remarkable. In a Lezgin village, Novi Frig, the Party had not allowed an electric bulb inside a privately owned cloche to be lit at night to 'save' electricity, so the much-needed plants were frost damaged. In Kriugh over supper, we attacked the Communist beliefs of our host, the 35-year-old new mayor, and questioned how the power balance would change now that there were deputies like him as well as the old Raikom, Obkom and Gorkom authorities – "No one knows what will happen." He had a horseshoe nailed to the threshold of his home. He was lucky, in that he had managed to join the Party cadre.

It was not always possible to join. Another morning in Akhti, everyone was arriving for the Party conference, except for one forlorn onlooker. He had been born in a village near Khunzakh, but had not returned there since he was eight. This was because his father had been killed in the war before his birth and his mother had died when he was eight. It seemed that he had no relatives to care for him as he was sent off to the orphanage in Makhachkala, where the Party often adopted low-level recruits. As he was bright, he went to the Institut, but could go no further, since he had no family connections in the Party. He was now a senior tour guide, which was as far as he would go. He admitted sympathy for Islam, but had missed out on a normal upbringing, with no grandmother to teach him.

Land leasing, or *arenda*, from the state farm to the private individual had just been permitted for the first time since Collectivisation in 1929. With only a savings bank system, where customers received two per cent interest but could not borrow, Davud and his sons and sons-in-law were the first *arenda* farmers near Archi. They previously worked at the state farm and started up three months ago in the ruins of an old farm. Before collectivisation, eleven families lived off the farm in these large buildings – four of them were deported for being *kulaks*, the peasants considered too wealthy by the Party and therefore purged, and the farm was abandoned. A tough 60, Davud had started to work two hectares of market gardening as well as a large area of grazing. He had 11

Soviet all-services Slavic boys poster with Gamzatov's cranes symbolising the souls of the fallen and mothers' despair. (Akhti archive)

July 1989 – first Shamil poster at the Avar National Festival in Khunzakh.

cows and 20 sheep. Two of his sons were picking caraway and mint for tea, to sell to the Azeris. He was the only supporter of Gorbachev that we found. As we drank his beer which tasted like sweet champagne and ate fried liver and stinging-nettle pancakes, he spoke of his worries about Gorbachev's survival and the chances of a new Stalin. "Who was ever secure in owning land?" he wondered.

On the way to the airport near Makhachkala, the Communist Party hotel for "special persons" was now up for rent and I was asked to look it over by a different Daniel, who was in charge of foreign tourism and a Party member too. He was smugly proud of it. For me, it was a long-awaited pleasure: "First, take down that plaster profile of Lenin from the entrance hall . . . the place looks like a gulag . . . the corridors look like a psychiatric hospital. Why is everything dirty and greasy? Why the stained, unwashed windows, streaked brown on the outside walls, and decapitated lamp posts in the untended concrete rectangles of garden? Is there a purpose in the consistently cracked plaster and cement around every internal fitting? Why the littered cigarette ends and burns, the cracked wastepipes, the blocked drain flooding the kitchens, and the rotten food left out next door? Who had designed the bedroom suites, crammed with crazy combinations of Finnish, New Orleans brothel Rococo and tacky Moscow furniture?" Grubby staff sat among the hidden luxury of the Party and its mediocre secrets.

ð.

Daghestan was overwhelmed by a thorough propaganda machine, from the lofty gaze of Soviet statues of Slav male and female athletes in cement, beckoning to the people of Makhachkala to pass through the Neo-Classical portals to the sports stadium, built in 1935, to the silver- and golden-painted concrete Lenins in every village. As a villager smilingly showed me a Raisa Gorbachova-faced grasshopper, it was touching, if pathetic, to see how people kept their sanity by turning their despair into jokes or folklore.

In Daghestan, unhappiness was connected with the Russian colours white and red: white for war and colonialisation, red for unification and suppression. In 1990, when the East Germans came to West Germany, they mused on their recent ideology. "Hitler was covered in shit up to his neck, while Stalin was only covered up to his knees." "Why only to his knees?" "Because he was standing on Lenin's shoulders."

The language of Stalinism was even the medium for its criticism – they knew nothing else. In front of the Tashpinar village Palace of Culture there was a silver painted statue of Lenin with a giving (or taking) arm, outstretched in international friendship. One night six years ago, Lenin's head and arm fell to the ground, but no one in the village had seen a thing. Local Party officials quickly stuck them on again. Over the years even Santa Claus occasionally appeared in village festivals as an ally of Leninisation and I saw village shops crazily filled with beautiful pyramids of Vietnamese Red River Hanoi cigarettes and Russian tinned fish which nobody bought.

Against this background and the particularly severe control of civilian life, it was hardly possible to believe in glasnost in Daghestan. One educated man guffawed as he read a one-page article in *Sovietskaya Rossia* about the KGB chief interviewed by deputies in 1989, while marvelling at a sports paper where it was reported, for the first time, that 340 people were killed in a football crush in Moscow back in 1982. The three-metre-long aluminium torpedo tubes, used as water tanks on the roofs of houses next to the Baku-Rostov railway line, were not jokes, merely an expression of the ideological dictatorship, where, according to the peeling tin slogan on the top of the Institute of History, Language and Literature building in Makhachkala: "Socialism and Science are indivisible."

On the propaganda front, by the mid-1930s the urban-based Soviet culture-crusher turned its attention to the village folk-dance. The brilliant virtuosity of the male dancer, mastered over centuries, was a rich and authentic folk art, which initially inspired Soviet-period folk-dancing on stage with its vitality and humour. But with the establishment of two professional ensembles, the State Ensemble of Song and Dance of Daghestan in 1935 and the ensemble Lezginka in 1959, folk-dance took a new direction.

"This intrusion did not always come about smoothly, but in the thirties one experiment took a simple folk tale and created a new popular form, which was admittedly within the great tradition," according to Alla Umakhanova. However, with the later Lezginka a move to innovate appeared, which was neither original nor justified. The overworked stereotypes debased the folk-dances, while posing and exaggeration of already sparkling movements distorted the originals. Flashy stage effects were often exaggerated by speeding up the tempo which ruined the traditional rhythm.

The Party maintained a close relationship with the dance theatre. Once in Makhachkala I was recommended to put on a tie and come to the Children's Concert. I found myself sitting in the row in front of the entire Party Secretariat. There were dazzling dancing displays by six to 11 year olds – far better than the Lezginka – and then there was a dance to Rasul Gamzatov's 'Poem of the Cranes', representing the spirits of young soldiers, who had been killed in the Second World War. Wraith-like figures appeared on stage in Red Army grey mackintoshes, which were discarded, one by one, to reveal rather well developed young girls in white tutus. The Party bosses held their breath – what on earth was going on? I felt bemused by a system which was happy to parade their children so proudly while there were no toys for them and in the villages like Andi boys had to play 'cars' with crushed tin cans or rocks on the dusty unpaved tracks.

One sad example of officially inspired waste was the secret garden of Botlikh. Magomedali Ubekhov was an old-style gentleman from Botlikh, whose grandfather owned one of the largest houses, and had opened his ground floor

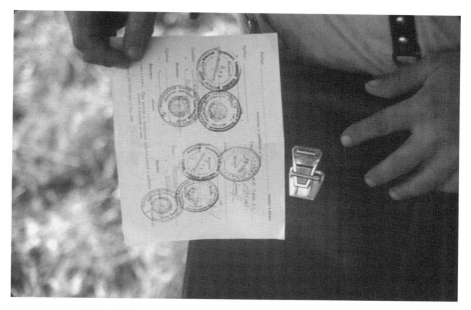

Author's 'kommanderovki' internal travel permits for Daghestan.

Poster for Lezgin First Furrow Festival combining Socialist tractors and ancient fire and fertility customs. (Akhti archive)

as a restaurant for Tsarist soldiers. They were a wealthy family and provided victuals for the army. During the 1920 war against the Red Army, all their fine goods, their gold and their chandeliers were taken. The purges of the *kulaks* under Stalin, starting in 1929, threatened Magomedali and his family with exile to Siberia. To escape this fate, they cut down their own rich orchard in their terraced garden, which like all private land was subsequently confiscated by the State in the form of the local Party. It turned out that he was spared exile for a different reason – it had all been an intentional bureaucratic bungle. He shrugged his shoulders and grinned. Somehow, he got his land back 40 years later and quietly replanted the orchard. It was all too late. When he built a house there for his wife, she did not want to live in it. His sons had already left Botlikh and his daughter and her husband had divorced. His story made the plums, ten different types of apple and three varieties of pears taste very sweet.

Collectivisation, the State seizure of all agricultural land, more than any other political act, degraded and destroyed the country. However, it was just as likely that something else equally nasty would have taken its place, as Collectivization was only one of several options for forcing a 'feudal' society into the 20th century. The Marxian idea of a proletariat had never existed in Daghestan, where there was no working class in the mainly village agrarian population, and little industry in the towns. Even in Baku, with its oil industry, the working class was more of an ethnic or religious than a political division.

The only way to get past the old propaganda lies was through research in the villages, the job of the Academy of Sciences. Magomedkhan spoke Avar, Arabic, Lak, Kumyk and Russian, and was well known, so we got fast and friendly treatment. He had studied ethnology at the University of Leningrad under the late Academician Yu. Bromlei (later chief advisor to the Soviet government and longstanding director of ethnography at the Academy of Sciences of the USSR) and he had been doing research fieldwork in Daghestan for nine years. The previous summer he had run a three-month expedition, looking after 34 specialists who worked round the Avar region in pairs.

Unusually for a Soviet ethnographer, he had written about inter-ethnic disagreements, how people ate and trade customs, using his official work on the effects of urbanisation of the villages of Daghestan to gather other information. He spoke of a mysterious "contemporary ethnic process." Process had been the Marxian euphemism for destruction. Soviet ethnographers (including, it was rumoured, an extremely reluctant and evasive Bromlei) had been more or less unwillingly used by the Stalinist authorities to provide background information which the state could use for more effective repression. Today ethnographers preferred to see themselves as agents for peaceful self-determinism, studying how people reacted with neighbouring nationalities. Lenin promised self-determinism, which he never delivered, so today they found themselves in a political-philosophical time-warp. Magomedkhan thought that "there was no point, however, in bringing back the *ochag* ('hearth') or *godekan* system ('men's village council')" as means of dialogue.

"Use local newspapers instead," I interrupted.

"But it is also possible to find some contemporary answers in traditions," replied Magomedkhan.

They had a systematic way of collecting information. Near Bezhta, Magomedkhan wanted to interview two villagers, whom Daniel-the-Historian knew. The academics had compiled lists of all the old people in the villages, whom they had interviewed on their summer expeditions over the years. In Bezhta there were about a hundred such informants with a larger number in the surrounding villages. Clearly, as they were over 65, every year there were fewer and the older they were, the less reliable their memory. Magomedkhan always needed the same story from three informants. But even if three said one thing, which yet a fourth contradicted, he put a question mark in his report.

Freedom of travel was one of the Human Rights agreed by the USSR at the Helsinki Conference. But it hardly happened in Daghestan, where it was compulsory to have a job and you could only travel if you had a *kommanderovki*, an authorisation from your employer. As a foreigner, I had to have dated stamps of arrival and departure in different republics, even within the Russian Federation, which I was always having done unofficially as I invariably forgot to register – it was alien to me. In addition, bus, train and air tickets were in short supply and usually only available to organisations, not individuals, except Moscow airtickets, but only if I paid ten times the rate in hard currency, which had recently became compulsory.

For the few lucky private or organisational car-owners, the rationed petrol supply was haphazard, even with ration coupons. Sometimes we waited an hour for 20 litres of petrol, other times there was only 72 octane kerosene as a substitute. It took me a while to catch on that we often got 19 litres of benzene on the pump (where the pointer started at four litres) for a 20 litre voucher. That explained why it was expensive to buy a job running a petrol pump. Sometimes we ended up hitching a lift by the roadside, which was quicker.

Every time I went to Daghestan it was as part of the UK-USSR Cultural Agreement, but nevertheless my trips were hindered both by their delays in providing a jeep and its poor condition, which must have been either intentional or culpably inefficient or both. First we had to get permission for the route and for my collaborator to be released to accompany me. Then there were authorisations to have a jeep, petrol coupons and a driver, who needed another permit to travel. Then everyone needed documents for money for expenses. Then we had to get a jeep. We were offered a jeep with no carburettor. We wanted a new one, strong enough for our long and bumpy journey to Bezhta. By 10am next day, even "our" old jeep had vanished with the driver, a lazy Russian, who was off on private business. He returned at 11 and we drove together back to our Institute to appeal to the director, who could not get us a new jeep either, so we rode back to the garage. In the end, we were obliged to keep the old jeep with a Volga engine, a dicky clutch and oil leaks.

Our first-choice driver – known as 'Anti-Freeze' – had disappeared, so we

The author feeling the weight of a Kalashnikov equipped with special night sight in the company of Gamid Gamidov, former wrestling champion and later Minister of Finance. Current lawlessness means that many officials need armed protection. It did not prevent Gamid being assassinated by a remote-control car bomb in October 1996 – Daghestan lost the best president they never had.

got another Dargin who needed a couple of hours to locate third and fourth gears – not his fault. Magomedkhan had to get more papers for the new driver, which had to be stamped at the Academy. We had planned to leave at eight in the morning four days earlier. Magomedkhan and I were so fed up with these regular delays, which always cost us from five to nine days of expedition on every one of my trips, that we decided to buy our own vehicle. To pay for half of one, I had brought a video-recorder to Makhachkala. First Magomedkhan was going to buy his uncle's Zaparozhnets, the local put-put, but it seemed that the air-cooled engine would overheat on mountain roads, so he then decided to buy an old jeep as scrap from the Filial. In theory it would cost 7000 roubles plus 22,000 to renew everything and then be worth 50,000. The director of transport for the Filial finally asked in vain for an invitation to London in return for providing or selling us the jeep. He subsequently became a failed banker.

Then we had to get there. There was no tread on the front left tyre and the back right was flat after a night journey on the rocky mountain roads. In the rain, when the 4-wheel drive didn't work, the Red Army jeep (a Ruf) immediately skidded and nearly toppled over on clay, but held on stones. The front right spring had also broken and grease was spraying from the overheated back wheels. Inside, the gearstick had to be removed three times to change gear with a crowbar, while the electrics cut out when the driver moved the gearstick, although the horn beeped at every bump. The back of my front seat broke, so I held on to the dashboard rail for the last 20 kilometres. The dashboard spontaneously heated up and the lights stopped working, while sulphurous fumes bubbled from the deformed battery, and the roof leaked from ever-changing places whenever it rained. The water boiled over going up most passes, but improved when my postcard of Madonna, the pop-goddess, was stuck on the windscreen.

The road to Bezhta had been built by slave labour, over 17 years, excluding the long snowy seasons. The rocks had been split by hammering in wooden wedges. The jeep stopped four times in six hours. A bus-full of girls ululated as they passed us. An unexpected advantage of a breakdown was that we sometimes borrowed a bus, which provided a cheerful way of gathering information from grateful passengers, who had been saved a long wait. Another year, after nine hours on the road, it was a landslide that forced us to turn back near Bezhta. It was frustrating. Once I returned to the unwelcoming hotel in Makhachkala at six in the evening, after losing yet another two days of a six-day trip. In despair, I reckoned that during one 42-day theoretical expedition, I had only spent 16 nights in the villages.

Air travel was also confused. There was no jet fuel in Moscow, so the flight to Makhachkala had left over eight hours late. This aeroplane was going to take me back to Moscow. While waiting at Makhachkala airport, I examined the amazing picture chart of forbidden weapons, which was next to the pictures of wanted men – no rewards offered – which looked like the election posters. It was lucky that I had passed on my savage knife from Koubachi. It was only openable with an impossibly stiff thumb press, and in any case would not have been allowed on the aeroplane. Neither were 19th-century *kinjal* daggers, 16th-century maces, giant wooden Hercules-style clubs, nor what appeared to be a studded cod-piece, which, I was told, was normally strapped into the palm for pushing into faces. No crucifixion-sized nails. No comprehensive range of switch blades, old hand guns, or something looking like bent old jeep parts with a wrist-sized loop at the small end. No alarming knuckle-dusters with baroque protrusions. Surprisingly, broken bottles were not included, but then no one would ever waste alcohol.

Ramazan had checked in my ticket and luggage. An hour and a half later, I was squeezed through to the hand luggage X-ray section and a woman controller said that I did not have a registration mark on my ticket.

"But then how could my luggage have been checked in?" I inquired. "Here are my reclaim tickets."

Then a young male official started on my visa: "Why, as the guest of the Academy of Sciences, did the visa have both their stamp and the Ministry of Culture's on the back? Why was there no hotel stamp?"

I was under arrest.

I decided to speak English. The real reason was that because of the start of the academic year – there was always some reason or other – the Academy would not have been able to get tickets. So I had asked Ramazan to get them. As director of the museums he was part of the Ministry of Culture, and needed the stamps to get me the ticket for roubles. Ramazan, Magomedkhan and two other friends accompanied me to the police room. It had comfortable seats, air-conditioning which worked and the Iraq news on television. The whisper went round that the official was a dreaded Lezgin, unlike my companions.

Magomedkhan and Ramazan filled in my charge sheet and signed for both organisations. They wrote that I did not know and was very sorry. One question asked if I was a member of the Communist Party. Of course I was, they exploded. ("Was it better or worse?" I wondered.) I signed once on each side of the sheet. I asked if I would ever be allowed into Daghestan again. The uniformed policeman – an Avar – made it clear to us that he thought the official was an idiot.

I was escorted by the Lezgin to the plane. He was from Rutul and religious. He had never before had the chance of practising his English: "Yes, your accent was wonderful and it has been a pleasure meeting – gerund or participle?"

We shook hands at the steps to the aeroplane. Then the stewardess would not let me on. She said that I had not been registered. I waited for her to return to the building to check with the other officials, whom I had already seen. The aeroplane looked full. It seemed a long time before she came back and apologised as I settled into Row 2, the ministerial seats. The small children were already screaming.

Daghestan people also often committed crimes against bureaucracy, or rather against the Party. We met Gapur Mogamedov at his recently built riverside cafe on the main road at Krasni Most, 'Red Bridge', near Gergebil. To cover the walls, he had commissioned large oil paintings of fantastic subjects such as Shamil and a slim Rasul Gamzatov brandishing his book *My Daghestan*, riding across the mountain plains together. One end of the room was spanned with a pierced tin arch of arabesques filled with wild animals. Even though the cafe was not to open for another month, his wife produced a delicious breakfast. Gapur as an expropriated shepherd apologised that he had no meat. As soon as he opened, he would run the state-controlled restaurant down the road out of business – but who cared anyway.

There was even real crime in Daghestan. Magomed Suleymanov, the Bezhta prosecutor, thought that patterns of criminality had changed in the village. He was proud that there had been no murders or stabbings – a residue of the inter-family blood-feud, banned by the Party in 1923. Also the level of reporting trivial crimes was lower than in Tsarist times, when it was a crime punishable by prison to pilfer ten kopeks. A lot of petty crime was dealt with privately, so he now found that he had too little work to provide the money to finish rebuilding his house. Before, when Magomed was a defence lawyer, he thought that there were too many cases. Reading between the lines, there seemed to be three legal systems in force – Soviet law, local Party extortion and the old customary law, *adat*.

Since 1992 there has been a fourth illegal system – mafia 'law'. This has been created by a combination of recent, inter-related events: the Russian war in Chechenia and the war and subsequent take-over of the Aliev regime in Azerbaijan, both leading to the increase in Russian troops in Daghestan; the blocking of communications by phone and transport with Moscow and St Petersburg; the closing down of all factories in Daghestan; and the break-up of the (inefficient) Soviet distribution system, immediately replaced by racketeering.

The Gamidov bomb assassination and a recent bomb in a military apartment block have taken events into an uncharted area. Whether the perpetrators are local mafia hit squads, Chechen exiles or Russian agent-provocateurs, the results and implications are nasty. The "troublous times" of the Russian 17th century have returned: there is enough food – almost nothing more.

Lenin flanked by Orzhonikidze ('Sergo the Butcher') and General Kirov in the centre of Gunib, once Shamil's stronghold (sculpture by local master).

· 13 ·

New nationalism for old nations

*I*t felt as if J. L. Borges was looking over my shoulder. He liked stories about mysterious libraries and there are about 1200 of them in Daghestan. In the larger libraries there is a door, discretely marked 'Service', which is where the non-books of non-history and old maps are kept. I have never seen this door, but I have been given books from there, such as *Songs of Stalin*, printed in Daghestan in 1949, which silently witnessed how nationalism was suppressed.

Borges also collected puzzling words. I found it difficult to understand the word 'nationalism' in the Soviet Union of today, where it could take on whatever meaning the writer or speaker wished to give it. There was little point in imposing some Western interpretation of this concept, rather it seemed more accurate and useful to allow an admittedly complicated idea to evolve from the local material.

I never went looking for nationalism, it came my way. There was Stalinism trying to suppress it, while heroes were evoked to encourage it. The Party manipulated the media and the main ten languages of Daghestan and forced urbanisation, combined with a ban on residential building, to make the peoples mix.

Over the past 15 years, the locals were only able to reply with festivals and stories, building blocks for some inner sense of identity. I pieced together stories of both more- and less-threatened ethnic minorities from the 33 indigenous peoples living in Daghestan, and developed ideas of a what must remain a philosophical opposition to the Communist regime. But I still have a feeling that the Party failed to destroy it, blanket-bombing a nebulous target which it never quite managed to define.

Songs of Stalin was a symbol of the denial of nationalism. As an elaborate literary insult, the best poets in the main languages of Daghestan were commissioned to write paeans about Stalin, parodies, set to the music of their own national songs, like these stanzas from the Kumyk national hymn:

New nationalism for old nations

He – Our Leader, He – Our Friend

Who is higher than the heavens, who is stronger than the storm? – Stalin!
Who is brighter than the fires of the sun? – Stalin!
Who is more immense than my land? – He, our Stalin!
Who is harder than the granite on it? – Only Stalin!

It is Stalin who is the genius of the wide oceans.
He leads his peoples to universal victory.

Skies, skies! Bow down before him! . . .

The portraits of Stalin, still stencilled on truck doors, his photographs adorning bus windscreens and chrome relief profiles on the walls of homes, express a supernationalism, perhaps his greatest success. This may be the point of view of the colonial rulers. But Daghestan desires for 'home rule' are linked to their perception of nationalism, though their eventual aspirations may stop well short of independence.

We had a practical lesson in Bezhta village, population 1500, which I visited with two ethnographers and a historian from the Daghestan Filial of the Academy of Sciences. When we had stayed there for over three days, in line with the usual custom, we had been politely invited to the Raikom building to answer written questions and share our learning with 40 Bezhtins. On a raised platform, we sat next to the Third Secretary at a long table, covered in a red furry cloth.

Tactfully, nationalism was first linked to their hero, Shamil. "Did Shamil come to Bezhta?" – "Yes, to negotiate with the Turks about Georgia." "Was he a hero?" – "Yes, today, but in the 1960s he was not. This was comparable to the Communist assessment of Napoleon, depending on whether he was seen to be fighting Tsarism or the people of Russia.* There was recently a conference for Soviet scholars on Shamil in Derbent, which turned into a celebration."

Then, homing in to the real subject, "What is the difference between *etnicheskaya gruppa*, ethnic group, and *narod*, a people?" – "Political, the former has only an internal role continuing its culture, the latter has outside relations with other *narodi*. Physical maps have been on sale in villages since 1989, but ethnic maps are still secret, nowadays probably to prevent nationalistic arguments. That is one reason why there is no paper for Gadji Gamzatov to print 20,000 planned copies of 65 ethnological maps of Daghestan."

The next step: "As Bezhta is a separate nation, what about independence for Bezhta?" – "No man is an island and neither is Bezhta, it needs to be part of a larger economic group, such as a country or federation."

---

* The retired Mikhail Gorbachev at a recent lecture in the Sheldonian, Oxford, used the word "Bonapartism" in a negative sense – so now I know.

Then the generalisation: "If we Bezhtin are aboriginals, does that mean that we are descended from monkeys? Did other tribes pass through here and what does the archaeological evidence indicate?" – difficult questions, followed by a probe, "What is the use of ethnography for Bezhta?" – I ducked this by sticking to a capitalist economic argument: "Trade is necessary as Bezhta is not self sufficient. Trade depends on trust and understanding customs and knowing about each other."

And the pay-off: "What could we trade?" – "Sell your untouched mushrooms from the woods to the Russians." "What if some are poisonous?" – "Sell them too. Sell your medicinal herbs, your carved wooden spoons and plates and grow your onions, carrots, potatoes and tomatoes under glass, as they grow and sell lemons near Akhti."

&

Awareness of nationalism is fostered by the treatment it is given in the media. The effect of recent external events has been dramatic. I sat next to a bemused Magomed Usienov, my host and a local party official in Bezhta – mayor since the March 1990 elections – as we watched a television documentary about the success of the Popular Front in the Baltic states on July 14, 1989. In Khunzakh, at the local First Secretary's comfortable large house, we watched the Olympic Games on TV, bounced off a nearby tall red dish aerial. The BBC World Service was also clear in the villages, but not in Makhachkala. They may understand English, but there are no short-wave radio sets.

The World Service speaks about the USSR usually seen from Moscow, for instance, giving the first news of Ligachev's demotion from the Politburo to lead the agricultural committee, but not about Daghestan. Daghestanis are oddly concerned about how Daghestan is thought of by westerners, and seem pleased with the usual platitudes of praise. Curiosity about foreigners must also explain why I had unexpectedly been approached and given the rights for exchange tours for small groups, breaking the state monopoly of Intourist, and introducing bed-and-breakfast to Daghestan. In the end, after much publicity in Britain, four people went. In 1988, during an interview for the conservative Daghestan Pravda, M. Aidunbekov, 35, asked the cliché *"Kak vash perspektiv?"* or "How do you see things?" When I answered "You can't make perestroika sitting down," he stopped.

After an interview on Avar radio, I asked about broadcasting in Daghestan. Each main language is allocated only eight hours a week, and most of that is filled with a translation from Russian of non-local programs. So the July 1989 editions of the Avar paper *Ba'arab Bairaq*, 'Red Flag', printed pages of

Facing page: Boy dancer wearing black cherkess flared jacket, with banderoles originally for gun powder across his chest and a silver encrusted dagger belt and long soft leather riding boots to protect his knees when he lands after a great leap.

interviews about the Avar festival at Khunzakh, described below, and the Kumyk paper, *Lenin Yolu*, 'Lenin's Way', printed my comments on Kumyk rugs as a nationalistic boast.

Soviet-controlled television and radio now reaches most mountain homes, but ignores Daghestan culture. There is only Russian, not local, language, music, songs, literature, children's cartoons, sport, films and of course, news. At 6pm, two local presenters read the Soviet news, with ten minutes of local Party news. This is followed by the weather forecast, where, unlike Tbilisi, Baku, Astrakhan, Erevan or Rostov, Makhachkala does not appear on the map, as it is part of the RSFSR or Russian Federation. During an average day's programme, local input amounted to 20 to 30 minutes, which has not changed recently. The village *klub* always shows Russian movies. It is not surprising that films and TV have proved addictive. In the most traditional village, Gagatl, we stayed with Akhmed Gadjibatyrov, a religious man, who did not drink but watched television reclining on his *takhta* (raised dais). During holidays, schoolchildren spend all day watching television.

Still more dangerous to local identity, especially since it is not recognised as such, are the recently permitted American and other non-Soviet television shows. The first bastion to fall is sexual taboo. Since 1988, a revolution has started which may change the family structure, by altering traditional patterns of relations between men and women. The pleasures of love – as opposed to courtship – have remained largely undiscovered in the mountain villages, where the purpose of intercourse was mainly for procreation, unlike in Moscow or London. Since glasnost, Soviet TV is now showing pop music every morning on *120 Minut* and pop is sexy, regularly including an East German all-girl romp group, a Romanian chanteuse, go-go dancing and Western pop videos. Most villages now have a *video zaal*, as the most popular co-operative venture, where it can only be a matter of time before the present supply of black and white kung-fu films will be supplemented by soft porn.

Village girls seem to like disco dancing. My gifts of samples of perfume, lipstick, make-up powder, eye shadow and skin lotions are treasured as promises of forbidden attraction. How that sudden change must affect the traditional modesty of mountain girls, many of whom now visit the towns, whether to study or see relatives. It is being accelerated by the introduction of Western televisual proof of another life. For example, Sabrina, the early nineties Italian sex bomb, introduced some quite new hip movements, wearing mainly a wide leather belt, while pouting "Boys, boys, boys" with obvious relish before a huge approving audience. Cut to a slightly embarrassed virginal Russian female announcer, who next introduced tame photographs of Soviet dress modes, followed by another Italian fashion queen, giving it to the viewers. "But how can I buy it?" the presenter asked.

Desire is born on television. I asked our generous host, the First Secretary of Khunzakh what effect go-go dancing would have on mountain village girls. He replied that they were out working in the fields during *120 Minut*, starting at

6.30am, so they would not see it. But that's hardly true: even Magomedkhan's three-year-old daughter rocked with the TV dancers.

Local languages are rarely heard on television, but there was one exception, a memorial programme to the Lezgin poet Etim Emin. All the main nationalities provided poets who praised his work in verse in their own languages before an ecstatic audience in Makhachkala. I heard Russian, Avar, Lak, Kumyk, Dargin, Lezgin, Nogai and there was also Tat, Tabassaran and Azeri. These ten languages are now taught locally, though children start learning Russian later, at the age of six. Three additional languages are now planned to be in print – Rutul, Tsakhur and Agul. Before the Russians took over in 1860, Arabic, Turkish and Persian were the written languages in Daghestan, while the 33 Caucasian tongues had rich oral traditions, which were passed on, in the family or the village, through epic poems and folktales.

The first collection was made by Baron von Uslar, a remarkable scholar, while he served as a German officer in the Russian army. He also wrote the first full Avar grammar in the late 19th century, which I found in a shop near the British Museum, taking refuge from the rain. There was another start collecting folktales in 1946, but they were not published until 1957-58 when Moscow policy stopped banning recognition of non-Russian cultures. Since then, about a couple of volumes in each of the major local languages have been published in small editions by the Daghestan Filial of the Academy of Sciences, where Dr A Abdurakhmanov and Professor M Abduhakim work. Between them they have collected over a thousand folk stories during 25 years from more than 80 informants. Their notebooks contain photographs of informants and record their name, age, village, and occupation.

I recorded them having a story-telling competition, Abdurakhman in Avar and Abdulhakim in Kumyk. Their work is the academic equivalent of the very old man whose job was to keep the poems and songs in Tindi village, or the 93 year old who chanted the Kumyk epic poem for an hour. With the recent upsurge in national feeling, more will be published to add to the 1990 collection of Avar folktales in Avar. The Filial is directly funded from Moscow and run as its subsidiary, unlike the Georgian and Azerbaijan Academies, which have their own budgets. In 1990 a Daghestan Scientific Centre was created to try and achieve academic and financial independence – in vain. The Filial had published several understandably covertly nationalistic books on physical remains in Daghestan, which fitted in with Soviet apolitical research into archaeology and material culture.

For example, there has been dogged work done by Paruk Debirov, recording carved wood and stone. The prizes, three 400-year-old giant wooden columns, almost Aeolian in style, are on display in Makhachkala. Other ancient colonnades were still found in mosques, which were potent symbols of local history, such as the Kumukh mosque. It was built in 778, when the Laks converted voluntarily to Islam (hence the old prefix Kazi-Kumukh, meaning 'Defender of the Faith'). There was another symbol there – a great Koran, too

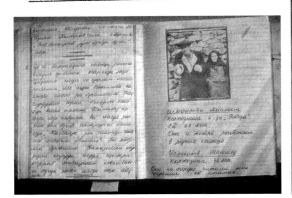

LANGUAGES OF DAGHESTAN
(Facing page, clockwise from top left): Laki translation of
Rasul Gamzatov's Avar writings; school reader in Avar
– one of the eleven languages taught in different regions
of Daghestan; Neo-Stalinist broadsheet, first edition,
August 1991; Dr A. Abdurakhmanov and Prof. A.
Adzhiev have collected the folklore of Daghestan over 25
years – two examples from their notebooks recording oral
material; both in Avar from farm workers in the Gunib district;
'Korsolh' Tat newspaper, published in Baku in 1922 (Tel-Aviv
archive, ack. Prof. M. Zand); Jewish prayer book in Aramaic
written in Hebrew letters, Derbent synagogue.
(This page, clockwise from top left): Early Soviet warning to the
women of Daghestan "under the power of adat customary law,"
offering Soviet feminism in exchange; an article about the
author in an Avar newspaper; an example of Avar verse,
written in modified Cyrillic with the distinctive 'I', used to
distinguish ejective consonants; Baron von Uslar the inspiration
behind 'Spornik . . .', collected essays of fieldwork in the
Caucasian Mountains from the 1870s – see Bibliography.

I ЦIАД АХIИ

Я-а-а-лагъу цIад баги,
ЦIад-цIалахъун магъилље,
Мегъ-мегъалда щущаги,
Щоб-щобазда биххаги!

Баги бечед чвахун цIад,
абхилъан иц баккизе,
Гъарзаго тIорцел цвезе,
Щвараб баракат лъезе!

245

heavy for one man to lift. Over the centuries, the mosque was rebuilt three times on its original plan, and it had just been restored. Local history reinforces nationalism and our guide, the garrulous Omar Ibragimovich Gaidarov, proudly recited that the mosque was supposed to be linked by an underground road, where 70 youths survived the Mongol sack in 1240, with the site of the 17th-century fort, Burgai Kala, part of the ancient fire-tower signal system. The walls were recently rebuilt from an old photograph, and inscribed in whitewashed stones "glory to the Communist Party." It was a jumbled flood of longing for identity and recognition. Through these more or less humble stories you can hear their striving for an elusive dignity and the primal howl of the dispossessed for an identity which we take for granted. It is not comfortable work.

The mythology of local heroes has proved equally resilient. The greatest is Shamil, the Avar imam who fought for independence, stopping the Tsarist armies from 1844 until 1859. Like Magomedkhan, every mountaineer would proudly pose for me in his *bourka*, in front of the hand-coloured picture of his bearded great-grandfather, an *alim*, or elder, of Shamil, with his sons, dressed in black *cherkess* flared coats, their hands restless on their *kinjal* daggers. Near Gunib, they point out Shamil's gorge and secret cave reached by rock track, accessible only to their horses. Beneath, his small band massacred 20,000 Russians under General Vorontsev in 1844. Later warrior icons which echo Shamil's mystique, are group photographs from the 1920s of hungry, unshaven, armed revolutionaries or partisans. Under Soviet rule (in addition to revolutionaries, war heroes and cosmonauts), wrestlers, poets and dancers took on the mantle of public folk heroes, keeping a sometimes ambivalent relationship with the authorities.

In the 1940s Gamzat Tsadasa became national poet, to be succeeded by his son Rasul Gamzatov, who became the token Daghestani – North Caucasian – on the USSR Supreme Soviet. Apotheosis, through proximity to Shamil, was achieved when Rasul related how, as a youth, he wrote a poem attacking him. Later in a dream, Shamil told him that of all his 20 wounds, the poem hurt the most. This caused Rasul, like another St Paul, to become a supporter of Shamil.

Another way to become a Daghestan hero and remain acceptable to the Soviets, was through wrestling, like Ali Aliev. At the 1959 world wrestling championships in Teheran, this relative-unknown first defeated the Iranian Olympic silver medallist, and then the famous Turk, Ahmen Bilek, to became world champion at 22. He was born in 1937 in Chokh, Gunibskii rayon, in the highlands of Daghestan. With a father in the army, the family moved about. Wherever they went, Ali worked hard to develop his strength, determined to be a wrestler. Disappointed, when he was not selected for a national youth contest, due to lack of endurance, he doubled his training to strengthen his stamina. By 1957 Aliev became champion of Daghestan and at the National games in 1958 he astonishingly defeated, one after the other, outstanding Soviet wrestlers to become lightweight champion of the USSR. In the years that followed, Aliev, as Master Sportsman of the USSR, became the first Daghestani to lead teams to the Olympics in Rome, Tokyo and Mexico. He was five times World and nine times USSR Champion. He is now a doctor.

All mountain boys who wrestle also dance, so it is traditional to have a dancer as hero too. Uslipat Abakarova was a Bagulaal Avar from Kapucha village, Tsuntinskii rayon. She was simply the best dancer of Daghestan and won prizes in far-away Paris and Warsaw. In a last photograph, when she was over 80, she sat strait-backed in a dazzling silk costume, set off by her special double earrings, surrounded by adoring pupils in every different Avar dress. She danced so lightly, Alla Umakhanova said, with small fluttering waves of her hands and very short steps, gliding on her knitted shoes. She danced until she died. These heroes are all Avar, reflecting an ascendancy of the largest ethnic minority, with over a quarter of the population of Daghestan. One curious result is that several peoples who speak different languages only have songs in Avar. Although this is resented by the other peoples, it is the Avar clans or *tukhums* that rule the country.

With no ethnic representation on television, festivals have become an important channel for asserting cultural identity. One morning I photographed the four A3-sized volume photo-archive of Akhti festivals assembled by Jamal Azizovich Shefiev. On my previous visit, I had misjudged the importance of what Jamal had done for his people. He was the first person to restart the traditional festivals in Daghestan in 1970 after a personally dangerous argument with the Communist Party apparatus, proving that the festivals were neither religious nor anti-Soviet. Obviously, they were pagan.

From one angle, Jamal is a symbol of the Soviet period. While he is chief of the cultural department of the Raiispolkom and member of the soviet of the region of Akhti, he wants to re-open the mosques, which is unusual in south Daghestan. He has already spent 10,000 roubles to restore one mosque, ostensibly for theatrical plays and he has now given it back to believers to use. Magomedkhan suggested that Jamal next collected funds to build a museum to house the mosque's collection.

≥≈

Daghestan has revived an unusually large number of annual festivals, as every nationality has their own version. For example, the Dargins have more than 13 celebrations a year, both solemnising the natural cycle and exalting the glory of man. There is the winter solstice feast, and then *Evla Ts'a*, the Zoroastrian spring fire ceremony. The primal agricultural festival of the First Furrow, *Kubyakhrumi*, when participants are ritually hosed with water to ensure fertility of the fields, is followed by others for planting trees, calling for rain, and commemorating weeding and harvest. Men's virility is celebrated in the Festivals of Victory, with the presentation to war veterans of the *kulucha* prize – a giant flat loaf, almost completely hidden behind a hundred painted eggs,

*The advent of technology could be so simple: It only costs $1000 a village for a fruit and
vegetable drying tunnel, a plastic bag sealing machine and a desk-top vacuum packer. Dried
and vacuum packed foods would supplement off-season diets.*

spiked onto the bread; of Mountain Skills, where the wrestling champion wears
the ritual *venkom* laurels of a great doughnut-shaped bread, resting on his
shoulders; of Chivalry, *Gulala-Aku-Vukon*, in Koubachi; of the Game, called
Ziduni in the village of Urakhi; and of Shepherds.

Frequently traditional and Soviet rituals have been combined, as in the
Lezgin Festival of Flowers, *Sukversovar*, which takes place in Akhti every June.
Local boys and girls climbed the mountain peak to gather magic flowers before
dawn. They took food and wine, and sang and danced all day. The best girl
worker in the *kolkhoz* was crowned queen, and danced with a clown in a tall
white sheepskin hat, differing from the older version, where a shah would
wrestle and fight the clowns with his *kinjal* dagger. Finally, the queen and her
attendants rode down the mountain with the flowers to give them to the old
villagers for luck. Celebrations continued until midnight. But they now wear
foreign costumes, because the festival must be international, and is organised
by the Party *khudozhnik samodetni*, or self-action artists, but without art, as Alla
Umakhanova commented. Another Lezgin festival, to celebrate the appearance
of sweet cherries, when young people danced in the orchards near Kasimkent

in 1986, is a bland version of the older *Karu*, named after the earth mother goddess, commemorated in a drawing in the Akhti archive, reminiscent of the many-breasted Diana of the Ephesians.

The Avar festival at Khunzakh on July 21 and 22, 1989 was the first unashamedly nationalist demonstration in Daghestan. Our jeep had two punctures, so at five in the morning Magomedkhan and I started waiting for a bus for Khunzakh in the middle of Botlikh, as instructed by the local woman Third Secretary. At about eight a very old bus appeared, driven by a very old man in his *karakoul* lambskin hat, khaki breeches and black riding boots next to his wife, who had an enigmatic smile. The Raikom had rented the thing to the elderly couple, who were the parents and grandparents of the ten-strong Botlikh Family Ensemble. Their children could not come because they were looking after the eldest son who was in hospital following a car crash. (Sadly, he later died, I heard in August 1990 when I met Mrs Shamkhal selling plums in Botlikh market. She wept and held my hand.)

However Shamkhal and his wife considered the festival too important to miss. Only eight days ago, he had towed the ex-Avar theatre bus from a well-earned retirement in Makhachkala. He had quickly fixed the engine, but not the body, the seats, the battery or the wheels, so it shook a lot. While driving in God's hands, Shamkal put on his green skullcap with a black tassel. When, as an act of charity, he stopped at Karakh, 50 excited people, young and old, jumped on the bus to get to the festival. About five kilometres further on, the engine stopped at the start of a long climb. Magomedkhan picked the moment when most of them had got off the bus to take a look, to tell them that they were too much weight. With his Archi mountain authority, he forbade them back on.

We arrived in Khunzakh about noon too late for the speeches (happily including my own, as I did not wish to be identified with the authorities). We met Kamil, from the Art Museum in Makhachkala, as arranged, whose 16-year-old sister was wearing a shimmering silver flamenco-style dress with a parasol. She practised her English on me and asked for a Rolling Stones cassette. I stayed with their cousin, Nurmagomed, who had made all the copper armour for the pageant in his home workshop – he then was elected mayor.

The festival was held to celebrate the 2400th anniversary of Khunzakh, capital town of the Avars. There was a historical pageant, ancient foods, a popular theatre traditional wedding and competitions for singing and dancing with about 150 entrants of all ages, the Lezginka National Dance group from Makhachkala, horseracing, a tightrope walker, a strong man and a cock fight put on for me as it was too hot for a dog fight. The crowd of 8000 was entirely Avar. For the first time in 70 years, Avar was the main language spoken by the announcers. The police allowed performers to carry arms. The old Raikom building was surrounded by newly built battlements, the scene of several warlike attacks during the performance.

There was the problem of what to do with a bust of Lenin which stood normally on top of the portal, in front of the target fortress. It would perhaps be misunderstood if Lenin were removed, so to prevent it being shot at, it was boxed in with boards, painted white. Windows in nearby houses were blown out when the cannons were fired. Battles were re-fought with streams of women prisoners from all periods of history. In chronological order, ancient pagan skirmishes were followed by Middle Ages battles with Khazars, 18th-century cavalry wearing *bourka* capes, repulsing Nadir Shah. But Hadji Murat and Shamil trotted past, without ambushing the Russians, which might have been misinterpreted. Finally, 1920s Civil War engagements with Daghestan and Russian partisans included girl soldiers, an idea foreign to Daghestan.

In between the fighting and explosions, cannon were drawn by oxen, a troika was pulled by horses and mothers sent their children to the Great Patriotic War and wept over long lists of the dead. Youths watched, spellbound, from roofs and walls overlooked by Shamil's portrait, flanked by his words "*Sudite o budushchem po proshedshemu? Tot ne khrabets kotoryi dumaet o posledstviakh!*" – "Can you judge the future from the past? He who thinks of the consequences is not brave!" On the second morning they finished judging the songs, music and dances. Then there was prize-giving and encores from the winners, with spontaneous prizes for some more popular losers. We set off back to reality at about four in the afternoon.

≈

The reality of nationalism begins with the disturbing displacement of ethnic groups from their archaic free villages (best thought of as an Ancient Greek *polis*). The village, a basic unit in Daghestan society, sometimes represented a whole nationality.

The Avar village of Charoda is growing empty. There are 250 Chadraal, and 170 more have emigrated to Makhachkala and 16 to Botlikh, but they do not sell their homes. The first village moved uphill when, as the legend goes, snakes ate the children. In contrast, the village of Ansalta, overlooking its fertile river flood plain, three kilometres from Charoda, has survived because it is twice as rich as nearby Botlikh. As usual, the villagers said that their village was the oldest, 2-3000 years old. As usual, the first house was two kilometres up the mountain. But the round arches and monolithic stone architecture are 19th-century work. Today, there are 400 inhabitants with four children and three or four cows in each family.

Tlyadal', like Ansalta, seemed to survive economically. When we arrived, the village accountant Djevatkhan Alievich Magomedov was doing the books. During 1988, *kolkhoz* sales were 2.4 million roubles, making 8-9 per cent gross profit, and a net profit of 140,000 roubles. State loans charge 2 per cent interest – they had to borrow 40,000 roubles once, in a bad year. Amortisation is over eight to 12 years, but the land and buildings are in the books at nil value. Eighty people work for the *kolkhoz* from the 120 households with 400 villagers. Most families have two or three cows and a kitchen garden.

The local king, Tazdin Debirov, estimated the village black market at four to five million roubles a year. In his garden, Tazdin grew carrots, pears, beans, sweet spring onions, apples, radishes, cucumber, dried pale green cumin tea for the heart, dill, the bitter, minty leafed herb *kinza*, wild garlic and St John's wort, and a dried golden medicinal herb for tea. He also had the best privy in Daghestan, down the end of the garden cooled by a gentle breeze, with a steady water trickle along a 30 degree downhill cast-iron gully, stopping before it reached the fast flowing river. He wanted his villagers to put in rain gutters to collect water for each house and so use the font for drinking, rather than washing water and so save carrying.

New ideas stopped after the persecution of the *kulaks* in the 1930s, which was obscenely ridiculous in Daghestan. Few *kulaks* lived in Daghestan since it was extremely poor, especially after the Civil War, but the quota had to be filled with an appropriately large number of deportations, so both old and new scores were settled. A deaf old woman was sitting alone in the road when some commissars arrived and asked her if there were any Trotskyists in the village, but she misheard the word as *traktoristi*, 'tractor drivers', and so sent them to her son and the others who would be able to help. They were all deported to Siberia.

Others were miserably exiled from their villages to the plains, and not allowed to return for 50 years on pain of punishment. In 1990 we stayed near Kasimkent with Ali Magomed, Magomedkhan's mother's cousin, who is about 70. He was forced to leave his village Archi in 1938 because the *kolkhoz* took his house, land and animals in 1936. His father was an invalid with a lame leg and with his wife and two children, they moved to Frig in Khivskii rayon when Ali was ten. In 1970 after the earthquake, they moved to a new village 15 km south of Derbent, called Novi Frig.

At last they are allowed to build their own houses. He also has a lively home economy, including about 50 sheep with lambs. His wife makes preserves in 600 litre barrels for sale and dry white wine. The wife and daughters also weave woollen *soumaks* and *palas* striped flatweaves.

Even before the 19th century, poverty forced mountain village men to go robbing or leave their families and move to towns to work. Nasir, one of Ali's sons, spoke Lezgin, and worked in Baku in the oil industry. He said that the border with Azerbaijan was open and he was fine with a passport in Baku, which was then under military rule. He had immediately tapped into a business opportunity: "Everything is expensive there except for flowers, which only cost ten kopeks each. On International Women's Day you can make a killing by taking a box of 1500 flowers to Makhachkala and selling them for 150 kopeks each – and because of the demand the price had also increased to 50 kopeks each in Baku then."

Some villages, like Gagatl, have twin suburbs built in the plains where there is work. Gagatl is 2500 metres high, with 700 hearths and 5000 people, mainly children, as there are five to a family. Seven hero-mothers (*geroi mat'*, a Soviet award for having over ten children) have ten children each and one 11. There are a similar number of Gagatl people settled in Novi Gagatl on the plain near Khasavyurt. Gagatl was the first village in Daghestan to rebuild their mosque, without permission in 1989.

Villages are both all the same and have odd identities. The bus from Botlikh to Gagatl left an hour late only after all the passengers had turned up. The main road to the Andi region and 60 km further north to Vedeno in Chechenia zigzags eight times, I lost count, up a steep mountain face. There were eight bulldozers clearing up after the rains, but we only stopped once as a machine gingerly moved ton rocks off the road, so as not to cause another rockslide onto the road below. It was tense work. In the back of the bus three young men and a girl were giggling all the time, as others scowled at them. When Magomedkhan asked why they were laughing, they said it was because they came from the village of Gunkho.

Many regions are emptying for economic reasons, like the rayon about Karata, Daniel's village. I was collecting more languages there, recording Karata, Akhwakh, Tilsi, 18km from Karata with 63 homes and 210 inhabitants, whose little-spoken language is a third Karata, and Toukhit'a village dialect, which is a third Akhwakh, and Anchikh, which is another dialect of Karata.

We were talking about how many people spoke the languages and it came out that the Karatinskii rayon has 10,300 inhabitants, down from 14,000 fifteen years ago. Today 40 per cent of the population are children and there are over 50 hero-mothers and most families have between three and seven children. Many moved to Sovietskaya near Khasavyurt for work and there is even a museum about Karata there. Mountaineers were politically encouraged to move to the plains after the earthquakes in the 1960s and 1970s, which were not reported.

Other ethnic regions were forcibly depopulated during the Stalin period. In 1944, the Chechens both in Daghestan and Chechenia were transported from many such villages to Central Asia, because Stalin feared they would join with the Germans to fight the Russians. This was a false pretext as the Germans had already retreated from Grozny. One night in Botlikh hotel, there was a knock on the door. A pretty Chechen girl from Jordan, with bad teeth, wanted to speak English. She had returned to study in Daghestan and, like some other students from Afghanistan there, she was not happy there.

After the revolution, many Chechens escaped to Jordan, Syria and Turkey and have prospered. There were rumours that the Aga Khan's secretary was a Chechen. When some Daghestani Chechens returned in 1958, they found their villages and homes settled by Avars and Laks – their 19th-century allies under Shamil. But Georgians and Cossacks who had also settled there had destroyed their cemeteries to eradicate their memory. More Chechens are now returning following the racial unrest in Central Asia and have succeeded in getting back their former lands in the Novolakskii rayon. Bagauddin Akhmedov, now Vice-President of Daghestan, resolved this, a rare feat, by giving the Laks land near Makhachkala.

Housing or rather the lack of it, is the barbed cause of inter-ethnic trouble. If your people can see that others have what you have not, but once had, the argument starts. Also house building costs vary wildly in Daghestan. Most expensive is Makhachkala where a good house can cost 100,000 roubles, in addition a bribe of 3000 roubles allegedly must be paid to the authorities to release the 'free' land. Near Magaramkent, land costs 3000 roubles a hectare and 50,000 roubles to build a nice house. State grants are worth 5-20,000 but to get one, you must pay a 2-3000 bribe. Akhti and its hamlets comprise one of the largest villages with 13,000 inhabitants – there it costs 20-30,000 roubles to build a nice house plus 2000 roubles for a hectare of land. The cheapest was Gagatl, where the unusually long houses only cost 5000 roubles. The villagers are famous builders and collect the conveniently shaped rocks themselves.

Legendary bard Mukhtar Tsagid Khuseinov strumming a 'pandur' with fellow Avar bard Magomed Rasul Khuchparu at the Khunzakh Festival.

But remember that inter-ethnic conflicts started before the sixth century, when successive waves of tribes from the north were blocked by the walls of Derbent, and forced already settled peoples to seek refuge in the mountains. The Laks have a saying that every time a Lak is born, it is a victory. A carved stone plaque built into the wall of the ruined mosque in Kriukh, dated probably 1800, commemorated an inter-ethnic battle between the small next-door villages Kiurukh and Rutul.

On a car trip with three Avars, I joked that with the new possibility of emigrating, the whole of Daghestan would declare themselves Jewish, a return to the Khazar period. Kamil's relative, who was there to help with our rug search, said that Avars would never become Jews! Temirkhan said that they would not leave either – they wanted the Russians to leave. He knew that there were 25 million *Russ* outside Russia itself, and as far as he was concerned both Russians and Ukrainians were equally unwanted. Kamil added that Jews were not the first enemy in Daghestan, Russians were.

Fifty years of Soviet policy of Russian settlement of Daghestan and dreams of intermarriage had failed, although even in Khunzakh, the Avar capital, Russians make up a tenth of the 2900 inhabitants. I was repeatedly told that if a

Daghestan girl married a Russian, her family would stab her before the wedding night. However, it is alright for Daghestan men to marry Russian women. A beautiful Kumyk song has a girl weeping for the boy she hopes to marry, who has gone away for army service and, she fears, will meet a Russian girl and not return.

In Derbent a wall was recently daubed with the slogan "Russians, Jews and Kumyks out!" Why Kumyks? They laughed: The Kumyks have been holding meetings and demonstrations demanding independence from the mountain people and putting forward pan-Turkic arguments.

In contrast, the people of Ginukh just survived extinction in 1944. From Bezhta, Magomedkhan and I drove to Ginukh village over the pass at about 2200 metres with our host, Magomed Useinov, who was born there. On one side springs rise which turn into the mighty Avar-Koisu river, on the other, the Andi-Koisu. The road was built in 1975 after two others had fallen down the mountain.

Ginukh is over 2000 metres high and is snow-covered for eight months of the year. The three-storey houses, built on a slope, have unusually long pitched roofs, covering summer quarters on the top, where hay is also stored in winter, when the temperature is -10 to -20 degrees centigrade out of the wind, with winter quarters on the second floor and animals on the ground. Electricity was connected in 1971.

Today there are 80 households, with five or six children in many houses, making a total population of 400. There is a new sports centre, club and cinema, and a well-stocked shop. The village smithy exports one domestic stove every day. Tobacco is grown for snuff, not cigarettes, as well as carrots, cabbage, onions, garlic, potatoes and cereals. Such industry is in marked contrast to Bezhta, 25 km over the pass.

We were guests of Abakhar, the local school teacher for a generation, and also the local historian, so his son, about 20, took me around the village. He thought that Ginukh was first mentioned in a seventh-century text and had an eventful religious history, described as pagan in a 13th-century Georgian manuscript, until conversion to Georgian Christianity in the 14th century. Three hundred years later, the church was destroyed by Muslims and the population of about 1000 converted to Sunni Islam. Villagers who were moved to other villages, were not allowed to speak their language and so only have a memory that their ancestors came from Ginukh.

Today everyone there speaks four languages and some, six: Ginukh, Dido in Tsunta or Kidero dialects, Bezhtin, Georgian, Avar and Russian. While I walked about, Magomedkhan sat on the *godekan* tree-trunk and quietly talked to Magomed Zakhayayev, aged 67, about the attempted genocide of his people and the Didoi. In the spring of 1944, when the population was about 300, they received a decree from the Obkom at Makhachkala that they were to be deported in three weeks. Those who refused were burnt in their homes by Daghestanis from another region and all the other houses were razed. They were forced from their alpine homes to a place near Vedeno in Chechen-Ingushetia, only 700 metres in altitude, where the population – the old, the children and even the healthy young adults – died of epidemic malaria and flu.

By 1948 the survivors adapted to the climate and regained their strength. About 300 returned in the spring of 1957 to find five houses that were still habitable. It later became known that the original decision of the Obkom was to deport two villages. One Debir Gadjiev, from Khunzakh, was the First Secretary of the Khunzakhskii Raikom and, following Stalin's deportation policy with zeal, gave the order for eight Dido villages to be evacuated and the inhabitants moved on foot to an unspecified destination, without consulting the Obkom bureaucrats, who condoned the deed. By chance, the people of Bezhta were spared.

Another small ethnic group living in Daghestan and north Azerbaijan are the Mountain Jews, also known as Tat, who speak their own language. Following recent emigration, less than 5000 still live there out of 50,000. Three synagogues are working in Daghestan and two more in neighbouring Azerbaijan. The Mountain Jews came from Persia, where they had settled after the destruction of the Second Temple, in two main waves of migration during the last 300 years. There is no evidence to support earlier settlement, which has been confused with survivals of the Khazars, who converted to Judaism in the eighth century.

Contrary to legend, Mountain Jews were not the Jews from ancient Babylon, who in fact survived until the 1950s in Baghdad. In the Caucasus, the appellation Tat was applied to Tat-speaking Muslims. Jews called themselves *juhur*, Avars and Kumyks called them *ju(h)ud* or *ju(h)ut* – a pejorative name. In both the Islamic and Russian worlds, the change of the initial *y* to *j* has a pejorative connotation, but was in such common usage that it became a pet name, merely implying inferiority. Professor Michael Zand* knew a family of four Mountain Jews, a father and two sons and their children, with three different official nationalities, and it is not known if they all had got what they wanted. The father and one son were *Gorskii Yevrei* 'Mountain Jews', the son's wife was Tatka 'Tat' like their children, and the other son who lived in European USSR was *Yevrei* 'Jewish'.

The story of how and why Mountain Jews came to be known as Tats provides an insight into the upside-down Soviet system, which unintentionally helped preserve an ethnic group, subjected to grass-roots persecution. From the late 18th century, identification papers required religion to be stated and the 1896 census, giving 95,056 Tats, is considered accurate. After the revolution, conflicting policies with regard to Jews led to unreliable census figures. However, unlike the Soviet civilian identity card which requires the bearer to enter his or her race, the military identity card only requires the

---

* The eminent authority on Soviet Judaica and co-author of the Russian *Encyclopaedia Judaica*, a tireless *refusenik* who eventually left the USSR.

bearer's religion to be stated. During the Great Patriotic War, there was violent anti-Semitism in the Red Army, so many Mountain Jews said they were Tat Muslims. This ruse was possible because conscripts were required to hand in their civilian documents, which were all lost by the army during the war. On demobilisation, it was possible to bribe the relevant local police official 50 roubles to change the nationality entry on a new identity card. Also by 1971 the Soviet government wanted to diminish the official size of the Jewish population to discourage local and international demands for emigration, so the Ethnographic Institute of the USSR Academy of Sciences gave a dispensation to a group of Mountain Jew intellectuals to change their nationality to Tat.

Magomedkhan has been repeatedly asked by the local government to write a report on the difference between Tats and Mountain Jews. He was suspicious of their motives and so has always said that they are all the same. Local Jews are confused as well. One said that in the late 1920s national schools and alphabets were only given to sufficiently large nationalities, as counted by ethnic language, so the Jews decided to become Tats. This is not true – 'Tatisation' only became national policy after 1979. Later they all changed back to Mountain Jews so they could emigrate. Most Jews have now emigrated to Israel, partly because of the increase in anti-Semitism in Russia and fears of the same in an increasingly Russian controlled state. However relations are relatively good in Daghestan and I met one Jewish Daghestan government official who had just been to Israel and returned without incident.

The original settlement was probably at Nyugdi, south of Derbent above the Samur river, because it is the only entirely Jewish village – all other places have a Jewish quarter. In fact, it is the only such intact settlement. Abshelomov published a folk legend about Nyugdi, which obscures the history, that the village was founded about 200 years ago by Jews fleeing from forcible conversion to Islam in the Tabassaran khanate. Mountain Jews are thought to have lived in 16 other villages mainly in south Daghestan, two of which are of interest. Near Jalkhan, south of Derbent, there was a settlement where they grew valuable madder for red dyes and Majalis village is reputed to have the oldest tombs, which were not to be found in the more recent Jewish cemetery where sheep grazed, but eight Tat families still live in the old Jewish *kvartal*. One family consisted of Nakhimal Ferenj, his wife Mikla, brother Jambulat (a Dargin name), son Dishi and daughter Safiat. They do not speak Hebrew nor do they go to synagogue, which Nakhimal strangely called *meschid* 'mosque' rather than the Judeo-Tat *namaz* or *numaz*, but they know the rabbi in Derbent. Ferenj said he spoke Tat, Tatar (probably meaning Turkic Azeri or Kumyk), Lezgin and Russian.

There was salted fish and calf's feet hanging in the shed in the courtyard of his single storey house, next to an old kilim and his two cars which probably didn't work. There was to be a Jewish wedding in Majalis on Sunday September 25, but the local First Secretary did not like me taking photos of the market that morning, unaccompanied, and made us leave immediately after

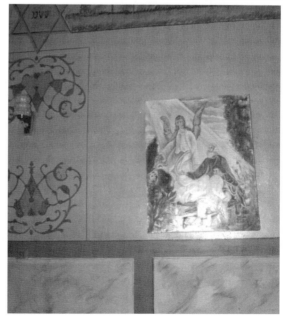

(Top left): 1988 – old Mountain Jews sitting in the courtyard of the small synagogue in Makhachkala. Then there were some 2500 Jews in Daghestan, now there are far fewer following emigration.
(Top right): One of the nine Mountain Jewish families living in Majalis – Nakhimal Ferenj, his wife Mitla, son Dishi and daughter Safiat.
(Centre): Oil painting of Moses and Aaron in Buinakst synagogue, with a dedicatory inscription for Magindovid Mahakhimovich K'iazavov, dated 1978.
(Bottom right): Local oil painting of the angel stopping Abraham from sacrificing Isaac, Makhach-kala synagogue, where the Party had moved the community from their former larger synagogue down the street.

breakfast. According to M R Ibraghimov at the Filial, Mountain Jews adopted Zoroastrian fire worship customs when they were in Persia, but these had died out or been assimilated long before. However, they did adopt local animist customs in Daghestan, such as the veneration of sacred trees and ghosts of natural spirits.

Another traditional Jewish festival was the busy Derbent Sunday market, filled with clothes, cars, bikes and about two hundred new carpets nailed on the walls. In front of the walls, on the roadside was the clothes market, with the wares laid out on the ground, under the eyes of Jewish and Azeri old women vendors. Nearby, the sons of a Tat family were doing up their house, *remont*, and we were talking when their father, Rambom Mikhaelov son of Ben Shalom, turned up in tracksuit bottoms. He explained that his family had lived there for 300 years (more likely 150) and when I asked him his nationality, he replied, "I am a Daghestani!"

Rasim Magomedov, a historian of his city Derbent, took me next door to the synagogue, where the Derbent rabbi greeted us with *"gesundheit!"* and said that only old people go to synagogue now there are 2500 Jews left there, following emigration to USA and Israel. They have no problems and want for nothing. The present synagogue was built in 1914 on the old site. There is a main room with another smaller synagogue for winter use, off the entrance porch, where there was a strange wooden tracery mimbar-like lectern, surrounded with electric candles. Rabbi Simon ben Shelbert said he was a Mountain Jew, not a Tat, like Danil ben Rabbi Shamoil, his assistant. They showed me their prayer book in Hebrew and Aramaic in Hebrew script, showing their Persian origins.

Back in Makhachkala, a Jewish Tat unofficial taxi driver said that life was really rather good for the Jews and gave me the address of the local synagogue. Like several others, he would not charge me. A 19th-century *shtetl* must have looked similar to the quiet tree-lined Kotrova Street, with single storey Russian-style houses and children playing in the road, on my way through the old Jewish quarter, past where there used to be a large synagogue, demolished 20 years ago, on what is now called Revolution Square. Nearby there is a small unannounced synagogue, at No. 111 Yermoshkina Street. The young Makhachkala rabbi, Shalumov Sherbchiv, who had studied at the Moscow yeshiva, said that both young and old came to his modest synagogue. He was just off to take some old people for a Sunday drive in a minibus. He repeated that there are now only 2500 Jews in Makhachkala after emigration. Inside was another recent (possibly heretical) oil painting of Moses and the Tablets of the Law. Past the three old men sitting in the leafy courtyard, was a spotless kosher butchery, recently transformed into a *kooperativ*.

While one plump chicken was patiently waiting in a basket, I asked the rabbi for a 20 kopek chit, as a souvenir, which shoppers used instead of giving him money for slaughtering. He added that the Buinakst synagogue was still working. The walled brick building, which has survived three earthquakes, is entered by a street gate, over which is written 1856, the date it was built. I arrived just before six when the Rabbi appeared with just enough men to make up a minyan for prayers. The ten included two boys and three young men. Inside, the large hall was filled with empty benches. Next to the magnificent painted Ark and brightly decorated platform, surrounded by red and white painted railings, was another heretical oil painting of 'God' giving Moses the tablets of the law, with a Russian inscription, "In memory of the Synagogue in the name of Iliazarov Magindovid Manakhimovich, May 1978." Under the painted ceiling, up on a wooden arcade, was the women's gallery from a time when there was a larger congregation.

The rabbi explained that only 120 households remained from over 1000. In contrast to Makhachkala, they seemed agitated. They needed help for everything, starting with Hebrew tuition books as they only had two, one a photocopy montage. He doubted that his letters abroad would get out of the USSR, or that it was legal to send him books. He had asked for help from the Jewish communities in Moscow and Makhachkala, but things were worse there. They felt cut off. Although I was there with two Avars, I told them that they should say what they wanted. Just before we drove off, they rushed out and asked me to write down Professor Zand's address. Next year, early one morning, I woke up the confused gateman to pass him a Tat magazine from Israel. It must be odd to be a Jew in Daghestan.

❧

It is hard to judge if internal ethnic problems are worse than those between republics, where sizeable minorities live. The first thing two men from different Caucasian republics did, like Emil, my ex-collaborator from Azerbaijan, and Magomedkhan, was to have long discussions of the Armenian problem, which has disturbed neighbouring Daghestan, raising questions of the meaning of 'homeland', when all their boundaries were made after the 1920s. The Armenian problem is bringing back the turbulent history of the nationalities. Even the executed Baku Commissars were Armenians under Stepan Shaumian. After 1920 the Karabagh Khanate was replaced by a small two-thirds Armenian and one third Azeri republic for a short time, to destabilise the *Mussavat* ('Egality') party in Azerbaijan. The capital was Khanikent near Stepanikent, so the whole dispute is based on false roots. A drunken Emil thinks that Azerbaijan and Turkey might unite from the Mediterranean to the Caspian. Magomedkhan went to a conference about origins of peoples with academics from the Caucasian republics of Georgia, Armenia, Chechen-Ingushetia and Azerbaijan. He listened to all the talks and then commented: "If I draw together your learned maps of historical Georgia, Armenia, Chechen-Ingushetia and Azerbaijan, then there is no room for Daghestan."

There was international trouble in Georgia, which we heard about in

Bezhta, just over the pass. While I was buying tomatoes, apricots and sunflower seeds at the private covered stall, Magomedkhan got talking to his former driver's brother, a young militia man from Tliarata, and a good fellow. He came around for supper with news from Georgia, where some of his family live. The militia were on alert, warned of a secret order to arm Georgian criminal prisoners to attack the Abkhaz. On television they announced 269 wounded, of whom 198 were in hospital and 19 had died. Near Ochamchira, where there are both Georgians and Abkhaz, there was a stand-off, with police and army trying to keep them apart. "We have enough forces to prevent unexpected events," the militia man said.

Georgia has many other unwanted minorities. On August 5, 1990 there was a meeting with 20,000 Avar, Kumyk, Chechen, Dargin, Laks and informal groups from Georgia, including Professor Abashidze, president of the Georgian Green party, to discuss what to do about Georgian harassment of 7000 Daghestanis settled in Georgia. Magomedkhan said that the Georgians had been buying them out, paying two or three times the going rate for their homes, so that now only 3-4000 remain. There is trouble too in Central Asia.

The typical murder of Magomedkhan's cousin is described elsewhere, but what I saw in Koubachi, where the men are normally confident and tough, was clear enough. Ibraghim, my *konak*, was host to a 30-year-old male guest, who was almost hysterical with worry over his wife and children, who were only in Makhachkala. He was one of 2-300 Koubachi families returning from Turkmenistan and Central Asia. They have been seriously frightened by the Uzbek–Kirgiz–Tajik violence and he was clearly in shock, obsessively pushing his papers about, asking everyone to inspect them. Meanwhile to the south, the Azerbaijanis want Derbent back, as they say it was one of the ten, or was it 12, cities of historic Azerbaijan. Daghestan wants Belokan and Zakatal rayons back from Azerbaijan as both Avar people and the Avar national shrine are there. It is as if the Romans, Danes and Normans were reclaiming Britain. And then in December 1994 the Russian-Chechen war began. The Russian bombardment of Grozny was six times as dense as Operation Desert Storm's bombardment of Basra. It dashed all former hopes for democratic or economic development of the region.

It may have been the only hope for Daghestan to withstand the internal and external chaos of inter-ethnic strife, emerging from the fall of the Soviet empire and the Communist party, to develop a Green party. In the West, Green usually refers the struggle to preserve natural resources, and several former causes have been incorporated into mainline political policy. So the Green Party in Europe and the USA is now diminished. However, the horrendous nuclear, chemical and environmental damage of the Soviet system remains in addition to military destruction in the Caucasus. In Daghestan there is the additional problem of spiritual pollution, which is frequently discussed in this book. By August 1990, after five years of theoretical perestroika, it is clear that local Popular or National Fronts or Social Democratic parties all have the same vague manifesto. The proposals are based on an uncomfortable mixture of racial purity, which would hopefully be irrelevant among the nationalities of Daghestan, and the Rights of Man, but contain nothing about actual government of which, naturally, the 90 per cent non-Communists have no experience. Something more specific, with teeth, is needed to catch local imagination. Environmental issues act as a first focus for new opposition to gain experience in exercising power and, as a result, throw up successful leaders.

ga

There was one false alarm. Up the valley towards the high mountains, upstream from the last villages grouped around Archi, Energo-Informatika, an Anglo-Soviet joint venture for importing computers, is building a 16-room hunting lodge complete with sauna and tennis courts for just two hunters at a time to use when they come to shoot the wild *tur* goats for their great horns. The lodge will be managed by the current construction boss, an aggressive 35-year-old from the distant Novolakskii rayon, who proudly showed me the plans, adding that they can charge US$5000 per *tur*.

Islambek, the naive director of the Archi *kolkhoz*, said that they would keep within the 20 *tur* a year they are allowed to shoot with permits. But how can it be controlled with such high rewards? There are about 2000 *tur* who live for 30-40 years and, it seems, differing numbers of permits for adjoining regions.

As part of a wider Soviet policy, there were no Archi people in charge of any local organisations. Some deal was made with the local *kolkhoz* after a charade of consulting a group of elders in Archi who gave permission for the building. But who has the right to give permission to build in an area of outstanding natural beauty? (With scrapyard mindlessness, the Soviets have built satellite receivers on mountain tops throughout Daghestan, part of widespread despoiling of the landscape.) The building will have a corrugated asbestos roof. There is bound to be an ugly fence around the whole area. What will happen to the ancient and still regularly used grazing routes for sheep and cattle which pass through the rich alpine meadowland?

The manager said that helicopters would bring people there and they also wanted to build a road there from Archi. They are paying a bribe-sized four times the normal rates for the stonework, 100 roubles a square metre, while the size of the building and facilities make the term *Dom Okhotnikov*, 'Hunters' House', sound like a lie. Plenty of old buildings could be restored down the valley in Archi. Magomedkhan was upset and angry that they were selling their birthright and went about, talking to everyone.

In 1991 the *kolkhoz* land reverts back to the village and it looks like this was a fast one to get the scheme in before then. He identified local opposition to the building and the Filial of the Academy of Sciences in Makhachkala is now against it. Ironically, Islambek, who is an Avar and married to a local woman, was so proud of the project that he arranged for us to ride on horseback for

Growing over 20,000 metres, Archi alpine flowers and herbs form part of Daghestan's rich herbal medicine traditions which compare with those of Tibet.

five km to see it. We then had a specially prepared feast of a boiled torn apart carcass of mutton, which looked grey and tasted dead, with white wine and *buza* for me. As we turned our backs to the howling wind to sip the bowls of hot mutton bouillon, it was hard to feel festive by the crashing torrent, as we wondered for how long the waters, which flow down to Archi, would remain clean. After one visitor, the hunting house remained empty six years later – an eerie monument to exchanging one awful future for another.

Water is scarce and precious. In some villages old water mills still work, while springs are still, as always, owned in common, not by the Communist Party. There is no piped water or sewage in the *auls*. Women traditionally fetch water, like our hostess in Bezhta, Khalema, who filled up the outdoor sink supply from a ten litre tinned copper ewer, which she filled several times a day, from a piped source a hundred metres down the road, making me appreciate the ease of releasing water by pressing the upward plunger into the Soviet aluminium cistern.

River power is also owned in common. There is a long-running project to build a hydro-electric plant past the dam at Chirkei. Reality is smaller scale. At the Bezhta water mill village women take turns to mill flour for customers who bring their own wheat. In Khunzakh, the regular sound of women shaking platters, skilfully tossing the baked apricot kernels to separate them from their skins indicates the presence of a water wheel, driving grinding stones to crush the kernels into *urbech*, the local Marmite.

There was more agriculture and irrigation before the Revolution, when water rationing was decreed by the Council of Elders and adhered to by the community. Spring watering began with the fields closest to the main canal and spread outwards, while summer watering, which continued until the harvest, started, not with the fields, but in the village gardens with four hours per house, timed by the sun, regardless of the size of an arable holding. There was a measure of water, the quantity needed to operate a Caucasian watermill for a fixed time, called a 'mill-water'. Night-time water, in contrast to day-time water, was only allocated to save crops from dryness.

Distribution of water in the fields was controlled from the minaret by the waving of a cloak, by day, and by lantern at night. Fairness was so important that in Igal there were three government posts connected with water. The 'Owner of the Water' took care of the use of water and smoothed out conflicts, the 'Manager of the Water' kept track of whose turn it was and checked the state of the canals, and the 'Keeper of the Books' had to be literate to keep records of the arable land, showing how much was ploughed and so needed water.

There is a ready ideological-Green replacement for Communism in the continuing and widespread tradition of mutual help, which is demonstrated proved by the existence of a word for it in every language in Daghestan. *Gvai* in Avar, *bilkha* in Dargin, *belki* in Chechen, *mel* in Lezgin and Rutul, *imajhi* in Tsakhur, *marshcha* in Lak, or *bulkha* in Kumyk, all meant that every household in the close communities knew it could depend on help, when needed. One such activity, combining work with leisure, was the clearing of the many communal springs after sowing, which also gave the younger generation a respectable chance to get together. Similarly, collection of white clay for whitewash took place in spring and autumn. Women and girls, in festive dress, left the village before daybreak, leading donkeys for the clay and the day ended with a party. Sometimes fines were imposed for failure to participate, such as in Nakhki, where a girl was fined 400g of butter, 800g of cheese, or 2400g of flour.

In the fields, many helping hands were needed because of primitive tools and difficult mountain terrain. There was also a limited time possible for weeding, spreading manure or ash fertiliser, harvesting crops, making hay ricks and threshing. In Khvarshin *gvai* for weeding, *ichila bakh*, was women's work, and two or three days in advance, the housewife would make the rounds of relatives and neighbours and casually mention her decision to weed her field of grain. A hint was enough for the women to gather on the appointed morning, bringing something for the dinner break in the field.

Threshing grain by a sled board was heavy work and always needed help and was sometimes (even) done by men, and winnowing required a specialist, who could throw shovels-full in the air so that the heavy grain and the light chaff fell in separate piles. Insufficient livestock in each smallholding made life potentially unstable, so two or three neighbouring smallholders would join together as a workforce and pool tools, in a *supriaga*.

To make sheep's cheese, ten households joined to share in the finished product, calculated according to the number of sheep – seven sheep gave one day's cheese. In another communal effort, wood for winter was chopped, brushwood and kindling gathered in one day, and on the next donkeys were loaded for transport to the village. The textile industry, sheep shearing, blanket, felt and cloth producing and making coats required communal work, as did house building. Material assistance was provided after disasters, such as fire or crop failures, and for expensive family feasts such as funerals or weddings.

Mutual aid may often have been abused by the wealthier to take advantage of free labour. Nevertheless, hard conditions made the custom an agricultural necessity, as well as an ethical duty, further compelling its observance in a small society. The community considered that *gvai* was given entirely free and, in fact, the beneficiary paid no money or kind for help (refreshments did not count as payment), but, following an unwritten rule, he or she was required to eventually pay with some kind of work in return.

This is no Prince Charlesian longing for a rural past from the armchairs of a wealthy society. The reality is that Daghestan (like most of the Caucasus) has no financial resources and no prospect of outside investment or support. Simple village-scale traditional development is the only possible means of survival in the medium to long term.

❧

In Daghestan, as every traveller cannot fail to see, nature is a majestic combination of mountains, torrents, wildlife and plants. In Tsofkra Vtoroi, the village of the tightrope-walkers, I was standing on the fragile fallen roof of the 15th-century mosque, gazing over the folded valleys, sweeping away beneath. When I looked up, I saw a movement in the air, first against the sky and then, less clearly, over the background of the mountains. I first saw three great birds, then ten. There were 50 eagles slowly circling in the sky. Some people say that the eagles were teaching their young to fly, others that the eagles were migrating. I felt that, after such a sight, there could be nothing more to see.

Near Akhti, where the Samur river broadens out, there were a dozen vultures perched on the river bed waiting for fish or floating dead animals. Next year, by the coast, Niamh saw two seals, which must have come down the river Volga, playing in the Caspian at Derbent. People said there were many more. In August, the fields are washed with wild flowers, and Niamh pressed those she saw in bloom. There was white campion, several types of vetch, catnip, purple loosestrife, red dead nettle, clover, bell flower, cornflower, chamomile, mint, viper's bugloss, forget-me-not, hardhead, thistle, and dandelion.

Daghestan is reputed to have almost as many medicinal herbs as Tibet – several hundred at least, depending on the method of classification. Near Ginukh, we passed boys gathering alpine yellow medicinal flowers, which, like others, are sold in village market stalls, downhill to Makhachkala and Derbent. Local belief in the purity of the herbs contrasts with fear of eating chemical fertilisers in vegetables.

More visible pollution always accompanies the much-needed industries and the best known, thanks to recent publicity, is the threat to sturgeon and their caviar from Azerbaijan oil and connected industrial waste, poisoning the Caspian Sea. The smaller industrial area near Makhachkala is also casting its pall over the town and the sea. Inland, there is heavy smoke pollution from the Kasimkent jam factory and the Buinakst tyre factory, just two examples. Because there are no spare parts, most industrial activity had ceased by 1996. While mountain forests are rich in conifers and deciduous trees, all construction outside towns, such as the Shamil-Kala hydro-electric project, causes trees to be killed, which are not replaced. From a bus window, you always see dead trees, where rocks and soil have been moved to build the much needed road, for example, by the Avar-Koisu river. Natural rockfalls, caused by heavy rains and spring thaws, frequently block the roads, since there are no retaining walls, like those in the Swiss Alps.

Lastly, there are environmental health problems. Dr Zulkip Magamedov, the 34-year-old, Leningrad-trained chief doctor of the Bezhtinskii rayon said that there was not even basic sanitary education provided at school. In Kumukh, there was a charming sign in Lak warning people not to make a mess of the water supply from the ancient two kilometres long underground aqueduct, except for respected guests. In Makhachkala, I saw an egg-sized white gall stone surrounded by a thin cuprous-blue ring, a common trophy from drinking the tap water. If, in the villages, Zulip continued, they had drainage and sewerage *kanalizatsiya*, there would be less stomach disease. If you eat meat from the dirty end of animals, such as the great delicacy, *kurdyuk*, the fat-tailed sheep's tail, you get infections which spread fast.

Men suffer from colitis. When there was a cholera epidemic in the 1950s, nearly half of the people of Koubachi died. Anaemia is widespread especially among women and is caused by lack of fresh fruit. But few women drink or smoke, unlike the men, who are more vulnerable to tuberculosis and killer flu. Zulip had no time to do research or even operate and, anyway, there was no equipment. It is hardly surprising that traditional folk medicine, using herbs, spring water and spells, is still popular.

Even before the Chechen War, there was a dearth of medical supplies. I once delivered a box of syringes to the main hospital in Makhachkala from a young British charity called BEARR, founded by Lady Gillian Braithwaite, wife of the UK ambassador to Russia. I felt ashamed that it was the first medical aid which Daghestan had received in living memory, and that such a small amount was written about it on the front pages of the newspapers. It was a measure of the desperate situation. Following the Chechen War and the collapse of distribution and manufacturing throughout Russia, the Daghestanis will need all their skills in traditional medicine as they are getting nothing from outside.

One-foot long triangular cloth-covered card talisman hanging in a newly-built house to protect the empty house from occupation by evil spirits. (Gumi village, Tabassaran)

· 14 ·

Afterword:
Daghestan avoids violence*
& the Russian–Chechen War

Daghestan only recently became known in Europe or America as a result of the war in neighbouring Chechenia (now dubbed 'Chechnya' since independence was declared). It has also achieved some prominence as a result of its position on the new southern border state of the Russian Federation as Russian troops in the spring of 1993 set up a military frontier with Azerbaijan. The stability of a historically volatile Daghestan in the increasing violence of the Caucasus must be a key to regional balance which also involves nearby Turkey, Iran and Iraq.

During Gorbachev's time and the few post-Soviet years the peaceful coexistence of Daghestan's multi-ethnic population has been accompanied by a limited evolution of democracy, including a circumscribed opposition. At the same time the first steps have been taken in developing an internal and exporting market economy. The Daghestan government is showing that it understands that these developments can only take place against a stable background. Such progress must be seen as happening against a series of increasingly unstable or violent incidents in other parts of the former Soviet Union which put a question mark over the long term success of mainly reactive government moves in Daghestan.

One reason why Daghestan has avoided violence is the survival of its complex social structure and traditional rules of behaviour. About the size of Scotland, the region, which takes its name from the Turkic for 'Land of the Mountains' is bordered by Azerbaijan to the south, Chechenia to the north, Georgia to the west and the Caspian Sea to the east. Over 60 per cent of the population of two million live in about 700 mountain and lowland villages. The population increased by 25 per cent during the ten years from 1979 to 1989. The capital city is Makhachkala with 350,000 inhabitants; there are six other towns with populations of over 50,000. The largest villages have about 10,000 inhabitants who are often spread in neighbouring hamlets; the smallest but a

* Written in collaboration with Magomedkhan Magomedkhanov. With further additions to take events to December 1996.

few hundred. There is additionally a Daghestani diaspora counted at 628,000, living in Azerbaijan, Russia and Central Asia, with a further 60,000 emigrés in Turkey, Jordan, Syria, Iraq, Saudi Arabia and Israel. Daghestan's 32 ethnic groups make it, in this way, a microcosm of the former USSR. The largest group is the Avars with over 600,000, and the smallest the Ginukhs with 400. There are also about 236,000 Russians, some of whom moved to Daghestan as early as the last century. This concentration of ethnic diversity is partly the residue of a number of aboriginal mountain tribes and partly the result of repeated invasions throughout Daghestan's violent history.

ð

April 1993 In addition to internal conflicts and shifting alliances, the mountain peoples of Daghestan were repeatedly pressed, attacked and frequently overrun by Persians from the south, Ottomans from the west, Turkic invaders from the south and north and Russians from the north. Derbent, with a population of 100,000 today, was founded 5,000 years ago at the narrowest point of the north-south route through the Caucasian mountains along the plain between the eastern extremities of the northern Caucasian mountain chain and the Caspian Sea. The vulnerability of Derbent was the reason why during the sixth century AD the Sassanian Persians built the surviving twin walls, reaching from the mountains to the sea. Derbent was on the main military route and accordingly the subject of continual attacks until the late 18th century when the Russians completed the Georgian military highway, opening up an alternative route through Tbilisi and the Kura river valley. From 1805 until 1859, the Tsar's armies were tied up fighting Daghestan who were among the last Caucasians to hold out. Imam Shamil was the leader of the Daghestan Islamic independence movement from 1832 until his honourable surrender in 1859 and in Daghestan he remains an inspiration and one of today's popular heroes. It was said that one Daghestan *djigit* or mounted warrior could handle a hundred Russian troops. This legendary prowess is a continuing reason for Russian fears about Daghestan.

During the Soviet period, Daghestan was virtually cut off from the rest of the Russian Federation of which it was an 'autonomous republic'.* With the exception of Kaspiisk, a Russian tourist camp on the Caspian, which handles the overflow from Sochi on the Black Sea, there are no international Intourist hotels. There are so few western visitors that most are interviewed on local television. Many people in Moscow think that Daghestan is 'primitive' and dangerous and do not wish to travel there, although it only takes two hours by aeroplane or, more tiringly, 44 hours by train via Rostov.

Russian anti-Daghestan prejudice has been noted for long in Daghestan. Yet

---

* The hollow status now enjoyed as the Republic of Daghestan, part of the Russian Federation, has changed nothing.

another such insult was received during the first weeks of April, 1993 when Daghestanis felt cheated by Russia and Yeltsin. Effectively at his request they decided not to form a National Guard only to hear that he has permitted the Cossacks to form their own National Guard. This may well be because there is to be an increase in the Red Army presence in Daghestan because it is now the southern border of the Russian Federation. However, these events must appear as a slight to the well-known military ability and machismo of Daghestan men. (With hindsight, was this part of the Russian build-up toward the Chechen War?)

ᔰ

Elections and politicians The 'democratic elections' of March 1990 showed the power of the old Communist party, which in turn had been infiltrated by the clan or *tukhum* system. The elections were significantly rigged, according to my eye-witness account which was published in *Central Asia and Caucasus Chronicle.**

The following brief sketch of the leading political players in Daghestan at the time shows who is locally considered significant. It is known that all of them had power under the Communists but this does not seem to be held against them. More important is the local perception of politicians as good or bad men. In addition, the ethnic diversity of the politicians has made Daghestanis feel that there is approximately fair ethnic representation, which was also the case during the Communist period.

Predsedatel' Prezidiuma Verkhovnogo Soveta Dagestana (President of the Praesidium of the Upper Assembly of Daghestan): Magomedali Magomedov (aged 65, Dargin). This is comparable to Khasbulatov's position in the Russian parliament.

Zam. Predsedatelia Prezidiuma Verkhovnogo Soveta Dagestana (Vice-President of the Praesidium of the Upper Assembly of Daghestan) (two): Bagauddin Akhmedov (50, Lezgin) and Mukhu Aliev (55, Avar), former first secretary of the Communist Party of Daghestan. They both have much to do and there is no rivalry apparent.

The *Verkhovnyi Sovet Dagestana* (Upper Assembly of Daghestan – VSD) consists of c.150 deputies, who were "elected" in March 1990. The VSD enacts laws and decrees, and confirms the budget. According to a previous arrangement, the budget for 1993 should have been presented in December 1992, after ratification by parliament in Moscow. But up to now (April 1993) the budget has been discussed but not confirmed by parliament in Moscow. So the VSD is proceeding as if it was confirmed.

The government, which holds executive power, is mostly made up of members of the VSD and appointed by the VSD.

* No. 9:4, pp 222-27.

The prime minister, Abdurazak Mirzabekov (60, Kumyk) has relevant experience, gained while he was the director of industry in Kizlyar region. There are three deputy prime ministers of whom Nabiulah Magomedov (55, Avar) is in charge of agriculture and Mr Amirov (55, Dargin), in charge of industry and foreign economic relations. There are about ten ministers, including Magomed Aburazakov (60, Avar), minister of the interior; a Russian (60), running the KGB; Dr Zaidullah Yuzbekov (55, Tabassaran), in charge of Goskomimushchestva, concerned with privatisation, *arenda* (a form of leasing) and so on; M. Gusaev (40, Lezgin) has a newly created department of international and external relations; an Avar (50) who is former first secretary of Komsomol and considered a bad man is minister of justice; Avadzi Omarov (65, Dargin) is head of the Supreme Court of Daghestan, and it is known that he resisted Communist pressure on his court. When the head of the *Raisovet* council of Kaiakent complained in the VSD in October 1992 that he had not been consulted over the appointment of the local judge, he was told to forget his corrupt ways by Omarov. One minister, Mr Khanilov, was recently shot, but no one could supply any reason for this.

It may seem strange that after such rigged elections the people have pragmatically accepted the politicians which they have and indeed they appear not to be doing too bad a job. The reason must be connected with maintaining the power balance of the clan system. In addition, there is little conspicuous consumption normally associated with 'corruption', with the exception of a few public celebrities who are locally considered to be deserving. The meteoric rise of Gamid Gamidov, finance minister since 1994, was cut short by his assassination aged 42 in October 1996.

&

Women in non-violent opposition   The women's hunger strike in November 1991, showed how non-violent protest has been used in Daghestan. Briefly, about 20 Daghestan people were murdered allegedly by KGB or government agents without anyone being charged. After many unsuccessful representations, local Avar and Kumyk women some of whom were relatives of the victims staged a hunger and thirst strike for seven days sitting under the statue of Lenin in the square opposite the government house. The government gave way to demands for dismissal of certain high officials in the ministry of interior and ministry of justice, threatened by further less peaceful mass demonstrations. However, later the government failed to fulfil most of these commitments. The whole episode is evidence of a sophisticated political sense from both government and opposition in Daghestan, which has continued to be evident in the methods of dealing with internal and external ethnic disputes described below.

&

Daghestan avoids violence

A negative   Besides the elections, the government (guided by Moscow) also
referendum   made a blundering step towards another aspect of democracy. A
           referendum was held in 1992. "If you want a wise answer, you
should ask a wise question," local humorists observed. In May 1992, the
Parliament of Daghestan, prompted by Moscow, asked two Delphic questions
on one sheet of paper. Each adult over 18 could answer "yes" or "no" or "don't
know" and there was also space for a written comment:

1. In your opinion, do we need presidential rule?
2. Are you in favour of private ownership of land (*chastnaia sobstvennost'
   na zemliu*)?

The first question prompted the following line of public discussion. "Surely
anyone who is familiar with the history of Daghestan could appreciate that
there was never a single person ruling Daghestan and that during peacetime
there was always a consensus. Even Shamil was just an imam, not a khan or
padishah. In the former USSR who could say what presidential rule meant?
Also which nationality would the president be? And why not from my nation?
(whichever of the 32 nations it was). And then, why was there no explanation
accompanying the question and what was the hidden agenda?" All the
intelligentsia knew the answer before the referendum; and that answer was
roughly 67% voting "no" with about a 90% turnout. The original reason for
the question came from outside Daghestan. Russia had elected a president and
Moscow wanted to know local reaction if the same model was used in
Daghestan. Of course, several other former republics and autonomous
republics now have presidents.

The second question seemed more stupid than the first. Collectivisation
(from c.1926) and consequent transportation of *kulaks* from their mountain
villages almost succeeded in breaking traditional Daghestan society. The
ubiquitous old but uncultivated mountain terraces witness that there has been a
decrease in agricultural land during this century. In spite of this, in Daghestan
there survives an old understanding of the nature of private land. Even now in
villages they can say that this piece of land belongs to that family and they
respect other's land. There are five types of land:

1. 'Fatherland', the name for fields for ploughing and growing hay are
   inherited by daughters (one part) and sons (two parts).
2. Common land, called *harim* – an Arabic word, describes pasture, forest
   and river to be used by a certain village or hamlet.
3. *Kolkhoz* and *sovkhoz* state farm land, which was partly new land often
   sited in the plains as well as on the old fatherland.
4. Mosque land.
5. The family house and the land between the house and the road which
   unofficially belonged to the house, excluding the road itself, which is
   common land.

Nobody understood which type of land was referred to in the question and again the answer was "no" by about the same margin. This was because all the villagers said "no," while many of the townspeople more under the sway of Russian propaganda said "yes." The Moscow and local democrats pushing for market reforms wanted to make radical land reform but they got the question wrong. Again, they had overlooked the fact that Daghestan traditional land structure in a mountainous region is different from the Russian model, and there is limited availability of land.

ঽ৶

Economic reform The 1993 budget for Daghestan is 50,000 million roubles (£1 = 1000 roubles in March 1993, when there appeared to be a lull in hyper-inflation), according to a local economist, and the significant local deficit is made up by Moscow. This is not as generous as it sounds, partly due to price fixing of valuable exports such as caviar, wool, oil and wine. For example, only 40% of total caviar production after tax is under Daghestan control. Caviar figures are not published and are considered a Moscow monopoly as is also the case for the railway, airline, shipping, power industries and so on.

In spite of the confused referendum, there has been limited land reform in Daghestan since spring 1992. It is now legal and allowed to rent agricultural land for ever with the right to pass it on to the next generation, but not for resale. Each man has the right to rent between one and ten hectares depending on the type of land, for instance rocky mountainous terraces or richer plains. The land can only be rented from the state farm property with the permission of the local council. The rent is very low. A result is the spread of one-family farms and the government is giving them credit to buy tractors, trailers, ploughs, seed and other equipment and consumables at 15% interest, which is far below the rate of inflation. Loans range from 100,000 to 10,000,000 roubles. In theory, a father with six married sons can have six times the area. However, unmarried sons are not counted, encouraging marriage, but, in a legal loophole, widows of all ages are allowed to claim their piece of land, although the local council usually doesn't give them permission. By March 1993, it was reported in the Daghestan parliament that the new association of farmers had over 6,000 members.

Private enterprise may have started slowly in Daghestan, but now men have become active in commerce both inside and outside Daghestan. Approximately 25% of all Daghestan people already live outside Daghestan in the former USSR, mainly in Azerbaijan, Russia and Central Asia, forming a ready-made commercial network, built around family ties. In addition perhaps 100,000 each year leave Daghestan as migrant workers, like shepherds in Kalmykia, Volgogradskaia and Rostovskaia oblasts; oil drillers in Turkmenistan; and builders in Kazakhstan and Siberia. Some of them are opening local ventures both in subcontracting, trade and manufacture (of tiles etc).

Daghestan avoids violence

Inside Daghestan, about a thousand private ventures have started up, with the most successful in housebuilding, furniture production, shoes and carpet-making. The majority though are in buying and selling, with countless commercial shops. This predominance of trading could be described as profiteering but it is also a necessary step on the road to a market economy to concentrate capital in the hands of the most able, who will in turn, solely for reasons of profit, set up manufacturing industries. Also so many people are involved in trading that the activity has taken on the form of a rapid educational process teaching fast brains, long subjected to enforced idleness, how money is made and lost.

Trade with Azerbaijan, Ukraine and Turkey is at a formative stage. The new southern border between the Russian Federation and Azerbaijan passes through Daghestan, which in future will help the economy of Daghestan. There has been a recent Russian government and presidential *ukaz* (decree) that Makhachkala airport, railway terminal and port should be developed to international status, replacing the role of Baku in the former USSR. This is now happening in Russia's new southernmost port on the Caspian. Because of Daghestan's relative poverty compared with Russia, a relatively small investment will have a significant economic effect in Daghestan. Many managers and skilled construction workers in the former USSR are Daghestanis, so it is expected that this development work will be done by local people.

There are several foreign joint projects afoot. A wealthy Turk has honour-ably given funds to build the new mosque in Makhachkala because his grandfather's spiritual mentor was from Daghestan. Other more down-to-earth Turkish businessmen are active as merchants exporting industrial wheels, wood, plastic granules, leather and wool from Daghestan. Basque businessmen came to Daghestan last summer and made a joint venture in the former military machine-making factory to now produce locks and diesel generators. They also plan to make equipment for dairy farmers. British, American and other oil companies have shown interest in the oil-bearing shelf in the Caspian Sea near Izberbash and there is a competition for the most ecologically clean project. Italian businessmen are negotiating at government level on wine and vegetable production.

Progress with internal ethnic pressures Internal ethnic pressures have been dealt with peacefully. The principle followed is that it is well worth paying for peace rather than paying for violence. This has led to an evolution of organisations and pressure groups of a decidedly democratic nature.

The government also consciously tries to defuse future causes of perceived ethnic insult and consequent stress by promoting languages and national festivals. While the government discussed what should be the state language in

1991, again imitating other parts of Russia and the former USSR, they intentionally avoided making any decision. If one language had been chosen then all the others would have been excluded. For many years there were nine languages and Russian taught in appropriate regional schools: Avar, Dargin, Lezgin, Kumyk, Lak, Tabassaran, Azeri, Tat and Nogai. After several years of discussion, there are attempts to make a Cyrillic alphabet, grammar and written language which is now being taught at schools for Agul, Rutul and Tsakhur. This is quite conscientious as for example, according to the 1989 census, a summary of which is appended, there are only 4000 Tsakhurs. The recent translation of the Bible into Andi and Bezhta (with 3000 speakers) languages has encouraged pressure for them to also be taught at schools along with more languages of other minorities.

There are several national organisations, each with a few thousand informal members, financed privately by voluntary contribution. They rent halls or organise outdoor meetings; they publish an irregular newsheet, depending on the current crisis; they were irregularly invited to participate in *kruglyi stol* ('round table') TV debates, at least ten times in 1992.

The Avar national front *Narodnyi Front im. Shamilia* ('Shamil People's Front'), which recently announced a moratorium on any activity until any other national movements take action.

The Lak front *Tsubars* ('New Star'), is more interested in developing Lak culture and national identity, so as not to be assimilated. At a large Lak conference held in one of the main halls in the centre of Makhachkala, the capital, in July 1992, the main slogan was "An Undivided Daghestan."

The Dargin front is *Tsadesh* ('Unity'). They follow everything which the Laks do.

The Lezgin movement is *Sadwal* (also meaning 'Unity'), has mainly political demands connected with about the 200,000 Lezgins living in Azerbaijan, that is more than half of the Lezgin peoples. In 1861 the Tsar included the Lezgin on the south side of the river Samur as part of the *Bakinskaia guberniia* and Stalin confirmed this divide and rule Russian policy. There is more written about this below.

The Kumyks now find themselves as a 22% ethnic minority in their own territory and so organised a national movement called *Tenglik* ('Equality'), with unrealistic but non-violent objectives – there is little that they can change.

The *Sotsial-Demokraticheskaia Partiia Dagestana* ('Social-Democratic Party of Daghestan') was born in 1990 out of *Klub Perestroika*, both of which were much vaunted by western observers in the early days. It published its manifesto and about 15 issues of a newsheet called *Majlis* ('Congress'), and went silent in 1993. It wanted to take an active part in elections and demanded a re-election of all the pro-Communist deputies, none of which happened.

All these movements and many officials in the Daghestan government support the Confederation of Mountain Peoples of the Caucasus (COMPOC), but internal problems in Daghestan described below mean that there is little that they can do. The COMPOC may develop rather like the Commonwealth into a responsible unifying organisation with influence but no official power.

The recent announcement from the Juma main mosque in Makhachkala that there are now 800 mosques, 30 *medreses* and two Islamic institutes working in Daghestan confirms a remarkable recovery. Before perestroika, a mere 17 working mosques were permitted, following closure and destruction of 2000 mosques and 700 *medreses* from 1928 and continuing during the 1930s.

After the dissolution of the Communist-sponsored North Caucasian Religious Board, Islamic organisation has fragmented in many ways mirroring the USSR. In Daghestan, there is the *Islamskaia Demokraticheskaia Partiia* ('Islamic Democratic Party'), who are unsurprisingly anti-Communist. They include some Avars living in the plains north of Makhachkala. Their activities on the newly formed Daghestan Muslim Religious Board had resulted by early 1992 in the setting up of different ethnic religious boards – one by the Dargins and Kumyks, keeping the traditional name *Kaziyat*, or religious court, and another, called the Kumyk Religious Board. The Laks and Lezgins are less religious and have not formed separate organisations. The national factor seems to be more important than religious unity.

At first glance, it may seem that the nationality problems of Transcaucasia are only relevant to the nationalities directly involved, but in fact North Caucasians have become involved in several ways. Firstly, many Armenians live in the North Caucasus in Kizlyar, Mozdok and south Georgia. Then, in Georgia, the main problem is that the Georgians are suppressing all other North Caucasian nationalities. Thirdly, a significant number of Daghestanis live in Azerbaijan, and as Azerbaijanis they are obliged to perform military service for two years.

In Daghestan, it is said that in the North Caucasus there are two main problems today:

1. The continuation and aftermath of the Ingush-Ossete conflict which became increasingly violent in February 1993 and has already resulted in several hundred deaths. This is outside the scope of this article.
2. The Chechens in Daghestan, where a non-violent solution is under way. In the whole former USSR this appears to be the only example of a non-violent solution to an ethnic crisis. It therefore deserves a more detailed account given below.*

In 1944 about 30,000 Chechens were transported from the former Aukhovskii rayon near Khasavyurt in north Daghestan to Kazakhstan by Stalin who pretended unreasonably that they would collaborate with the Nazis. The Nazis may have reached the city limits of Grozny in 1942 but had already been driven back far away by 1944. Stalin was irrationally prejudiced against the Chechens,

* This was before the Chechen War, whose effects on Daghestan are outlined further on.

perhaps because the Chechens had enjoyed an understanding with Beria, Stalin's NKVD chief (and, like Stalin, a fellow Caucasian).

Later in 1944 some 15,000 Laks had been forced to settle in the former Aukhovskii rayon when the rayon was renamed Novolakskii. They moved into the Chechen villages and over the years they looked after them well, building new houses, schools, hospitals and so on.

In 1957-58 when the Chechens returned to their homes – there are now 65-70,000 – they found that according to the laws of the time they had been dispossessed and they resettled in Khasavyurtovskii rayon in an area several times larger than the former Aukhovskii rayon: but it was not their home. In 1990, after perestroika, it was possible to discuss a solution. Following various demands, schemes and threats, in 1992 the Laks responsibly agreed to resettle elsewhere in Daghestan. All parties in Daghestan feared that the problem would escalate into a Daghestan-Chechen conflict. The problem was complicated by the economic cost of resettlement and consequent problems with the Kumyks whose ethnic territory north of Makhachkala was chosen by the Daghestan government as the Laks' new home. The Novolaks had no interest in returning to their old mountain villages which had long been abandoned and had fallen into ruin.

Nationalists and extremists from both sides from Grozny and Makhachkala created artificial tensions around this sad problem, demanding immediate resolution which was unrealistic in a country in the midst of an economic crisis. From spring 1991 the state has been building houses and communal buildings for them north of Makhachkala and they are about 40% ready but not yet habitable. The government hopes to finish the houses in a few years. The Chechens are also keeping their existing houses in Khasavyurt and have therefore won handsomely. It is a price which the Daghestanis are prepared to pay to avoid conflict which is materially more expensive and would also last for a longer time. In different areas of Daghestan the attitude is always to do anything to prevent ethnic conflict. In the meantime the situation is under control.

The resettlement of the Laks led to a consequent problem for the Kumyks. The Kumyks, as do many other Daghestan peoples, have ethnic problems concerned with immigrants from Avar, Dargin and Lezgin mountain villages who were forcibly settled in the barren plains from the 1950s onwards. The Kumyks now find themselves as a 22% ethnic minority in their own territory but there is little that they can change.

During summer 1992, there was a problem between the Laks and the Kumyks about resettling Laks from the Novolakskii rayon in Kumyk land to the north of Makhachkala, which was already worked by a Lak *kolkhoz* named after Garun Saidov. The Kumyks stopped the Rostov-Baku trains and put armed guards around the border of "their" territory. There was a stand-off between the Laks and the Kumyks. The police were called. At the height of the crisis, one police officer announced, "If you want to beat someone, beat me!"

Daghestan avoids violence

This was an unexpected move and made both sides think. Also the religious authorities from both sides and from other Daghestan peoples all decided to intervene to strike a *maslahat*, or an agreement. This resulted in peace. In fact the religious leaders have played a similar role in other potential conflicts. They have influence both for religious reasons and because they are older and therefore command traditional respect.

&

External ethnic fire-fighting The imagination and persistence of the Daghestan government in buying time or resolving internal ethnic problems was also evident in external ethnic problems involving Daghestanis. However, the external problems were obviously relatively outside Daghestani control. Excluding the Chechen War, there were five problem areas: the Lezgins in Azerbaijan, the Avars expelled from Georgia, the attacks on transport in Chechenia, the Dargin shepherds in the southern Steppes, and the attacks on Daghestani oil workers in Tiumen' in Siberia.

1. The Lezgin problems intensified in 1992. There was already pressure during 1991, caused by the return of 300 Lezgin families as refugees from Novyi Uzen' in Kazakhstan. In October 1992, the Lezgins were worried about the creation of a border between Russia and Azerbaijan along the river Samur dividing their territory. They were also concerned about their position in Azerbaijan as an ethnic minority with no form of self rule. Under the initiative of the Russian government, a militarily controlled border with customs was set up, and the Lezgins have had to live with this fact. The Daghestan government delegation, led by Ramazan Abdulatipov, an Avar, head of the Soviet of Nationalities in the Russian Parliament, has negotiated with the Azerbaijan government about the various Daghestan minorities in Azerbaijan, with positive results for the development of their cultures and languages. The situation is stable. Although the Lezgins are dissatisfied, they are not considered to be suffering. It is well known to both Lezgins and Azeris that if a major instability occurred in north Azerbaijan, then all Daghestan would become involved.

2. Indigenous Avars were expelled from Georgia in 1992. The 1989 official census identified 5000 Daghestanis in Georgia, mainly Avar with a few from Bezhta and Gunzib. They were treated as a nationalist problem by the Georgian authorities. They were settled in about ten villages on their historic ethnic land on the east bank of the river Alazan and in two towns – Lagodekh and Kuareli. The Georgians closed all roads to their villages. Propaganda was made telling them to go back to Daghestan. There was even a doctorate written investigating the optimal way of resettling these Avar people to their 'fatherland'. At the same time, the Georgians were renting 300,000 hectares of pastureland near Kizlyar and Kochubei and during the winter grazing season the Georgian population there grew from 1500 to 10,000. So the Georgians

had much to lose by expelling the Daghestanis. The Daghestan government sent and received delegations for five rounds of negotiation with the last in July 1992. By September 1992, it became obvious that the Georgians would not change their position and Avar refugees continued to arrive, mainly settling in the Kizlyar region without government support. But from then the Daghestan government undertook to give them land near Iuzhno-Sukhokumsk in north Daghestan. The Georgians had made the Avars sell their houses at a low price in the summer of 1992, for 2-300,000 roubles compared to a market price of five to ten times higher. The Daghestan government is now giving them credit to build homes on favourable terms. Now the Georgians are disappearing from their rented pastures, which must be bad for both economies. Even with this situation in Georgia, there was no prejudice and no attacks occurred against Georgians in Daghestan.

3. Armed guards now protect trains from Moscow to Makhachkala and Baku. Originally the Moscow train went through Grozny, but when Chechenia declared independence, it was dangerous to go through Grozny because of robbery and gross interference with passengers being unofficially searched, and the route was changed in January 1993 to pass through Mozdok in Adige and Gudermes in south-east Chechenia. In December 1992, the Daghestan parliament decided to have armed guards and OMON (*Otdelennie Militsii Osobogo Naznacheniia*) police on the trains, with more than ten guards on passenger trains and several guards on the long goods trains. So now, when you buy a ticket from Makhachkala to Moscow, costing 3000 roubles, you pay an extra 200 roubles for guard expenses. But even now people are worried when the train or bus passes through Chechenia and there are plans to build a new railway through Kizlyar joining the Astrakhan line. On television there have been reports of buses from Daghestan burnt by Chechens, and beaten-up drivers and so on. In February, when the Chechen president Djokhar Dudayev was interviewed by Gadji Abashilov in *Komsomolets Dagestana* about train attacks, he curiously answered that they were controlling the situation and that none of the bands which had been arrested contained Chechens.

4. During 1992 and continuing till the present, in the southern Steppes there are 20,000 shepherds and their families who are increasingly suffering from anti-Caucasian racism. They are mostly Dargins and some Avars who work in Stavropol'skii kray, Kalmykia, Rostovskaia oblast and Volgogradskaia oblast. Local criminals are stealing their livestock and so the shepherds are beginning to return to Daghestan. This must also be bad for the local economies, where there are no local skilled shepherds.

5. In Tumenskaia oblast in Siberia, well known for its oil potential, there are 1500 Lezgin and Avar oil workers. There have been sporadic attacks from local Russians since 1991. This does not bode well for much needed stability in a region whose industry is essential to any Russian economic recovery.

❧

To conclude... The people of Daghestan are by tradition modest and would perhaps be surprised to hear that their virtually unplanned avoidance of inter-ethnic strife and consequent bloodshed might hold some lessons for other parts of the former USSR. Current problems which have yet to be addressed are health, hunger and housing. Because of the relative social stability, a grassroots approach to these problems, which are soluble, could slowly transform Daghestan into a reasonably prosperous and a happier place. Their journey will be fraught with difficulties. Unlike the case in many other parts of the former USSR, very few people desire to leave or are emigrating from Daghestan.

ta

The Russian- The Russian-Chechen War had little effect on Western
Chechen War attitudes. Initial Western lack of interest and ignorance of the region gave way to a flood of journalistic coverage. It was fortunate for the Chechens that Western television journalists were in Grozny when the Russian invasion took place. The Chechens handled the public relations war brilliantly. In contrast, the 1994 Queen's Christmas message which went out during the battle, showed her visting a Russian Orthodox service with that nice President Boris Yeltsin. This curiosity elicited no comment in Britain. I wondered what international reaction would be if the British Air Force bombed the Bogside in Belfast – an equivalent act with greater provocation as the Chechens had not bombed Moscow. It was symbolic of Western official attitudes to a Russian "internal matter." The attitude appeared to be that Yeltsin must be supported to maintain stability in Russia. The continuing payments of international aid to Russia by agencies of the World Bank and the European Union must have given the Russians comfort to massacre their own civilians following a policy which can hardly be reconciled with the "good governance" which nowadays is supposed to be a precondition for aid. In practice, the Russian fiasco in Chechenia probably will prove to be a destabilising influence in the region.

The sole question to me from the American Christian Science Monitor Radio during the final grotesque bombardment of the presidential palace was: "What is the significance of the presidential palace in Grozny anyway?" As usual the answer was complicated: "It is the place where General Dudayev was democratically and overwhelmingly elected president three years ago with the mandate to make Chechenia independent of the Russian empire like other former colonies such as Ukraine, Georgia or Estonia.

"But the building in the provincial Stalinist style was also once the Communist Party HQ. The totalitarian Soviets were always afraid of uprisings in the Caucasus – Daghestan rebelled in 1937 – and built a fortress of reinforced concrete decorating the facade with mounded cement like a monstrous wedding-cake. So, in military terms, the Presidential Palace is the only tall fortress-like building in the centre of Grozny. Until recently the first objective in attacking a city was to capture the TV station. But that is no longer relevant, since Grozny, like most of the Eastern Caucasus, is under the footprint of several communications satellites, so all that is needed is a hand-held camera, a briefcase-sized transmitter and a small aerial.

"Capturing Grozny, which by the way means 'terrible' in Russian, is of more significance to the Russian's wooden military tactics than to the well-disciplined and motivated Chechens. But any Russian triumph would be short-lived: the Chechens are mountain villagers and historically freemen. The Russians will have to fight for the town of Argun and other villages to the south of Grozny, where through the mists and snow they will see the real Chechen heartlands – the northern chain of the Great Caucasian Mountains. It would be easier to bomb the Rocky Mountains."

In contrast, for Daghestan the tragic, violent and turbulent story of the Russian war in Chechenia from the destruction of Grozny and many other towns and villages to the Lebed-Maskhadov peace accord and Russian troop withdrawal in December 1996 (see Appendix 1) had the following results, isolating Daghestan from Russia and the outside world. Daghestan is unwittingly under siege:

1. The new Daghestan telephone network supplied by Samsung has been virtually disconnected, making international calls impossible and calls to Russia intermittent.
2. There has been a decrease of train and aeroplane services to Moscow and St Petersburg, as well as difficulties of road transport and obtaining petrol.
3. The border to Azerbaijan is virtually sealed by Russian troops and there is no passport office there, so it is difficult for foreigners to enter Daghestan by this route, taking advantage of international flights to Baku. However, there are now regular flights from Istanbul to Makhachkala.
4. Anti-Caucasian racism and prejudice in Moscow and St Petersburg makes any business relations almost impossible.
5. Yeltsin never delivered any promised aid – new airport, seaport, stations, industrial development – no factories are working, there are no spare parts and no fuel. While there is international interest in oil in other areas by the Caspian Sea – particularly Azerbaijan and Kazakhstan – Daghestan has not attracted any significant investors (see Appendix 2).
6. The Daghestanis have always given all possible humanitarian aid to the Chechens. Since the war there have always been 50,000 to 150,000 Chechen refugees in Daghestan. There are no refugee camps because the Chechens were taken in by families who have had to sacrifice much to feed them.

Daghestan avoids violence

There is enough food to survive, but otherwise prospects look grim. Sources suggest that Daghestan will overwhelmingly vote for the Communist presidential candidate, Y. Zuganov, for three reasons: firstly, there is no trust for Yeltsin, which is understandable judging him on his record; secondly, old Communists imagine they will get a better deal from the new Communists; and thirdly, there is a possibility that if the vote is close throughout Russia, then their vote will marginally help create a hung result, so the Russians will be busy fighting each other and not have time or interest to interfere in the Caucasus. Yeltsin won the elections with General Lebed's support – Yeltsin appointed Lebed to make peace in Chechenia and then sacked him. The people of Daghestan will need to use all their internal strengths and perseverance to cope with their isolation.

There are three pivotal events which have hardened their attitude to the Russians from peaceful co-existence to a fear and breakdown of the little trust which had previously existed. Firstly, over Christmas 1994 Russian tanks rolled into Grozny, transforming a psychological threat into physical action, which to date has resulted in an estimated 20,000 Chechen deaths (see Appendix 3). Secondly, in March 1996, Russian artillery bombed a Daghestani village after Magomed Aliev, the president of Daghestan, had personally appealed to Yeltsin not to do so. The Chechens had taken hostages to Kizlyar in western Daghestan. On their way back to Chechenia they were blocked on the Daghestan side of the border at a small village, named ironically Pervomayskaya ('First of May/May Day'), which the Russians bombarded, besieged and overran. Most of the 80-odd Chechen fighters escaped. It must have made the president and citizens of Daghestan wonder what exactly it meant to be a 'Republic' in the new Russian Federation.

Thirdly, two bombings in Makhachkala, capital of Daghestan may signal the start of a determined attempt to destabilise Daghestan. The first was the assassination of Gamid Gamidov, a charismatic John Kennedy figure, who was Minister of Finance and at 42 the best president Daghestan would never have. Many others died from the car bomb as he was reported to be talking with friends next to his car. Rumours suggest that he was about to bring to book a social security finance scandal involving government officials. The second was the bombing of an apartment block which housed military officers killing more than 20 people. It has not been established who was responsible and it is unlikely that the same people were behind both bombs. There would appear to be three possibilities. While there is a problem with Chechen criminals infiltrating with refugees in Daghestan, either bombing was hardly in their interests. The Women's Hunger Strike was about alleged secret police-inspired killings. If the bombs were not the work of Chechen or Daghestani mafias, that leaves the possibility of Russian-backed agents provocateurs or agents of factions in the Daghestan government. If Russia's apparent policy towards the Caucasus is indeed as described below, then the motive is there. At present the verdict must remain open.

≈

Events are continually developing. A November 1996 fax to *Oxford Analytica:*

Event: Yeltsin's heart operation.
Consequence for the Caucasus: Very little on the now-sporadic Chechen conflict and other Caucasian countries' attitudes to Moscow.

It is premature to comment on Lebed's Chechen peace proposals because:
1. The proposals appear to be in a pro-forma shape rather like heads of agreement in a contract without working details – ie sector boundaries or government statuses.
2. The amended proposals are being used as a political football in Moscow to satisfy varying aspirations of Russsian nationalism, inter-ministry rivalry, war weariness and to a far lesser extent western aid conditions.
3. Yeltsin distanced himself from the proposals and Chernomyrdin appeared to half endorse them which can be interpreted as a power-play for Yeltsin's successor – chosen or not.
4. Lebed has been sacked by Yeltsin.

Back to first principles: what is Russia's interest in the Caucasus?
1. The Caucasus is a historic buffer region to keep Iran and Turkey away from the Russian southern flank.
2. Memory of the 1800-1860 Russian-Caucasian war, the Civil War and anti-Soviet uprising as late as 1937.
3. A gut-level Russian hatred of non-Slavs, non-Christians, swarthy dark handsome people, coupled with Russian jealousy of Caucasian flair, fighting prowess, independence of spirit
4. Oil and oil routes; Russia wants a larger share and control in Azerbaijan and Kazakhstan production; the Caspian Sea boundaries for offshore drilling and extraction; Russia wants her pipeline options, with charges and costs via Russia and Chechenia, not via Georgia and Turkey, or via Iran.
5. Russia wants to control communications: internet, fax, telephone, rail and road routes. Russia wants to reinforce the southern border to prevent the possible influx of arms, soldiers, drugs and criminal activity from Iran and Turkey.
6. Frozen Moscow's need of temperate Caucasian food meat vegetables and fruit.

How does the Chechen war compare with other recent Caucasian ethnic conflicts? There are many factors in common:
1. All arms are Russian. Any non-Russian arms would have been

exhibited on Russian television. That implies that directly or indirectly the Russian army and the Russian state has supplied arms for all the Caucasian conflicts.

2. The ethnic conflicts are usually based on unresolved territorial disputes caused by mass forced transportation of Caucasians during the Soviet period and subsequent internal displaced persons (IDPs) problems. There are now estimated two million IDPs in the Caucasus.

3. Both sides are helped at different times to keep the conflict going by direct or indirent Russian materiel or personnel.

4. Eventually the Russians say that the local peoples are incapable of governing themselves so that Russian troops can move in to keep order.

5. The country is laid waste and virtually no external humanitarian aid is allowed in.

6. The new 'policy' of dispersion of ethnic groups instead of genocide or mass transportation to dilute an effective concerted voice of dissent and consequent foreign objections.

Either the Russians are acting in a haphazard bull-in-a-china-shop way or there is a mediaeval-style policy of reducing the Caucasus for the foreseeable future. The different Caucasian countries have cause to think it is the latter. What is their attitude to the Chechen war?

1. Everyone was shocked and amazed by the ferocity of the Russian attack on Grozny. UK analysts estimated the artillery to be six times the frequency and volume of the Desert Storm attack on Basra.

2. Georgia remembers Russian aid to the Abkhaz as well as resenting Chechens fighting with the Abkhaz. The Russians had little difficulty forcing the Georgians to close borders with Chechenia. Note that there are about 250,000 to 400,000 Azeris and Armenians in southern Georgia. Georgia has one of the two oil pipeline routes which will only be built if foreign investors are comfortable with local stability.

3. The Russians have closed the Daghestan-Azerbaijan border and there is no immigration post hindering Azerbaijan trade. The Azerbaijan Lukoil-BP deal may well be revised as the Russian government keeps changing the authorised negotiator ministries.

4. There has been no movement or resolution to the Ingush reclamation of the east bank of Vladikavkas the North Ossetian capital, whence they were transported by the Soviets in 1944. The Russian threat to withdraw support from the Ossetes keeps them in line over Chechnia.

5. A recent experienced European visitor noted that the Tatars had become completely subdued and were afraid to even discuss events as if the Soviet repressions had returned.

6. The Russians are ready to use the widely spread Cossacks who make up less than 27% of the population in the Terek, Don and Kuban regions.

They have started to be encouraged to have national aspirations which have been satisfied in a preliminary way by their host countries but they are open to Russian influence and have a warlike history.

7. Daghestan is virtually under siege from Russia as described above.

The prognosis is grim for the Caucasus. In the unlikely event of a signed detailed peace agreement in Chechenia, the practical intricacies mean that it will soon be broken and the conflict restart. There are still estimated half to a million Russian troops with nowhere to stay in Russia. All neighbouring Caucasian countries are wary of Russian military intentions. With Ukraine, Belorussia, Kazakstan all but rejoined to the Union, there is an inevitability that sooner or later non-volunteer regions will be coerced. The sight of Grozny, a capital city the size of Coventry, Lyons or Atlanta razed to the ground has evaporated local thoughts of independence, especially in the light of Western governmental indifference to an "internal Russian matter." Hardline Russians encouraged in this way, and noting NATO disarray over recent events in Iraq, must next be making calculations about reannexation of the pre-Baltic states.

Maskhadov won the (internationally observed) democratic elections for president of Chechenia with over 60% of the vote in a heavy turn-out. Russia refused visas for the representatives of various countries to attend the inauguration in February 1997.

ֶֶ

Both Daghestan and Chechenia need substantial development aid. Daghestan is, of course, part of the Russian Federation and, *de facto*, so is Chechenia, in that Russia permits no external relations or development aid there. Unlike, for example, Scotland, which as a European Community region receives EC aid independently of the rest of the UK, Daghestan and Chechenia are entirely dependent on Moscow for economic, budgetary, development and finanancial infrastructure aid. Russia's own economic problems – in addition to its unethusiastic attitude towards Daghestan and Chechenia – means that not only is little aid arriving, but that local industry is almost at a standstill, unemployment is chronic and migrant work in Baku and Central Asia is affected by border closures.

There is a grim time ahead: it seems that the North Caucasians are damned if they fight the Russians and damned if they don't.

ֶֶ

Further reading

*Balkhar village boy displaying buffalo skull
decorated with sun-sign and spots, 1985
(photo: P. Gamzatova)*

One of the first 'zikrs' in public in modern Daghestan, which took place in Andi village, July 1992. (photo: M. Aglavov)

Appendix 1

As requested, I sent the following draft to 'Oxford Analytica', a news service, on October 8, 1996:

The Lebed-Maskhadov accord quoted (apparently in full) in the investigative *Moskovski Komsomolets* of 3 Sept 1996 is quite brief and set out in military rather than diplomatic or political language, entitled:

Principles of the determination of a basis for mutual relations between the Russian Federation (RF) and the Chechen Republic (CR)

1. An agreement about the bases for mutual relations between the RF and CR, determined in compliance with universally recognised principles and norms of international law, is to be concluded by December 31, 2001.

2. Not later than 1 October 1996 a Joint Commission is to be formed representing the organs of state power of the RF and CR, with the following aims:

a) To put into practice the [necessary] controls to fulfil the Decree of the President of the Russian Federation dated 25 June 1996 No. 985 and to prepare proposals for the complete withdrawal of troops;

b) The preparation of agreed [legal] measures to combat [organised] crime, terrorism and displays of national and religious hostilities and to control the implementation [of such measures].

c) The preparation of proposals for reestablishment of mutual relations with regard to foreign currency-finance and budgetary [matters].

d) The preparation and enactment of RF legislation for a [financial] program to reestablish the socio-economic infrastructure of the CR.

e) Control over agreed reciprocal organs of state power and relevant organisations for the provision of the population's food and medicine.

3. The legislation of the CR is to be based upon observation of human and citizens' rights and rights of national self-determination, principles of legal equality of [all] national [ethnic] groups, the provision of peaceful borders, international treaties and the security of those living on the territory of the CR to be citizens independent of nationality, religion or other differences.

4. The Joint Commission is to conclude its work according to mutual agreement.

Comment

The nationalist elements of the Russian press thought it was a sell-out; yet it is not a treaty or even an agreement; merely preliminary principles requiring much interpretation by two sides who have entirely differing views. There are in addition a variety of inconsistencies:

1. It is not clear if the Joint Commission includes Zafgaev, the Russian appointed governor of Chechenia, and if so in what capacity. Also who would have the casting vote on the Joint Commission.

2. While the right of national self-determination is conceded by the Russians, and presumably means that the Chechens would choose "independence," the aid package which would take some time to implement implies that it is self-determination within a Russian framework.

3. It is not even clear if a Russian veto could block the self-extinction of the Joint Commission and thus keep the new CR in limbo.

4. Furthermore what are the unspecified penalties for each side for not agreeing by the set date? It appears that the Chechens would lose the agreement and return to the status before the agreement and the Russians would breach the agreement and also return to the same status – that is, the Chechens would lose both ways.

Joint Commissions

The history of Joint Commissions is not encouraging, *interalia:*

1. The Vichy government-Nazi Joint Commission 'worked' because De Gaulle was in London.

2. The Berlin Joint Commission resulted in the Wall.

3. The Northern Ireland Joint Commission has never been established because of essential disagreement on representation and voting.

4. The Yugo-Slav Joint Commission resulted in civil war.

Playing for time

Chernomyrdin's comment that the accord needed more work is self-evident; however it is also in both sides interests to play for time. The Chechen separatists need time to regroup both militarily and politically following Dudayev's death. The Russians need to delay until there is clear presidential direction. The ceasefire gives both sides a breathing space.

Appendix 2

The businessman's brief of 'How ordinary people live in the west Caspian region' is taken from a talk I gave at London University at the SOAS-MENAS conference 'Oil and Caviar in the Caspian' in 1995. It summarises an entirely different view of the whole book:

An investor who is considering joint ventures in the west Caspian region needs to be able to estimate the degree of local stability, which can and has been affected by the following two external factors:

1. Local attitudes towards Russia whether the region is within the Russian Federation, like Daghestan or Chechenia or nominally independent like Azerbaijan. While there is often hostility for legitimate historical reasons connected with Russsian conquest, there is more or less reluctant co-operation which admits to the political realities.

2. Local attitudes towards foreign investment are coloured by initial fantasies about the riches of the West which will rescue them from the repressive Russians (who in reality are unwilling to be excluded from potential money-making deals in the former USSR).

Further reading

To understand and assess these risks is not solely a theoretical problem. It is also necessary to understand the internal forces at work, namely who the west Caspian people are and how they live. It may prove critical not to offend local ethnic sensibilities in an area already under both economic pressure and stress from ethnic disputes which could lead to conflict. Here I will be discussing briefly Chechens, Daghestanis and Azerbaijanians. They are quite different both from Russians and western and central Europeans in the various ways outlined below. The following five aspects may be considered as the main components in the loyalty structures of these multi-ethnic societies. Obviously, these are important to appreciate for the investor who wants to create a successful and lasting enterprise. The multi-ethnicity and languages of the region are reinforced by the prevailing religions. The mountain village tradition is still the bed-rock of social life centring on the family and clan system. Finally, parts of the traditional legal system have informally survived, making for complications in land ownership, which is often a factor in inter-ethnic disputes.

1. Ethnicity and language

The Caucasians are descended from the 26 Albani tribes known to classical authors from ancient times. Most complex are the 32 ethnic groups in Daghestan (with 1989 population of 2 million+ living in a mountainous area about the size of Scotland), all local except for Kumykhs (descended from Kipcak Turks) and Nogais (descended from the Golden Horde), Azeris descended from Selcuk Turks and Sassanian Persians, Tats (both Persians and Mountain Jews) and local ethnic Russians.

While each group speaks their own language as different as English is to German, and eleven languages are taught in different primary schools, Russian is the lingua franca. Azerbaijan is also multi-ethnic with 1989 population of 6.5 million+, with the Azeris in the majority and small settlements of Daghestani ethnic groups and a few Armenians who have stayed. In 1989 Chechenia was made up of 1 million+ Chechens and 250,000 Russians, many of whom have left during the past four years. Together with 250,000 Ingush now living in Ingushetia, they formerly made up the Russian Federation Republic of Chechen-Ingushetia. The historic ethnic mosaic which was in many cases maintained during the Soviet period has been severely upset by conflicts during the past four years.

In addition to blind racist hatred and historical "unfinished business," local inter-ethnic problems have been caused by forced resettlement by the Soviet regime, (mountain people being forcibly moved into towns on the coastal plains during the 1960s) and the recent refugee problems caused by conflicts and returnees from Soviet-created exile – both mass deportation of the Chechens and Ingush and extensive deportation from the 1920s of supposed 'kulaks' or rich peasants.

Estimates of refugee numbers are 500,000+ in Azerbaijan (Azeris from Armenia, Azeris from Nagorno-Karabagh, Mesketian Turks from Central Asia), 100,000+ in Daghestan (Chechens from Groznyi, Chechen returnees from deportation to Kazakhstan, Daghestani returnees from internal forced migrations during the 1930s-1960s, Avars expelled from Georgia), and 300,000+ in Chechenia (Chechen and some Russian ethnic war refugees from Grozny now in mountain villages). There are estimated to be more than 2 million refugees in the whole Caucasus, few of whom have any desire or possibility to return home. Their hospitable host governments cannot afford to support them for long because of their own extreme economic difficulties, and this has the potential to lead to future instability or conflict.

2. Religion

Religion after Soviet suppression is mainly Sunni Muslim in Daghestan and Chechenia, with inherited membership of Sufi mystical orders, and in Azerbaijan the majority are Shiite Muslim with the remainder Sunni. There are a limited number of Russian-Arabic Korans in circulation, though many people are not very 'religious'.

During the 1930s most of the mosques (for example 2000 in Daghestan) and religious schools (for example 800 in Daghestan) were closed down or destroyed. About a third have been rebuilt since perestroika. This reaction is not 'fundamentalist' which seems to be the adjective used by Russian government alarmist propaganda.

There has been virtually no support for the Caucasus from other Islamic countries. It is instead rather a similar cultural reaction which would appear in England if all the parish churches had been closed down for fifty years by an authoritarian government. However in Chechenia the existing Sufi brotherhood organisations must have had some influence on the extraordinary discipline shown by Chechen fighters against the Russians.

3. Village tradition

Except for the cosmopolitan inhabitants of Baku, the rest of the people are at heart independent mountain villagers. Apart from the large industrial cities (Baku with a population of 2 million+, Grozny with a former population of 400,000 and Makhachkala with a population of 350,000) and a dozen or so large towns of over 50,000, most of the population do indeed live in mountain or lowland villages (for example there are 700 villages in Daghestan).

Almost all urban dwellers, apart from those in Baku, have a village family home as well. In the mountains, villages survive and are growing, living on subsistence terraced agriculture, livestock herding and their well-known handicrafts. Traditionally, after harvest and weddings, mountain men migrate to work in the towns or formerly went raiding for booty.

The villages, many of which were destroyed and moved down from the highest slopes after the Russian conquests from 1830 to 1860, were first settled over 2500 years ago. Until the Russian conquests, most villages were made up of *uzden* or freemen living in an Ancient-Greek *polis* city-state democracy, ruled by an elected council or *jamat* of male elders. The infrastructure of this system has often survived and most villages have a *godekan* or bench where the council sits. Contrary to Communist propaganda, there was no proletariat at the time of the Revolution apart from within the Baku oil industry, nor was there a peasant class as in Russia.

While the people are proud and generous, in economic terms they are not rich. The current average wage for those in work is about $US 10-20 a month. GDP per capita is estimated to lie between $US 500 and 1500, with hunger level at about $US 580 (1989 values). In spite of the dramatic rates of inflation (2000% p.a. in 1992) and the conflicts, there do not seem to be hungry children in the villages, largely thanks to the extended family-clan system. Most nutritional deficiencies are due to adherence to a traditional flour-rice-meat-garlic-cheese-apricot kernel paste-fresh herb and potato diet which needs supplementing by citrous fruit (locally grown but exported), more winter vegetables and dried summer produce. Although market prices have increased dramatically over the past five years, bread – for example – still costs 3 to 5 pence a loaf, in contrast to the Turkish price of 40 pence, illustrating that there is still a lot of inflation left in these economies.

4. Social ties

The family and the clan are the most important social units. Traditional customs of hospitality are observed which sometimes may appear to outsiders to be more for the benefit of the host than the guest. Guests are an excuse for late night feasts with large numbers of lengthy and macho toasts which mean that a colossal amount of alcohol is consumed by British standards. But the acceptance of hospitality is seen as a way of bonding and giving guarantees of welcome and necessary protection to the guest.

There is a healthy mistrust of foreign businessmen based on a history of exploitation by one-shot swindlers, and in turn today's businessman must also beware of being considered fair game by jealous locals who do not belong to his protection clan(s). At the same time his friends or *konaks* will prove true as has been my experience over a decade in Daghestan. There are often hidden obligations on the guest which will include helping with medicines, educating children and arranging visits abroad. When you do business in the Caucasus you become part of the family within a culture of favours.

The birth rate is very high with most ethnic groups' population increasing by 20-25% during each decade ending in 1979 and 1989. There is little birth control except for abortion though many women are unhappy about the situation. Marriage feasts usually last three days with 500-1000 guests and represent major financial expenditure. During the past four years building anew and *remont* or doing-up private houses, which was forbidden since the 1930s, have also become a major item of pride and expenditure.

To sum up, these proud peoples see life in a romantic-historic context. This can be explained as the only way to preserve their identity during the hellish years of Soviet rule. They have a fund of folklore and given a chance they are story-telling, joking and warm people, yet their mood may swiftly change to offence and anger, which may initially appear inexplicable to outsiders. The energetic men of Daghestan and Chechenia are builders, farmers, shepherds, wrestlers, dancers, singers, and above all fighters, while the Azeris are traditionally more relaxed and referred to as "tea-drinkers" by their northern neighbours. Many Daghestanis and Chechens work in Baku. The women who appear to be ruthlessly exploited by their menfolk are nevertheless the main upholders of tradition. However US TV is accomplishing what Stalin failed to do, which is to penetrate every home with images of women's liberation. There is a new essential and developing role for women in capitalism as the bookkeepers, turning into the accountants, and ultimately the finance directors of the future. It is ironic that the women of Azerbaijan had the vote before the women of Britain.

5. Land ownership

In addition to the confusion surrounding the recent transformation from Soviet to Russian law, there are some local legal-cultural differences which the investor should note. In many business dealings, *adat* or local customary law, rather than Soviet law, new Russian law or *shariat* Islamic law is often followed. *Adat* is a type of 'eye-for-an-eye' legal system which was recorded in detail by tsarist Russian ethnographers at the end of the last century. *Adat* covers business dealings, all types of compensation for damage to property up to murder, and everything else of local import including sexual offences. One of the most destabilising aspects of *adat* is the inter-clan blood feud, which has begun to reappear in Chechenia. This is a potential minefield for an outsider and it is easy to unwittingly commit some offence which is another reason why it is important to have the strong local protection mentioned above.

Specifically, local land ownership is complicated. When the people of Daghestan were asked by referendum in 1992 if they wanted land reform, the question was considered so unclear that they voted "no." They could not understand which "land" was being referred to: 1. State farms created by the Soviet system from confiscated land; 2. Regional rayon ex-Communist Party appropriated property; 3. Traditional "national lands" of an ethnic group. This is the subject of the current Osete-Ingush conflict in North Osetia, and the Chechen-Lak-Kumykh dispute in Daghestan; 4. Traditional common land in and near villages; 5. Traditional Mosque land; 6. Private land and houses; and 7. The land between private houses and the road, which is considered as an extension of the house. A certain amount of land reform has occurred in Daghestan with more than 20,000 private farmers leased five to ten hectares each by the state. Who owns the land over which new or existing oil or gas pipes pass and what the owners' rights are make for interesting future problems.

This summary merely gives a brief taste of the complexity of the west Caspian region while pointing out some areas where the foreign investor must proceed with care.

Appendix 3

Brussels, Tuesday 24 January, 1995 – Aslanbek Kadiev was "Special Representative of the President of the Republic of Chechenia," he could write and speak English not quite fluently. We spoke in Russian and English. He is 30-35, fit-looking with military bearing, short with a typical Dudayev moustache. He was impressive, professional, not emotional, bright and fast. He was accompanied by a young Dutchman of Chechen origin who did not speak Russian but spoke English. Kadiev apologised for not having a visiting card, explaining that it was hard for him to leave Russia via Moscow and that as he was searched before boarding they would have found his cards and detained him. He answered all the eight questions which I had prepared.

1. *Where is the front-line?* He marked the roads controlled by Russian troops in yellow on my large-scale 1990 map and destroyed villages/suburbs with a circle. The Russians control routes, not areas. The Russians only control the north bank of the river Sunja in Grozny and nothing to the east of Grozny. He marked the only southwards road from Grozny, the R-305, which remains open after Russian bombardment, and said that it was 50/50 possible to travel on it.

2. *Refugee numbers and location?* 30-50,000 in Khasavyurt in Daghestan and 30-50,000 in Nazran in Ingushetia. The majority, more than 300,000 (including ethnic Russians with Chechen friends) have moved to the mountain villages in the south. Only 50,000 out of 400,000 remain in Grozny. Refugees have also come from the destroyed towns Argun, Pervomayskaya and Pervopavlovskaya. The mountain villages have no medical supplies or equipment and very few doctors. Much medical material was destroyed in Grozny and doctors were killed in bombed hospitals. He has fixed an appointment to see the International Red Cross in Geneva. (I later discovered from Dieter Pfaff, who was the Red Cross Chechen desk officer, that the Red Cross had been consistently refused access to Chechenia by the Russians so that less than 10% of their humanitarian aid had reached Chechen civilians in Chechenia).

3. *How many dead?* About 1000 Chechen military have been killed and 20,000 Chechen civilians. He did not know how many Russian soldiers had been killed. The Chechens had captured 1500 of whom 200 were in the cellars of the presidential palace.

4. *Communications?* The TV mast in Grozny had been destroyed so they can only pick up radio, including the BBC World Service.

5. *What would happen if the Russians set up a puppet government in Grozny?* Out of the question. It would never work.

6. *Is there an alternative government which could be set up perhaps without Dudayev which could be acceptable to the Russians?* Dudayev does not see himself as indispensable. In any case democratic elections are due in late 1995 and they are ready to hold elections earlier with or without Dudayev.

7. *How are relations with Daghestan and Georgia? Because of snow and/or Russian border troops there is no contact with Daghestan or Georgia?* Both say good things about Chechenia, but there is no help, we are on our own; the Russians would like to publish photos of (dead or captured) Daghestanis or Georgians fighting with us, but there are none.

8. *Are the Chechens planning reprisals in the Moscow metro or power stations?* Categorically not, the Chechens refuse to take part in any terrorism which will harm civilians. They intend to become part of the international community and so are behaving according to international standards. If they use terrorism, how could they ask for international support?

❧

Haberdashery for sale at the Gagatl 'international' market. Here come people from Chechenia, Khunzakh, Botlikh . . . in fact, everywhere!

Sources and further reading

While there is a large Russian bibliography on Daghestan, for accessibility I have listed some English, German, French and Italian language books first. Then a section on bibliographies. Two major English publications by John Baddeley in 1940 and Louis Luzbetac in 1951 which have comprehensive bibliographies are listed first. As the books can be found in university libraries it seemed unnecessary to repeat their bibliographies. Next brief notes of the catalogues in the Academy of Sciences library in Makhachkala and the two recent bibliographies published by them. The three Russian-language series published by the Russian Imperial Academy from the 1870s until the Revolution are noted next. Then notes on local films and museums. I have also formed a substantial photo archive.

I then list a selection of mainly post-1951 Russian-language publications. Most authors' work appeared as articles in collections forming single books or annual series, so I have only indicated the name of the whole book or series as appropriate. In practice, if the further reader consults 'Daghestan' or 'Caucasus' in university library indexes outside Russia, only part of the bibliography will likely be found. The trail is often more tortuous: Baddeley's library and *Index Caucasica* was bequeathed to the London Library where it appears under 'Topography'.

English, German, French and Italian selected reading

Abdulrahmanov A., ['Animal totemism in Daghestan and north Caucasian folklore'], in *Proceedings 5th colloquium Societas Caucasologica Europea*, London, 1990.

Allen W.E.D., *A History of the Georgian People*, London, 1932.

Baddeley J., *The Rugged Flanks of the Caucasus*, OUP, London, Humphrey Milford, 1940.

Bailey H.W., *North Iranian problems*, SOAS Bulletin, London, 1979.

Bashchkirov A.S., *Iskusstvo Dagestana*, Ranion, M., 1931 (English summary and plate list).

Bennigsen A. & Enders Wimbush S., *Muslims of the Soviet Empire*, Hurst, London, 1986.

Bennigsen A. & Enders Wimbush S., *Mystics and Commissars: Sufism in the Soviet Union*, Hurst, London, 1985.

Bennigsen A. & Lemercier-Quelquejay C., 'Muslim religious conservatism and dissent in the USSR', in *Religion in Communist Lands*, 1978.

Bennigsen A. & Lemercier-Quelquejay C., 'Politics and linguistics in Daghestan', in *Socio-linguistic perspectives on Soviet national languages*, Mouton, Berlin, New York Amsterdam, 1985.

van den Berg H., *A Grammar of Hunzib*, Leiden, 1995.

Blanch L., *The Sabres of Paradise*, Quartet, London, 1978.

Bleichsteiner R., 'Rossweihe und Pferdeopfer im Totenkult der kaukasischen Volker', *Weiner Beitrage zur Kulturgeschichte und Linguistik*, 4, Salzburg-Leipzig, 1936.

Bleichsteiner R., 'Die Volker das Kaukasus', *Asien-Berichte*, V, 1944.

Broxup M., 'Islam in Daghestan since Gorbachev', *Religion in Communist Lands*, 1990.

Byhan A., *La civilisation caucasienne*, Paris, 1936.

Chenciner, R., *Kaitag: Textile art from Daghestan*, London, 1993.

Chenciner R., 'Daghestan Elections', *Central Asia and Caucasus Chronicle*, Society for Central Asian Studies, London, 1992.

Chenciner R., *Textiles of Daghestan*, Mimar, London, March 1990.

Chenciner R., *Daghestan Today*, Zamana, London, 1989.

Chenciner R., 'Hospitality and the ram-gut sausage', *World Gastronomy Journal*, 1989.

Chenciner R., & Salmanov, E., 'Little known aspects of North East Caucasian Mountain Ram and other dishes', *Oxford Symposium on Food & Cookery*, Prospect, London, 1987.

Chirkov, D., *Dekorativnoe isskustvo Dagestana*, Makhachkala, 1971.
Crisp S., 'The formation and development of literary Avar', *Contributions to the Sociology of Language*, 40, Mouton de Gruyter, 1985.
Crisp, S., 'Language planning and the orthography of Avar', *Folia Slavica*, 7, 1984.
Crisp, S., *Language Planning and the development of written Avar syntax*, thesis, Oxford University, 1982.
Dalgat, B. (trans), 'Die alte Religion der Tschetschenen', *Anthropos*, III, 1908.
Dirr, A., (whole bibliography), d.1930.
von Erkert R., *The Caucasus and Its Peoples*, Leipzig, 1888.
Field H., *Contributions to the Anthropology of the Caucasus*, Cambridge, Mass., 1953.
Gammer M., *Muslim Resistance to the Tsar*, Cass, London, 1994.
Gamzatov R., trans. Katzer J., *My Daghestan*, Roman-Gazeta, M., 1970.
Gamzatov R., Magomedov D., Mikailov R., Shakhmardanova L., Geibatova-Sholokhova Z., Gamzatova P., *Isskustvo Dagestana* (English summary and plate list), Sovetskii Khudozhnik, M., 1981.
Geiger B., Halasi-Kun T., Kuipers A., Menges K., *Peoples and Languages of the Caucasus*, Columbia University, Mouton & Co. 'S-Gravenhage, 1959.
Ivanov A., *Isskustvo Kubachi* (English summary and plate list), Khudozhnik RSFSR, L., 1976.
Lermontov M., trans. Foote P., *A hero of our time*, Penguin, 1966.
Luzbetak L., 'The Family in Caucasia', *Studia Instituti Anthropos*, 3, St. Gabriel's Mission Press, Vienna-Modling, 1951.
Magomedkhanov M., Luguev S., Chenciner R. (ed.), 'Traditional Table Manners in Daghestan', *Oxford Symposium on Food & Cookery*, Prospect, London, 1989.
Magomedkhanov M., edited by Chenciner R., 'Feasting after Fasting in Archib village, Daghestan ASSR', *Oxford Symposium on Food & Cookery*, Prospect, London, 1990.
Nioradze G., *Begrabnis und totenkult bei den chevssuren*, Strecker u Schroeder, Stuttgart, 1931.
Nioradze G., *Die Berg-Ossen*, Berlin, 1923.
Plaetschke B., *Die Tschetschenen*, Hamburg, 1929.
Rilli N., Italian essays in *L'Universo, Rivista dell'Instituto Geografico Militare*, Firenze, 1952-1955.
Salmanov E. & Chenciner R., '*Davaghin* and *dumi* rugs of Daghestan', *Oriental Carpet & Textile Studies*, III, Part 1, Hali OCTS, London, 1987.
Salmanov E., 'Ancient vegetariamism: staple foods and customs in Azerbaijan', *Oxford Symposium on Food & Cookery*, Prospect, London, 1989.

Bibliographies

The bibliographies of the following include historical material from classical antiquity:

Baddeley J., *The Rugged Flanks of the Caucasus*, OUP, London, Humphrey Milford, 1940.
Luzbetak L., 'The family in Caucasia', *Studia Instituti Anthropos*, 3, St. Gabriel's Mission Press, Vienna-Modling, 1951, pp 23-26 [classical literary chronology].

Catalogues in Academy of Sciences Daghestan Library, Makhachkala

1 box of cards cataloguing D.Z. Pisarevskii's library
4 boxes of cards cataloguing Lavrov's library
15 boxes on Daghestan

The Daghestan Filial of the Academy of Sciences also published two bibliographies:
Katalog pechatnykh knig i publikatsii na yazykakh narodov Dagestana – dorevolyutsionnyi period), ed A.A. Isaev M'kala, 1989.
Izdaniya instituta istorii, yazika i literatury, im. G. Tsadasy za 60 let 1924-1984, Makhachkala 1986, ed L.N. Sebova.

Further reading

Others

The three multi-volumed, largely annual, Tsarist Russian ethnographic sources are known by their initials below. They appeared after the conquest of Daghestan in 1859 and continued until the Revolution. An enlightened Russian scholar-officer Baron P. von Uslar was the coordinating force behind this massive work – starting with his own 699-page quarto Avar grammar and dictionary:

SMOMPK (Sbornik materialov dlya opisaniya mestnostey i plemen Kavkaza); almost 50 vols 1881-1929, vol xlvi and more?).

SSKG (Sbornik svedeniy o kavkazskikh gortsakh), 10 vols, 1868-81.

ZKO (Zapiski kavkazskago otdela imperatorskogo russkago geografishcheskago obshchestva) – the Imperial Russian Geographical Society was founded in 1831, well before the Royal Geographical Society – 1862-1917.

There are also four ethnographic-historical locally-produced colour films for the Academy in Daghestan – director, editor & cameraman, Marc Yeremeyyevich Wilenskii:
1. 'Women's traditional costume in Daghestan', 1983, S. Gadjieva consultant, 30 mins.
2. 'Stones talk', 20 minutes.
3. 'Towers of Daghestan', 20 minutes.
4. 'Derbent', 20 minutes.

Museums

The Daghestan museum collections have grown constantly over the last 20 years and now have assembled more than 15,000 objects. The St Petersburg Ethnographical Institute also has large holdings collected from the 1860s onwards.

Russian selected reading (1951 onwards)

Abaev V., *'Narty' epos osetinskogo naroda*, Makhachkala, 1957.

Abakarova F.O. sost., *Dagestanskii Fol'klore vo vzaimosvyazyakh s inoetnicheskim fol'klorum*, Makhachkala, 1985.

Abdulazizov A.I. (ed.), *Byulleten' Ateista*, No.3, Makhachkala, 1979.

Abdurakhmanov A.M., *Formirovanie i razvitie zhanra basni v Dagestanskoi literature*, Makhachkala, 1986.

Abdurahmanov A.M., [Animal characters in folktales of Daghestan & north Caucasus], 1980? ms.

Agapov F.A., *Fizicheskaya kul'tura i sport u gorskikh narodov severnogo Kavkaza*, Makhachkala, 1971.

Agashirinova S., *S Patronimia u Lezgin, uchen zap In-ta IIAL im G.Tzadas*, Makhachkala, 1965.

Aglarov M.A., [Village communities in the mountains of Daghestan], Makhachkala, 1987.

Aglarov M.A., *Andiskaia Gruppa Narodnostei: Dis. kand. ist. nauk.*, Makhachkala, 1967.

Aitberov T.M., *Drevnii Khunzakh i Khunzakhtsy*, Makhachkala, 1990.

Akhmedov M.-Sh., *Znamenostsy Dagestanskogo sporta*, Makhachkala, 1972.

Alieva A.K. (ed.), *Ateisticheskoe vospitanie naseleniya*, Makhachkala, 1977.

Bagabov I.M., *Musul'manskii konfessionalizm*, Makhachkala, 1985.

Bromlei Yu. V., *Ocherki teoria etnosa*, Makhachkala, 1983.

Bulatova A.G., *Laktzy*, Makhachkala, 1975.

Bulatova A.G., *Traditsionnye prazdniki i obryady narodov gornogo Dagestana v XIX – n.XX veka*, Nauka, 1988.

Chursin G.F., *Magia v borbe c zasukhoi u kavkazskikh narodov. – Biul. Kavkaz. ist. arkheolog. In-ta*, Tbilisi, 1930.

Dalgat E.M., *Istoriografiya istorii Dagestana dosovetskogo perioda*, Makhachkala,1986.

Davidov O.M., [Daghestan culture of Early Iron Age], Makhachkala, 1974.

Debirov P.M., *Rez'ba po kamniu v Dagestane*, Nauka, Makhachkala, 1966.

Debirov P.M., *Rez'ba po derevu v Dagestane*, Nauka, Makhachkala, 1982.

Debirov P.M., *Arkhitekturnaia rez'ba Dagestana*, Nauka, Makhachkala, 1966.

Djavrishvili D., *Grunzinskie Narodnie Tantzi*, Tbilisi, 1958.

Dubrovin N., *Istoriya voyny ...*, vol 1, SPb, 1871.

Egorova V.P., *Iz Narodnykh Traditzii Dagestana, Vapros Ist. Etno. Dag.*, Dagosuniv, Makhachkala, 1970.

Gadlo A.V., [Ethnic history of the North Caucasus: fourth-tenth centuries], L. U., 1979.

Goldshtein A., *Bashni v gorakh*, Sov. Khud., Makhachkala, 1977.

Gadzhiev M.G., *Etnokulturniye protsessi v drevnem Dagestane*, Makhachkala, 1987.

Gadjieva S.Sh., *Sem'ya i brak u narodov Dagestana v XX-nach XX v. M.*, Nauka, 1985.

Gadjieva S.Sh., *Traditsionnyi zemledel'cheskii kalendar' i kalendarnye obryady Kumykov*, Makhachkala, 1989.

Gadjieva S.Sh. (ed.), *Dagestanskii etnograficheskii sbornik*, 1, Makhachkala, 1974.

Gadjieva S.Sh. (ed.), *Sovremennaya kul'tura i byt narodov Dagestana*, Nauka, Makhachkala, 1971.

Gadjieva S.Sh., *Odezhda narodov Dagestana*, Makhachkala, 1981.

Gadjieva S.Sh., *Kumiki*, Ist.-etno. Isled., Makhachkala, 1961.

Gadjieva S.Sh., Osmanov M.O., & Pashayeva A.G., *Mat. Kultura Dargintzev*, Makhachkala, 1967.

Gadjieva S.Sh., *Materialnaya kultura Nogaitsev v XIX- n. XX v Nauka*, Makhachkala, 1976.

Gadjieva V.G. (ed.), *Istochnikovedenie istorii dosovetkogo Dagestana*, Makhachkala,1987.

Ganieva A.M., *Zhanr skazki v fol'klore narodov Dagestana*, Makhachkala, 1987.

Islamagomedov A.I., *Mujskie sobrania 'gorko rukI' u avartsev, tez. dokl. nauch. ses. posviash. itogam ekspedits. isled. In-ta. IIAL. v 1984-1985 gg*, Makhachkala 1986.

Islamagomedov A.I., *Traditzion. i novoe v sovrem, Bytu Dagestantsev-pereselentzev*, Makhachkala, 1981.

Islamegomedov A.I. (otv. red.), *Aguly*, Makhachkala, 1975.

Istoria Dagestana, T.I, Makhachkala, 1967.

Kadryadzhiev K.S., *Struktura i genezis Kumykskikh mifologicheskikh elementov paleotiurskovo proiskhozhdenia, mifologia narodov Dagestana*, Makhachkala, 1984.

Kaloev B.A., *Aguly*, TIE, 1962.

Kasumov S. & Illaev A. (sost.), *Kulinariya narodov Dagestana*, Makhachkala, 1994.

Khalilov Kh.M. (ed.), *Semeino-obryadovaya poeziya severnogo Kavkaza*, Makhachkala, 1985.

Khan-Magomedov S.O., *Lezginskoe narodnoe zodchestvo*, Nauka, Makhachkala, 1969.

Khashchaev Kh., *Zanyatiya naseleniya Dagestana v XIX v*, Makhachkala, 1959.

Kilchevskaya E.V., *Dekorativnoe isskustvo aula Koubachi*, Makhachkala, 1962.

Kosven M.O., Lavrov L.I., Nersesov G.A., & Khashchaev KH.O. (eds)., *Narody Kavkaza*, vols. 1-2, Nauk, Makhachkala, 1960.

Krachkovskaia V.A. *Iz. Epigraficheskikh Motivov Mecheti v aule Koubachi, Sb. pamiati N.Ya. Marr, In-ta iazyka i myshlenia*, L., 1938.

Lavrov L.I., et al. (ed.), *Kazkazkii etnograficheski sbornik*, vols 1-7. Makhachkala, c.1955 v.I, 1972 v.V, 1976 v.VI, 1980 v.VII.

Lavrov L.I., *Doislamkie Verovania Adygeitsev i Kabardintsev*, TIE.T.L.M., 1959.

Lavrov L.I., *Epigraficheskie Pamiatniki Severnovo Kavkaza*, 3 pts. Makhachkala, 1966, 1980.

Libirov M., *Narodny Igry i sport Dagestane*, Makhachkala, 1968.

Luguev S.A., *Relikty Mujskikh Soyouzov v obshchestvenom byte Laktsev*, Vsesoyuz. ses. po itogam polevyh etnogr. isled. 1980-1981 gg posviash. 60 let obrazovania SSSR: Tez. Dokl. Nalchik, 1982.

Luguev S.A., *Obshchestveny byt Laktsev, vo 2-oi pol. XIX – nach. XX v. Avtoref. dis. kand.ist.nauk.* Makhachkala, 1982.

Luguev S.A. sost., *Voprosi obshestvennogo bita naradov Dagestana v XIX – n. XX v Makhachkala*, 1987.

Luguev S.A., *Gosteprimstvo i Kunachestvo i Laktsev vtor. pol. XIX-nach.XXvv, Semeinuiy byt naradov Dagestana v XIX-nach.XXvv*, Makhachkala, 1980.

Luybimova G.N. & Khan-Magomedov S.O., *Narodnaya arkhitektura yuzhnogo Dagestana*, Makhachkala, 1956.

Magomedov A., *Dagestan i Dagestantsy v mire*, Yupiter, Makhachkala, 1994.

Further reading

Magomedov D.M., *Ideino-Khudozhestvennye problemy sovremennogo iskusstva Dagestana*, Makhachkala, 1982.

Magomedov D.M. & Gadjiev A. Yu., *Isskustvo Dagestana*, Makhachkala, 1981.

Magomedov N.A., *Economicheskoe razvitie derbentskogo khanstva v XVIII v.*, Nalchik, 1985.

Magomedov R.M., *Legendy i fakty o Dagestane*, Makhachkala, 1963.

Magomedov R.M., *Khronologiya istorii Dagestana*, Makhachkala, 1959.

Marshchaev R. & Butaev B., *Istoriya Laktsev*, Makhachkala, 1991.

Materiale Kultura Avartzev, Makhachkala, 1967.

Narochnitskii A.L. ed, *Istoria narodov severnogo Kavkaza k. XVIII v.- 1917 g.*, Nauka, Makhachkala, 1988.

Ocherki nauchnevo ateizma, Makhachkala, 1972.

Orazaev G.M.-R. & Shikhsaidov A.R ed., *Istochnikovedenie srednevekogo Dagestana*, Makhachkala, 1986.

Orbeli I.A., *Albanski Relefy i Bronzovye Kotly*, Izbr. Trudy, Erevan, 1963.

Osmanov G.G., *Sotsialno-ekonomicheskoe Razvitie Dagestanskovo Dokolkhoznovo Aula*, Makhachkala, 1965.

Osmanov G.G., *Genezis Kapitalizma v Sel'skom khozaistve Dagestana*, Makhachkala, 1984.

Pikul M.I., *Epokha ranevo zheleza v Dagestane*, Tez.dokl.Arkheologii Dagestana, Makhachkala, 1959; 1967.

Piotrovskii B.B., *Istoria narodov severnogo kavkaza – XVIII v.*, Nauka, Makhachkala, 1988.

Ramazanova Z.B., *Zemledelie Laktsev v k. XIX- n. XX v.*, Nauka, L., 1988.

Shilling E.M., *Koubachintsi i ikh kultura*, Nauk, L., 1949.

Shilling E.M., *Dagestanskaia Expedisia*, KSIE, 1949.

Sovetskii Dagestan [bi-monthly journal], Makhachkala, 1965-1991.

Spravochnik telefonov, upravlenie delami soveta ministrov Dagestanskoi ASSR Makhachkala, 1983.

Tatayev V.A., *Dekorativno-prikladnoe isskustvo Checheno-Ingushetii*, Grozny, 1974.

Tuganov M.S., *Osetinskie Narodnie Tantzy*, Stalinir Tzinvali, 1957.

Tultseva L.A., *Sovremennye prazdniki i obryadi narodov SSSR*, Nauka, Makhachkala, 1985.

Vereshchagina V., 'Lezginka: Dagestan Tanetz', *Djivopisnaya Rossia*, SPb, 1883.

Yaralov Yu.S. (ed.), *Zodchestvo Dagestana Makhachkala*, 1974.

Yusupova Ch.S. (ed.), *Problemy mifologii i verovanii naradov Dagestana*, Makhachkala, 1988.

Zalov G. (ed.), *Pesn' o Staline*, Makhachkala, 1949.

Zand M., 'Dagestan v gody velikogo terrora', in Nisim Ilishchaev (ed.), *Nakazanie bez prestupleniya*, Tel-Aviv, Shch. Segal, 1982.

Horse being presented to mountaineer corpse laid on carpet to speed his journey to the next world – a Caucasian survival of Scythian horse sacrifice at funerals. (Photo: G. Nioradze, c.1920s)

Census of the peoples of Daghestan 1959, 1970, 1979 & 1989

In thousands	1959	1970	1979	*%	1989	p%
Total population	1062	1429	e.1600		2000	25
Dagh. in USSR	–	1365	1657		2072	25[a]
Daghestanis	736	1061	1267	76	1585	25
incl. Avars	239	349	419	87	524	25
Dargins	148	208	247	86	314	27
Kumyks	121	169	202	89	249	23
Lezgins	109	163	189	49	231	22
Laks	53	72	83	83	98	18
Tabassarans	34	53	72	95	94	31
Nogais	15	22	25	42	32	27
Rutuls	7	12	14	95	19	38
Aguls	6	9	11	95	18	65
Tsakhurs	4	4	5	34	7	49
Azeris	38	54	68		84	24
Chechens	13	40	49		62[b]	27
Tats	–	6	8		11	37
Tatars	–	6	6		6	7
Ossetes	–	2	2		2	10
Total Muslim origin	–	1169	e.1400		e.1750	
% of total pop.	–	82%	88%		88%	
Russians	214	210	224		236	6
Mountain Jews	–	–	9		20[c]	108
Jews	21	22	–		– ?[d]	–
Ukrainians	-	9	9		9	4
Armenians	–	7	8		9	12
Georgians	–	2	2		2	12

[a] census figure   [b] low-returnees   [c] including Azerbaijan   [d] now called Mountain Jews

Further reading

Notes to Daghestan Census information

These figures were taken from the following sources:

1. There was an all Soviet Union census every ten years. Some results of the January 1989 census are available through Ann Sheehy (1990), from a photocopy of part of *Natsional'nyi sostav naseleniya*, chast' II (Moscow, 1989), published reportedly "for official use." Source for 1959, 1970 and 1979: A. Bennigsen & S. Enders Wimbush, *Muslims of the Soviet Union – a guide*, (1985); with acknowledgements to Marie Broxup & the Society for Central Asian Studies. In addition, the entire 1989 raw census by oblast is available in Britain on disc.

2. To convert the recent incomplete census figures to be comparable to the earlier census results, the following estimates and calculations were done. All numbers have been rounded up to the nearest thousand, all percentages have been rounded up to the nearest percent (e.g. 7.5% rounded up to 8%).

3. *% is the percentage of Daghestani peoples of the Soviet Union living in the Daghestan ASSR in 1979 – a significant proportion of Daghestanis live in other Soviet Republics, mainly Azerbaijan SSR, Georgia SSR and Kazakhstan SSR, but there are current uncharted movements back home due to the desire to return home and/or local nationalism – for example, Chechens returning from Kazakhstan.

4. p%. At present we only have the numbers in all the USSR for 1989, so the 1989 purely Daghestan numbers are obtained by multiplying 100% plus the 1979-89 all USSR percentage increase – p% – by the 1979 purely Daghestan number. To crosscheck, when the resulting number was divided by the 1979 percentage living in Daghestan – *% -, the numbers were within 1% of the 1989 all USSR numbers, except for the three smallest – 5%, where there were possibly rounding up variations.

5. For non-Daghestan nationalities living in Daghestan we have used the all USSR rates of change. This is probably true for Caucasian groups like Azeris, but there must be less confidence in the growth rates of other groups like Russians or Ukrainians. Local sources believe that while the former have decreased, the latter have taken their place. Mountain Jews, Jews and Tats are a special case because of emigration.

6. The census has omitted a number of smaller peoples, each with their own language. Numbers for the main Daghestani peoples include numbers of the following smaller, yet distinct ethnic groups: Akhvakh, Andi, Archi, Bagulaal, Bezhtin, Botlikh, Chamalal, Dido, Ginukh, Godoberi, Kaitag, Kapucha, Karata, Khunzal, Khvarshi, Koubachi, Tindi (Geiger, Halasi-Kun, Kuipers & Menges, *Peoples & Languages of the Caucasus*, Janua Linguarum VI, 1959). A growth rate much over 25% implies that the basis of identification may have changed, i.e. smaller peoples have been included.

Seljuk Turks, Mongols, Persians and Ottomans in the Parade of Conquerors of the Caucasus at the Khunzakh Festival.

Languages of Daghestan

NORTH CAUCASIAN		SOUTH CAUCASIAN	INDO-EUROPEAN

NORTH CAUCASIAN
NORTH-CENTRAL
1   CHECHEN
2   INGUSH
3   BATS
NORTH-EAST
Avar-Andi-Dido:
4   AVAR
5   ANDI
6   BOTLIKH
7   GODOBERI
8   KARATA
9   AKHVAKH
10 BAGULAAL
11 TINDI
12 CHAMALAL

13 DIDO (TSEZ)
14 KHVARSH
15 BEZHTI
     (KAPUCH)
16 HUNZIB
Lak-Dargin:
17 LAK
18 DARGIN
Lezgin:
19 LEZGIN
20 AGHUL
21 TABASSARAN
22 BUDUKH
23 KRYZ
24 RUTUL
25 TSAKHUR

26 UDI
27 ARCHI
28 KHINALUG
NORTH-WEST
29 KABARDIAN

SOUTH CAUCASIAN
30 GEORGIAN

ALTAIC
MONGOLIAN
31 KALMYK
     (OIRAT)
TURKIC
Kipchak:
32 KUMYK

33 KARACHAI-
     BALKAR
34 NOGAI
Oghuz:
35 AZERBAIJANI
36 TURKMEN

INDO-EUROPEAN
IRANIAN
37 TAT
38 OSSETE
ARMENIAN
39 ARMENIAN
SLAVONIC
40 RUSSIAN

Most languages are now spoken in Makhachkala.

Index

Index

Index

*Postcard-size view of
Derbent, 1730 from I.B.
Homann, Nürnberg.
(Royal Geographical Society,
London)*

*The walls of Derbent, originally built by the Persian Sassanians
during the sixth century AD. (Photo: A. Koudniatsev)*

(Right to left from top): Roadside Laki children at Shangoda village, built on a precipice; stirring the Rasoulov wedding soup in Bezhta; Knitted boots from Bezhta; archaic horn-shaped armchair, late 19th c., Duakar village (photo: Paruk Debirov); Maisarat Magomedkhan making butter in Archi; carpet knotting from a cartoon drawn on squared paper at the Derbent carpet manufactory; hobby-horse used in masked mummer performances in Koubachi (given to Leningrad Ethnographic Museum by E.M. Schilling).